SAME-SEX MARRIAGE

Contemporary Issues

Series Editors: Robert M. Baird & Stuart E. Rosenbaum

Volumes edited by Robert M. Baird and Stuart E. Rosenbaum
unless otherwise noted.

SAME-SEX MARRIAGE

The Moral and Legal Debate

SECOND EDITION

edited by

ROBERT M. BAIRD & STUART E. ROSENBAUM

Prometheus Books

59 John Glenn Drive
Amherst, New York 14228-2197

Published 2004 by Prometheus Books

Inquiries should be addressed to
Prometheus Books
59 John Glenn Drive
Amherst, New York 14228–2197
VOICE: 716–691–0133, ext. 207
FAX: 716–564–2711
WWW.PROMETHEUSBOOKS.COM

08 07 06 05 04   5 4 3 2 1

Library of Congress Cataloging-in-Publication Data

Same-sex marriage : the moral and legal debate / edited by Robert M. Baird and Stuart E.
    Rosenbaum. — 2nd. ed.
        p. cm.
    Includes bibliographical references.
    ISBN 1–59102–274–6 (pbk. : alk. paper)
    1. Same-sex marriage—Moral and ethical aspects—United States. 2. Same-sex
marriage—Law and legislation—United States. I. Baird, Robert M., 1937–
II. Rosenbaum, Stuart E.

HQ1034.U5S25   2004
306.84'8—dc22   2004016580

CONTENTS

5

6   Contents

PART TWO. THE EMOTIONAL DIMENSIONS
OF THE DEBATE

APPENDIXES

INTRODUCTION

On May 17, 2004, the state of Massachusetts began performing marriages of same-sex couples. On the front page of the May 18 *New York Times* was a picture of a gay couple, Joe Rogers and Tom Weikle, walking away from Boston's city hall after having been united in marriage by Boston city clerk Rosaria Salerno. Many such marriages were performed that same day in cities throughout Massachusetts. Opponents of same-sex marriage had been unable to turn aside this consequence of the Massachusetts Supreme Judicial Court's 4-to-3 decision, issued in November 2003, in the *Goodridge* case.

In April 2001 attorney Mary Bonauto filed *Goodridge v. Department of Public Health*, arguing that refusal to grant marriage licenses to same-sex couples violated Massachusetts's constitutional guarantee of equal treatment under the law. The trial court ruled against her, but the state's Supreme Judicial Court ruled 4-to-3 in her favor while granting a 180-day stay until May 17. Following the Supreme Judicial Court's ruling, state legislators sought ways to diminish the impact of the ruling but were told by the four-member majority of the court that the ruling was a matter of constitutional interpretation rather than of social policy subject to political strategies.[1] The legislative body of the state of Vermont had earlier, with the apparent encouragement of that state's supreme court, modified a similar, earlier Vermont court decision to allow same-sex couples to join in civil unions rather than in marriages. The Massachusetts court, however, refused to back away from its decision that the Massachusetts Constitution required, as a condition of equal treatment, that same-sex couples be granted the opportunity to marry.

Shortly after the *Goodridge* decision, the mayor of San Francisco, Gavin Newsom, began authorizing same-sex marriages in San Francisco. Newsom believed that the right to marry was fundamental because of the California Constitution's banning of discrimination. Approximately four thousand same-sex marriages were performed as many Californians took advantage of Newsom's activist perspective. The California Supreme Court, however, on August 12, 2004, voided those marriages and ruled that Newsom had overstepped his mayoral authority in issuing marriage licenses to those couples. That court did not decide, however, on the constitutionality within California of same-sex marriage, though the court will undoubtedly issue a ruling on this issue as soon as a case raising that issue comes before it.

More than a decade earlier the Hawaii Supreme Court had come to a similar decision in *Baehr v. Lewin*. On May 5, 1993, that court declared that Hawaii's refusal to grant marriage licenses to same-sex couples violated the equal protection provision of the state constitution. The state had, according to the court, failed to demonstrate any compelling state interest in denying marriage licenses to the same-sex couples petitioning for them. The court ordered that the petitioning couples were entitled to an evidentiary hearing to determine whether Lewin, commissioner of the state's Department of Health, could demonstrate "compelling state interests" in applying the relevant statute to discriminate against them and other same-sex couples. In November 1998, before the proceedings of this hearing concluded, the voters of Hawaii adopted a constitutional amendment banning same-sex marriage. The *Baehr* decision, more than a decade before same-sex marriages became legal in Massachusetts, spurred a heated debate entered by activists of every stripe who expressed strong and diverse opinions about the central issue: should marriages between same-sex couples be authorized, sanctioned, or recognized by the state?

Hawaii's decision rested on its constitutional provision for equal protection. The Massachusetts decision, handed down on November 18, 2003, rested on both the equal protection provision of its constitution and the due process provision: "Limiting the benefits, and obligations of civil marriage to opposite-sex couples violates the basic premises of individual liberty and equality under the law protected by the Massachusetts Constitution."

These state courts handed down judgments on an issue that is as divisive as any ever adjudicated in the history of American constitutional interpretation, and the future will likely yield a United States Supreme Court confrontation over this same issue that is, in the wake of the Massachusetts decision, now working its way through judicial venues in several additional states. How should reasonable people think or feel about this issue? President George W. Bush has demeaned these court decisions as products of "activist judges," suggesting that he believes there are no real constitutional grounds for these courts' decisions; his view is rather that the judges issuing these decisions have peculiar, unrepresentative ideologies that preclude their offering reasonable interpretations of the various states' constitutions and of the US Constitution. In order to counteract the peculiar and unrepresentative decisions such judges deliver, Bush has proposed a constitutional amendment to limit marriage to the union of one man and one woman.

Are court decisions that go against widely held sentiment, as the Massachusetts court's *Goodridge* decision does, constitutionally inappropriate? Are they products of narrow ideologies that must be countermanded at all costs—even through the device of a constitutional amendment—in order to preserve social and cultural order and basic human values? The fundamental issue here is that of the integrity of the various courts and of the men and women holding positions as judges who issue the controversial opinions that frequently change, or refuse to change, American culture. Although this question is not a focus for this volume of essays and reflections, it must always, especially in light of Bush's charges and his proposal to amend the Constitution, remain a background issue of great importance. The ramifications of this background issue are also of great importance; they open up virtually every significant issue about the relationship among the three large branches of government, the executive, the legislative, and the judicial. Although it is beyond the scope of this collection, this issue deserves careful thought by all Americans.

The largest dimensions of this fundamental issue of the integrity of the judicial branch of government are those of the extent to which individuals must conform their lives and actions to the judgment of others—either to the expectations of a majority culture, or to the behaviors and actions of others of which one strongly and fundamentally disapproves. According to Bush and others who believe as he does, "activist judges" require the majority culture to tolerate what that majority strongly believe is intolerable, contrary to nature, or in direct opposition to what is morally or religiously appropriate. According to Mary Bonauto and others like her, their natural sexual dispositions should not disqualify them, in spite of disapproval by a majority culture, from customary and normal marital relationships, along with all the normal social and personal benefits that are a part of those normal marital relationships.

This issue of tension between minority rights and majority opinion appears in many different cases adjudicated throughout US judicial history, and it has always been central in American social and cultural change. This same issue will continue to hold its central place in thought about the American cultural and political context. Changes in social norms and practices will come in the future, as they have come in the past, by virtue of court decisions that seek to make coherent in some current context the intricacies of legal precedent and cultural tradition. For the present collection of essays and documents, that context is the issue of same-sex marriage.

If this issue is resolved, as now appears likely, that in accord with the *Goodridge* decision same-sex marriages will become common in Massachusetts and eventually also in additional states, a great social and cultural change will have been wrought. Comparisons frequently made involve the 1954 *Brown v. Board of Education* decision, making racial integration of public schools mandatory throughout America, and the *Loving v. Virgina* decision constitutionally legitimizing interracial marriages. In response to each of these decisions, the social and cultural fabric of the United States has become dramatically different from what it would otherwise have been; our public schools are now thoroughly integrated racially, and our neighbors are more and more frequently interracial couples. American society and culture are different as a result of these court decisions, but only a very small minority of Americans would choose life in the society America would have been without those decisive moments in judicial history. In another fifty years, American society will likely become as thoroughly acclimated to same-sex marriage as it is now to racial integration and interracial marriage.

For some this vision of the future in the United States is welcome; for others it is offensive. Consequently, apart from the basic documents expressing the relevant court rulings and the reasoning that led to those rulings, this collection includes trenchant and diverse expressions of opinion. The essays that appear here are representative of the most prevalent strands of thought and opinion that motivate Americans entertaining the issue of same-sex marriage. As we did with the first collection of essays about this issue, published in 1996, we have divided this revised collection into three sections. The first section deals with the *Goodridge* decision and includes a wide variety of responses to that decision, some acutely thoughtful, some less thoughtful, and some humorous. A second section deals most prominently with the emotional dimensions of the debate about same-sex marriage, and a third section deals primarily with the philosophical, theological, and moral dimensions of the issue.

The *Goodridge* decision itself, along with the dissenting opinions, is important reading; anyone who holds an opinion about the issue of same-sex marriage has a responsibility to read—and to read carefully—these basic documents. If "activist judges" are responsible for these decisions that change the fabric of American culture, then the evidence for that claim is embedded in these basic documents. The majority opinion, the supporting opinions, and the dissenting opinions in *Goodridge* are thoughtful expressions of people chosen to be judges because of their legal skill and knowledge, and their wisdom and integrity. One may disagree with any one of them—one may disagree with the majority opinion—still, one may not prudently dismiss the court's decision as nothing more than an aberrant expression of narrowly ideological, liberal, or "activist" judges. Responsible individuals who hold opinions about this issue must engage these primary documents.

Becoming familiar with these basic documents naturally invites engagement with other issues. Why would any homosexual individual want to marry? What would motivate someone who did not have any hope or expectation of bringing progeny into the world to seek legal recognition as part of a family? American culture has for a very long time acknowledged the ubiquity of sexual activity outside of marriage, even glamorizing such activity. Marriage is not glamorous. In Hollywood, where intense sexual relationships are a presumed norm, marriage is often not regarded as particularly desirable. Why would homosexuals, perhaps one of the most deeply countercultural groups in American society, seek the legal sanction of marriage for their relationships? Several of the selections included here, especially in part 2, address these questions.

One of the selections included in this section is an autobiographical narrative by an anonymous woman titled "I Left My Husband for the Woman I Love." Jane Doe left her marriage of twenty-five years and her two children because of an intense love relationship that developed between her and another woman. As Doe's narrative begins, a female friend asks, "Are you going to marry the person you left him for?" Her response is simply, "The person is a woman," as though that remark settled conclusively the issue of marriage. She simply took for granted that because "the person is a woman," marriage was impossible. (We are curious to know, and would be interested in discovering, whether or not the Jane Doe who authored this narrative is still with the lover for whom she left her family, and whether or not she would, now that it has become legally available, contemplate marriage to this female lover.)

The selections in part 2 focus generally on how people who are not heterosexual confront the emotional issues involved in coming to grips personally with their sexual orientation, what it means for their futures and for the general structures of their lives. Beyond the personal, emotional issue of how one puts together a meaningful life, there are the larger philosophical, theological, and moral issues that seek to circumscribe the possible ways one may go about putting together a meaningful life. How *ought* one deal with the fact of one's homosexuality? Indeed, is one's homosexuality a biological fact that one simply must, because of one's biological constitution, accommodate? Is there a moral reality, one knowable through philosophical, reflective thought, that requires and prohibits certain behaviors of everyone, regardless of their own personal, emotional constitutions? Is there a natural law that our behaviors and our legal reasoning should seek to accommodate? Do religious authorities have insights into moral reality that should be acknowledged in our behavior and in our laws? These more theoretical issues are the focus of part 3 of this collection.

Just after the Hawaii decision in 1993, Robert Knight, then director of cultural studies for the Family Research Council, said, "No law that contradicts the fundamental moral law is legitimate. This means that the court has now acted lawlessly. . . ."[2] Conservative heterosexuals frequently see same-sex marriage as a threat to family values. From their perspective, the idea of same-sex marriage is part of the corruption of contemporary culture, a culture that makes tolerance its only moral ideal. In making tolerance its only ideal, contemporary culture loses respect for the natural law that has traditionally been present, more or less adequately, in various human societies. The idea that we should tolerate aberrations from traditional societal norms is an idea that has increasingly acquired legitimacy in America; but according to heterosexuals like Knight, tolerance of such aberrations as same-sex marriage only further undermines traditional family values rooted in natural law. The bottom line for these heterosexuals is erosion of the traditional family and of the values inseparable from it. Hence, the idea of same-sex marriage, for these traditionalists, is only one more threat to the values that made America great, to the values rooted in American families with two parents, and to values rooted also in a whole battery of cultural institutions—among them churches and schools—

that mutually reinforce each other. Same-sex marriage, for these traditional heterosexuals, is as destructive, if not more destructive, of traditional family values as are drugs, absentee fathers, and easy access to abortion.

Another response to the Hawaii decision came from Kerry Lobel, then executive director of the National Gay and Lesbian Task Force: "This decision is one small but crucial step forward in a long march toward civil equality for lesbian, gay, bisexual, and transgendered people. . . . We seek the same rights and responsibilities of marriage that heterosexual people enjoy."[3] According to Lobel, the fundamental moral dimension of that decision was its motion toward greater equality of treatment for homosexuals. Consistency in applying our commitments to treating different humans equally is, for Lobel and a large number of interested parties, the relevant moral principle that should determine social policy.

These reactions to the earlier Hawaii decision were reactions of principle; they were reactions that appealed to "fundamental moral law" as showing that the very idea of same-sex marriage is illegitimate, and to "civil equality" for homosexuals as showing that homosexuals should be allowed to participate equally in this basic institution of American culture.

Beyond these two responses of those who think that same-sex marriage either accords or does not accord with obvious principles of morality, a third group think, again as a matter of principle, that the very idea of marriage is objectionable, that marriage is a corrupt, patriarchal institution that should be abandoned by reasonable or well-informed people. Among representatives of this minority view, the most prominent are gay, lesbian, and feminist thinkers. The selection by Paula Ettlebrick expresses this perspective. For Ettlebrick and others, same-sex marriage is undesirable and so is heterosexual marriage; the institution of marriage itself, through its patriarchal relations of dominance and submission, distorts the human condition and leaves a social trail of unnecessary abuse and misery.

The advocates of these three perspectives about same-sex marriage believe their positions are justified by basic human values. Needless to say, these advocates appeal to different basic values. For many radical gays, lesbians, and feminists—those who deride the desire of some homosexuals to marry—the oppressiveness of a paternalistic society justifies their rejection of marriage. For those gay and lesbian couples who *want* to marry, the tradition of family along with the social normalcy it represents is their justification; they want the same normalcy their parents and grandparents enjoyed. For those couples, the corruption of paternalistic institutions is too abstract to override their concrete desire for normal lives. Furthermore, they believe that nothing about their sexual orientation should disqualify them from having the normal lives they want. They are not criminals. They see themselves to be "following nature" in the same way their heterosexual peers do. Why should they not have the same opportunities for social recognition?

For the majority of conservative heterosexuals, those who object to same-sex marriage, what is at stake is civilized society itself; these traditionalists fear the disintegration of the traditional family and the vital cultural values inseparable from it. The motivating values of each group are different. Which set of motivating values is preferable, more rational, more productive, more just, or more in accord with other deeply rooted traditions of Western culture? This question, in all its various guises, is critical to constructive conversation about same-sex marriage.

All these conflicts of principle are embodied in real people living in real social situations in which many futures hang in the balance: their own futures as well as those of their children, of their grandchildren, and of their friends. But beyond these fears, hopes, and cares for themselves and other individuals, these conflicts of principle derive from different understandings of what an ideal society should be. Conservative, Christian heterosexuals who believe for scriptural reasons that same-sex marriage is wrong undoubtedly also believe that permitting same-sex marriage will produce a society even further removed from the Christian ideal than American society is currently. Similar concerns about ideals motivate the other perspectives discussed in these essays. Those who think marriage is a corrupt, paternalistic institution believe that crucial social ideals are critically at stake in decisions about same-sex marriage. Those homosexuals who want to marry seek a society in which all may feel at home, no matter their sexual orientation; they want normalcy for those who do not fit statistical norms of sexual preference. In addition to personal lives, social ideals and hopes for the larger human future are also involved in the issue of same-sex marriage.

The task of mediating among these competing ideals for the future and of opening or closing possibilities for personal futures falls most frequently on our courts. Ideals, traditions, statutes, and precedents come to a focus in individual court cases that must be decided by individual judges to whom we typically entrust such decisions. In seeking an appropriate mediation of these competing claims, the courts must take into account a large body of legal tradition as well as the particulars of the case at issue.

A distinct lineage of court cases informs every far-reaching court decision. In *Goodridge*, that lineage includes those decisions that bring more autonomy to individuals as they seek to build what they consider a desirable life in the face of social constraints imposed by tradition or by a majority culture. In 1965, for example, in *Griswold v. Connecticut*, the United States Supreme Court legitimated individual rights to the use of birth control devices in spite of a state law prohibiting them. The Catholic majority in the state disapproved of the use of birth control, and Connecticut law had previously embodied and preserved the traditional values of that majority. After *Griswold*, the individual right to choose birth control in spite of the moral and religious objections of the majority was legally secure. In the 1986 case, *Bowers v. Hardwick*, on the other hand, in which the legal issues seemed quite similar to those in *Griswold*, the Court upheld a Georgia law prohibiting homosexual behavior. In 2003, however, that 1986 decision was overturned in *Lawrence v. Texas*; Justice Anthony Kennedy's majority opinion in *Lawrence* explicitly repudiated the earlier *Bowers* decision. The *Griswold* case found a fundamental constitutional right of privacy to cover individuals' choices whether or not to use birth control; the *Bowers* case denied that individuals had a constitutional right to engage in homosexual behavior; and the *Lawrence* case again rejected the idea of majority control of individual sexual behaviors. These tensions among traditions, ideals, and individual rights are a normal part of life in a democratic community. The responsibility of our courts is to adjudicate among these competing cultural currents for the benefit of individuals caught in those currents.

In *Goodridge*, the Massachusetts Supreme Judicial Court took the responsibility of extending the idea of equal protection of the law to individuals who desire to marry others of their own sex. Consequently, same-sex families are likely to become as common in American society as are married interracial couples.

Some parts of American society have long been ready for same-sex families. After the Hawaii Supreme Court's decision in 1993, there appeared a spate of media responses to the mere possibility of same-sex marriage. In November 1996, *Newsweek* featured a cover picture of singer Melissa Etheridge and her pregnant partner, Julie Cypher, in mutual embrace and staring defiantly toward the camera. The caption read: "We're Having a Baby," with subcaptions, "Can Gay Families Gain Acceptance?" and "What It's Like for the Kids." Similarly, in that same month *Harper's* magazine featured a cover picture of two gay men, one nuzzling the other; the title of the cover story was "Wedded to an Illusion: Do Gays and Lesbians Really Want the Right to Marry?"

Politicians, if they do not exactly relish such controversies, hurry to exploit them. Just as Bush in the wake of *Goodridge* proposed a constitutional amendment defining marriage as the union of one man and one woman, President Bill Clinton had earlier signed the Defense of Marriage Act permitting states not to recognize same-sex marriages performed in other states and denying federal benefits to same-sex married couples.

The goal of this volume is to present a representative sample of diverse and well-informed opinions about the issue of same-sex marriage. We believe the coverage offered here of the various perspectives on this issue is fair and comprehensive, and we hope readers will be able to come to terms in constructive ways with all significant dimensions of this issue. We believe that each American, no matter how intensely he might disagree with other Americans, should seek to understand the perspectives of those others. We also believe that each American should acknowledge that most Americans, even those who have interests and traditions very different from his own, are persons of integrity who seek to understand and accommodate, to the extent that they are able with integrity to do so, the interests and traditions of Americans unlike themselves.

Waco, Texas
May 2004

NOTES

1. See David J. Garrow, "Toward a More Perfect Union," *New York Times Magazine*, May 9, 2004, included as chapter 2 in this volume. Garrow's essay is useful and informative, especially about some legal developments relevant to this issue.

2. Knight was quoted in a press release on the Family Research Council Web site. The contact listed on the Web site was Kristi S. Hamrick (202-393-2100, ext. 3017).

3. Lobel was quoted in a press release on the National Gay and Lesbian Task Force Web site. Contacts listed on the press release were Robert Bray (rbray@ngltf.org) and Tracey Conaty (tconaty@nglft.org).

Part One.

THE MASSACHUSETTS DECISION AND REACTIONS

1.

GOODRIDGE V. MASSACHUSETTS DEPARTMENT OF PUBLIC HEALTH

Massachusetts Supreme Judicial Court

MARSHALL, C.J.

Marriage is a vital social institution. The exclusive commitment of two individuals to each other nurtures love and mutual support; it brings stability to our society. For those who choose to marry, and for their children, marriage provides an abundance of legal, financial, and social benefits. In return it imposes weighty legal, financial, and social obligations. The question before us is whether, consistent with the Massachusetts Constitution, the commonwealth may deny the protections, benefits, and obligations conferred by civil marriage to two individuals of the same sex who wish to marry. We conclude that it may not. The Massachusetts Constitution affirms the dignity and equality of all individuals. It forbids the creation of second-class citizens. In reaching our conclusion we have given full deference to the arguments made by the commonwealth. But it has failed to identify any constitutionally adequate reason for denying civil marriage to same-sex couples.

We are mindful that our decision marks a change in the history of our marriage law. Many people hold deep-seated religious, moral, and ethical convictions that marriage should be limited to the union of one man and one woman, and that homosexual conduct is immoral. Many hold equally strong religious, moral, and ethical convictions that same-sex couples are entitled to be married, and that homosexual persons should be treated no differently than their heterosexual neighbors. Neither view answers the question before us. Our concern is with the Massachusetts Constitution as a charter of governance for every person properly within its reach. "Our obligation is to define the liberty of all, not to mandate our own moral code."

Whether the commonwealth may use its formidable regulatory authority to bar same-sex couples from civil marriage is a question not previously addressed by a Massachusetts appellate court. It is a question the United States Supreme Court left open as a matter of federal law in *Lawrence* [*v. Texas*, 2003] where it was not an issue. There, the Court affirmed that the core concept of common human dignity protected by the Fourteenth Amendment to the United States Constitution precludes government intrusion into the deeply personal realms of consensual adult expressions of intimacy and one's choice of an intimate partner. The Court also reaffirmed the central role that decisions whether to marry or have children bear in shaping one's identity. The Massachusetts Constitution is, if anything, more protective of individual liberty and equality than the federal Constitution; it may demand broader protection for fundamental rights; and it is less tolerant of government intrusion into the protected spheres of private life.

Barred access to the protections, benefits, and obligations of civil marriage, a person who enters into an intimate, exclusive union with another of the same sex is arbitrarily deprived of membership in one of our community's most rewarding and cherished institutions. That exclusion is incompatible with the constitutional principles of respect for individual autonomy and equality under law.

I

The plaintiffs are fourteen individuals from five Massachusetts counties. As of April 11, 2001, the date they filed their complaint, the plaintiffs Gloria Bailey, sixty years old, and Linda Davies, fifty-five years old, had been in a committed relationship for thirty years; the plaintiffs Maureen Brodoff, forty-nine years old, and Ellen Wade, fifty-two years old, had been in a committed relationship for twenty years and lived with their twelve-year-old daughter; the plaintiffs Hillary Goodridge, forty-four years old, and Julie Goodridge, forty-three years old, had been in a committed relationship for thirteen years and lived with their five-year-old daughter; the plaintiffs Gary Chalmers, thirty-five years old, and Richard Linnell, thirty-seven years old, had been in a committed relationship for thirteen years and lived with their eight-year-old daughter and Richard's mother; the plaintiffs Heidi Norton, thirty-six years old, and Gina Smith, thirty-six years old, had been in a committed relationship for eleven years and lived with their two sons, ages five years and one year; the plaintiffs Michael Horgan, forty-one years old, and David Balmelli, forty-one years old, had been in a committed relationship for seven years; and the plaintiffs David Wilson, fifty-seven years old, and Robert Compton, fifty-one years old, had been in a committed relationship for four years and had cared for David's mother in their home after a serious illness until she died.

The plaintiffs include business executives, lawyers, an investment banker, educators, therapists, and a computer engineer. Many are active in church, community, and school groups. They have employed such legal means as are available to them—for example, joint adoption, powers of attorney, and joint ownership of real property—to secure aspects of their relationships. Each plaintiff attests a desire to marry his or her partner in order to affirm publicly their commitment to each other and to secure the legal protections and benefits afforded to married couples and their children.

The Department of Public Health (department) is charged by statute with safeguarding public health. Among its responsibilities, the department oversees the registry of vital records and statistics (registry), which "enforce[s] all laws" relative to the issuance of marriage licenses and the keeping of marriage records, and which promulgates policies and procedures for the issuance of marriage licenses by city and town clerks and registers. The registry is headed by a registrar of vital records and statistics (registrar), appointed by the Commissioner of Public Health (commissioner) with the approval of the public health council and supervised by the commissioner.

In March and April 2001, each of the plaintiff couples attempted to obtain a marriage license from a city or town clerk's office. As required, . . . they completed notices of intention to marry on forms provided by the registry and presented these forms to a Massachusetts town or city clerk, together with the required health forms and marriage license fees. In each case, the clerk either refused to accept the notice of intention to marry or denied a marriage license to the couple on the ground that Massachusetts does not recognize same-sex marriage. Because obtaining a marriage license is a necessary prerequisite to civil marriage in Massachusetts, denying marriage licenses to the plaintiffs was tantamount to denying them access to civil marriage itself, with its appurtenant social and legal protections, benefits, and obligations.

On April 11, 2001, the plaintiffs filed suit in the Superior Court against the department and the commissioner seeking a judgment that "the exclusion of the [p]laintiff couples and other qualified same-sex couples from access to marriage licenses, and the legal and social status of civil marriage, as well as the protections, benefits, and obligations of marriage, violates Massachusetts law." . . .

The department, represented by the attorney general, admitted to a policy and practice of denying marriage licenses to same-sex couples. It denied that its actions violated any law or that the plaintiffs were entitled to relief. The parties filed cross motions for summary judgment.

A Superior Court judge ruled for the department. In a memorandum of decision and order dated May 7, 2002, he dismissed the plaintiffs' claim that the marriage statutes should be construed to permit marriage between persons of the same sex. . . . Turning to the constitutional claims, he held that the marriage exclusion does not offend the liberty, freedom, equality, or due process provisions of the Massachusetts Constitution, and that the Massachusetts Declaration of Rights does not guarantee "the fundamental right to marry a person of the same sex." He concluded that prohibiting same-sex marriage rationally furthers the legislature's legitimate interest in safeguarding the "primary purpose" of marriage, "procreation." The legislature may rationally limit marriage to opposite-sex couples, he concluded, because those couples are "theoretically . . . capable of procreation," they do not rely on "inherently more cumbersome" noncoital means of reproduction, and they are more likely than same-sex couples to have children, or more children.

After the complaint was dismissed and summary judgment entered for the defendants, the plaintiffs appealed. Both parties requested direct appellate review, which we granted.

II

Although the plaintiffs refer in passing to "the marriage statutes," they focus, quite properly, on G.L. c. 207, the marriage licensing statute, which controls entry into civil marriage. . . .

General Laws c. 207 is both a gatekeeping and a public records statute. It sets minimum qualifications for obtaining a marriage license and directs city and town clerks, the registrar, and the department to keep and maintain certain "vital records" of civil marriages. The gatekeeping provisions of G.L. c. 207 are minimal. They forbid marriage of individuals within certain degrees of consanguinity, and polygamous marriages. They prohibit marriage if one of the parties has communicable syphilis, and restrict the circumstances in which a person under eighteen years of age may marry. The statute requires that civil marriage be solemnized only by those so authorized. . . .

In short, for all the joy and solemnity that normally attend a marriage, G.L. c. 207, governing entrance to marriage, is a licensing law. The plaintiffs argue that because nothing in that licensing law specifically prohibits marriages between persons of the same sex, we may interpret the statute to permit "qualified same-sex couples" to obtain marriage licenses, thereby avoiding the question whether the law is constitutional. This claim lacks merit.

We interpret statutes to carry out the legislature's intent, determined by the words of a statute interpreted according to "the ordinary and approved usage of the language." The everyday meaning of "marriage" is "[t]he legal union of a man and woman as husband and wife," *Black's Law Dictionary* 986 (7th ed., 1999), and the plaintiffs do not argue that the term "marriage" has ever had a different meaning under Massachusetts law. This definition of marriage, as both the department and the Superior Court judge point out, derives from the common law. Far from being ambiguous, the undefined word "marriage," as used in G.L. c. 207, confirms the General Court's intent to hew to the term's common-law and quotidian meaning concerning the genders of the marriage partners.

The intended scope of G.L. c. 207 is also evident in its consanguinity provisions. Sections 1 and 2 of G.L. c. 207 prohibit marriages between a man and certain female relatives and a woman and certain male relatives, but are silent as to the consanguinity of male-male or female-female marriage applicants. The only reasonable explanation is that the legislature did not intend that same-sex couples be licensed to marry. We conclude, as did the judge, that G.L. c. 207 may not be construed to permit same-sex couples to marry.

III

A

The larger question is whether, as the department claims, government action that bars same-sex couples from civil marriage constitutes a legitimate exercise of the state's authority to regulate conduct, or whether, as the plaintiffs claim, this categorical marriage exclusion violates the Massachusetts Constitution. We have recognized the long-standing statutory understanding, derived from the common law, that "marriage" means the lawful union of a woman and a man. But that history cannot and does not foreclose the constitutional question.

The plaintiffs' claim that the marriage restriction violates the Massachusetts Constitution can be analyzed in two ways. Does it offend the constitution's guarantees of equality before the law? Or do the liberty and due process provisions of the Massachusetts Constitution secure the plaintiffs' right to marry their chosen partner? In matters implicating marriage, family life, and the upbringing of children, the two constitutional concepts frequently overlap, as they do here.

Much of what we say concerning one standard applies to the other.

We begin by considering the nature of civil marriage itself. Simply put, the government creates civil marriage. In Massachusetts, civil marriage is, and since precolonial days has been, precisely what its name implies: a wholly secular institution. No religious ceremony has ever been required to validate a Massachusetts marriage.

In a real sense, there are three partners to every civil marriage: two willing spouses and an approving state. While only the parties can mutually assent to marriage, the terms of the marriage—who may marry and what obligations, benefits, and liabilities attach to civil marriage—are set by the commonwealth. Conversely, while only the parties can agree to end the marriage (absent the death of one of them or a marriage void *ab initio*), the commonwealth defines the exit terms. . . .

In broad terms, it is the legislature's power to enact rules to regulate conduct, to the extent that such laws are "necessary to secure the health, safety, good order, comfort, or general welfare of the community."

Without question, civil marriage enhances the "welfare of the community." It is a "social institution of the highest importance." Civil marriage anchors an ordered society by encouraging stable relationships over transient ones. It is central to the way the commonwealth identifies individuals, provides for the orderly distribution of property, ensures that children and adults are cared for and supported whenever possible from private rather than public funds, and tracks important epidemiological and demographic data.

Marriage also bestows enormous private and social advantages on those who choose to marry. Civil marriage is at once a deeply personal commitment to another human being and a highly public celebration of the ideals of mutuality, companionship, intimacy, fidelity, and family. "It is an association that promotes a way of life, not causes; a harmony in living, not political faiths; a bilateral loyalty, not commercial or social projects." Because it fulfills yearnings for security, safe haven, and connection that express our common humanity, civil marriage is an esteemed institution, and the decision whether and whom to marry is among life's momentous acts of self-definition.

Tangible as well as intangible benefits flow from marriage. The marriage license grants valuable property rights to those who meet the entry requirements, and who agree to what might otherwise be a burdensome degree of government regulation of their activities. The benefits accessible only by way of a marriage license are enormous, touching nearly every aspect of life and death. The department states that "hundreds of statutes" are related to marriage and to marital benefits. . . .

It is undoubtedly for these . . . reasons, as well as for its intimately personal significance, that civil marriage has long been termed a "civil right."

Without the right to marry—or more properly, the right to choose to marry—one is excluded from the full range of human experience and denied full protection of the laws for one's "avowed commitment to an intimate and lasting human relationship." Because civil marriage is central to the lives of individuals and the welfare of the community, our laws assiduously protect the individual's right to marry against undue government incursion. Laws may not "interfere directly and substantially with the right to marry."

Unquestionably, the regulatory power of the commonwealth over civil marriage is broad, as is the commonwealth's discretion to award public benefits. Individuals who have the choice to marry each other and nevertheless choose not to may properly be denied the legal benefits of marriage. But that same logic cannot hold for a qualified individual who would marry if she or he only could.

B

For decades, indeed centuries, in much of this country (including Massachusetts) no lawful marriage was possible between white and black Americans. That long history availed not when the Supreme Court of California held in 1948 that a legislative prohibition against interracial marriage violated the due process and equality guarantees of the Fourteenth Amendment, *Perez v. Sharp* (1948), or when, nineteen years later, the United States Supreme Court also held that a statutory bar to interracial marriage violated the Fourteenth Amendment, *Loving v. Virginia* (1967). As both *Perez* and *Loving* make clear, the right to marry means little if it does not include the right to marry the person of one's choice, subject to appropriate government restrictions in the interests of public health, safety, and welfare. In this case, as in *Perez* and *Loving*, a statute deprives individuals of access to an institution of fundamental legal, personal, and social significance—the institution of marriage—because of a single trait: skin color in *Perez* and *Loving*, sexual orientation here. As it did in *Perez* and

Loving, history must yield to a more fully developed understanding of the invidious quality of the discrimination.

The Massachusetts Constitution protects matters of personal liberty against government incursion as zealously, and often more so, than does the federal Constitution, even where both constitutions employ essentially the same language. That the Massachusetts Constitution is in some instances more protective of individual liberty interests than is the federal Constitution is not surprising. Fundamental to the vigor of our federal system of government is that "state courts are absolutely free to interpret state constitutional provisions to accord greater protection to individual rights than do similar provisions of the United States Constitution."

The individual liberty and equality safeguards of the Massachusetts Constitution protect both "freedom from" unwarranted government intrusion into protected spheres of life and "freedom to" partake in benefits created by the state for the common good. Both freedoms are involved here. Whether and whom to marry, how to express sexual intimacy, and whether and how to establish a family—these are among the most basic of every individual's liberty and due process rights. And central to personal freedom and security is the assurance that the laws will apply equally to persons in similar situations. "Absolute equality before the law is a fundamental principle of our own Constitution." The liberty interest in choosing whether and whom to marry would be hollow if the commonwealth could, without sufficient justification, foreclose an individual from freely choosing the person with whom to share an exclusive commitment in the unique institution of civil marriage.

The Massachusetts Constitution requires, at a minimum, that the exercise of the state's regulatory authority not be "arbitrary or capricious." Under both the equality and liberty guarantees, regulatory authority must, at very least, serve "a legitimate purpose in a rational way"; a statute must "bear a reasonable relation to a permissible legislative objective." Any law failing to satisfy the basic standards of rationality is void.

The plaintiffs challenge the marriage statute on both equal protection and due process grounds. With respect to each such claim, we must first determine the appropriate standard of review. Where a statute implicates a fundamental right or uses a suspect classification, we employ "strict judicial scrutiny."

For all other statutes, we employ the "'rational basis' test." For due process claims, rational basis analysis requires that statutes "bear[] a real and substantial relation to the public health, safety, morals, or some other phase of the general welfare." For equal protection challenges, the rational basis test requires that "an impartial lawmaker could logically believe that the classification would serve a legitimate public purpose that transcends the harm to the members of the disadvantaged class."

The department argues that no fundamental right or "suspect" class is at issue here, and rational basis is the appropriate standard of review. For the reasons we explain below, we conclude that the marriage ban does not meet the rational basis test for either due process or equal protection. Because the statute does not survive rational basis review, we do not consider the plaintiffs' arguments that this case merits strict judicial scrutiny.

The department posits three legislative rationales for prohibiting same-sex couples from marrying: (1) providing a "favorable setting for procreation"; (2) ensuring the optimal setting for child rearing, which the department defines as "a two-parent family with one parent of each sex"; and (3) preserving scarce state and private financial resources. We consider each in turn.

The judge in the Superior Court endorsed the first rationale, holding that "the state's interest in regulating marriage is based on the traditional concept that marriage's primary purpose is procreation." This is incorrect. Our laws of civil marriage do not privilege procreative heterosexual intercourse between married people above every other form of adult intimacy and every other means of creating a family. General Laws c. 207 contains no requirement that the applicants for a marriage license attest to their ability or intention to conceive children by coitus. Fertility is not a condition of marriage, nor is it grounds for divorce. People who have never consummated their marriage, and never plan to, may be and stay married. People who cannot stir from their deathbed may marry. While it is certainly true that many, perhaps most, married couples have children together (assisted or unassisted), it is the exclusive and permanent commitment of the marriage partners to one another, not the begetting of children, that is the sine qua non of civil marriage.

Moreover, the commonwealth affirmatively facilitates bringing children into a family regardless of whether the intended parent is married or unmarried, whether the child is adopted or born into a family, whether assistive technology was used to conceive the child, and whether the parent or her partner is heterosexual, homosexual, or bisexual. If procreation were a necessary component of civil marriage, our statutes would draw a tighter circle around the permissible bounds of nonmarital childbearing and the creation of families by noncoital means. The attempt to isolate procreation as "the source of a fundamental right to marry," . . . overlooks the integrated way in which courts have examined the complex and overlapping realms of personal autonomy, marriage, family life, and child rearing. Our jurisprudence recognizes that, in these nuanced and fundamentally private areas of life, such a narrow focus is inappropriate.

The "marriage is procreation" argument singles out the one unbridgeable difference between same-sex and opposite-sex couples, and transforms that difference into the essence of legal marriage. Like "Amendment 2" to the Constitution of Colorado, which effectively denied homosexual persons equality under the law and full access to the political process, the marriage restriction impermissibly "identifies persons by a single trait and then denies them protection across the board." *Romer v. Evans* (1996). In so doing, the state's action confers an official stamp of approval on the destructive stereotype that same-sex relationships are inherently unstable and inferior to opposite-sex relationships and are not worthy of respect.

The department's first stated rationale, equating marriage with unassisted heterosexual procreation, shades imperceptibly into its second: that confining marriage to opposite-sex couples ensures that children are raised in the "optimal" setting. Protecting the welfare of children is a paramount state policy. Restricting marriage to opposite-sex couples, however, cannot plausibly further this policy. "The demographic changes of the past century make it difficult to speak of an average American family. The composition of families varies greatly from household to household." Massachusetts has responded supportively to "the changing realities of the American family," and has moved vigorously to strengthen the modern family in its many variations. Moreover, we have repudiated the common-law power of the state to provide varying levels of protection to children based on the circumstances of birth. The "best interests of the child" standard does not turn on a parent's sexual orientation or martial status.

The department has offered no evidence that forbidding marriage to people of the same sex will increase the number of couples choosing to enter into opposite-sex marriages in order to have and raise children. There is thus no rational relationship between the marriage statute and the commonwealth's proffered goal of protecting the "optimal" child rearing unit. Moreover, the department readily concedes that people in same-sex couples may be "excellent" parents. These couples (including four of the plaintiff couples) have children for the reasons others do—to love them, to care for them, to nurture them. But the task of child rearing for same-sex couples is made infinitely harder by their status as outliers to the marriage laws. While establishing the parentage of children as soon as possible is crucial to the safety and welfare of children, same-sex couples must undergo the sometimes lengthy and intrusive process of second-parent adoption to establish their joint parentage. While the enhanced income provided by marital benefits is an important source of security and stability for married couples and their children, those benefits are denied to families headed by same-sex couples. While the laws of divorce provide clear and reasonably predictable guidelines for child support, child custody, and property division on dissolution of a marriage, same-sex couples who dissolve their relationships find themselves and their children in the highly unpredictable terrain of equity jurisdiction. Given the wide range of public benefits reserved only for married couples, we do not credit the department's contention that the absence of access to civil marriage amounts to little more than an inconvenience to same-sex couples and their children. Excluding same-sex couples from civil marriage will not make children of opposite-sex marriages more secure, but it does prevent children of same-sex couples from enjoying the immeasurable advantages that flow from the assurance of "a stable family structure in which children will be reared, educated, and socialized."

No one disputes that the plaintiff couples are families, that many are parents, and that the children they are raising, like all children, need and should have the fullest opportunity to grow up in a secure, protected family unit. Similarly, no one disputes that, under the rubric of marriage, the state provides a cornucopia of substantial benefits to married parents and their children. The preferential treatment of civil marriage reflects the legislature's conclusion that marriage "is the foremost setting for the education and socialization of children" precisely because it "encourages parents to remain committed to each other and to their children as they grow."

In this case, we are confronted with an entire, sizable class of parents raising children who have absolutely no access to civil marriage and its protections because they are forbidden from procuring a marriage license. It cannot be rational under our laws, and indeed it is not permitted, to penalize children by depriving them of state benefits because the state disapproves of their parents' sexual orientation.

The third rationale advanced by the department is that limiting marriage to opposite-sex couples furthers the legislature's interest in conserving scarce state and private financial resources. The marriage restriction is rational, it argues, because the General Court logically could assume that same-sex couples are more financially independent than married couples and thus less needy of public marital benefits, such as tax advantages, or private marital benefits, such as employer-financed health plans that include spouses in their coverage.

An absolute statutory ban on same-sex marriage bears no rational relationship to the goal of economy. First, the department's conclusory generalization—that same-sex couples are less financially dependent on each other than opposite-sex couples—ignores that many same-sex couples, such as many of the plaintiffs in this case, have children and other dependents (here, aged parents) in their care. The department does not contend, nor could it, that these dependents are less needy or deserving than the dependents of married couples. Second, Massachusetts marriage laws do not condition receipt of public and private financial benefits to married individuals on a demonstration of financial dependence on each other; the benefits are available to married couples regardless of whether they mingle their finances or actually depend on each other for support.

The department suggests additional rationales for prohibiting same-sex couples from marrying, which are developed by some amici. It argues that broadening civil marriage to include same-sex couples will trivialize or destroy the institution of marriage as it has historically been fashioned. Certainly our decision today marks a significant change in the definition of marriage as it has been inherited from the common law, and understood by many societies for centuries. But it does not disturb the fundamental value of marriage in our society.

Here, the plaintiffs seek only to be married, not to undermine the institution of civil marriage. They do not want marriage abolished. They do not attack the binary nature of marriage, the consanguinity provisions, or any of the other gatekeeping provisions of the marriage licensing law. Recognizing the right of an individual to marry a person of the same sex will not diminish the validity or dignity of opposite-sex marriage, any more than recognizing the right of an individual to marry a person of a different race devalues the marriage of a person who marries someone of her own race. If anything, extending civil marriage to same-sex couples reinforces the importance of marriage to individuals and communities. That same-sex couples are willing to embrace marriage's solemn obligations of exclusivity, mutual support, and commitment to one another is a testament to the enduring place of marriage in our laws and in the human spirit.

It has been argued that, due to the state's strong interest in the institution of marriage as a stabilizing social structure, only the legislature can control and define its boundaries. Accordingly, our elected representatives legitimately may choose to exclude same-sex couples from civil marriage in order to assure all citizens of the commonwealth that (1) the benefits of our marriage laws are available explicitly to create and support a family setting that is, in the legislature's view, optimal for child rearing, and (2) the state does not endorse gay and lesbian parenthood as the equivalent of being raised by one's married biological parents. These arguments miss the point. The Massachusetts Constitution requires that legislation meet certain criteria and not extend beyond certain limits. It is the function of courts to determine whether these criteria are met and whether these limits are exceeded. In most instances, these limits are defined by whether a rational basis exists to conclude that legislation will bring about a rational result. The legislature in the first instance, and the courts in the last instance, must ascertain whether such a rational basis exists. To label the court's role as usurping that of the legislature . . . is to misunderstand the nature and purpose of judicial review. We owe great deference to the legislature to decide social and policy issues, but it is the traditional and settled role of courts to decide constitutional issues.

The history of constitutional law "is the story of the extension of constitutional rights and protections to people once ignored or excluded." *United States v. Virginia* (1996). This statement is as true in the area of civil marriage as in any other area of civil rights. As a public institution and a right of fundamental importance, civil marriage is an evolving paradigm. The common law was exceptionally harsh toward women who became wives: a woman's legal identity all but evaporated into that of her husband. Thus, one early-nineteenth-century jurist could observe matter of factly that, prior to the abolition of slavery in Massachusetts, "the condition of a slave resembled the connection of a wife with her husband, and of infant children with their father. He is obliged to maintain them, and they cannot be separated from him." But since at least the middle of the nineteenth century, both the courts and the legislature have acted to ameliorate the harshness of the common-law regime. Alarms about the imminent erosion of the "natural" order of marriage were sounded over the demise of antimiscegenation laws, the expansion of the rights of married women, and the introduction of "no-fault" divorce. Marriage has survived all of these transformations, and we have no doubt that marriage will continue to be a vibrant and revered institution.

We also reject the argument suggested by the department, and elaborated by some amici, that expanding the institution of civil marriage in Massachusetts to include same-sex couples will lead to interstate conflict. We would not presume to dictate how another state should respond to today's decision. But neither should considerations of comity prevent us from according Massachusetts residents the full measure of protection available under the Massachusetts Constitution. The genius of our federal system is that each state's constitution has vitality specific to its own traditions, and that, subject to the minimum requirements of the Fourteenth Amendment, each state is free to address difficult issues of individual liberty in the manner its own constitution demands.

Several amici suggest that prohibiting marriage by same-sex couples reflects community consensus that homosexual conduct is immoral. Yet Massachusetts has a strong affirmative policy of preventing discrimination on the basis of sexual orientation.

The department has had more than ample opportunity to articulate a constitutionally adequate justification for limiting civil marriage to opposite-sex unions. It has failed to do so. The department has offered purported justifications for the civil marriage restriction that are starkly at odds with the comprehensive network of vigorous, gender-neutral laws promoting stable families and the best interests of children. It has failed to identify any relevant characteristic that would justify shutting the door to civil marriage to a person who wishes to marry someone of the same sex.

The marriage ban works a deep and scarring hardship on a very real segment of the community for no rational reason. The absence of any reasonable relationship between, on the one hand, an absolute disqualification of same-sex couples who wish to enter into civil marriage and, on the other, protection of public health, safety, or general welfare, suggests that the marriage restriction is rooted in persistent prejudices against persons who are (or who are believed to be) homosexual. "The Constitution cannot control such prejudices but neither can it tolerate them. Private biases may be outside the reach of the law, but the law cannot, directly or indirectly, give them effect." *Palmore v. Sidoti* (1984). Limiting the protections, benefits, and obligations of civil marriage to opposite-sex couples violates the basic premises of individual liberty and equality under law protected by the Massachusetts Constitution.

IV

We consider next the plaintiffs' request for relief. We preserve as much of the statute as may be preserved in the face of the successful constitutional challenge.

Here, no one argues that striking down the marriage laws is an appropriate form of relief. Eliminating civil marriage would be wholly inconsistent with the legislature's deep commitment to fostering stable families and would dismantle a vital organizing principle of our society. We face a problem similar to one that recently confronted the Court of Appeal for Ontario, the highest court of that

Canadian province, when it considered the constitutionality of the same-sex marriage ban under Canada's federal constitution, the Charter of Rights and Freedoms (Charter). Canada, like the United States, adopted the common law of England that civil marriage is "the voluntary union for life of one man and one woman, to the exclusion of all others." In holding that the limitation of civil marriage to opposite-sex couples violated the Charter, the Court of Appeal refined the common-law meaning of marriage. We concur with this remedy, which is entirely consonant with established principles of jurisprudence empowering a court to refine a common-law principle in light of evolving constitutional standards.

We construe civil marriage to mean the voluntary union of two persons as spouses, to the exclusion of all others. This reformulation redresses the plaintiffs' constitutional injury and furthers the aim of marriage to promote stable, exclusive relationships. It advances the two legitimate state interests the department has identified: providing a stable setting for child rearing and conserving state resources. It leaves intact the legislature's broad discretion to regulate marriage.

In their complaint the plaintiffs request only a declaration that their exclusion and the exclusion of other qualified same-sex couples from access to civil marriage violates Massachusetts law. We declare that barring an individual from the protections, benefits, and obligations of civil marriage solely because that person would marry a person of the same sex violates the Massachusetts Constitution. We vacate the summary judgment for the department. We remand this case to the Superior Court for entry of judgment consistent with this opinion. Entry of judgment shall be stayed for 180 days to permit the legislature to take such action as it may deem appropriate in light of this opinion.

So ordered.

GREANEY, J. (CONCURRING)

I agree with the result reached by the court, the remedy ordered, and much of the reasoning in the court's opinion. In my view, however, the case is more directly resolved using traditional equal protection analysis.

(a) Article 1 of the Declaration of Rights, as amended by art. 106 of the Amendments to the Massachusetts Constitution, provides:

> All people are born free and equal and have certain natural, essential and unalienable rights; among which may be reckoned the right of enjoying and defending their lives and liberties; that of acquiring, possessing and protecting property; in fine, that of seeking and obtaining their safety and happiness. Equality under the law shall not be denied or abridged because of sex, race, color, creed or national origin.

This provision, even prior to its amendment, guaranteed to all people in the commonwealth—equally—the enjoyment of rights that are deemed important or fundamental. The withholding of relief from the plaintiffs, who wish to marry, and are otherwise eligible to marry, on the ground that the couples are of the same gender, constitutes a categorical restriction of a fundamental right. The restriction creates a straightforward case of discrimination that disqualifies an entire group of our citizens and their families from participation in an institution of paramount legal and social importance. This is impermissible under art. 1.

Analysis begins with the indisputable premise that the deprivation suffered by the plaintiffs is no mere legal inconvenience. The right to marry is not a privilege conferred by the state, but a fundamental right that is protected against unwarranted state interference. This right is essentially vitiated if one is denied the right to marry a person of one's choice.

Because our marriage statutes intend, and state, the ordinary understanding that marriage under our law consists only of a union between a man and a woman, they create a statutory classification based on the sex of the two people who wish to marry. That the classification is sex based is self-evident. The marriage statutes prohibit some applicants, such as the plaintiffs, from obtaining a marriage license, and that prohibition is based solely on the applicants' gender. As a factual matter, an individual's choice of marital partner is constrained because of his or her own sex. Stated in particular terms, Hillary Goodridge cannot marry Julie Goodridge because she (Hillary) is a woman. Likewise, Gary Chalmers cannot marry Richard Linnell because he (Gary) is a man. Only their gender prevents Hillary and Gary from marrying their chosen partners under the present law.

A classification may be gender based whether or not the challenged government action apportions benefits or burdens uniformly along gender lines. This is so because constitutional protections extend to individuals and not to categories of people. Thus, when an individual desires to marry, but cannot marry his or her chosen partner because of the traditional opposite-sex restriction, a violation of art. 1 has occurred. I find it disingenuous, at best, to suggest that such an individual's right to marry has not been burdened at all, because he or she remains free to chose another partner who is of the opposite sex.

The equal protection infirmity at work here is strikingly similar to (although, perhaps, more subtle than) the invidious discrimination perpetuated by Virginia's antimiscegenation laws and unveiled in the decision of *Loving v. Virginia*. In its landmark decision striking down Virginia's ban on marriages between Caucasians and members of any other race on both equal protection and substantive due process grounds, the United States Supreme Court soundly rejected the proposition that the equal application of the ban (i.e., that it applied equally to whites and blacks) made unnecessary the strict scrutiny analysis traditionally required of statutes drawing classifications according to race. That our marriage laws, unlike antimiscegenation laws, were not enacted purposely to discriminate in no way neutralizes their present discriminatory character.

With these two propositions established (the infringement on a fundamental right and a sex-based classification), the enforcement of the marriage statutes as they are currently understood is forbidden by our Constitution unless the state can present a compelling purpose further by the statutes that can be accomplished in no other reasonable manner. This the state has not done. The justifications put forth by the state to sustain the statute's exclusion of the plaintiffs are insufficient for the reasons explained by the court. . . .

A comment is in order with respect to the insistence of some that marriage is, as a matter of definition, the legal union of a man and a woman. To define the institution of marriage by the characteristics of those to whom it always has been accessible, in order to justify the exclusion of those to whom it never has been accessible, is conclusory and bypasses the core question we are asked to decide. This case calls for a higher level of legal analysis. Precisely, the case requires that we confront ingrained assumptions with respect to historically accepted roles of men and women within the institution of marriage and requires that we reexamine these assumptions in light of the unequivocal language of art. 1, in order to ensure that the governmental conduct challenged here conforms to the supreme charter of our commonwealth. "A written constitution is the fundamental law for the government of a sovereign state. It is the final statement of the rights, privileges, and obligations of the citizens and the ultimate grant of the powers and the conclusive definition of the limitations of the departments of state and of public officers. . . . To its provisions the conduct of all governmental affairs must conform. From its terms there is no appeal." I do not doubt the sincerity of deeply held moral or religious beliefs that make inconceivable to some the notion that any change in the common-law definition of what constitutes a legal civil marriage is now, or ever would be, warranted.

But, as matter of constitutional law, neither the mantra of tradition, nor individual conviction, can justify the perpetuation of a hierarchy in which couples of the same sex and their families are deemed less worthy of social and legal recognition than couples of the opposite sex and their families.

(b) I am hopeful that our decision will be accepted by those thoughtful citizens who believe that same-sex unions should not be approved by the state. I am not referring here to acceptance in the sense of grudging acknowledgment of the court's authority to adjudicate the matter. My hope is more liberating. The plaintiffs are members of our community, our neighbors, our coworkers, our friends. As pointed out by the court, their professions include investment advisor, computer engineer, teacher, therapist, and lawyer. The plaintiffs volunteer in our schools, worship beside us in our religious houses, and have children who play with our children, to mention just a few ordinary daily contacts. We share a common humanity and participate together in the social contract that is the foundation of our commonwealth. Simple principles of decency dictate that we extend to the plaintiffs, and to their new status, full acceptance, tolerance, and respect. We should do so because it is the right thing to do. The union of two people contemplated by G.L. c. 207 "is a coming together for better or for worse, hopefully enduring, and intimate to the degree of being sacred. It is an association that promotes a way of life, not causes; a harmony in living, not political faiths; a bilateral loyalty, not commercial or social projects. Yet it is an association for as noble a purpose as any involved in our prior decisions."

SPINA, J.
(DISSENTING, WITH WHOM SOSMAN AND CORDY, JJ., JOIN)

What is at stake in this case is not the unequal treatment of individuals or whether individual rights have been impermissibly burdened, but the power of the legislature to effectuate social change without interference from the courts. The power to regulate marriage lies with the legislature, not with the judiciary. Today, the court has transformed its role as protector of individual rights into the role of creator of rights, and I respectfully dissent.

1. Equal protection. Although the court did not address the plaintiffs' gender discrimination claim, G.L. c. 207 does not unconstitutionally discriminate on the basis of gender. A claim of gender discrimination will lie where it is shown that differential treatment disadvantages one sex over the other. General Laws c. 207 enumerates certain qualifications for obtaining a marriage license. It creates no distinction between the sexes, but applies to men and women in precisely the same way. It does not create any disadvantage identified with gender as both men and women are similarly limited to marrying a person of the opposite sex.

Similarly, the marriage statutes do not discriminate on the basis of sexual orientation. As the court correctly recognizes, constitutional protections are extended to individuals, not couples. The marriage statutes do not disqualify individuals on the basis of sexual orientation from entering into marriage. All individuals, with certain exceptions not relevant here, are free to marry. Whether an individual chooses not to marry because of sexual orientation or any other reason should be of no concern to the court.

The court concludes, however, that G.L. c. 207 unconstitutionally discriminates against the individual plaintiffs because it denies them the "right to marry the person of one's choice" where that person is of the same sex. To reach this result the court relies on *Loving v. Virginia*, and transforms "choice" into the essential element of the institution of marriage. The *Loving* case did not use the word "choice" in this manner, and it did not point to the result that the court reaches today. In *Loving*, the Supreme Court struck down as unconstitutional a statute that prohibited Caucasians from marrying non-Caucasians. It concluded that the statute was intended to preserve white supremacy and invidiously discriminated against non-Caucasians because of their race. The "choice" to which the Supreme Court referred was the "choice to marry," and it concluded that with respect to the institution of marriage, the state had no compelling interest in limiting the choice to marry along racial lines. The

Supreme Court did not imply the existence of a right to marry a person of the same sex. To the same effect is *Perez v. Sharp*, on which the court also relies.

Unlike the *Loving* and *Sharp* cases, the Massachusetts legislature has erected no barrier to marriage that intentionally discriminates against anyone. Within the institution of marriage, anyone is free to marry, with certain exceptions that are not challenged. In the absence of any discriminatory purpose, the state's marriage statutes do not violate principles of equal protection. This court should not have invoked even the most deferential standard of review within equal protection analysis because no individual was denied access to the institution of marriage.

2. Due process. The marriage statutes do not impermissibly burden a right protected by our constitutional guarantee of due process implicit in art. 10 of our Declaration of Rights. There is no restriction on the right of any plaintiff to enter into marriage. Each is free to marry a willing person of the opposite sex.

Substantive due process protects individual rights against unwarranted government intrusion. The court states, as we have said on many occasions, that the Massachusetts Declaration of Rights may protect a right in ways that exceed the protection afforded by the federal Constitution. However, today the court does not fashion a remedy that affords greater protection of a right. Instead, using the rubric of due process it has redefined marriage. . . .

Although this court did not state that same-sex marriage is a fundamental right worthy of strict scrutiny protection, it nonetheless deemed it a constitutionally protected right by applying rational basis review. Before applying any level of constitutional analysis there must be a recognized right at stake. Same-sex marriage, or the "right to marry the person of one's choice" as the court today defines that right, does not fall within the fundamental right to marry. . . . In this commonwealth and in this country, the roots of the institution of marriage are deeply set in history as a civil union between a single man and a single woman. There is no basis for the court to recognize same-sex marriage as a constitutionally protected right.

3. Remedy. The remedy that the court has fashioned both in the name of equal protection and due process exceeds the bounds of judicial restraint. . . .

Courts have authority to recognize rights that are supported by the Constitution and history, but the power to create novel rights is reserved for the people through the democratic and legislative processes. . . .

By extending constitutional protection to an asserted right or liberty interest, we, to a great extent, place the matter outside the arena of public debate and legislative action. We must therefore "exercise the utmost care whenever we are asked to break new ground in this field," lest the liberty protected by the Due Process Clause be subtly transformed into the policy preferences of the members of this court. . . .

The court has extruded a new right from principles of substantive due process, and in doing so it has distorted the meaning and purpose of due process. The purpose of substantive due process is to protect existing rights, not to create new rights. . . .

SOSMAN, J.
(DISSENTING, WITH WHOM SPINA AND CORDY, JJ., JOIN)

In applying the rational basis test to any challenged statutory scheme, the issue is not whether the legislature's rationale behind that scheme is persuasive to us, but only whether it satisfies a minimal threshold of rationality. Today, rather than apply that test, the court announces that, because it is persuaded that there are no differences between same-sex and opposite-sex couples, the legislature has no rational basis for treating them differently with respect to the granting of marriage licenses. Reduced to its essence, the court's opinion concludes that, because same-sex couples are now raising children, and withholding the benefits of civil marriage from their union makes it harder for them to raise those children, the state must therefore provide the benefits of civil marriage to same-sex couples just as it does to opposite-sex couples. Of course, many people are raising children outside the confines of traditional marriage, and, by definition, those children are being deprived of the various benefits that would flow if they were being raised in a household with married parents. That does not mean that the legislature must accord the full benefits of marital status on every household raising children. Rather, the legislature need only have some rational basis for concluding that, at present, those alternate family structures have not yet been conclusively shown to be the equivalent of the marital family structure that has established itself as a successful one over a period of centuries. People are of course at liberty to raise their children in various family structures, as long as they are not literally harming their children by doing so. That does not mean that the state is required to provide identical forms of encouragement, endorsement, and support to all of the infinite variety of household structures that a free society permits.

Based on our own philosophy of child rearing, and on our observations of the children being raised by same-sex couples to whom we are personally close, we may be of the view that what matters to children is not the gender, or sexual orientation, or even the number of the adults who raise them, but rather whether those adults provide the children with a nurturing, stable, safe, consistent, and supportive environment in which to mature. Same-sex couples can provide their children with the requisite nurturing, stable, safe, consistent, and supportive environment in which to mature, just as opposite-sex couples do. It is therefore understandable that the court might view the traditional definition of marriage as an unnecessary anachronism, rooted in historical prejudices that modern society has in large measure rejected and biological limitations that modern science has overcome.

It is not, however, our assessment that matters. Conspicuously absent from the court's opinion today is any acknowledgment that the attempts at scientific study of the ramifications of raising children in same-sex couple households are themselves in their infancy and have so far produced inconclusive and conflicting results. Notwithstanding our belief that gender and sexual orientation of parents should not matter to the success of the child-rearing venture, studies to date reveal that there are still some observable differences between children raised by opposite-sex couples and children raised by same-sex couples. Interpretation of the data gathered by those studies then becomes clouded by the personal and political beliefs of the investigators, both as to whether the differences identified are positive or negative, and as to the untested explanations of what might account for those differences. (This is hardly the first time in history that the ostensible steel of the scientific method has melted and buckled under the intense heat of political and religious passions.) Even in the absence of bias or political agenda behind the various studies of children raised by same-sex couples, the most neutral and strict application of scientific principles to this field would be constrained by the limited period of observation that has been available. Gay and lesbian couples living together openly, and official recognition of them as their children's sole parents, comprise a very recent phenomenon, and the recency of that phenomenon has not yet permitted any study of how those children fare as adults and at best minimal study of how they fare during their adolescent years. The legislature can rationally view the state of the scientific evidence as unsettled on the critical question it now faces: Are families headed by same-sex parents equally successful in rearing children from infancy to adulthood as families headed by parents of opposite sexes? Our belief that children raised by same-sex couples should fare the same as children raised in traditional families is just that: a passionately held but utterly untested belief. The legislature is not required to share that belief but may, as the creator of the institution of civil marriage, wish to see the proof before making a fundamental alteration to that institution.

Although ostensibly applying the rational basis test to the civil marriage statutes, it is abundantly apparent that the court is in fact applying some undefined stricter standard to assess the constitutionality of the marriage statutes' exclusion of same-sex couples. While avoiding any express conclusion as to any of the proffered routes by which that exclusion would be subjected to a test of strict scrutiny—infringement of a fundamental right, discrimination based on gender, or discrimination against gays and lesbians as a suspect classification—the opinion repeatedly alludes to those concepts in a prolonged and eloquent prelude before articulating its view that the exclusion lacks even a rational basis. . . . In short, while claiming to apply a mere rational basis test, the court's opinion works up an enormous head of steam by repeated invocations of avenues by which to subject the statute to strict scrutiny, apparently hoping that that head of steam will generate momentum sufficient to propel the opinion across the yawning chasm of the very deferential rational basis test.

Shorn of these emotion-laden invocations, the opinion ultimately opines that the legislature is acting irrationally when it grants benefits to a proven successful family structure while denying the same benefits to a recent, perhaps promising, but essentially untested alternate family structure. Placed in a more neutral context, the court would never find any irrationality in such an approach. For example, if the issue were government subsidies and tax benefits promoting use of an established technology for energy efficient heating, the court would find no equal protection or due process violation in the legislature's decision not to grant the same benefits to an inventor or manufacturer of some new, alternative technology who did not yet have sufficient data to prove that that new technology was just as good as the established technology. That the early results from preliminary testing of the new technology might look very promising, or that the theoretical underpinnings of the new technology might appear flawless, would not make it irrational for the legislature to grant subsidies and tax breaks to the established technology and deny them to the still unproved newcomer in the field. While programs that affect families and children register higher on our emotional scale than programs affecting energy efficiency, our standards for what is or is not "rational" should not be bent by those emotional tugs. Where, as here, there is no ground for applying strict scrutiny, the emotionally compelling nature of the subject matter should not affect the manner in which we apply the rational basis test.

Or, to the extent that the court is going to invoke such emotion-laden and value-laden rhetoric as a means of heightening the degree of scrutiny to be applied, the same form of rhetoric can be employed to justify the legislature's proceeding with extreme caution in this area. In considering whether the legislature has a rational reason for postponing a dramatic change to the definition of marriage, it is surely pertinent to the inquiry to recognize that this proffered change affects not just a load-bearing wall of our social structure but the very cornerstone of that structure. Before making a fundamental alteration to that cornerstone, it is eminently rational for the legislature to require a high degree of certainty as to the precise consequences of that alteration, to make sure that it can be done safely, without either temporary or lasting damage to the structural integrity of the entire edifice. The court today blithely assumes that there are no such dangers and that it is safe to proceed, an assumption that is not supported by anything more than the court's blind faith that it is so.

More importantly, it is not our confidence in the lack of adverse consequences that is at issue, or even whether that confidence is justifiable. The issue is whether it is rational to reserve judgment on whether this change can be made at this time without damaging the institution of marriage or adversely affecting the critical role it has played in our society. Absent consensus on the issue (which obviously does not exist), or unanimity amongst scientists studying the issue (which also does not exist), or a more prolonged period of observation of this new family structure (which has not yet been possible), it is rational for the legislature to postpone any redefinition of marriage that would include same-sex couples until such time as it is certain that that redefinition will not have unintended and undesirable social consequences. Through the political process, the people may decide when the benefits of extending civil marriage to same-sex couples have been shown to outweigh whatever risks—be they palpable or ephemeral—are involved. However minimal the risks of that redefinition of marriage may seem to us from our vantage point, it is not up to us to decide what risks society must run, and it is inappropriate for us to abrogate that power to ourselves merely because we are confident that "it is the right thing to do."

As a matter of social history, today's opinion may represent a great turning point that many will hail as a tremendous step toward a more just society. As a matter of constitutional jurisprudence, however, the case stands as an aberration. To reach the result it does, the court has tortured the rational basis test beyond recognition. I fully appreciate the strength of the temptation to find this particular law unconstitutional—there is much to be said for the argument that excluding gay and lesbian couples from the benefits of civil marriage is cruelly unfair and hopelessly outdated; the inability to marry has a profound impact on the personal lives of committed gay and lesbian couples (and their children) to whom we are personally close (our friends, neighbors, family members, classmates, and coworkers); and our resolution of this issue takes place under the intense glare of national and international publicity. Speaking metaphorically, these factors have combined to turn the case before us into a "perfect storm" of a constitutional question. In my view, however, such factors make it all the more imperative that we adhere precisely and scrupulously to the established guideposts of our constitutional jurisprudence, a jurisprudence that makes the rational basis test an extremely deferential one that focuses on the rationality, not the persuasiveness, of the potential justifications for the classifications in the legislative scheme. I trust that, once this particular "storm" clears, we will return to the rational basis test as it has always been understood and applied. Applying that deferential test in the manner it is customarily applied, the exclusion of gay and lesbian couples from the institution of civil marriage passes constitutional muster. I respectfully dissent.

CORDY, J.
(DISSENTING, WITH WHOM SPINA AND SOSMAN, JJ., JOIN)

The court's opinion concludes that the Department of Public Health has failed to identify any "constitutionally adequate reason" for limiting civil marriage to opposite-sex unions, and that there is no "reasonable relationship" between a disqualification of same-sex couples who wish to enter into a civil marriage and the protection of public health, safety, or general welfare. Consequently, it holds that the marriage statute cannot withstand scrutiny under the Massachusetts Constitution. Because I find these conclusions to be unsupportable in light of the nature of the rights and regulations at issue, the presumption of constitutional validity and significant deference afforded to legislative enactments, and the "undesirability of the judiciary substituting its notions of correct policy for that of a popularly elected legislature" responsible for making such policy, I respectfully dissent. Although it may be desirable for many reasons to extend to same-sex couples the benefits and burdens of civil marriage (and the plaintiffs have made a powerfully reasoned case for that extension), that decision must be made by the legislature, not the court.

If a statute either impairs the exercise of a fundamental right protected by the due process or liberty provisions of our state constitution, or discriminates based on a constitutionally suspect classification such as sex, it will be subject to strict scrutiny when its validity is challenged. If it does neither, a statute "will be upheld if it is 'rationally related to a legitimate State purpose.'" . . .

The Massachusetts marriage statute does not impair the exercise of a recognized fundamental right, or discriminate on the basis of sex in violation of the equal rights amendment to the Massachusetts Constitution. Consequently, it is subject to review only to determine whether it satisfies the rational basis test. Because a conceivable rational basis exists upon which the legislature could conclude that the marriage statute furthers the legitimate state purpose of ensuring, promoting, and supporting an optimal social structure for the bearing and raising of children, it is a valid exercise of the state's police power.

A. Limiting marriage to the union of one man and one woman does not impair the exercise of a fundamental right. Civil marriage is an institution created by the state. In Massachusetts, the marriage statutes are derived from English common law and were first enacted in colonial times. They were enacted to secure public interests and not for religious purposes or to promote personal interests or aspirations. As the court notes in its opinion, the institution of marriage is "the legal union of a man and woman as husband and wife," and it has always been so under Massachusetts law, colonial or otherwise.

The plaintiffs contend that because the right to choose to marry is a "fundamental" right, the right to marry the person of one's choice, including a member of the same sex, must also be a "fundamental" right. While the court stops short of deciding that the right to marry someone of the same sex is "fundamental" such that strict scrutiny must be applied to any statute that impairs it, it nevertheless agrees with the plaintiffs that the right to choose to marry is of fundamental importance ("among the most basic" of every person's "liberty and due process rights") and would be "hollow" if an individual was foreclosed from "freely choosing the person with whom to share . . . the . . . institution of civil marriage." Hence, it concludes that a marriage license cannot be denied to an individual who wishes to marry someone of the same sex. In reaching this result the court has transmuted the "right" to marry into a right to change the institution of marriage itself. This feat of reasoning succeeds only if one accepts the proposition that the definition of the institution of marriage as a union between a man and a woman is merely "conclusory" rather than the basis on which the "right" to partake in it has been deemed to be of fundamental importance. In other words, only by assuming that "marriage" includes the union of two persons of the same sex does the court conclude that restricting marriage to opposite-sex couples infringes on the "right" of same-sex couples of "marry."

The plaintiffs ground their contention that they have a fundamental right to marry a person of the same sex in a long line of Supreme Court decisions . . . that discuss the importance of marriage. In context, all of these decisions and their discussions are about the "fundamental" nature of the institution of marriage as it has existed and been understood in this country, not as the court has redefined it today. Even in that context, its "fundamental" nature is derivative of the nature of the interests that underlie or are associated with it. An examination of those interests reveals that they are either not shared by same-sex couples or not implicated by the marriage statutes.

Supreme Court cases that have described marriage or the right to marry as "fundamental" have focused primarily on the underlying interest of every individual in procreation, which, historically, could only legally occur within the construct of marriage because sexual intercourse outside of marriage was a criminal act. In *Skinner v. Oklahoma*, the first case to characterize marriage as a "fundamental" right, the Supreme Court stated, as its rationale for striking down a sterilization statute, that "[m]arriage and procreation are fundamental to the very existence of the race." In concluding that a sterilized individual "is forever deprived of a basic liberty," the Court was obviously referring to procreation rather than marriages. Similarly, in *Loving v. Virginia*, in which the United States Supreme Court struck down Virginia's antimiscegenation statute, the Court implicitly linked marriage with procreation in describing marriage as "fundamental to our very existence." In *Zablocki v. Redhail*, the Court expressly linked the right to marry with the right to procreate, concluding that "if [the plaintiffs] right to procreate means anything at all, it must imply some right to enter the only relationship in which the state . . . allows sexual relations legally to take place." . . . Because same-sex couples are unable to procreate on their own, any right to marriage they may possess cannot be based on their interest in procreation, which has been essential to the Supreme Court's denomination of the right to marry as fundamental.

Supreme Court cases recognizing a right to privacy in intimate decision making, e.g., *Griswold v. Connecticut* (striking down statute prohibiting use of contraceptives) and *Roe v. Wade* (striking down statute criminalizing abortion), have also focused primarily on sexual relations and the decision whether or not to procreate, and have refused to recognize an "unlimited right" to privacy.

What the *Griswold* Court found "repulsive to the notions of privacy surrounding the marriage relationship" was the prospect of "allow[ing] the police to search the sacred precincts of marital bedrooms for telltale signs of the use of contraceptives." When Justice [Arthur] Goldberg spoke of "marital relations" in the context of finding it "difficult to imagine what is more private or more intimate than a husband and wife's marital relations[hip]," *Griswold v. Connecticut*, he was obviously referring to sexual relations. Similarly, in *Lawrence v. Texas* (2003), it was the criminalization of private sexual behavior that the Court found violative of the petitioners' liberty interest. . . .

The marriage statute, which regulates only the act of obtaining a marriage license, does not implicate privacy in the sense that it has found constitutional protection under Massachusetts and federal law. It does not intrude on any right that the plaintiffs have to privacy in their choices regarding procreation, an intimate partner, or sexual relations. The plaintiffs' right to privacy in such matters does not require that the state officially endorse their choices in order for the right to be constitutionally vindicated.

Although some of the privacy cases also speak in terms of personal autonomy, no court has ever recognized such an open-ended right. "That many of the rights and liberties protected by the Due Process Clause sound in personal autonomy does not warrant the sweeping conclusion that any and all important, intimate, and personal decisions are so protected. . . ." Such decisions are protected not because they are important, intimate, and personal, but because the right or liberty at stake is "so deeply rooted in our history and traditions, or so fundamental to our concept of constitutionally ordered liberty" that it is protected by due process. Accordingly, the Supreme Court has concluded that while the decision to refuse unwanted medical treatment is fundamental, because it is deeply rooted in our nation's history and tradition, the equally personal and profound decision to commit suicide is not because of the absence of such roots.

While the institution of marriage is deeply rooted in the history and traditions of our country and our state, the right to marry someone of the same sex is not. No matter how personal or intimate a decision to marry someone of the same sex might be, the right to make it is not guaranteed by the right of personal autonomy. . . .

Insofar as the right to marry someone of the same sex is neither found in the unique historical context of our Constitution nor compelled by the meaning ascribed by this court to the liberty and due process protections contained within it, should the court nevertheless recognize it as a fundamental right? The consequences of deeming a right to be "fundamental" are profound, and this court, as well as the Supreme Court, has been very cautious in recognizing them. Such caution is required by separation of powers principles. If a right is found to be "fundamental," it is, to a great extent, removed from "the arena of public debate and legislative action"; utmost care must be taken when breaking new ground in this field "lest the liberty protected by the Due Process Clause be subtly transformed into the policy preferences of [judges]."

"[T]o rein in" the otherwise potentially unlimited scope of substantive due process rights, both federal and Massachusetts courts have recognized as "fundamental" only those "rights and liberties which are, objectively, 'deeply rooted in this nation's history and tradition,' . . . and 'implicit in the concept of ordered liberty.'" In the area of family-related rights in particular, the Supreme Court has emphasized that the "Constitution protects the sanctity of the family precisely because the institution of the family is deeply rooted."

Applying this limiting principle, the Supreme Court, as noted above, declined to recognize a fundamental right to physician-assisted suicide, which would have required "revers[ing] centuries of legal doctrine and practice, and strik[ing] down the considered policy choice of almost every state." While recognizing that public attitudes toward assisted suicide are currently the subject of "earnest and profound debate," the Court nevertheless left the continuation and resolution of that debate to the political arena, "as it should be in a democratic society." . . .

This is not to say that a statute that has no rational basis must nevertheless be upheld as long as it is of ancient origin. However, "[t]he long history of a certain practice . . . and its acceptance as an uncontroversial part of our national and state tradition do suggest that [the court] should reflect carefully before striking it down." As this court has recognized, the "fact that a challenged practice 'is followed by a large number of states . . . is plainly worth considering in determining whether the practice "offends some principle of justice so rooted in the traditions and conscience of our people as to be ranked as fundamental.""'"

Although public attitudes toward marriage in general and same-sex marriage in particular have changed and are still evolving, "the asserted contemporary concept of marriage and societal interests for which [plaintiffs] contend" are "manifestly [less] deeply founded" than the "historic institution" of marriage. Indeed, it is not readily apparent to what extent contemporary values have embraced the concept of same-sex marriage. Perhaps the "clearest and most reliable objective evidence of contemporary values is the legislation enacted by the country's legislatures." No state legislature has enacted laws permitting same-sex marriages; and a large majority of states, as well as the United States Congress, have affirmatively prohibited the recognition of such marriages for any purpose.

Given this history and the current state of public opinion, as reflected in the actions of the people's elected representatives, it cannot be said that "a right to same-sex marriage is so rooted in the traditions and collective conscience of our people that failure to recognize it would violate the fundamental principles of liberty and justice that lie at the base of all our civil and political institutions. Neither . . . [is] a right to same-sex marriage . . . implicit in the concept of ordered liberty, such that neither liberty nor justice would exist if it were sacrificed." The one exception was the Alaska Superior Court, which relied on that state's constitution's express and broadly construed right to privacy. In such circumstances, the law with respect to same-sex marriages must be left to develop through legislative processes, subject to the constraints of rationality, lest the court be viewed as using the liberty and due process clauses as vehicles merely to enforce its own views regarding better social policies, a role that the strongly worded separation of powers principles in art. 30 of the Declaration of Rights of our Constitution forbids, and for which the court is particularly ill suited. . . .

B. The marriage statute, in limiting marriage to heterosexual couples, does not constitute discrimination on the basis of sex in violation of the Equal Rights Amendment to the Massachusetts Constitution. In his concurrence,

Justice Greaney contends that the marriage statute constitutes discrimination on the basis of sex in violation of art. 1 of the Declaration of Rights as amended by art. 106 of the Amendments to the Constitution of the Commonwealth, the Equal Rights Amendment (ERA). Such a conclusion is analytically unsound and inconsistent with the legislative history of the ERA.

The central purpose of the ERA was to eradicate discrimination against women and in favor of men or vice versa. Consistent with this purpose, we have construed the ERA to prohibit laws that advantage one sex at the expense of the other, but not laws that treat men and women equally (assuming that "separate but equal" treatment of males and females would be constitutionally permissible). The Massachusetts marriage statute does not subject men to different treatment from women; each is equally prohibited from precisely the same conduct. . . .

There is no evidence that limiting marriage to opposite-sex couples was motivated by sexism in general or a desire to disadvantage men or women in particular. Moreover, no one has identified any harm, burden, disadvantage, or advantage accruing to either gender as a consequence of the Massachusetts marriage statute. In the absence of such effect, the statute limiting marriage to couples of the opposite sex does not violate the ERA's prohibition of sex discrimination. . . .

C. The marriage statute satisfies the rational basis standard. The burden of demonstrating that a statute does not satisfy the rational basis standard rests on the plaintiffs. It is a weighty one. "[A] reviewing court will presume a statute's validity, and make all rational inferences in favor of it. . . . The Legislature is not required to justify its classifications, nor provide a record or finding in support of them." The statute "only need[s to] be supported by a conceivable rational basis."

"[I]t is not the court's function to launch an inquiry to resolve a debate which has already been settled in the legislative forum. '[I]t [is] the judge's duty . . . to give effect to the will of the people as expressed in the statute by their representative body. It is in this way . . . that the doctrine of separation of powers is given meaning.'

"This respect for the legislative process means that it is not the province of the court to sit and weigh conflicting evidence supporting or opposing a legislative enactment. . . .

"Although persons challenging the constitutionality of legislation may introduce evidence in support of their claim that the legislation is irrational . . . they will not prevail if 'the question is at least debatable' in view of the evidence which may have been available to the legislature."

The "time-tested wisdom of the separation of powers" requires courts to avoid "judicial legislation in the guise of new constructions to meet real or supposed new popular viewpoints, preserving always to the legislature alone its proper prerogative of adjusting the statutes to changed conditions."

In analyzing whether a statute satisfies the rational basis standard, we look to the nature of the classification embodied in the enactment, then to whether the statute serves a legitimate state purpose, and finally to whether the classification is reasonably related to the furtherance of that purpose. With this framework, we turn to the challenged statute, G.L. c. 207, which authorizes local town officials to issue licenses to couples of the opposite sex authorizing them to enter the institution of civil marriage.

1. Classification. The nature of the classification at issue is readily apparent. Opposite-sex couples can obtain a license and same-sex couples cannot. The granting of this license, and the completion of the required solemnization of the marriage, opens the door to many statutory benefits and imposes numerous responsibilities. The fact that the statute does not permit such licenses to be issued to couples of the same sex thus bars them from civil marriage. The classification is not drawn between men and women or between heterosexuals and homosexuals, any of whom can obtain a license to marry a member of the opposite sex; rather, it is drawn between same-sex couples and opposite-sex couples.

2. State purpose. The court's opinion concedes that the civil marriage statute serves legitimate state purposes, but further investigation and elaboration of those purposes is both helpful and necessary.

Civil marriage is the institutional mechanism by which societies have sanctioned and recognized particular family structures, and the institution of marriage has existed as one of the fundamental organizing principles of human society. Marriage has not been merely a contractual arrangement for legally defining the private relationship between two individuals (although that is certainly part of any marriage). Rather, on an institutional level, marriage is the "very basis of the whole fabric of civilized society," and it serves many important political, economic, social, educational, procreational, and personal functions.

Paramount among its many important functions, the institution of marriage has systematically provided for the regulation of heterosexual behavior, brought order to the resulting procreation, and ensured a stable family structure in which children will be reared, educated, and socialized.

Admittedly, heterosexual intercourse, procreation, and child care are not necessarily conjoined (particularly in the modern age of widespread effective contraception and supportive social welfare programs), but an orderly society requires some mechanism for coping with the fact that sexual intercourse commonly results in pregnancy and childbirth. The institution of marriage is that mechanism.

The institution of marriage provides the important legal and normative link between heterosexual intercourse and procreation on the one hand and family responsibilities on the other. The partners in a marriage are expected to engage in exclusive sexual relations, with children the probable result and paternity presumed. Whereas the relationship between mother and child is demonstratively and predictably created and recognizable through the biological process of pregnancy and childbirth, there is no corresponding process for creating a relationship between father and child. Similarly, aside from an act of heterosexual intercourse nine months prior to childbirth, there is no process for creating a relationship between a man and a woman as the parents of a particular child. The institution of marriage fills this void by formally binding the husband-father to his wife and child, and imposing on him the responsibilities of fatherhood. The alternative, a society without the institution of marriage, in which heterosexual intercourse, procreation, and child care are largely disconnected processes, would be chaotic.

The marital family is also the foremost setting for the education and socialization of children. Children learn about the world and their place in it primarily from those who raise them, and those children eventually grow up to exert some influence, great or small, positive or negative, on society. The institution of marriage encourages parents to remain committed to each other and to their children as they grow, thereby encouraging a stable venue for the education and socialization of children. More macroscopically, construction of a family through marriage also formalizes the bonds between people in an ordered and institutional manner, thereby facilitating a foundation of inter-connectedness and interdependency on which more intricate stabilizing social structures might be built. . . .

It is difficult to imagine a state purpose more important and legitimate than ensuring, promoting, and supporting an optimal social structure within which to bear and raise children. At the very least, the marriage statute continues to serve this important state purpose.

3. Rational relationship. The question we must turn to next is whether the statute, construed as limiting marriage to couples of the opposite sex, remains a rational way to further that purpose. Stated differently, we ask whether a conceivable rational basis exists on which the legislature could conclude that continuing to limit the institution of civil marriage to members of the opposite sex furthers the legitimate purpose of ensuring, promoting, and supporting an optimal social structure for the bearing and raising of children.

In considering whether such a rational basis exists, we defer to the decision-making process of the legislature, and must make deferential assumptions about the information that it might consider and on which it may rely.

We must assume that the legislature (1) might conclude that the institution of civil marriage has successfully and continually provided this structure over several centuries; (2) might consider and credit studies that document negative consequences that too often follow children either born outside of marriage or raised in households lacking either a father or a mother figure, and scholarly commentary contending that children and families develop best when mothers and fathers are partners in their parenting; and (3) would be familiar with many recent studies that variously: support the proposition that children raised in intact families headed by same-sex couples fare as well on many measures as children raised in similar families headed by opposite-sex couples; support the proposition that children of same-sex couples fare worse on some measures; or reveal notable differences between the two groups of children that warrant further study.

We must also assume that the legislature would be aware of the critiques of the methodologies used in virtually all of the comparative studies of children raised in these different environments, cautioning that the sampling populations are not representative, that the observation periods are too limited in time, that the empirical data are unreliable, and that the hypotheses are too infused with political or agenda-driven bias.

Taking all of this available information into account, the legislature could rationally conclude that a family environment with married opposite-sex parents remains the optimal social structure in which to bear children, and that the raising of children by same-sex couples, who by definition cannot be the two sole biological parents of a child and cannot provide children with a parental authority figure of each gender, presents an alternative structure for child rearing that has not yet proved itself beyond reasonable scientific dispute to be as optimal as the biologically based marriage norm. Working from the assumption that a recognition of same-sex marriages will increase the number of children experiencing this alternative, the legislature could conceivably conclude that declining to recognize same-sex marriages remains prudent until empirical questions about its impact on the upbringing of children are resolved.

The fact that the commonwealth currently allows same-sex couples to adopt does not affect the rationality of this conclusion. The eligibility of a child for adoption presupposes that at least one of the child's biological parents is unable or unwilling, for some reason, to participate in raising the child. In that sense, society has "lost" the optimal setting in which to raise that child—it is simply not available. In these circumstances, the principal and overriding consideration is the "best interests of the child," considering his or her unique circumstances and the options that are available for that child. The objective is an individualized determination of the best environment for a particular child, where the normative social structure—a home with both the child's biological father and mother—is not an option. That such a focused determination may lead to the approval of a same-sex couple's adoption of a child does not mean that it would be irrational for a legislator, in fashioning statutory laws that cannot make such individualized determinations, to conclude generally that being raised by a same-sex couple has not yet been shown to be the absolute equivalent of being raised by one's married biological parents.

That the state does not preclude different types of families from raising children does not mean that it must view them all as equally optimal and equally deserving of state endorsement and support. For example, single persons are allowed to adopt children, but the fact that the legislature permits single-parent adoption does not mean that it has endorsed single parenthood as an optimal setting in which to raise children or views it as the equivalent of being raised by both of one's biological parents.

The same holds true with respect to same-sex couples—the fact that they may adopt children means only that the legislature has concluded that they may provide an acceptable setting in which to raise children who cannot be raised by both of their biological parents. The legislature may rationally permit adoption by same-sex couples yet harbor reservations as to whether parenthood by same-sex couples should be affirmatively encouraged to the same extent as parenthood by the heterosexual couple whose union produced the child.

In addition, the legislature could conclude that redefining the institution of marriage to permit same-sex couples to marry would impair the state's interest in promoting and supporting heterosexual marriage as the social institution that it has determined best normalizes, stabilizes, and links the acts of procreation and child rearing. While the plaintiffs argue that they only want to take part in the same stabilizing institution, the legislature conceivably could conclude that permitting their participation would have the unintended effect of undermining to some degree marriage's ability to serve its social purpose.

As long as marriage is limited to opposite-sex couples who can at least theoretically procreate, society is able to communicate a consistent message to its citizens that marriage is a (normatively) necessary part of their procreative endeavor; that if they are to procreate, then society has endorsed the institution of marriage as the environment for it and for the subsequent rearing of their children; and that benefits are available explicitly to create a supportive and conducive atmosphere for those purposes. If society proceeds similarly to recognize marriages between same-sex couples who cannot procreate, it could be perceived as an abandonment of this claim, and might result in the mistaken view that civil marriage has little to do with procreation: just as the potential of procreation would not be necessary for a marriage to be valid, marriage would not be necessary for optimal procreation and child rearing to occur. In essence, the legislature could conclude that the consequence of such a policy shift would be a diminution in society's ability to steer the acts of procreation and child rearing into their most optimal setting.

The court recognizes this concern, but brushes it aside with the assumption that permitting same-sex couples to marry "will not diminish the validity or dignity of opposite-sex marriage," and that "we have no doubt that marriage will continue to be a vibrant and revered institution." Whether the court is correct in its assumption is irrelevant. What is relevant is that such predicting is not the business of the courts. A rational legislature, given the evidence, could conceivably come to a different conclusion, or could at least harbor rational concerns about possible unintended consequences of a dramatic redefinition of marriage.

There is no question that many same-sex couples are capable of being good parents, and should be (and are) permitted to be so. The policy question that a legislator must resolve is a different one, and turns on an assessment of whether the marriage structure proposed by the plaintiffs will, over time, if endorsed and supported by the state, prove to be as stable and successful a model as the one that has formed a cornerstone of our society since colonial times, or prove to be less than optimal, and result in consequences, perhaps now unforeseen, adverse to the state's legitimate interest in promoting and supporting the best possible social structure in which children should be born and raised. Given the critical importance of civil marriage as an organizing and stabilizing institution of society, it is eminently rational for the legislature to postpone making fundamental changes to it until such time as there is unanimous scientific evidence, or popular consensus, or both, that such changes can safely be made.

There is no reason to believe that legislative processes are inadequate to effectuate legal changes in response to evolving evidence, social values, and views of fairness on the subject of same-sex relationships. Deliberate consideration of, and incremental responses to, rapidly evolving scientific and social understanding is the norm of the political process—that it may seem painfully slow to those who are already persuaded by the arguments in favor of change is not a sufficient basis to conclude that the processes are constitutionally infirm. The advancement of the rights, privileges, and protections afforded to homosexual members of our community in the last three decades has been significant, and there is no reason to believe that that evolution will not continue. Changes of attitude in the civic, social, and professional communities have been even more profound. Thirty years ago, the *Diagnostic and Statistical Manual,* the seminal handbook of the American Psychiatric Association, still listed homosexuality as a mental disorder. Today, the Massachusetts Psychiatric Society, the American Psychoanalytic Association, and many other psychiatric, psychological, and social science organizations have joined in an amicus brief on behalf of the plaintiffs' cause. A body of experience and evidence has provided the basis for change, and that body continues to mount. The legislature is the appropriate branch, both constitutionally and practically, to consider and respond to it. It is not enough that we as justices might be personally of the view that we have learned enough to decide what is best. So long as the question is at all debatable, it must be the legislature that decides. The marriage statute thus meets the requirements of the rational basis test.

D. Conclusion. While "the Massachusetts Constitution protects matters of personal liberty against government intrusion at least as zealously, and often more so than does the federal Constitution," this case is not about government intrusions into matters of personal liberty. It is not about the rights of same-sex couples to choose to live together, or to be intimate with each other, or to adopt and raise children together. It is about whether the state must endorse and support their choices by changing the institution of civil marriage to make its benefits, obligations, and responsibilities applicable to them. While the courageous efforts of many have resulted in increased dignity, rights, and respect for gay and lesbian members of our community, the issue presented here is a profound one, deeply rooted in social policy, that must, for now, be the subject of legislative not judicial action.

2.

TOWARD A MORE PERFECT UNION

David J. Garrow

Mary Bonauto vividly remembers her first day as a lawyer at Gay and Lesbian Advocates and Defenders (GLAD), the small public-interest law office that represents gays and lesbians in the six New England states. "When I came here on March 19, 1990," she recalled not long ago, "one of the things waiting for me on my desk was a request from a lesbian couple in western Massachusetts who wanted to get married." At that time, though, she believed a lawsuit seeking a right to gay marriage had no chance of success in any American appellate court. "It was absolutely the wrong time," she told me, "and I said no."

A generation or two from now, March 19, 1990, may appear in history books the same way that another date appears in accounts of *Brown v. Board of Education*: October 6, 1936, the day that Thurgood Marshall accepted a full-time job at the NAACP Legal Defense Fund. Marshall, too, said no—for more than a decade—to petitioners who asked him to challenge public-school segregation in the South. Only in 1950, as the legal landscape began to shift, did Marshall finally say yes.

For Bonauto, the wait was shorter but the outcome no less momentous. "I said no to many people over the years," she remembered, "until I finally said yes." In 1997, Bonauto and two other attorneys, Beth Robinson and Susan Murray, filed a lawsuit attacking the constitutionality of Vermont's exclusion of gay and lesbian couples from the institution of civil marriage. The case went all the way to the Vermont Supreme Court, which in December 1999 ruled in their favor but invited the state legislature to devise a remedy. The legislature responded by creating the country's first-ever "civil unions," which extended to same-sex couples all the legal benefits of marriage without granting the actual name.

As historic as the Vermont decision was, Bonauto will forever be remembered for her more important victory last November, when the Massachusetts Supreme Judicial Court, in response to a lawsuit she filed on behalf of seven same-sex couples seeking marriage licenses, handed down a landmark decision, *Goodridge v. Department of Public Health*, ending the exclusion of gay and lesbian couples from civil marriage in the state. The ramifications of *Goodridge* have been felt throughout the country: public officials in San Francisco; Portland, Oregon; New York State; and New Jersey were inspired to grant marriage licenses to same-sex couples (all such licensing has since been halted), and a political backlash took form, culminating in President George W. Bush's call in late February for a federal constitutional amendment to "protect marriage," as he put it, from "activist judges and local officials."

Just as with the society-wide desegregation of American life that slowly followed from *Brown v. Board of Education* fifty years ago this month, what will occur on May 17, when Massachusetts begins issuing full-fledged marriage licenses to same-sex couples, will mark the beginning of a new social era. Kevin Cathcart, executive director of Lambda Legal Defense and Education Fund, America's oldest gay rights law group, observes that once fully credentialed gay marriages become a reality, "you can't put the toothpaste back in the tube." Many individuals and organizations have helped usher in the era of marriage equality, but Bonauto's contribution has been exceptional. Kate Kendell, executive director of the National Center for Lesbian Rights, says that "Massachusetts has had the success it did because of Mary Bonauto." Bonauto's patient, quietly passionate yet self-effacing advocacy may have as far-reaching an effect on America as did that of Thurgood Marshall. As Beth Robinson notes, the marriage-equality movement "doesn't stand on the shoulders of any one person," but there is no doubt that "the one individual person who's done the most for marriage is Mary."

A native of Newburgh, New York, Bonauto grew up with her three brothers in what she describes as a "highly Catholic" family. Her father worked as a pharmacist and her mother as a teacher. Bonauto first came to terms with her lesbian identity as an undergraduate at Hamilton College in Clinton, New York, but only during her first year of law school at Northeastern University in Boston in 1984–85 did she come out to her parents. When she joined a small law firm in Portland, Maine, in 1987, Bonauto was one of only three openly gay lawyers in private practice in the state. In Portland, she also met her life partner, Jennifer Wriggins, now a professor at the University of Maine School of Law.

The late 1980s were an auspicious time for a young lawyer in New England with a commitment to gay equality. In 1989, Massachusetts became the second state, after Wisconsin, to provide antidiscrimination protection to gays in employment, housing, and public accommodations. When GLAD advertised for a lawyer to help enforce the new law, Bonauto jumped at the opportunity and moved back to Boston, accompanied by Wriggins. Bonauto's work at GLAD in the early 1990s taught her, she says, "how to build, brick by brick, protections for gay folks," even while she continued to say no on marriage.

But the marriage question was still very much on her mind. GLAD was inundated with requests from gays and lesbians for help with legal difficulties—child custody and adoption, health-benefits coverage, inheritance and Social Security survivor benefits—that would not have existed if same-sex couples enjoyed the legal protections and benefits of marriage. Some of those requests, Bonauto says, are "seared into my soul" because they came from "people who are calling me sobbing from a pay phone because their partner of twenty-four years has just died and the so-called family is in the house cleaning it out." But prudence prevailed. "I would have loved to have been married myself and would have loved to have filed a marriage case," she says, but "you have to apply your strategic sensibility to it."

In the early 1990s, the strategic and political discussions among gay lawyers about marriage were intense. The most outspoken marriage advocate was Evan Wolfson, a Lambda lawyer who had written a prescient student paper at Harvard Law School in 1983 titled "Same-Sex Marriage and Morality: The Human Rights Vision of the Constitution." A similarly obscure article, by a little-known lawyer named Nathan Margold, first set forth the constitutional game plan that Thurgood Marshall followed all the way to *Brown v. Board of Education*. Wolfson's deep commitment to pursuing the marriage issue ran into opposition from his colleagues and peers. Some of them argued that marriage was so unappealing an institution that access to it should not be a gay civil rights priority; others claimed that irrespective of its desirability, pursuing a right to marriage was an unattainable goal. These disagreements often were articulated at meetings of the Roundtable, a twice-yearly national gathering of gay rights litigators that originated in the mid-1980s. When Bonauto attended her first meeting in April 1990, Wolfson gained a crucial ally. "I remember Evan coming over and introducing himself," she recalls. "He and I, at that point I think, were two of the very few people who felt like marriage was something that needed to be fought for in the courts."

The disagreements crystallized in 1991, when several same-sex couples in Hawaii persuaded an attorney named Dan Foley, a former legal director of the American Civil Liberties Union's Hawaii affiliate, to file a constitutional case there. Both the ACLU and Lambda declined to support the challenge, but Wolfson took an active role. Most gay lawyers gave the case little thought, but two years after Foley initiated it, the Hawaii Supreme Court issued a surprising ruling that the state would have to demonstrate a "compelling" reason—the same legal standard applied in race-discrimination cases—in order to continue excluding same-sex couples from civil marriage.

"Once the Hawaii court ruled, we were in a different world," Wolfson says. "There was this sense of possibility, this sense of hope, this sense of empowerment." Bonauto, too, saw it as a sea-change moment, especially for previously ambivalent gay lawyers: "It was really when the Hawaii Supreme

Court ruled in May 1993 that people said we have to stand up and take notice of this. If a court is going to stand with us, shouldn't we be standing up for our own community?" The high court returned the case to a lower court for trial, but few expected that the state could meet the exacting standard the court had imposed. Wolfson celebrated what he called a "seismic win" and declared that gay Americans stood "on the verge of victory."

But more than three years passed before a trial judge finally ruled that the state indeed had not met the Hawaii Supreme Court's test. In the meantime, political opposition mushroomed, both nationally and in Hawaii. In Washington, opponents of gay marriage won the support of President Bill Clinton in passing into law the federal Defense of Marriage Act, which limits federal recognition to male-female marriages and decrees that no state has to recognize same-sex marriages that are performed elsewhere. In Honolulu, the state legislature voted in early 1997 to place a constitutional amendment on the November 1998 state ballot that would give it the exclusive power to define marriage.

Proponents of gay marriage eagerly awaited a decisive affirmation by Hawaii's top court, but months passed with no ruling. The court still had not spoken when Hawaii voters adopted the anti–gay marriage constitutional amendment by a margin of 69 to 29 percent. Foley and Wolfson's much-heralded victory had turned into a sour defeat.

As disheartening as Hawaii was, the original constitutional victory was an encouraging indication of the persuasiveness of the equality argument. Early in the Hawaii struggle, Wolfson urged Bonauto and others to hold off on filing another marriage case in a second state, but as the Hawaii logjam dragged into 1997, Bonauto's patience waned. "I was really uncomfortable with leaving Hawaii out there alone," she recalls. "I just felt that this can't be about one state."

In July 1997, as the Hawaii case languished, Bonauto, Robinson, and Murray filed their case in Vermont. Hawaii had demonstrated that a well-wrought lawsuit, strong constitutional arguments, and a sympathetic court could produce a victory but were not necessarily sufficient to protect and preserve it. Vermont, by contrast, had several decisive advantages. Three years earlier, the state supreme court issued a pioneering opinion approving second-parent adoption for same-sex couples, thus evidencing sympathy for gay families. What's more, Vermont's state constitution, unlike Hawaii's, was difficult to amend, creating a high hurdle for anyone eager to overturn a state constitutional judicial decision. In addition, Robinson and Murray had begun laying crucial political groundwork by creating the Vermont Freedom to Marry Task Force, which conducted public education work of a sort that had never occurred in tandem with the Hawaii case.

The case that Bonauto and her colleagues filed asserted that under the "common benefits" clause in the state constitution (Vermont's more expansive version of the federal equal-protection clause), the exclusion of gay couples from the rights and benefits of marriage was unconstitutional. A trial judge rejected their complaint, but on appeal the Vermont Supreme Court endorsed their challenge to the state's discriminatory conduct. That December 1999 ruling, *Baker v. State*, was a gay rights landmark, but it nonetheless left the lawyers "crushed," Robinson remembers, because the high court called for legislative action rather than ordering that marriage licenses be issued to gay couples. "It was a political decision and not a legal decision," Robinson says. When the Vermont legislature took up the court's invitation, a result was "civil unions," in which the legal benefits of matrimony were extended to gay couples but the all-powerful term—"marriage"—was withheld. The distinction evoked a phrase that Thurgood Marshall knew all too well: "separate but equal," the pre-*Brown* label for the fictional fairness of segregation.

Bonauto decided to try again, this time in Massachusetts, where both the state constitution and the high court offered advantages similar to those of Vermont. A summer 2000 meeting of the state's gay activists endorsed her resolve, and in April 2001 she filed *Goodridge*, her second right-to-marry case, in Boston. On behalf of seven same-sex couples, Bonauto asserted that the state's refusal to grant licenses to gay and lesbian life partners violated Massachusetts's constitutional equality provisions. The trial court again said no, and Bonauto appealed to the Massachusetts Supreme Judicial Court. When she argued her case to the seven justices on March 4 of last year, she beseeched them not to dodge the question. Fearful of how Vermont's high court had rendered a decision that allowed for a remedy that stopped short of actual marriage, Bonauto insisted that "civil unions" would not satisfy the requirements of the Massachusetts Constitution. "The Vermont approach is not the best approach for this Court to take," she emphasized, for "when it comes to marriage, there really is no such thing as separating the word 'marriage' from the protections it provides. The reason for that is that one of the most important protections of marriage is the word, because the word is what conveys the status that everyone understands as the ultimate expression of love and commitment." To follow Vermont, she continued, by "creating a separate system, just for gay people, simply perpetuates the stigma of exclusion that we now face because it would essentially be branding gay people and our relationships as unworthy of this civil institution of marriage."

While Bonauto waited for a decision, the legal climate improved. In the early summer of 2003, the Canadian provinces of Ontario and British Columbia joined Belgium and the Netherlands in authorizing same-sex marriages. Late in June, the United States Supreme Court, in *Lawrence v. Texas*, emphatically reversed its infamous 1986 decision *Bowers v. Hardwick*, which had upheld the criminalization of private, consensual gay and lesbian sex. The high court's voiding of Texas's antisodomy law surprised almost no one, but most observers expected a narrow ruling striking down only those laws, like Texas's, that expressly singled out gays. Instead, Justice Anthony M. Kennedy's majority opinion overturned all remaining American sodomy laws and explicitly repudiated *Bowers*. Kennedy energetically deplored government hostility toward homosexuals, and his expansive language seemed to open the door to full legal equality for gay Americans just as *Brown* in 1954 had opened wide the door to racial equality.

Although Kennedy stated that *Lawrence* "does not involve whether the government must give formal recognition to any relationship that homosexual persons seek to enter," he also wrote that sodomy prohibitions "seek to control a personal relationship that, whether or not entitled to formal recognition in the law, is within the liberty of persons to choose." The phrase "whether or not" was expressly suggestive, and an angry dissent by Justice Antonin Scalia declared that the majority's opinion destroyed the possibility of a constitutional distinction between heterosexual and homosexual marriages.

Five months later, the Massachusetts Supreme Judicial Court handed down the ruling for which Bonauto had been waiting: an unparalleled 4-to-3 decision ending the exclusion of gay couples from marriage. The moral influence of the *Lawrence* decision on the Massachusetts court was made explicit at the very beginning of the *Goodridge* majority opinion, in which Massachusetts Chief Justice Margaret H. Marshall cited *Lawrence* three times in her first three paragraphs. As Matt Coles, head of the American Civil Liberties Union's Lesbian and Gay Rights Project, observes, *Goodridge* "answered that question that *Lawrence* begged." And while "*Goodridge* is the earthquake," Coles says, "*Goodridge* is the earthquake because of *Lawrence*." Bonauto was surprised when some observers interpreted the Massachusetts Supreme Judicial Court's 180-day stay of the ruling, until May 17, as an unspoken invitation to Massachusetts politicians to substitute Vermont-style civil unions for actual marriage licenses. But when legislators formally asked the court for its opinion on such a maneuver, the four-member majority brusquely reiterated that *Goodridge* was "not a matter of social policy but of constitutional interpretation." That February 4 announcement made gay marriage a legal certainty in Massachusetts come May 17, notwithstanding the efforts of Gov. Mitt Romney to block implementation of the court's mandate.

Bonauto remains warily prepared to head off any last-minute effort by the governor. She emphasizes that "my first priority is maintaining this victory here on the ground in Massachusetts." Most opponents of gay marriage are reluctantly backing a constitutional amendment in Massachusetts that would prohibit gay marriages while establishing fully equivalent civil unions, but the measure must obtain majority support in the 2005–2006 session of the legislature and then win a popular majority on the November 2006 statewide ballot. Opponents can also put a more extreme measure, simply banning gay marriages and civil unions, before Massachusetts voters, but not until November 2008. Thus gay marriages will have been hometown realities in Massachusetts for at least two years, if not four, before ballots to overturn *Goodridge* can be cast. Statewide polls show that 40 percent of Massachusetts residents already support gay marriages, and another 11 percent express no interest in the issue. Bonauto says those numbers will increase once voters see that "gay families have been strengthened, and nothing has been taken away from your family" in the months and years after May 17.

"Massachusetts was the breakthrough we had been building all these ten or twelve years of work to achieve," Wolfson says. The impact of *Goodridge* on gay people, Bonauto adds, is immeasurable. "It has taken my breath away," she says, "to have so many people come up to me and say: 'I had no idea all the ways in which I had incorporated my second-class-citizen status and didn't even know it. For the first time I actually realize I am a full and equal citizen, and I didn't even realize all the accommodations I had been making.' That, I think, is what is transformative."

But *Goodridge*'s impact was felt not only by gays. Hostile reaction followed just as with Hawaii a decade ago, including critical words by President Bush in his State of the Union address on January 20. Among those in the audience that evening was the newly elected San Francisco mayor, Gavin Newsom, and Bush's remarks started Newsom thinking.

Two weeks later, Newsom instructed his top aides to look into how San Francisco could start issuing marriage licenses to homosexual couples. Newsom's chief of staff, Steve Kawa, phoned Kate Kendell of the San Francisco–based National Center for Lesbian Rights late on the afternoon of Friday, February 6. "The mayor wants to begin issuing marriage licenses to lesbian and gay couples," Kawa told an astounded Kendell. On Monday, Kendell suggested to Newsom's staff that the pioneering lesbian rights activists Phyllis Lyon and Del Martin become the city's first legally wed gay couple. Three days later, on February 12, Lyon and Martin, ages seventy-nine and eighty-three, were married at City Hall. Literally overnight, Newsom's initiative transformed the gay-marriage story from dry reports of court rulings into vivid pictures of hundreds of homosexual couples standing in line, sometimes in the rain, outside San Francisco City Hall in order to follow in Lyon and Martin's footsteps.

President Bush upped the political ante on February 24 when, warning that the 1996 federal Defense of Marriage Act might not withstand judicial scrutiny, he endorsed a federal constitutional amendment to define marriage as a "union of a man and a woman." Reaction to Bush's declaration was largely lukewarm, even among some Republican congressional leaders. But when the gay men and women of the Roundtable assembled on March 1 for a long-scheduled meeting, many worried that federal intervention could upset their careful state-level strategy. Evan Wolfson pushed his colleagues to respond to the dramatic acceleration of events by intensifying their own litigation initiatives. Some disagreed, worried that further events, on top of Massachusetts and San Francisco, could fuel a reactionary backlash.

No consensus emerged, but two days later another unexpected chapter in the struggle opened in Portland, Oregon, when the Multnomah County Commission authorized the issuance of marriage licenses to same-sex couples. The Portland events received far less media attention than San Francisco's, but the Multnomah marriages soon looked more legally secure than the California ones. On March 11 the state supreme court ordered San Francisco officials to stop issuing licenses to same-sex couples, and joyous scenes at San Francisco City Hall came to an abrupt and tearful end after 4,037 same-sex marriages. The California court is now considering whether to hold the San Francisco marriages null and void, and a ruling disallowing the licenses is possible sometime this summer. In Oregon, a trial judge has upheld the Multnomah marriages but also ordered the county to halt such licensing at least temporarily. Accelerated appellate review may put the question before the Oregon Supreme Court this fall, but conservatives hope to force a popular vote on an anti–gay marriage state constitutional amendment either this November or in 2006.

The gay and lesbian Roundtable litigators envision first Massachusetts and then perhaps Oregon embracing full marriage equality within the next twelve months. Lambda also has potentially promising constitutional challenges pending in New Jersey, New York, and Washington state courts that could prove successful within the next few years. Longer-shot marriage cases—some of them brought by attorneys not acting in concert with the Roundtable organizations—are also under way in Arizona, Florida, Indiana, and North Carolina.

But rather than dwell on state-by-state prognoses, Bonauto and other gay and lesbian litigators privately focus upon delaying any federal court consideration of same-sex marriage issues for a good many years. "What's happened in Massachusetts has been a beacon of fairness, hope, and equality across the country," Bonauto says, but "I think that what it boils down to is avoiding the federal piece" for as long as possible. "I have tried to plead with lawyers not to get overly ambitious about going into court and challenging the federal Defense of Marriage Act," she says. "I think a lot of times these cases would arise as tax cases by wealthy individuals" who pay disproportionate sums because of the unavailability of marriage. "I can't think of a less sympathetic prospect," Bonauto says. "I would like the opportunity for states to wrestle with this before we have to go into federal court."

One immediate challenge Bonauto faces is an attempt by Governor Romney to order local officials to enforce a long-ignored 1913 statute that proscribes the issuance of marriage licenses to out-of-state couples whose marriage would be "void" in their home state. Romney wants town clerks to begin demanding proof of residency from marriage applicants, but individual clerks will face the choice of how to apply the state instructions, couple by couple.

That's exactly the context Evan Wolfson wants. After May 17, he predicts, "for a period of time there will be a patchwork in which couples have this mix of experiences, and in which nongay people, primarily, sitting on the other side of those desks at the bank, at the clerk's office, at the school registrar's, are going to have to now look at a real family and say, 'Am I going to be the one to say they're not married?'"

Wolfson says that firm but polite insistence will prevail. "These couples are married," he says. "They're as married as any people on the planet. They are legally married." And first in Massachusetts, and then probably in Oregon and elsewhere, the evidence rapidly will mount, in a phrase both Bonauto and

Wolfson spontaneously employ, that "the sky doesn't fall" once gay couples receive unquestionably valid state marriage licenses. "Moving it from a hypothetical, when it's easy to be 'against it,' to a reality of 'these are real people, and who does it hurt?'" Wolfson predicts, will fundamentally alter the debate.

Bonauto says that the struggle that will climax on May 17 is strengthening America. "Because of gay folks wanting to get married," she says, "the rest of the country is having a teach-in about what marriage is." The most important lesson Massachusetts illustrates, she adds, is that "it's marriage itself that is so valuable as an institution, and that it's more than the sum of its legal parts."

When asked to talk about herself, Bonauto insists that "it's totally not about me." Since she and her partner Jennifer Wriggins—and their two-year-old twin daughters, to whom Bonauto gave birth during the early litigation of *Goodridge*—now live in Maine rather than Boston, Bonauto and Wriggins's desire to marry may fall victim to Massachusetts's nonresident statutory restriction. Beth Robinson emphasizes Bonauto's "modesty and humility," but insiders who fully appreciate how a very small network of gay lawyers has brought America to the threshold of another civil rights milestone know whom to credit. Disclaiming any desire for an "architect" label, Bonauto says, "I'm happy to be a bricklayer."

Wolfson says, "I really believe we are going to win," and Bonauto agrees. "I'm very confident what the outcome is going to be," she says. She is uncertain how many years will pass before gay marriage triumphs nationally, but, she emphasizes: "I really think that time is absolutely on our side here. That's part of why there's such a rush from our opponents to amend the federal Constitution." Opponents of gay rights, just like the Roundtable litigators, can read the public-opinion data showing how heavy majorities of younger Americans readily support same-sex marriage.

Lambda's Kevin Cathcart cites that polling data in explaining "why I can be confident and sleep soundly at night." He acknowledges that "it's very difficult right now to predict what's going to happen" in the months and years immediately ahead, but he also says that without a doubt "in the long run we win," a sentiment shared by Wolfson and Bonauto.

"I'm a little less sanguine than a lot of people," Cathcart admits, about the very long odds that marriage-equality opponents face in pushing for an anti–gay marriage federal constitutional amendment. Bonauto acknowledges that the possibility of statewide votes in Massachusetts in 2006 or 2008 actually impedes the mustering of anti–gay marriage forces at the national level, but at her weakest moments she, too, focuses on the long-term demographic implications of current polling data. "The times when I'm struggling," she says, "I think, Do I have to wait until those people who are now ten years old are fifty-five before we have equality for all gay and lesbian families in this country? And that's a possibility, but even if that is true, that's forty-five years from now."

Looking back fifty years to *Brown v. Board of Education*, most Americans have no difficulty in distinguishing the legacies of Thurgood Marshall, Martin Luther King Jr., and John F. Kennedy from those of the segregationist governors Orval Faubus, Ross Barnett, and George Wallace. And fifty years from now, the odds are that Americans will have little difficulty in distinguishing the legacies of Evan Wolfson, Mary Bonauto, and Gavin Newsom from those who oppose gay equality. As Kevin Cathcart asks, "Which side of history do you want to be on?"

3.

A CALL FOR A CONSTITUTIONAL AMENDMENT PROTECTING MARRIAGE

President George W. Bush

Good morning. Eight years ago, Congress passed, and President Clinton signed, the Defense of Marriage Act, which defined marriage for purposes of federal law as the legal union between one man and one woman as husband and wife.

The act passed the House of Representatives by a vote of 342 to 67, and the Senate by a vote of 85 to 14. Those congressional votes and the passage of similar defensive marriage laws in thirty-eight states express an overwhelming consensus in our country for protecting the institution of marriage.

In recent months, however, some activist judges and local officials have made an aggressive attempt to redefine marriage. In Massachusetts, four judges on the highest court have indicated they will order the issuance of marriage licenses to applicants of the same gender in May of this year. In San Francisco, city officials have issued thousands of marriage licenses to people of the same gender, contrary to the California family code. That code, which clearly defines marriage as the union of a man and a woman, was approved overwhelmingly by the voters of California. A county in New Mexico has also issued marriage licenses to applicants of the same gender. And unless action is taken, we can expect more arbitrary court decisions, more litigation, more defiance of the law by local officials, all of which adds to uncertainty.

After more than two centuries of American jurisprudence, and millennia of human experience, a few judges and local authorities are presuming to change the most fundamental institution of civilization. Their actions have created confusion on an issue that requires clarity.

On a matter of such importance, the voice of the people must be heard. Activist courts have left the people with one recourse. If we are to prevent the

---

Speech delivered on February 24, 2004.

meaning of marriage from being changed forever, our nation must enact a constitutional amendment to protect marriage in America. Decisive and democratic action is needed, because attempts to redefine marriage in a single state or city could have serious consequences throughout the country.

The Constitution says that full faith and credit shall be given in each state to the public acts and records and judicial proceedings of every other state. Those who want to change the meaning of marriage will claim that this provision requires all states and cities to recognize same-sex marriages performed anywhere in America. Congress attempted to address this problem in the Defense of Marriage Act, by declaring that no state must accept another state's definition of marriage. My administration will vigorously defend this act of Congress.

Yet there is no assurance that the Defense of Marriage Act will not, itself, be struck down by activist courts. In that event, every state would be forced to recognize any relationship that judges in Boston or officials in San Francisco choose to call a marriage. Furthermore, even if the Defense of Marriage Act is upheld, the law does not protect marriage within any state or city.

For all these reasons, the Defense of Marriage requires a constitutional amendment. An amendment to the Constitution is never to be undertaken lightly. The amendment process has addressed many serious matters of national concern. And the preservation of marriage rises to this level of national importance. The union of a man and woman is the most enduring human institution, honoring—honored and encouraged in all cultures and by every religious faith. Ages of experience have taught humanity that the commitment of a husband and wife to love and to serve one another promotes the welfare of children and the stability of society.

Marriage cannot be severed from its cultural, religious, and natural roots without weakening the good influence of society. Government, by recognizing and protecting marriage, serves the interests of all. Today I call upon the Congress to promptly pass, and to send to the states for ratification, an amendment to our Constitution defining and protecting marriage as a union of man and woman as husband and wife. The amendment should fully protect marriage, while leaving the state legislatures free to make their own choices in defining legal arrangements other than marriage.

America is a free society, which limits the role of government in the lives of our citizens. This commitment of freedom, however, does not require the redefinition of one of our most basic social institutions. Our government should respect every person and protect the institution of marriage. There is no contradiction between these responsibilities. We should also conduct this difficult debate in a manner worthy of our country, without bitterness or anger.

In all that lies ahead, let us match strong convictions with kindness and goodwill and decency.

4.

BUSH'S CASE FOR SAME-SEX MARRIAGE

Jonathan Rauch

In endorsing the passage of a constitutional amendment that would restrict marriage to the union of men and women, President Bush established himself as the country's most prominent advocate of same-sex marriage.

To be more precise, he established himself as the most prominent advocate of the best arguments for gay marriage, even as he roundly rejected gay marriage itself. Consider the words that he spoke in the Roosevelt Room of the White House on February 24.

"The union of a man and woman is the most enduring human institution . . . honored and encouraged in all cultures and by every religious faith." Correct. Marriage is indeed the bedrock of civilization. But why would the establishment of gay matrimony erode it? Would millions of straight spouses flock to divorce court if they knew that gay couples, too, could wed? Today, a third of all American children are born out of wedlock, with no help from homosexual weddings; would the example gays set by marrying make those children's parents less likely to tie the knot?

Children, parents, childless adults, and marriage itself are all better off when society sends a clear and unequivocal message that sex, love, and marriage go together. Same-sex marriage affirms that message. It says that whether you're gay or straight—or rich or poor, or religious or secular, or what have you—marriage is the ultimate commitment for all: the destination to which loving relationships naturally aspire.

"Ages of experience have taught humanity that the commitment of a husband and wife to love and to serve one another promotes the welfare of children and the stability of society." Correct again. And the commitment of gay partners to love and serve each other promotes precisely those same goals.

First published on March 7, 2004, in the *New York Times Magazine*. Reprinted with permission.

A solitary individual lives on the frontier of vulnerability. Marriage creates kin, someone whose first "job" is to look after you. Gay people, like straight people, become ill or exhausted or despairing and need the comfort and support that marriage uniquely provides. Marriage can strengthen and stabilize their relationships and thereby strengthen the communities of which they are a part. Just as the president says, society benefits when people, including gay people, are durably committed to love and serve one another.

And children? According to the 2000 census, 27 percent of households headed by same-sex couples contain children. How could any pro-family conservative claim that those children are better off with unmarried parents?

"Marriage cannot be severed from its cultural, religious, and natural roots without weakening the good influence of society." By "roots," Bush had in mind marriage's traditional definition as male-female. But at least as deep as marriage's roots in gender are its roots in commitment. Marriage takes its ultimate meaning not from whom it excludes but from what it obliges: "To have and to hold from this day forward, for better, for worse, for richer, for poorer, in sickness and in health, till death do us part." For gay people to join other Americans in embracing that vow only strengthens "the good influence of society."

Yes, letting same-sex couples wed would in some sense redefine marriage. Until a decade ago, no Western society had ever embraced or, for the most part, even imagined same-sex marriage. But until recently, no Western society had ever understood, to the extent most Americans do today, that a small and more or less constant share of the population is homosexual by nature. Homosexuals aren't just misbehaving heterosexuals. Fooling straight people into marrying them is not an option. Barring them from the blessings of marriage is inhumane and unfair, even if that is a truth our grandparents did not understand.

So today's real choice is not whether to redefine marriage but how to do so: as a club only heterosexuals can join or as the noblest promise two people can make. To define marriage as discrimination would defend its boundaries by undermining its foundation.

"Government, by recognizing and protecting marriage, serves the interests of all." Correct yet again. A marriage license uniquely bestows many hundreds of entitlements and entanglements that publicly affirm the spouses' mutual responsibility and that provide them with the tools they need to care for each other. Far from being just a piece of paper, a marriage license both ratifies and fortifies a couple's bonds. And marriage, like voting and other core civic responsibilities, is strongest when universal. It best serves the interests of all when all are eligible and welcome to serve.

"Our government should respect every person and protect the institution of marriage. There is no contradiction between these responsibilities." Indeed, there is not. Allowing and expecting marriage for all Americans would show respect for the welfare and equality of all Americans, and it would protect the institution of marriage from the proliferation of alternatives (civil unions,

domestic-partner benefits, and socially approved cohabitation) that a continued ban on same-sex marriage will inevitably bring—is, in fact, bringing already.

The logic of Bush's speech points clearly toward marriage for all. It is this logic, the logic of marriage itself, that Bush and other proponents of a constitutional ban defy in their determination to exclude homosexuals.

"In all that lies ahead, let us match strong convictions with kindness and goodwill and decency." Amen. And let us have the courage to follow where our convictions and our compassion logically lead.

5.

HOW GOOD IS *GOODRIDGE*? An Analysis of *Goodridge v. Department of Public Health*

Glenn T. Stanton

If preachers who judge are unsavory, judges who preach are worse still. But that is exactly what we have in four justices of Massachusetts's Supreme Judicial Court and their recent creation of same-sex marriage as a new constitutional right. While the US Supreme Court drew on European law this summer in finding a right to sodomy, the Massachusetts Supreme Judicial Court found their new right to gay marriage more locally: the personal sentimentality of four justices. Dissenting justice Martha Sosman says the majority's opinion is fraught with "emotion-laden invocations."

In creating this new right, the majority in *Goodridge* makes little of their own admission that civil marriage is *not* the domain of the court, but is "created and regulated through exercise of . . . the commonwealth's lawmaking authority." Dissenting justice Francis Spina observes "the remedy the court has fashioned . . . exceeds the bounds of judicial restraint." He explains "the court has extruded a new right."

In fact, a panel of Harvard law professors, assembled to discuss the *Goodridge* decision in an academic setting shortly after it was handed down, offered some sharp criticism. Prof. Richard Parker lamented the decision oozed with "self-intoxicating narcissism and arrogance right on the surface. . . . [A]s sloppy of an opinion as you could want to read." The *Harvard Crimson* reported Prof. Laurence Tribe "was a minority of one" in his favor of the decision, although he admitted it created "a plethora of legal anomalies."[1]

Let us examine some of the primary problems with the approach and reasoning of this decision.

From www.family.org, a Web site of Focus on the Family. © 2004, by Focus on the Family. All rights reserved. International copyright secured. Used by permission. Glenn T. Stanton is senior analyst for Marriage and Sexuality at Focus on the Family and the coauthor of *Marriage on Trial: The Case against Same-Sex Marriage and Parenting*, published by InterVarsity Press.

MARRIAGE ARBITRARILY DEFINED

The court defines marriage as a "vital social institution," which is an "exclusive commitment of two individuals to each other" that "nurtures love and mutual support; it brings stability to our society." Elsewhere, it is explained that "the exclusive and permanent commitment of the marriage partners to one another . . . is the sine qua non of civil marriage." With no mention of the fundamental and humanly universal male-female part of marriage, the majority's definition is very selective, and no effort is made to show how this curious definition is rooted in law or tradition. They just state it.

While elsewhere the majority recognizes *Black's Law Dictionary*'s definition of marriage as "[t]he legal union of a man and woman as husband and wife," they do not incorporate this in their working definition of marriage.

The court then laments that current law, confining marriage to male-female couples, rests on "no rational reason," and "arbitrarily deprive[s]" same-sex couples access to marriage. Dissenting justice Sosman questions how the majority finds "the legislature is acting *irrationally* when it grants benefits to a proven successful family structure while denying the same benefits to a recent, perhaps promising, but essentially untested alternate family structure."

It is a bold show of arrogance and judicial fiat for the majority to claim that Massachusetts's traditional definition of marriage, rooted in the law, long tradition, and experience of the commonwealth—paralleling the law and tradition of forty-nine other states and all developed nations—is arbitrary and that *their* very selective and completely unfounded definition of marriage is the reasonable one.

MARRIAGE ROOTED IN BIGOTRY?

While the court says the state's traditional definition of marriage is derived arbitrarily, it admits this definition is not completely arbitrary and irrational. This court makes the astonishing accusation that the male-female definition of marriage is suspect because it is "rooted in persistent prejudices against persons who are (or who are believed to be) homosexual." And, of course, the "Constitution cannot control such prejudices, but neither can it tolerate them." So, of course, current marriage law must change.

Are these justices capable of considering that there might be reasons other than animus toward homosexuals that marriage is and has always been defined in *every* society as between men and women? And current marriage law does not discriminate against homosexuals, for homosexuals, like heterosexuals, can marry according to law. But both homosexuals and heterosexuals are prohibited from marrying someone of the same sex. So this is not about fairness or discrimination, but how we define marriage.

In fact, Justice Sandra Day O'Connor, writing this summer with the majority in the US Supreme Court's *Lawrence* sodomy decision, recognizes a "legitimate state interest . . . in preserving the traditional institution of marriage," and these reasons exist "beyond mere moral disapproval of an excluded group."[2]

But we must understand that biology itself is prejudiced against same-sex coupling, given that reproduction and proper child development demand binary human coupling.

COURT PLAYS THE EMOTION CARD

The court's judicial activism is revealed in the way it introduces the reader to the issue at hand; it explains that the fourteen plaintiffs make up seven same-sex couples who have all "been in a committed relationship" for anywhere from four to thirty years. We are told that many of them care for children together, and one couple even nursed an ailing mother before she passed away. Their respectable professional careers and activity in church and community groups are also touted.

Justice must be blind, and not swayed by the feelings of the judges or the likeability of the plaintiffs. The plaintiffs' rights are not more substantive because they are admirable citizens. Would their case be less compelling if they were day laborers or unemployed?

Why does the court feel the need to pad their rationale with information that is irrelevant to the question of justice?

LECTURED ON THE PLAINTIFFS' PURE INTENTIONS

After learning how nice the plaintiffs are, we are lectured on the purity of their intentions. The court instructs us that the plaintiffs seek only to be married and "not to undermine the institution of civil marriage." But as Stanley Kurtz brilliantly documents in a recent article, a "faction of gay rights advocates actually favors gay marriage as a step toward the abolition of marriage itself.[3]

But how did the court discern the plaintiffs' pure intentions? Did it ask? And what difference do the plaintiffs' intentions make toward the constitutional question of being able to "marry the person of one's choice"?

The court then moves from comforting us with the plaintiffs' pure intent to calming our fears over the outcome of such redefinition, explaining that "[r]ecognizing the right of an individual to marry a person of the same sex will not diminish the validity or dignity of opposite-sex marriage."

To the contrary, many believe that when something valuable is changed to become something else, the original thing tends to lose its meaning and significance.

But again, there's that haunting question, How does the lack of negative outcome for regular marriage make the right to same-sex marriage more substantial? If that right exists, it exists independent of its effect on another thing. Our best recent example was striking down state bans on interracial marriage, which was not contingent on the absence of negative impact upon whites marrying whites or blacks marrying blacks. It stood on its own merit.

IS RACE THE SAME AS SEXUAL ORIENTATION?

The court reminds us that expanding marriage to same-sex couples does not harm marriage "any more than recognizing the right of an individual to marry a person of a different race devalues the marriage of someone who married someone of her own race." Traditionalists are to be comforted by recognizing that actually, "extending civil marriage to same-sex couple reinforces the importance of marriage."

The court stakes its case strongly on this interracial point. Since the 1967 US Supreme Court case *Loving v. Virginia* struck down state bans on interracial marriage "because of a single trait," the commonwealth's court contends that homosexuals cannot be denied access to marriage because of their single trait. So, we are to conclude, a black man's wife being white is just like his "wife" being a man. Ergo, homosexuality is just like race.

However, the court doesn't establish this as fact; it just assumes it. But they *cannot* establish it, just as no other United States court or academic institution in the world has ever established that race and homosexuality are similar. This court simply assumes it as truth and builds on that assumption.

But there are a few things to consider here.

1. The *Goodridge* decision is nothing like the *Loving* decision. The latter *affirms* marriage by stating that any *man and woman* have a right to marry each other, regardless of race. *Goodridge*, however, *redefines* marriage. What is more, children growing up with interracial parents do not suffer the serious negative developmental consequences that children do when deprived of a mother or a father.
2. Interracial bans were clearly motivated by animus toward blacks and therefore completely unrelated to any effort to protect or maintain the underlying purpose and nature of marriage.
3. The applicability of *Loving* to same-sex marriage has been before the courts in the 1971 Minnesota case *Baker v. Nelson*. The Minnesota Supreme Court declared "in commonsense and in a constitutional sense, there is a clear distinction between a marital restriction based merely on race and one based on the fundamental difference in sex." The case was appealed to the US Supreme Court, which refused to hear the case, agreeing with and upholding Minnesota's conclusion. Curiously, the majority in *Goodridge* failed to mention this important piece of legal history.

COURT DECLARES NATURE UNCONSTITUTIONAL

Another key to the court's decision was rejecting the state's explanation that marriage is special because only opposite-sex marriage can produce children. The court denounces this as mean-spirited because it exploits "the one unbridgeable difference between same-sex and opposite-sex couples" and denies citizens access to same-sex marriage based on "a single trait."

If the only "unbridgeable" difference dividing same-sex and opposite-sex couples is the "single-trait" of being able to procreate without outside assistance, then the court reduces the value and uniqueness of femininity and masculinity to mere egg and sperm.

Every other apparent difference between male and female is, as the court says, "bridgeable." In fact, a concurring justice laments that the plaintiffs are hindered from marrying each other by "only their genders." And every man is prevented from being a mother for the very same reason.

But we understand and live out our humanity as members in one of two genders, for we understand humanity in male and female. They are far more than cultural constructs, for male and female traits and characteristics are manifest universally across time and culture. Of course there are variations, but there are more constants. However, the court deconstructs humanity by saying male or female just don't matter.

In fact, Sosman concludes, the court "is persuaded that there are *no differences* between same-sex and opposite-sex couples" (emphasis added). But can any husband, wife, or child admit that his or her spouse or parent could be replaced by someone of any sex? Is emotional attachment all there is to these relationships?

What is more, the court recognizes that without the right to marry whom one chooses, a citizen is "excluded from the full range of human experience." But the court fails to recognize that nature itself excludes same-sex couples from experiencing one of the fullest human experiences of joining sexually, becoming one flesh, creating new life from that beautiful union, and cooperatively seeing that glorious common fruit of humanity fully grow and mature. Same-sex couples can only *try* to imitate this wonder.

In effect, Massachusetts's Supreme Judicial Court has declared nature unconstitutional.

IGNORING WHAT CHILDREN NEED

The court recognizes that "protecting the welfare of children is a paramount state policy." However, they make the remarkable assertion that restricting marriage to male and female coupling "cannot plausibly further this policy." This statement exhibits a severe lack of understanding of what healthy child development demands.

Offering no documentation from any child development or social science scholars to support this, the court says moms or dads are unnecessary; all kids need are any loving parents. But the fallout of three decades of growing father-lessness in our nation has demonstrated how deeply kids need mothers and fathers. Child well-being decreases markedly in *every* important measure when a child lives separate from his or her biological mother and father.[4]

A recent study in the journal *Pediatrics* indicates that children residing in a home with a stepparent are *eight times* more likely to *die* of maltreatment than children living with biological parents.[5] It is impossible for children living in same-sex homes to live with both biological parents, and therefore they are dramatically at risk. It is never compassionate, but rather quite dangerous, to intentionally deny children their mother or father, which is exactly what every same-sex family does.

Sosman recognizes this omission of research from the majority: "Conspicuously absent from the court's opinion today is any acknowledgment that the attempts at scientific study of the ramifications of raising children in same-sex couple households are themselves in their infancy and have so far produced inconclusive and conflicting results." She continues, "Studies to date reveal that there are still some observable differences between children raised by opposite-sex couples and children raised by same-sex couples."[6]

This research compels dissenting justice Robert J. Cordy to caution the legislature that declining to recognize "same-sex marriage remains prudent until empirical questions about its impact on the upbringing of children are resolved." Sosman agrees, instructing, "it is rational for the legislature to postpone any redefinition of marriage that would include same-sex couples until such time as it is certain that that redefinition will not have unintended and undesirable social consequences. . . . However minimal the risk of the redefinition of marriage may seem to us from our vantage point, it is not up to us to decide what risks society must run."

The Massachusetts legislature would do well to heed the cautionary advice of Justices Cordy and Sosman. Their argument provides a very principled place to stand *for* the coming generations of children in the commonwealth (and the other forty-nine states) and against the judicial overreach of the Supreme Judicial Court.

CAN SAME-SEX AND OPPOSITE-SEX COUPLES BE SOCIALLY EQUAL?

While the court at the outset explains its mission as "to define the liberty of all, not to mandate our own moral code," an avant garde moral code is exactly what they put forth. One of the most stunning "sermonettes" in this decision is found in Justice John Greaney's concurrence. It is quoted at length:

I am hopeful that our decision will be accepted by those thoughtful citizens who believe that same-sex unions should not be approved by the state. I am not referring here to acceptance in the sense of grudging acknowledgment of the court's authority to adjudicate the matter. My hope is more liberating. The plaintiffs are members of our community, our neighbors, our coworkers, our friends. As pointed out by the court, their professions [are noble professional positions]. The plaintiffs volunteer in our schools, worship beside us in our religious houses, and have children who play with our children, to mention just a few ordinary daily contacts. We share a common humanity. . . . Simple principles of decency dictate that we extend to the plaintiffs, and to their new status, full acceptance, tolerance, and respect. We should do so because it is the right thing to do.

Justice Greaney believes he has served an important social function by letting us know who the good people and the bad people are in this issue. But can we logically "accept, tolerate, and respect" the plaintiffs' new status? Can we see same-sex unions as morally equal to marriage? We cannot and here is why.

Marriage is just as much about the community as it is about the couple. Marriage serves an important social good of regulating adult domestic and sexual behavior and providing mothers and fathers for children. No society can ever suffer from too much marriage between men and women.

To the contrary, society can suffer from *too much* homosexual marriage. Science cannot tell us how much is too much, but logic tells us there is certainly a troubling saturation point. Too much same-sex coupling will threaten the creation and development of the next generation. Too much will also threaten the necessary values of monogamy, the social necessity of men caring for and protecting women and women domesticating men. These important tasks will become optional.

Likewise, too little same-sex marriage has never been a problem for any society, but too little heterosexual marriage certainly is.

Therefore, we cannot logically fulfill Greaney's hope for full acceptance of same-sex "marriage" because it would not be "liberating" but, rather, humanly and culturally stifling.

The question of same-sex marriage is not just a moral question, but a social one as well. It is a question of the very nature of humanity.

WHAT WILL *GOODRIDGE* ALLOW?

In light of their ruling that barring couples of the same-sex from marrying is unconstitutional, Massachusetts's Supreme Judicial Court gave the Massachusetts legislature 180 days (from November 18, 2003, to May 17, 2004) "to take such action as it may deem appropriate." So what could the legislature do?

Reading the court's decision, it looked as if anything less than full-blown same-sex marriage would be judged unconstitutional because the majority concludes the Constitution will not tolerate the "protections, benefits, and obligations conferred by civil marriage" being denied to same-sex couples. But would it tolerate civil unions? Not according to the next line of the decision, which says the Massachusetts Constitution affirms the equality of all individuals and "forbids the creation of second-class citizens." Allowing civil unions, but not marriage, would certainly be seen as treating same-sex couples as second class by this court.

And that is exactly how the Supreme Judicial Court directed the Massachusetts legislature on February 3, 2003. The Massachusetts Senate had asked the Supreme Judicial Court on December 12, 2003, whether civil unions satisfied the requirement the court demanded in *Goodridge*. The court's simple answer: "No." The court explained, "Segregating same-sex unions from opposite-sex unions cannot possibly be held rationally to advance or 'preserve' what we stated in *Goodridge*."

CONCLUSION

This brings us to the fundamental legal questions here:

Who holds rights?
What is equality?

This is not about whether Massachusetts's citizens—homosexual or heterosexual—are treated equally under the law. It is not about homosexuals as a class of people being arbitrarily barred from marriage. Spina recognizes that as they stand, "the marriage statutes do not discriminate on the basis of sexual orientation."

All citizens of Massachusetts enjoy full access to marriage as long as they meet the criteria set forth by law:

1. One cannot already be married.
2. One must be an adult and must marry an adult.
3. One cannot marry a close family member.
4. One's spouse must be of the opposite sex.

Current marriage law is blind regarding sexual orientation. It does not treat homosexuals differently than heterosexuals, for homosexuals have absolute access to marriage as it has always existed, just as any other citizen does. Yes, current law keeps them from marrying members of the same sex, but it also keeps heterosexuals from doing the same. Marriage treats all citizens equally.

This helps us understand the question at hand. This debate is not about fair *access* to marriage. It is about *redefining* marriage, for that is exactly what these plaintiffs and the court have done.

This is exactly what Justice Cordy recognizes: "In reaching this result, the court transmuted the "right" to marry into a right to change the institution itself." And so, Massachusetts's marriage law, along with that of the other forty-nine states, did not draw an unequal line "between men and women or between heterosexuals and homosexuals, any of whom can obtain a license to marry a member of the opposite sex; rather, it is drawn between same-sex couples and opposite-sex couples." And that is the primary difference, for as Spina observes, "constitutional protections are extended to *individuals*, not *couples*," and "whether an individual chooses not to marry because of sexual orientation or any other reason should be of no concern to the court" (emphasis added).

So, with the question being about redefinition, we must ask, Who can redefine marriage? The court admits it is their role to "define the liberty of all" and protect "equality under the law" according to the Constitution. Marriage law, prior to *Goodridge*, honored these values, and the plaintiffs made no charge that it did not. If the citizens of the commonwealth desire to change the legal criteria for marriage itself, the legislature provides them that opportunity, as this court recognized.

But as the dissenting justices cautioned, the legislature should not do so until it is sure such a fundamental social change will not have deep negative consequences for children, women, men, and the larger society. This is an important warning because a remarkably conclusive body of social science research published over the last forty years indicates that *any* straying away from the ideal of man and woman joining together for life in marriage and raising their common children significantly diminishes the most important measures of human well-being and the health of children and society.[7]

NOTES

1. Daniel L. Hemel, "HLS Panel Mulls Over Gay Marriage," *Harvard Crimson*, February 6, 2004.

2. *Lawrence v. Texas* (02-102) 41 S.W.3d 349 (2003), p. 7.

3. Stanley Kurtz, "Beyond Gay Marriage," *Weekly Standard*, August 4, 2003, p. 26.

4. David Popenoe, *Life without Father: Compelling Evidence That Fatherhood and Marriage Are Indispensible for the Good of Children* (New York: Free Press, 1997); Glenn T. Stanton, *Why Marriage Matters: Reasons to Believe in Marriage in Postmodern Society* (Colorado Springs, CO: Pinon Press, 1997); Sara McLanahan and Gary Sandefur, *Growing Up with a Single Parent: What Hurts, What Helps* (Cambridge, MA: Harvard University Press, 1994); Deborah Dawson, "Family Structure and Children's Health and Well-Being: Data from the 1988 National Health Interview Survey on Child Health," *Journal of Marriage and the Family* 53 (1991): 573–84; Michael Gottfredson and Travis Hirschi, *A General Theory of Crime* (Stanford, CA: Stanford University Press, 1990), p. 103; Richard Koestner et al., "The Family Origins of Empathic Concern: A Twenty-Six-Year Longitudinal Study," *Journal of Personality and Social Psychology* 58 (1990): 709–17; E. Mavis Hetherington, "Effects of Father Absence on Personality Development in Adolescent Daughters," *Developmental Psychology* 7 (1972): 313–26; Irwin Garfinkel and Sara McLanahan, *Single Mothers and Their Children: A New American Dilemma* (Washington, DC: Urban Institute Press, 1986); Ronald J. Angel and Jacqueline

Worobey, "Single Motherhood and Children's Health," *Journal of Health and Social Behavior* 29 (1988): 38–52; L. Remez, "Children Who Don't Live with Both Parents Face Behavioral Problems," *Family Planning Perspectives* (January/February 1992); Judith Wallerstein and Sandra Blakeslee, *Second Chances: Men and Women a Decade after Divorce* (New York: Ticknor & Fields, 1990); Judith Wallerstein et al., *The Unexpected Legacy of Divorce: A 25-Year Landmark Study* (New York: Hyperion, 2000); Nicholas Zill, Donna Morrison, and Mary Jo Coiro, "Long-Term Effects of Parental Divorce on Parent-Child Relationships, Adjustment, and Achievement in Young Adulthood," *Journal of Family Psychology* 7 (1993): 91–103.

5. Michael Stiffman et al., "Household Composition and Risk of Fatal Child Maltreatment," *Pediatrics* 109 (2002): 615–21.

6. A 2001 *American Sociological Review* study reports 64 percent of young adults raised by lesbian mothers reported considering having same-sex erotic relationships either in the past, now, or in the future. Only 17 percent of young adults in heterosexual families reported the same thing. The study concludes there is "evidence of a moderate degree of parent-to-child transmission of sexual orientation." This study also reported that heterosexual mothers were significantly more likely to desire their boys engage in masculine activities and their daughters in feminine ones, however, "lesbian mothers had no such interest. Their preference for their child's play was gender-neutral." See Judith Stacey and Timothy Biblarz, "(How) Does the Sexual Orientation of Parents Matter?" *American Sociological Review* 66 (2001): 159–83.

7. Many of these studies are either presented or represented in: Popenoe, *Life without Father*; Stanton, *Why Marriage Matters*; Ronald P. Rohner and Robert A. Veneziano, "The Importance of Father Love: History and Contemporary Evidence," *Review of General Psychology* 5, no. 4 (2001): 382–405; Kyle D. Pruett, *Fatherneed: Why Father Care Is as Essential as Mother Care for Your Child* (New York: Free Press, 2000); David Blankenhorn, *Fatherless America: Confronting Our Most Urgent Social Problem* (New York: Basic Books, 1994); McLanahan and Sandefur, *Growing Up with a Single Parent*; Ellen Bing, "The Effect of Child-Rearing Practices on the Development of Differential Cognitive Abilities," *Child Development* 34 (1963): 631–48; Dawson, "Family Structure and Children's Health and Well-Being"; Scott Coltrane, "Father-Child Relationships and the Status of Women: A Cross-Cultural Study," *American Journal of Sociology* 93 (1988): 1088; Gottfredson and Hirschi, *A General Theory of Crime*, p. 103; Koestner et al., "The Family Origins of Empathic Concern"; Hetherington, "Effects of Father Absence on Personality Development in Adolescent Daughters"; Garfinkel and McLanahan, *Single Mothers and Their Children*, pp. 30–31; Sara L. McLanahan, "Life without Father: What Happens to Children?" Center for Research on Child Well-being Working Paper #01-21, Princeton University, August 15, 2001; Paul R. Amato and Fernando Rivera, "Paternal Involvement and Children's Behavior Problems," *Journal of Marriage and the Family* 61 (1999): 375–84; David Ellwood, *Poor Support: Poverty in the American Family* (New York: Basic Books, 1988), p. 46; Angel and Worobey, "Single Motherhood and Children's Health"; Remez, "Children Who Don't Live with Both Parents Face Behavioral Problems"; Wallerstein et al., *The Unexpected Legacy of Divorce*; Zill, Morrison, and Coiro, "Long-Term Effects of Parental Divorce on Parent-Child Relationships, Adjustment, and Achievement in Young Adulthood"; Jan Stets and Murray A. Strauss, "The Marriage License as a Hitting License: A Comparison of Assaults in Dating, Cohabiting, and Married Couples," *Journal of Family Violence* 4 (1989): 161–80; Jan Stets, "Cohabiting and Marital Aggression: The Role of Social Isolation," *Journal of Marriage and the Family* 53 (1991): 669–80; Michael Gordon, "The Family Environment of Sexual Abuse: A Comparison of Natal and Stepfather Abuse," *Child Abuse and Neglect* 13 (1985): 121–30; Michael Stiffman et al., "Household Composition and Risk of Fatal Child Maltreatment," *Pediatrics* 109 (2002): 615–21; Frank Putnam, "Ten-Year Research Update Review: Child Sexual Abuse," *Journal of the American Academy of Child and Adolescent Psychiatry* 42 (2003): 269–79; David Popenoe, "The Evolution of Marriage and the Problems of Stepfamilies: A Biosocial Perspective," in *Stepfamilies: Who Benefits? Who Does Not?* ed. Alan Booth and Judy Dunn (Hillsdale, NJ: Lawrence Erlbaum Associates, 1994); Nicholas Zill, "Understanding

Why Children in Stepfamilies Have More Learning and Behavior Problems Than Children in Nuclear Families," in *Stepfamilies: Who Benefits? Who Does Not?* p. 98; Martin Daly and Margo Wilson, "Child Abuse and Other Risks of Not Living with Both Parents," *Ethology and Sociobiology* 6 (1985): 197–210; Martin Daly and Margo Wilson, *Homicide* (New York: de Gruyter, 1988), pp. 87–88; Margo Wilson and Martin Daly, "Risk of Maltreatment of Children Living with Stepparents," in *Child Abuse and Neglect: Biosocial Dimensions*, ed. R. Gelles and J. Lancaster (New York: de Gruyter, 1987), p. 230; Michael Stiffman et al., "Household Composition and Risk of Fatal Child Maltreatment," *Pediatrics* 109 (2002): 615–21; "Shuttle Diplomacy," *Psychology Today* (July/August 1993): 15; Douglas B. Downey, "Understanding Academic Achievement among Children in Stephouseholds: The Role of Parental Resources, Sex of Stepparent, and Sex of Child," *Social Forces* 73 (1995): 875–94; William L. MacDonald and Alfred DeMaris, "Parenting Stepchildren and Biological Children: The Effect of Stepparent's Gender and New Biological Childen," *Journal of Family Issues* 17 (1996): 5.

6.

THE ROAD TO GAY MARRIAGE

New York Times *Editorial*

When Massachusetts's highest court ruled that gays have a right to marry, it opened a floodgate.

From San Francisco to New Paltz, New York, thousands of gay couples have wed, and the movement shows no sign of slowing. There has been opposition, from the White House down, but support has come from across the nation and the political spectrum. Arnold Schwarzenegger, the Republican governor of the most populous state, said it would be "fine" with him if California allowed gay marriage. The student newspaper at Baylor, the world's largest Baptist university, ran a pro–gay marriage editorial.

At an anti–gay marriage meeting in Washington last week, Senator Bill Frist, the majority leader, warned that the "wildfire" of same-sex marriages will spread unless opponents mobilize. But even if they do, it is unlikely gay marriage can or will be halted. Opponents are pinning their hopes on a federal constitutional amendment, but even many Americans who are skittish about gay marriage do not want to enshrine intolerance as one of the nation's fundamental principles. The founders made it extremely hard to amend the Constitution, and it is unlikely this effort will succeed.

With allies in the White House and both houses of Congress, gay marriage opponents want the issue decided in Washington. But it appears we are embarking on fifty national conversations, not one. Following the lead of Vermont, which has civil unions, and Massachusetts, other states will weigh what rights to accord same-sex couples, and how to treat marriages and unions from other states. When the federal government does act, it is likely that, as with the Supreme Court's 1967 ruling on interracial marriage, it will be to lift up those states that failed to give all their citizens equal rights.

The idea of marriage between two people of the same sex is still very new,

Reprinted with permission from the *New York Times*, March 7, 2004.

and for some unsettling, but we have been down this road before. This debate follows the same narrative arc as women's liberation, racial integration, disability rights, and every other march of marginalized Americans into the mainstream. Same-sex marriage seems destined to have the same trajectory: from being too outlandish to be taken seriously, to being branded offensive and lawless, to eventual acceptance.

THE FLOOD OF GAY MARRIAGES

The television images from San Francisco brought gay marriage into America's living rooms in a way no court decision could. Mayor Gavin Newsom's critics called his actions lawless, but the law was, and still is, murky. When California's attorney general asked the state supreme court to address same-sex marriage, it declined to stop the city from performing the ceremonies right away, or to invalidate those already performed. When New Paltz's mayor began performing same-sex marriages, New York law seemed similarly uncertain.

The rebellious mayors have so far acted honorably. Testing the law is a civil rights tradition: Jim Crow laws were undone by blacks who refused to obey them. Visible protests of questionable laws can, as the Reverend Dr. Martin Luther King Jr. wrote in "Letter from Birmingham Jail," "dramatize" an issue so "it can no longer be ignored." The mayors have succeeded in dramatizing the issue. But for them to defy court orders requires a far greater crisis than is present here. If courts direct officials not to perform gay marriages, they should not.

THE ROLE OF "ACTIVIST JUDGES"

Opponents of gay marriage have tried to place all of the blame for recent events on "activist judges." Senator John Cornyn, a Texas Republican, has called for a congressional investigation of "judicial invalidation of traditional marriage laws." The judiciary, however, is only one part of a much larger story. Gay rights and gay marriages are being driven by an array of social forces and institutions. In California, the driving force has been an elected mayor, with the support of his constituents. In that case, it is gay marriage opponents who are asking judges to step in.

To the extent that the courts do have a leading role, it is perfectly natural. Gay marriage opponents like to portray judges as alien beings, but state court judges are an integral part of state government. They were elected, or appointed by someone who was. The founders created three equal branches, and a Constitution setting out broad principles, at both the national and state levels. Courts are supposed to give life to phrases like "equal protection" and "due process." Much of the nation's progress, from integration to religious freedom, has been won just this way.

THE EMERGING LEGAL PATCHWORK

As more courts and legislatures take up the issue, the rules for gay civil unions and marriages will most likely vary considerably across the nation. More states can be expected to follow Vermont's lead and allow civil unions that carry most of the rights of marriage. Others may allow gay marriage. This is hardly unusual, since states have historically made their own marriage and divorce rules. Currently, some people, such as first cousins, can marry in some states but not others.

The last great constitutional transformation of marriage in this country, the invalidation of laws against interracial marriage, moved slowly. In 1948 California became the first state in the nation to strike down its laws against interracial marriages. It was not until 1967 that the Supreme Court held Virginia's law unconstitutional, and created a rule that applied nationally.

THE BATTLE FOR INTERSTATE RECOGNITION

Popular attention is now on wedding ceremonies for people of the same sex, but a no less important issue is whether states will recognize gay marriages and unions performed in other states. In 1996 Congress passed the Defense of Marriage Act, which says no state can be forced to recognize gay marriages. But the law has not been tested, and it should eventually be found to violate the constitutional requirement that states respect each other's legal acts. As a practical matter, the nation is too tightly bound today for people's marriages to dissolve, and child custody arrangements to change, merely because they move to another state.

Whether or not they have to recognize other states' civil unions and gay marriages, states clearly have the option to. Whether they will is likely to be the next important chapter of the gay marriage story. Couples who are married or who have civil unions will return to their home states, or move to new ones, and seek to have their status recognized. Attorney General Eliot Spitzer of New York, in an opinion last week, strongly suggested New York's law requires it to recognize gay marriages and civil unions entered into elsewhere. At least one New York court has already reached this conclusion.

FINAL DESTINATION

The controversy over same-sex weddings has obscured the remarkable transformation in opinion over civil unions. Less than twenty years ago, the United States Supreme Court enthusiastically upheld a Georgia law making gay sex a crime. Last year, the court reversed itself, and a national consensus seems to be forming that gay couples have a right to, at the least, enter into civil unions that carry the same rights as marriage. Even President Bush, who has endorsed a constitutional amendment to prohibit gay marriage, has suggested he had no problem with states recognizing civil unions.

Civil unions, with rights similar to marriage, are a major step, but ultimately only an interim one. As both sides in the debate agree, marriage is something more than a mere bundle of legal rights. Whatever else the state is handing out when it issues a marriage license, whatever approval or endorsement it is providing, will ultimately have to be made available to all Americans equally.

To the Virginia judge who ruled that Mildred Jeter, a black woman, and Richard Loving, a white man, could not marry, the reason was self-evident. "Almighty God created the races white, black, yellow, Malay, and red, and he placed them on separate continents," he wrote. "And but for the interference with his arrangement there would be no cause for such marriages." Calling marriage one of the "basic civil rights of man," the Supreme Court ruled in 1967 that Virginia had to let interracial couples marry. Thirty-seven years from now, the reasons for opposing gay marriage will no doubt feel just as archaic, and the right to enter into it will be just as widely accepted.

7.

TIME FOR A
NEW BOSTON TEA PARTY

Pat Buchanan

"John Marshall has made his decision. Now let him enforce it," thundered Andrew Jackson of the legendary chief justice.

From the sublime to the ridiculous, we have one Margaret Marshall, chief justice of the Massachusetts Supreme Judicial Court, ordering the state legislature to enact, in 180 days, a law giving homosexuals the right to marry. What is to be done with this Justice Marshall?

The legislature and Gov. Mitt Romney should ignore the court, defy the order, and submit to Massachusetts voters a constitutional amendment declaring that marriage is between a man and woman, as God and nature intended.

Massachusetts has been given an opportunity to lead the nation as it did in the 1770s, in breaking the power of a tyranny. If Bay State legislators will refuse to pass the law demanded by the court, and Romney will refuse to sign such a law and orders the bureaucracy to ignore the court, what could the court do? Order his arrest? Declare him in contempt? So what? Reasonable people already hold the Massachusetts court in contempt.

It is time for elected representatives to take back powers that were never constitutionally granted to any court. For the issue here is not, What is decided? but, Who decides? In a republic, the power to write laws is given to elected representatives, not judges or justices.

In every state, marriage has been between a man and woman and restrictions have been set by the legislature. One cannot practice bigamy or polygamy or polyandry. One cannot marry children. One cannot marry a member of one's own family.

What the Massachusetts court did was to declare that, from now on, it would decide such matters. The Massachusetts court has just usurped the power of the elected branches, and they should slap the court down.

This is an issue of power as well as law. Governor Romney can make himself a national figure by refusing to propose or to sign any law regarding marriage that he and the people of the Bay State believe to be rooted in ignorance, illogic, and immorality.

The opportunity afforded by this absurd decision is not confined to Massachusetts. Legislatures across America should enact laws defining marriage as between a man and woman. Voters should petition to have identical referenda put on the ballot.

Congress should reenact the Defense of Marriage Act and amend it to deny the Supreme Court any right of review. Congress's power to restrict the appellate review jurisdiction of the Supreme Court was granted in Article III of the Constitution for a purpose. This is it.

President Bush should make the preservation of marriage the social issue of 2004. Every candidate, including Governor Dean if nominated by the Democrats, should be forced to declare himself for or against the idea that marriage is restricted to men and women.

Gay activists and their media auxiliaries will denounce this as the politics of divisiveness and hate. But America has begun to catch on to the tactic of smearing as bigots and haters any who resist this new social revolution. And the nation has begun to see through the strategy of imposing that revolution not through the democratic process of winning hearts, minds, and votes, but through the dictatorial process of getting collaborator-judges to issue court degrees.

"The worse the better" is an old revolutionary slogan. The more stupid, arrogant, and oppressive a regime becomes, the more the people turn to revolution to be rid of it. The principle applies to counterrevolutions, as well. The more insolent, arrogant, and dictatorial judges become, the more they build up the cordite of counterrevolution.

In a half century, we have watched judges and justices arbitrarily strike down laws against pornography, denying communities the power to prevent the pollution of cultures. We have seen the killing of unborn children declared a constitutional right. We have seen children forcibly bused across cities to meet some jurist's idea of what is the proper racial balance.

Judges have declared the Pledge of Allegiance to be a violation of the Constitution. They have ordered high school teams not to pray before games. They have ordered students not to say a prayer at graduation. They have told teachers what they may and may not teach about God and man. They have declared homosexual sodomy a constitutional right.

Time to go to the root of America's social crisis: the power usurped by judges and imposed against the will of the people and their chosen representatives.

Legislatures and executives should begin recapturing their lost powers, or we should find new legislators and executives with the courage to restore the constitutional balance of the Founding Fathers. Let the counterrevolution begin where that first revolution began, with a new Boston Tea Party.

8.

THE POWER OF MARRIAGE

David Brooks

Anybody who has several sexual partners in a year is committing spiritual suicide. He or she is ripping the veil from all that is private and delicate in oneself, and pulverizing it in an assembly line of selfish sensations.

But marriage is the opposite. Marriage joins two people in a sacred bond. It demands that they make an exclusive commitment to each other and thereby takes two discrete individuals and turns them into kin.

Few of us work as hard at the vocation of marriage as we should. But marriage makes us better than we deserve to be. Even in the chores of daily life, married couples find themselves, over the years, coming closer together, fusing into one flesh. Married people who remain committed to each other find that they reorganize and deepen each other's lives. They may eventually come to the point when they can say to each other: "Love you? I *am* you."

Today marriage is in crisis. Nearly half of all marriages end in divorce. Worse, in some circles, marriage is not even expected. Men and women shack up for a while, produce children, and then float off to shack up with someone else.

Marriage is in crisis because marriage, which relies on a culture of fidelity, is now asked to survive in a culture of contingency. Today, individual choice is held up as the highest value: choice of lifestyles, choice of identities, choice of cell phone rate plans. Freedom is a wonderful thing, but the culture of contingency means that the marriage bond, which is supposed to be a sacred vow till death do us part, is now more likely to be seen as an easily canceled contract.

Men are more likely to want to trade up when a younger trophy wife comes along. Men and women are quicker to opt out of marriages, even marriages that are not fatally flawed, when their "needs" don't seem to be met at that moment.

Reprinted with permission from the *New York Times,* November 22, 2003.

Still, even in this time of crisis, every human being in the United States has the chance to move from the path of contingency to the path of marital fidelity—except homosexuals. Gays and lesbians are banned from marriage and forbidden to enter into this powerful and ennobling institution. A gay or lesbian couple may love each other as deeply as any two people, but when you meet a member of such a couple at a party, he or she then introduces you to a "partner," a word that reeks of contingency.

You would think that faced with this marriage crisis, we conservatives would do everything in our power to move as many people as possible from the path of contingency to the path of fidelity. But instead, many argue that gays must be banished from matrimony because gay marriage would weaken all marriage. A marriage is between a man and a woman, they say. It is women who domesticate men and make marriage work.

Well, if women really domesticated men, heterosexual marriage wouldn't be in crisis. In truth, it's moral commitment, renewed every day through faithfulness, that "domesticates" all people.

Some conservatives may have latched onto biological determinism (men are savages who need women to tame them) as a convenient way to oppose gay marriage. But in fact we are not animals whose lives are bounded by our flesh and by our gender. We're moral creatures with souls, endowed with the ability to make covenants, such as the one Ruth made with Naomi: "Where you go I will go, and where you stay I will stay. Your people will be my people and your God my God. Where you die I will die, and there I will be buried."

The conservative course is not to banish gay people from making such commitments. It is to expect that they make such commitments. We shouldn't just allow gay marriage. We should insist on gay marriage. We should regard it as scandalous that two people could claim to love each other and not want to sanctify their love with marriage and fidelity.

When liberals argue for gay marriage, they make it sound like a really good employee benefits plan. Or they frame it as a civil rights issue, like extending the right to vote.

Marriage is not voting. It's going to be up to conservatives to make the important, moral case for marriage, including gay marriage. Not making it means drifting further into the culture of contingency, which, when it comes to intimate and sacred relations, is an abomination.

9.

WHY THE "M" WORD MATTERS TO ME

Andrew Sullivan

As a child, I had no idea what homosexuality was. I grew up in a traditional home—Catholic, conservative, middle class. Life was relatively simple: education, work, family. I was raised to aim high in life, even though my parents hadn't gone to college. But one thing was instilled in me. What mattered was not how far you went in life, how much money you earned, how big a name you made for yourself. What really mattered was family and the love you had for one another.

The most important day of your life was not graduation from college or your first day at work or a raise or even your first house. The most important day of your life was when you got married. It was on that day that all your friends and all your family got together to celebrate the most important thing in life: your happiness—your ability to make a new home, to form a new but connected family, to find love that put everything else into perspective.

But as I grew older, I found that this was somehow not available to me. I didn't feel the things for girls that my peers did. All the emotions and social rituals and bonding of teenage heterosexual life eluded me. I didn't know why. No one explained it. My emotional bonds to other boys were one-sided; each time I felt myself falling in love, they sensed it, pushed it away. I didn't and couldn't blame them. I got along fine with my buds in a nonemotional context, but something was awry, something not right. I came to know almost instinctively that I would never be a part of my family the way my siblings might one day be. The love I had inside me was unmentionable, anathema. I remember writing in my teenage journal one day, "I'm a professional human being. But what do I do in my private life?"

I never discussed my real life. I couldn't date girls and so immersed myself in schoolwork, the debate team, school plays, anything to give me an excuse not to confront reality. When I looked toward the years ahead, I couldn't see a future. There was just a void. Was I going to be alone my whole life? Would I ever have a most important day in my life? It seemed impossible, a negation, an undoing. To be a full part of my family, I had to somehow not be me. So, like many other gay teens, I withdrew, became neurotic, depressed, at times close to suicidal. I shut myself in my room with my books night after night while my peers developed the skills needed to form real relationships and loves. In wounded pride, I even voiced a rejection of family and marriage. It was the only way I could explain my isolation.

It took years for me to realize that I was gay, years more to tell others, and more time yet to form any kind of stable emotional bond with another man. Because my sexuality had emerged in solitude—and without any link to the idea of an actual relationship—it was hard later to reconnect sex to love and self-esteem. It still is. But I persevered, each relationship slowly growing longer than the last, learning in my twenties and thirties what my straight friends had found out in their teens. But even then my parents and friends never asked the question they would have asked automatically if I were straight: So, when are you going to get married? When is your relationship going to be public? When will we be able to celebrate it and affirm it and support it? In fact, no one—no one—has yet asked me that question.

When people talk about gay marriage, they miss the point. This isn't about gay marriage. It's about marriage. It's about family. It's about love. It isn't about religion. It's about civil marriage licenses. Churches can and should have the right to say no to marriage for gays in their congregations, just as Catholics say no to divorce, but divorce is still a civil option. These family values are not options for a happy and stable life. They are necessities. Putting gay relationships in some other category—civil unions, domestic partnerships, whatever—may alleviate real human needs, but by their very euphemism, by their very separateness, they actually build a wall between gay people and their families. They put back the barrier many of us have spent a lifetime trying to erase.

It's too late for me to undo my past. But I want above everything else to remember a young kid out there who may even be reading this now. I want to let him know that he doesn't have to choose between himself and his family anymore. I want him to know that his love has dignity, that he does indeed have a future as a full and equal part of the human race. Only marriage will do that. Only marriage can bring him home.

10.

MARRIAGE
Mix and Match

Nicholas Kristof

Shakespeare's *Othello* used to be among the hardest plays to stage in America. Although the actors playing Othello were white, they wore dark makeup, and audiences felt "disgust and horror," as Abigail Adams said. She wrote, "My whole soul shuddered whenever I saw the sooty heretic Moor touch the fair Desdemona."

Not until 1942, when Paul Robeson took the role, did a major American performance use a black actor as Othello. Even then, Broadway theaters initially refused to have such a production.

Fortunately, we did not enshrine our "disgust and horror" in the Constitution—but we could have. Long before President Bush's call for a "constitutional amendment protecting marriage," Rep. Seaborn Roddenberry of Georgia proposed an amendment that he said would uphold the sanctity of marriage.

Roddenberry's proposed amendment, in December 1912, stated, "Intermarriage between Negroes or persons of color and Caucasians . . . is forever prohibited." He took this action, he said, because some states were permitting marriages that were "abhorrent and repugnant," and he aimed to "exterminate now this debasing, ultrademoralizing, un-American and inhuman leprosy."

"Let this condition go on if you will," Roddenberry warned. "At some day, perhaps remote, it will be a question always whether or not the solemnizing of matrimony in the North is between two descendants of our Anglo-Saxon fathers and mothers or whether it be of a mixed blood descended from the orangutan-trodden shores of far-off Africa." (His zoology was off: Orangutans come from Asia, not Africa.)

In Bush's call for action last week, he argued that the drastic step of a con-

Reprinted with permission from the *New York Times*, March 3, 2004.

stitutional amendment is necessary because "marriage cannot be severed from its cultural, religious, and natural roots without weakening the good influence of society."

Roddenberry also worried about the risks ahead: "This slavery of white women to black beasts will bring this nation to a conflict as fatal and as bloody as ever reddened the soil of Virginia."

That early effort to amend the Constitution arose after a black boxer, Jack Johnson, ostentatiously consorted with white women. "A blot on our civilization," the governor of New York fretted.

In the last half century, there has been a stunning change in attitudes. All but nine states banned interracial marriages at one time, and in 1958, a poll found that 96 percent of whites disapproved of marriages between blacks and whites. Yet in 1997, 77 percent approved. (A personal note: My wife is Chinese American, and I heartily recommend miscegenation.)

Bush is an indicator of a similar revolution in views—toward homosexuality—but one that is still unfolding. In 1994, Bush supported a Texas antisodomy law that allowed the police to arrest gays in their own homes. Now the Bushes have gay friends, and Bush appoints gays to office without worrying that he will turn into a pillar of salt.

Social conservatives like Bush are right in saying that marriage is "the most fundamental institution in civilization." So we should extend it to America's gay minority—just as marriage was earlier extended from Europe's aristocrats to the masses.

Conservatives can fairly protest that the gay marriage issue should be decided by a political process, not by unelected judges. But there is a political process under way: state legislatures can bar the recognition of gay marriages registered in Sodom-on-the-Charles, Massachusetts, or anywhere else. The Defense of Marriage Act specifically gives states that authority.

Yet the Defense of Marriage Act is itself a reminder of the difficulties of achieving morality through legislation. It was, as Slate noted, written by the thrice-married Rep. Bob Barr and signed by the philandering Bill Clinton. It's less a monument to fidelity than to hypocrisy.

If we're serious about constitutional remedies for marital breakdowns, we could adopt an amendment criminalizing adultery. Zamfara, a state in northern Nigeria, has had success in reducing AIDS, prostitution, and extramarital affairs by sentencing adulterers to be stoned to death.

Short of that, it seems to me that the best way to preserve the sanctity of American marriage is for us all to spend less time fretting about other people's marriages—and more time improving our own.

11.

THE BELLS ARE RINGING ...
Marriage, Marriage, Everywhere

John O'Sullivan

As same-sex couples from neighboring jurisdictions and even states besiege San Francisco's city offices clamoring to be wed, one is half-tempted to grant them what they say they want—the stability of lifelong marriage. Suppose same-sex marriages were introduced by legislation that also made divorce much harder to obtain: How many same-sex couples would then be rushing to join San Francisco's wedding carnival? My suspicion is that lesbians would heavily outnumber gay men and that there would be a great many grooms left waiting at the municipal altar. It is not lifelong commitment that the couples are seeking (except in moments of romantic fantasy), but the revolving door of modern marriage with no-fault divorce. And it tells us a great deal that legislation to make marriage both gender free and permanent would have no chance whatsoever of passing—while gay marriage is almost upon us.

Whatever its conservative advocates may argue, gay marriage would be not a move toward greater stability in homosexual relationships, but just another domino falling in the slow-motion collapse of marriage in the Western world. Radical advocates of gay marriage support it for that very reason. As Stanley Kurtz has persuasively demonstrated, the end result of this trend is visible in Scandinavia—where marriage is gradually dying away, replaced by cohabitation, family dissolution, and child rearing by the welfare state. Gay marriage in Scandinavia has done nothing to halt these trends. Indeed, they have accelerated in the period since gay marriages and civil unions were legalized.

Yet unless an amendment to the US Constitution is passed, same-sex marriage is likely to become a reality in America. The Massachusetts supreme court has effectively ordered the legislature to allow gay couples to marry. Even before that, the Canadian Supreme Court's discovery of a right to same-sex marriage—though hotly contested in Ottawa—was presented in the US media as an indicator of where the United States is heading on the grounds that, well, Canada is a more progressive version of America. And Justice Sandra Day O'Connor laid the groundwork for direct legal influence when she argued in favor of citing the decisions of overseas courts as precedents in US court decisions. Judges will naturally pick and choose among these decisions, generally preferring to cite Scandinavia over Saudi Arabia, so that individual judicial decisions will become quite arbitrary while their overall drift is in a left-progressive direction. Such easygoing arbitrariness seems to be catching. In San Francisco, even the mayor is legislating—though the courts may well rebuff this challenge to their monopoly.

It is far from certain that even a federal amendment would halt this juggernaut. Although the Equal Rights Amendment failed to pass into law, the courts subsequently imposed a great many of its provisions by judicial fiat. And it is not hard to imagine determined ideological judges somehow circumventing the amendment, however cleverly it is drafted, to make gay marriage exist in all but name. That would not satisfy its advocates, of course, for whom absolute equality between gays and straights in "marriage rights" is the goal. But how long could that goal be denied once marriages and "civil partnerships" were for practical purposes identical arrangements? Judges who found ingenious ways to interpret the amendment as mandating gay marriage—don't laugh until you have studied how the 1964 Civil Rights Act came to mandate racial preferences—would have the grave nodding agreement of the *New York Times* and all the other arbiters of cultural and social fashion.

Is this analysis defeatist? No, because I will propose ways to outwit these trends. But it is pessimistic, because it suggests that some form of gay marriage is inevitable unless there are two great revolutions simultaneously. The first is a religious revival. As Stanley Kurtz has pointed out, both gay marriage and the decline of heterosexual marriage tend to appear where religion, especially Catholicism, becomes weak and socially timid. The second is a successful political campaign to limit judicial review severely and to restore legislative and democratic authority on political questions. (Neither revolution is likely, but a religious revival does at least have the consolation of being unpredictable.)

Conservatives should advocate three broad principles on the marriage issue. First, marriage should be hard to get out of—and if there are children under sixteen in the family, it should be *very* hard to get out of. Second, since society recognizes that marriage is a serious mutual sharing of responsibilities for the lives of others, mainly children, marriage should be given real fiscal and social advantages over the single life and nonmarital living arrangements. (Once very substantial, these advantages have atrophied in recent years under the influence of feminism, individualism, and liberal theories of fiscal nondiscrimination.) Third, there should be no reforms that seem to grant social or governmental approval for nonmarital sexual partnerships.

If gay marriage is to be forced on us by nondemocratic bodies, we should seek to embed these counteracting principles in legislation. One of the conso-lations this might provide is the actual rescue of traditional marriage from descent into a cold Scandinavian hell. A few months ago, I suggested that we might end up with three competing institutions: (1) Church marriages, inde-pendent of the state, and confined to heterosexual couples, with much stricter rules for divorce than exist in civil marriages; (2) civil marriages, open now to same-sex couples; and (3) household partnerships open to any grouping of people under one roof—perhaps a widowed mother and her unmarried son, or two crusty old bachelors sharing a household for convenience, or two lesbians uncertain about the permanence of their relationship. Such partnerships could enjoy certain legal rights, tax arrangements, and rights to hospital visitation and insurance, but the state would take absolutely no interest in the sleeping arrangements of those in the household, and there would be no presumption that the households were essentially sexual relationships.

In this scenario, traditional marriage would be entirely in the purview of the churches, in opposition to the radical modernizing state—and traditional marriage could well emerge as the winner from this evolutionary competition, if only because such marriages would tend to produce more children and thus to reproduce themselves.

This modest proposal of mine aroused a fair amount of criticism. Blogger Noah Millman, my most severe critic, raised several points of interest—notably that if the churches no longer insisted that their marriages be recog-nized by the state, then there would be no legal means whereby spouses could hold their partners to their vows. I am not inclined to be overawed by these criticisms—the modern state does not enforce all the religious vows of spouses married in church today, merely the diminishing number of them that coincide with the regulations of the government—but I am not inclined to dismiss them either. I would therefore amend my proposal as follows. In order to per-suade the churches not to cut their links with civil marriage, the state would introduce a new version of it with much stricter rules for divorce—the so-called covenant marriages created some years ago in Louisiana. Couples in covenant marriages would also enjoy much more generous fiscal benefits, as a recognition that they have taken on a more arduous task. The churches in turn would agree to solemnize only such covenant marriages. The other two in-stitutions—current civil marriage and household partnerships—would remain as described above.

There is, however, one drawback to this scheme from a traditionalist and religious standpoint. As a form of civil marriage in a gender-free legal envi-ronment, covenant marriage would presumably have to be open to same-sex couples. That would, however, return us to the question with which we began: Just how many gay and lesbian couples would sign up for a marriage that really was lifelong? It would be a searching test of consistency. And it would also settle the question of whether gays seeking marriage are seeking public commitment or merely equality of esteem.

12.

"SANCTITY" AND SANCTIMONY

Jennifer Black

I just don't get it. I've listened to the arguments and considered the ramifications. I still don't understand the logic behind the anti–gay marriage movement. Take the "it violates the sanctity of marriage" argument. Please.

In the 1960s, Liz and Dick pretty much summed up how much "sanctity" we could expect from the institution. Now we've got J. Lo, Britney, and Woody Allen. But how about regular folk? The 'til death do us part vow doesn't seem to work so well for them, either.

Depending on which set of statistics you read, the divorce rate is anywhere from 29 percent to 50 percent for first marriages, while 61 percent to 76 percent of second marriages fail. According to the "All about Families" newsletter, a whopping 87 percent of third marriages and 93 percent of fourth marriages fail. It seems we heterosexuals haven't done so well in the sanctity department.

And why is government in the sanctity business anyway? Religions are well within their rights to deny the benefits of marriage as they see fit. A government founded on the principle of separation of church and state just might need to rethink that one.

Then there's the domino-effect argument. The fear that—egads—if we let homosexuals marry, we won't be able to prevent unions between a man and two women or a woman and three men. I'll admit, that had me stumped at first. But the more I thought about it, the more I came to this conclusion: the number of participants—or sexual orientation—in someone else's marriage has no relevance to me or you—or the government.

MARRIAGE HAS CHANGED

Think of the money we'd save just by avoiding legal cases against polygamists in Utah and gay couples in Texas. If they pay their taxes, don't beat their children, and keep their cars off their front lawns, I'm all in favor of "alternative" marriage partners moving into my neighborhood.

The reality is that marriage has changed, whether we like it or not. Once a primarily economic institution, marriage is now primarily an emotional connection, based on love and hopes of fidelity. People once feared interracial marriage. But *Loving v. Commonwealth of Virginia*, the landmark 1967 Supreme Court case that reversed three hundred years of antimiscegenation laws, showed us that opening doors strengthens bonds—and opens minds.

Then there's the "sin" argument, as in "we can't condone sin." Never mind state-led lotteries that fund our education coffers, state-taxed prostitution in Nevada, and mixed-weave linens that regularly cross state lines.

Mixed-weave linens? Just check out Leviticus. Gay marriage opponents frequently cite Leviticus 18:22, but I went a bit further. In fact, 19:19 might lead to protests against the whole garment industry for the no-no of "mingling linen and woolen," and I'm pretty sure it also gives us constitutional amendment fodder against genetically engineered foods and hybrid meats.

Sure, Leviticus tells us that homosexuality is wrong. It also ranks adultery equally on the "sin" meter. And I don't see any constitutional amendments to prevent adulterers from being eligible for second marriages.

Most important, though, a constitutional amendment should increase people's rights, not codify prejudices. Our Bill of Rights protects us as citizens, voters, even as criminals. It protects us from racism and sexism, overzealous and unscrupulous law enforcement officials, and an overreaching military.

It allows me to write this column, even if it does contradict our current president, and it allows protesters to carry all the biblical signs they want. Even on my street.

A constitutional amendment denying rights to homosexuals while pretending merely to define marriage is harmful to who we are as a nation. It's an attempt to impose a religious way of life on civic matters. That way lies the burka, folks. The America I love is bigger than that.

13.

NO COURT RULING CAN CHANGE THE FACT THAT MARRIAGE IS ABOUT ONE MAN AND ONE WOMAN

Ron Crews

In the three weeks since the Massachusetts Supreme Judicial Court reinterpreted the state constitution to order up "marriage" for homosexuals, there's been a lot of discussion, public and private. Polls show that opposition to same-sex "marriage"—despite massive media efforts to the contrary—has actually risen since that ruling was made—and for good reason.

The four justices who've imposed their view of what marriage should be on the people of Massachusetts—and by extension, the rest of America—said that opposition to homosexual "marriage" is rooted in an outdated bigotry that the state may not be able to control, but cannot tolerate. In doing so, the court didn't just hijack a major decision that, by rights, belongs solely to the voters of Massachusetts through their elected representatives in the legislature, and it didn't just completely rewrite the state constitution.

It lied to us.

As the Alliance Defense Fund has pointed out, the Massachusetts courts began this descent twenty years ago, when a state court ruled that a person's sexual orientation or marital status is not relevant to a custody decision about what is in the best interest of a child. Ten years ago, a Massachusetts court said the state must permit homosexual couples to adopt children. Seeming to forget that since this situation would not exist unless the court had ordered that up, too, the court is now saying that since homosexual couples have adopted children, the state must give them marriage licenses. In my view that's circular reasoning, not common sense. It is the Supreme Judicial Court that created the slippery slope down which we're sliding.

The English term "marriage" dates back to the fourteenth century, but the institution itself has existed since the dawn of time. Marriage is not, as the

Supreme Judicial Court opined, merely the creation of the state. Nor is it solely a creation of the Judeo-Christian worldview. Marriage is ingrained on the human conscience as existing solely between a man and a woman. That is why this is the only commonly accepted arrangement found across all spectrums of religion, race, and culture.

Marriage between men and women has been maintained by all major religions through the ages, and subsequently by the state, because it is the only arrangement that benefits society. Marriage has never been solely about affirming the love between two partners; historically, it's always been about benefiting society. It began in ancient times even in completely pagan cultures as a way to domesticate men, to force them to take responsibility for the children they helped create. Modern research bears out the wisdom of that idea: children raised in two-parent homes where both a mother and a father are present grow up having better education, fewer physical and mental health problems, and are less likely than others to commit violent crimes as adults.

When society loses perspective on what marriage is—the permanent bonding of one man and one woman—these benefits are lost. If the court's ruling that marriage means whatever the court says it means is allowed to stand, it will be virtually impossible to deny marriage licenses to those seeking legal recognition of other "arrangements." Once limitations on the sex of marriage partners are overturned, activists favoring polygamy and "group marriage" will have an effective argument against limitations on the number of partners. Ultimately, women and children will pay the price: Women will become objects to be collected and used—not to be committed to, cherished, and loved. Children will be denied either a mother or a father 100 percent of the time—and that is never compassionate.

All that's standing between the permanent loss of the unique benefits marriage brings to the citizens of Massachusetts are the citizens of Massachusetts.

The Vatican has made its views clear twice this year alone, writing in "Considerations Regarding Proposals to Give Legal Recognition to Unions between Homosexual Persons" that "to vote in favour of a law so harmful to the common good is gravely immoral." That's what all voters in the state need to tell their representatives when the legislature reconvenes next session. That's when it will vote on the Massachusetts Marriage Affirmation and Protection Amendment—which is the ultimate remedy for keeping the Supreme Judicial Court from destroying marriage. Speak up. Marriage belongs to us, the people—not the court.

14.

WEDDINGS ONCE FORBIDDEN
Obstacles to Gay Marriage
Evoke Mixed-Marriage Bans

Derrick Z. Jackson

To be sure, Massachusetts attorney general Thomas Reilly is no friend of gay marriage. But when Gov. Mitt Romney asked Reilly to seek a stay of the Massachusetts Supreme Judicial Court ruling that will make same-sex marriage legal on May 17, [2004,] Reilly said no.

"Whether the governor likes it or not or whether I agree with the decision, the plaintiffs have won their case," Reilly said. "They're entitled to the right that they've won, and I will not stand in their way."

But then Reilly announced that no out-of-state gay or lesbian couple can come to Massachusetts to get married. He cited a 1913 law that forbids marriage to an out-of-state couple if that couple is banned from marriage back home.

The most obvious usage of such laws back then was to limit interracial marriages. Massachusetts lifted its own ban on interracial marriage in 1843. But as late as 1952, thirty of the forty-eight states still had laws on the books banning interracial marriage. It was not until 1967 that the Supreme Court struck down bans on interracial marriage for good.

It is ridiculously fitting that today, a similar number of states—thirty-eight—stand arrayed against gay marriage.

FEARS OF RACE-MIXING

Anyone with the least sense of history knows that interracial marriage bans came about because of white fears of race-mixing. Black people were often falsely accused of lusting after white women. According to statistics compiled by Tuskegee Institute, 25 percent of the estimated forty-seven hundred lynchings in the United States involved charges of rape or attempted rape.

That hate was alive in 1958 when Mildred and Richard Loving, a black woman and a white man, faced police officers who burst into their house in the middle of the night in a small town in Virginia. "What are you doing in bed with this lady?' Sheriff R. Garnett Brooks asked Richard Loving. The husband pointed to their marriage certificate on the wall. Brooks said, "That's no good here."

The Lovings were jailed for five days. They then faced county judge Leon Bazile, who berated them by saying, "Almighty God created the races white, black, yellow, Malay, and red, and he placed them on separate continents, and but for the interference with his arrangement, there would be no cause for such marriages." Bazile gave the Lovings the choice of spending a year in prison or going into exile from Virginia for twenty-five years.

The Lovings moved momentarily to Washington, but then launched a legal challenge that resulted in the 1967 Supreme Court decision that ruled Virginia's ban unconstitutional. Like a lot of ordinary people who are thrown into extraordinary circumstances, Mildred Loving said she fought the case because "it was thrown in my lap. What choice did I have? We weren't bothering anyone."

"SPARROWS AND ROBINS"

As extraordinary as was the strength of the Lovings was the stubbornness of the sheriff who arrested them. Even in 1992, Brooks told the *New York Times*, "I was acting according to the law at the time and I still think it should be on the books. I don't think a white person should marry a black person. I'm from the old school. The Lord made sparrows and robins, not to mix with one another. . . . If they'd been outstanding people, I would have thought something about it. But with the caliber of those people, it didn't matter. They were both low-class."

The stubbornness of Brooks ought to be instructive to today's politicians. Married gay couples are not bothering anyone. Yet politicians and preachers reach for their holy scriptures to say the Lord made sparrows and robins.

While acknowledging the victory of gay and lesbian couples in Massachusetts, the state power structure is resurrecting an old law that represents the worst of American history.

15.

THE ABOLITION OF SEX DON'T WORRY— ONLY IN THE LAW. ONLY!

John Derbyshire

With recent events in Massachusetts and California, homosexual marriage—an idea that seems not to have occurred to anyone at all in the entire span of human history until about five years ago—is now a daily topic in our newspapers and TV programs. While there is certainly a great deal to be said about homosexual marriage, I have come to believe that this issue is merely an epiphenomenon, the visible manifestation of some deeper trend. To be precise, I think that what is under way here is a program to purge the very notion of sex from all our laws. This is not just a campaign to permit men to marry men, and women, women; it is a campaign for the abolition of sex. Nor is it the homosexualists who are in the vanguard here, but the *trans*sexualists—persons who wish to be not the sex nature, in forming their bodies, intended them to be, but the other one.

I had better clarify my usage. I don't mean that we are witnessing an attempt to stamp out the intimate act. Probably nothing could be further from the minds of the activists promoting this revolution. No: Here I am using "sex" in the first of the senses offered by *Merriam-Webster*'s Third: "one of the two divisions of organic, especially human, beings respectively designated male or female." In what passes for academic literature in this field, the word "gender" is now commonly used with this denotation. If I were more modern-minded, I would say "the abolition of gender." However, when I have used "gender" in this sense in the past, I have got angry letters and e-mails from fellow conservatives. After reading through several dozen of these, I have concluded that my correspondents are correct.

Furthermore, if you read much of the propaganda of transsexualist agitators, you realize that there is, for them, a key distinction between "sex" and "gender." "Sex" is what someone else thinks you are, based on some objective criterion (visual inspection, chromosome count, biochemical analysis); "gender" is what you feel yourself to be, tests and evidences notwithstanding. The latter notion, being subjective, is of course good; the former is correspondingly bad. See how the wheel has turned: "Sex" is once again a dirty word!

So my argument is that these recent shenanigans at top right and bottom left of our country are the first battles in a much broader war, a war to expunge sex from the public sphere altogether.

This came to me in a flash of understanding while I was reading the Gender Recognition Bill, which was passed by Britain's House of Lords last month. This bill, the fruit of many years' lobbying by transsexualist groups, is a remarkable document. The essence of it is that if you are a man who wishes to be known as a woman (or, of course, vice versa), the public authorities will oblige you. They will even issue you a new birth certificate, with your new sex written in. You will thenceforth be a woman, for all legal and political purposes.

There will be some formalities to be gone through. The bill requires that you present yourself to a Gender Recognition Panel, armed with a certificate from either "a registered medical practitioner practising in the field of gender dysphoria, or . . . a chartered psychologist practising in that field." You must offer some evidence that you have been living as a member of your new sex for two years. You do not, however, need to have undergone sex-reassignment surgery. A man with a full set of tackle can now be a woman under British law. He and another man, similarly equipped, could present themselves as man and woman at a church, and be married. You see why I believe the homosexual-marriage issue to be a secondary phenomenon here.

This bill has, as I said, passed the House of Lords. The debates were not without some droll moments.

> *Lord Tebbit:* Clause 16 provides that if an earl reregisters himself as a woman, he fortunately does not have to become a countess. That is a most liberal part of the bill; for such small mercies we should be grateful. I therefore presume that if a king should undertake gender reassignment, he could rule as a woman, but he would still be a king. I must say that that would raise some curious thoughts.
>
> *Earl Ferrers:* My Lords, my noble friend's speech is so fascinating that it has stimulated my thoughts. What happens if an earl becomes a woman? Does his son then become the earl?
>
> *Lord Tebbit:* My Lords, I really do not know. Presumably, as he would remain an earl rather than becoming a countess, his son would have other problems on his mind than whether he would immediately succeed to the title.
>
> *Baroness O'Cathain:* My Lords, let us hope that my noble friend is not going to do it.

Lord Tebbit: Indeed, my Lords, we hope that my noble friend's interest in the matter is not entirely personal.

At the time this issue of *National Review* goes to press, the bill, having passed the House of Lords, is being debated in Commons.

Baroness O'Cathain attempted to introduce an amendment to the bill, specifying that "a body which exists for the purposes of organised religion may prohibit or restrict the participation in its religious activities or ceremonies of persons whose gender has become the acquired gender under this Act . . . if the prohibition is necessary to comply with the doctrines of the religion." This amendment was defeated on a vote, 144 to 149. (Nobody who follows Church of England affairs will be much surprised to learn that opposition to this amendment was led by the Right Reverend Peter Selby, bishop of Worcester.)

Another amendment was proposed by old Thatcherite warhorse Lord Tebbit, specifying that "no two persons each possessing XX chromosomes nor each possessing XY chromosomes, nor each possessing genitalia appropriate to the same sex, may be married the one to the other." That one went down 46 to 121. Not only does the Gender Recognition Bill open the door to homosexual marriage, it effectively prohibits a clergyman from refusing to conduct such a marriage. And if, after conducting a marriage between two people he assumed to be of opposite biological sex, the clergyman discovers that they were, in fact, of the same sex, he may not tell anyone of his discovery. Should he do so, he will have broken the law, and will face a £5,000 fine!

In line with the thinking of most British citizens, while religion was given short shrift by the assembled peers, sport occupied a great deal of their time. If Hulk Hogan were to get himself "recognized" as a woman in British law, could a women's wrestling team exclude him without opening itself to a discrimination lawsuit? Their lordships pondered mightily before passing a subtle amendment permitting sports bodies to make their own determinations of sex, where considerations of safety or fair competition might otherwise be compromised. You could practically hear Britain's swelling legion of trial attorneys rubbing their hands with glee at this point.

As an American friend remarked when I explained the bill to him: "Presumably the next step is to allow individual men or women to legally declare themselves to be trees or turnips." Presumably so; though that step will of course require parliament to first pass a Species Recognition Bill.

Part Two.

THE EMOTIONAL DIMENSIONS
OF THE DEBATE

16.

GAY MARRIAGE TAKES HEART
One Couple's Story

Chivas Sandage

Antonin Scalia was right about something *when he wrote in his* Lawrence v. Texas *dissent that decriminalizing gay sodomy in the Lone Star State would make it more difficult for courts to continue denying marital rights to gays and lesbians. In the past year, the issue of gay marriage seems to have reached a tipping point in the United States as well as in Canada: First, two Canadian provinces legalized gay marriage, then in November the high court of Mass-achusetts ruled that gay weddings were legal. An expected backlash has greeted these rulings—a constitutional amendment to prevent gay marriage was introduced by Senator Wayne Allard (R-CO), right after the Massachusetts ruling. Right-wing extremists will undoubtedly attempt to use this as a divisive "wedge" issue in the 2004 elections.*

But for those availing themselves of the new marriage rights, those whose unions are now recognized on the social pages of the New York Times *as well as in a handful of government buildings, the issue is more than political. These personal stories touch on family, acceptance, and yes, love. Here's one Massachusetts woman's story. . . .*

When I wrote my mother in Texas to remind her that my upcoming civil union in Vermont was soon to become a reality, she wrote back, "Just how legal is this going to be?"

My sister, trying to help, told Mom that it was just a piece of paper once we crossed back over the state line to return home, thirty miles away in Mass-achusetts (this was before the state high court's pro–gay marriage ruling). Mom's letters made no further comment about the marriage, so I wrote ask-ing for one word, *Congratulations.* No answer, so I wrote again: "Mom, please support me." Still no answer.

Finally she replied: "I *have* been supportive. *I never said a word.* I just wanted to know how legal it was. I'm relieved; your sister says it's not."

"Your silence cannot help me," I wrote back. "Mom—not being able to legally marry profoundly affects my life and the lives of my partner and child. There's no peace of mind to be found in my family and property not being protected through this basic civil right."

"Why don't you move to Vermont?" she wrote back. "I want you to be happy, not militant."

I was touched—it was a breakthrough, it was endearing—but I was confused. Had I become "militant" by asking her to talk about my marriage? In further letters, Mom kept using that word, and I kept thinking that militant implies an aggressive, combative attitude. Aggression implies the intention to dominate in disregard for others' rights. Why were my efforts, and those of other lesbians pursuing the right to marry, so often interpreted as the desire to argue and dominate? Was this a twist on the same old feminist question: Why is a man assertive but a woman is a bitch? *Unhappy, militant, feminist, lesbian,* and *bitch*—when did these words become synonymous?

My six-year-old daughter understood our desire to marry. She wrote a small book of fairy tales in which girls marry girls *or* boys, as they see fit. The stories ended with: "and they married themselves." Our wedding wasn't a question for her at all—as long as she was allowed to wear a fancy dress to it. In fact, she wanted us to marry so that my partner "will not go away." Even for a child whose parents separated when she was two, marriage still connotes longevity and security.

My mother finally came around, too. Memories of her own work for black civil rights—she was a teenager in Little Rock, Arkansas, during the 1957 desegregation riots there—as well as her love for me, helped her fully open her heart to my commitment. These days, she sends *me* articles about gay marriage!

At this threshold in history, I hope people will remember that it wasn't until 1967 that the US Supreme Court decided once and for all, in *Loving v. Virginia,* that black and white Americans had the legal right to intermarry. Going back a century further, black slaves lacked the right to marry each other—so they would hold small community gatherings instead, ritually jumping over a broom to mark the moment of union.

When I married my sweetheart on June 13, 2002, we marked the moment of union by jumping over a long piece of driftwood, carved by the work of water and time. In that instant, I wasn't thinking of myself as a gay woman. I was thinking of myself as any woman—any *person*—in love.

17.

A (PERSONAL) ESSAY ON SAME-SEX MARRIAGE

Barbara J. Cox

Very little since Stonewall,* and the break from accepting the status quo that those riots symbolize, has challenged the lesbian and gay community as much as the debate we have had over the past several years on whether seeking the right to marry should be the focus of our community's efforts, political influence, and financial resources. As is often true in most such political debates, both "sides" to the debate make important arguments about the impact that the right to marry will have on each member of our community, on the community as a whole, and on our place in society. . . .

One way to expand this debate is to read the interviews of lesbian and gay couples, some of whom have chosen to have public ceremonies celebrating their commitment and some of whom have chosen to keep their commitment private.

The debate continues to rage, as seen from the recent articles contained in the *Virginia Law Review*'s symposium issue. Without resolving the debate here, it seems clear that obtaining the right to marry will drastically impact the lesbian and gay civil rights movement. My response to the debate is best expressed in the following short (and personal) essay, explaining the vital political change that can result from the simple (and personal) act of same-sex marriage.

Yes, I know that weddings can be "heterosexual rituals" of the most repressive and repugnant kind. Yes, I know that weddings historically symbolized the loss of the woman's self into that of her husband's, a denial of her

This article originally appeared as notes 10, 11, and 12 in Barbara J. Cox, "Same-Sex Marriage and Choice-of-Law: If We Marry in Hawii, Are We Still Married When We Return Home?" *Wisconsin Law Review* (1994): 1033. Copyright 2003 by the Board of the Regents of the University of Wisconsin System. Reprinted by permission of the *Wisconsin Law Review*.

*The gay and lesbian riot began early in the morning of June 28, 1969, when police raided the Stonewall bar in Greenwich Village. It sparked gay and lesbian activity around the world. (Eds.)

existence completely. Yes, I know that weddings around the world continue to have that impact on many women and often lead to lives of virtual slavery. Yes, I know. Then how could a feminist, out, radical lesbian like myself get married a year ago last April? Have I simply joined the flock of lesbians and gay men rushing out to participate in a meaningless ceremony that symbolizes heterosexual superiority?

I think not.

When my partner and I decided to have a commitment ceremony, we did so to express the love and caring that we feel for one another, to celebrate that love with our friends and family, and to express that love openly and with pride. It angers me when others, who did not participate or do not know either of us, condemn us as part of a mindless flock accepting a dehumanizing ceremony. But more, it distresses me that they believe their essentialist vision of weddings explains all—because they have been to weddings, both straight and queer, they can speak as experts on their inherent nature.

Perhaps these experts should consider the radical aspect of lesbian marriage or the transformation that it makes on the people around us. As feminists, we used to say that "the personal is political." Have we lost that vision of how we can understand and change the world?

My commitment ceremony was not the mere "aping" of the bride that I supposedly spent my childhood dreaming of becoming. (In fact, I was a very satisfied tomboy who never once considered marriage.) My ceremony was an expression of the incredible love and respect that I have found with my partner. My ceremony came from a need to speak of that love and respect openly to those who participate in my world.

Some of the most politically "out" experiences I have ever had happened during those months of preparing for and having that ceremony. My sister and I discussed for weeks whether she would bring her children to the ceremony. Although I had always openly brought the women I was involved with home with me, I had never actually sat down with my niece and nephews to discuss those relationships. My sister was concerned that her eldest son, particularly, might scorn me, especially at a time when he and his friends tended toward "faggot" jokes. After I expressed how important it was for me to have them attend, she tried to talk with her son about going to this euphemistically entitled "ceremony." He kept asking why my partner and I were having a "ceremony" and she kept hedging. Finally he just said, "Mom, Barb's gay, right?" She said yes, they all came, and things were fine. Her youngest son sat next to me at dinner after the ceremony trying to understand how it worked. "You're married, right?" "Yes." "Who's the husband?" "There is no husband." "Are you going to have children?" "No." "So there's no husband and no children but you're married, right?" "Yes." "Okay," and he happily turned back to his dinner.

My partner invited her large Catholic family to the ceremony. We all know how the pope feels about us. Despite that, her mother and most of her siblings, some from several states away, were able to attend. Her twin brother later told us that our ceremony led him to question and resolve the discomfort that had plagued his relationship with his sister for many years.

As a law professor leaving town early for the ceremony, I told my two classes (one of ninety-five and one of twenty students) that I was getting "married" to my partner, who is a woman. (I actually used "married" because saying I was getting "committed" just didn't quite have the right ring to it.) The students in one of my classes joined together to buy my partner and myself a silver engraved frame that says "Barb and Peg, Our Wedding." My colleagues were all invited to the ceremony and most of them attended. One of them spoke to me of the family discussion explaining to their children that they were going to a lesbian wedding.

How can anyone view these small victories in coming out and acceptance as part of flocking to imitate, or worse join, an oppressive heterosexual institution? Is it not profoundly transformative to speak so openly about lesbian love and commitment? The impact was so wide-ranging, not just on my partner and myself, but on our families, our friends, and even the clerks in the jewelry stores when we explained we were looking for wedding rings for both of us. Or on the two hundred people who received my mother's annual xeroxed Christmas letter with a paragraph describing the ceremony. Or the clerk in the store who engraved the frame for my students. Or the young children who learned that same-sex marriage exists.

Yes, we must be aware of the oppressive history that weddings symbolize. We must work to ensure that we do not simply accept whole-cloth an institution that symbolizes the loss and harm felt by women. But I find it difficult to understand how two lesbians, standing together openly and proudly, can be seen as accepting that institution. What is more antipatriarchal and rejecting of an institution that carries the patriarchal power imbalance into most households than clearly stating that women can commit to one another with no man in sight? With no claim of dominion or control, but instead of equality and respect. I understand the fears of those who condemn us for our weddings, but I believe they fail to look beyond the symbol and cannot see the radical claim we are making.

18.

ADAM AND EVE, NOT ADAM AND HENRY

Jeffrey Hart

Being nasty to homosexuals is certainly not on the agenda of any decent person. Whatever it is homosexuals do in private is best left private. Our problem at the moment, however, is homosexual cultural aggression.

One major segment of that is the drive to make homosexual companionships legally "marriages." The focus has been the recent legal fight in Hawaii.*

But before we get into that, a point about the nature of language:

Language is normative. Its meanings and connotations communicate values. Thus everyone knows what the word "marriage" means. It means what it has always meant.

Millennia of human experience have demonstrated that marriage is the best arrangement for bringing up children and communicating to them the substance of a culture.

Recently, the old truths have been reinforced by researchers, who have marked the disastrous results of single-parent upbringing, dysfunctional families, and so forth.

Aside from the civilizational value of marriage, it does not take much experience to discern that females and males are naturally complementary.

But along comes Hawaii, where a state court is expected this summer [1996] to legalize homosexual "marriages."

If the state court does hand down the decision, it likely would be appealed to the Supreme Court, where no one knows what will result.

If homosexual "marriages" become legal in Hawaii, the other forty-nine states might well have to honor—if that is the word—such arrangements. The US Constitution requires that each state afford "full faith and credit" to "the public acts, records, and judicial proceedings of every other state."

    *See appendix 3.

Viewing that prospect with distaste, nineteen state legislatures are considering legislation that would bar out-of-state homosexual marriages.

Just what is at stake?

Currently, homosexuals living together can avail themselves of most of the practical benefits of a genuine marriage arrangement. They can endorse any sort of a legal contract binding upon both of them, such as agreed-upon penalties if they stop living together. They can put one another in their wills, or they can agree to leave joint property to any charity or trust they desire. They can own property together, under agreed-upon terms about what happens to it. They can make each other the beneficiary of life insurance.

The homosexuals pushing for legalized "marriage" know all that. What they want is legal and social equality with what has always been understood to be marriage.

Homosexuality in virtually all cultures has been frowned upon and sometimes condemned. The universal vote of human experience has gone against it.

It certainly is true throughout the Hebrew Bible. The paradigmatic couple in Genesis is named "Adam and Eve." The representation is valid not just because it is in the Bible, but in the Bible because it is valid. It is amusing to imagine what would have been the response from the rabbis in the Temple of Jerusalem if a theological poet had shown up with a proposal for Genesis featuring a first couple named "Adam and Henry."

In Canto XV of Dante's *Inferno,* he writes a great poem of personal love and pity for his older master in literature, Brunetto Latini. He loves Brunetto for his writing, but pities him and condemns him for his crime against nature. He is in Dante's *Inferno* because in life he was in his private inferno.

In Elizabethan England, homosexual acts were punishable by death.

Perhaps strange to say, Oscar Wilde can be understood as participating in the general negative judgment. His paradoxical wit consisted of jokes against the norm. He said things such as "Niagara Falls would be more interesting if it flowed upward." If Dante's Brunetto was tragic, Wilde's sense of homosexuality was comic. In his homosexual persona he was a society clown.

Human culture, for millennia, has been "homophobic"—a strange new coinage that tries to make disapproval of homosexuality equivalent to an illness, or phobia. That is, the normal is "ill."

No one would worry much about homosexuals today if so many of them had not become so aggressive. They want their aberration projected into education at all levels, celebrated in popular culture, and honored in so-called marriages.

Well, the cup runneth over. It is time for legal, political, and cultural resistance to homosexual aggression.

19.

A LESBIAN FAMILY

Lindsy Van Gelder

Sarah is in most ways your basic five-year-old: a watcher of Charlie Brown videos, a reader of Richard Scarry books, a crayoner of cotton-puff clouds and fat yellow suns with Tinkertoy-spoke rays. Like every other piece of kindergarten artwork ever made, her portrait of "My Family" contains stick-figurey construction paper people, all holding hands and looking jolly. Except her family is a little different: there's Sarah, there's "Daddy," there's "Mommy" . . . and there's Amy, Mommy's lover.

Sarah's "cubby" at school is special, too. While the other kids hang their windbreakers and lunch boxes next to photos of one parent, or two, Sarah has three. She takes this embarrassment of riches in stride—which is to say, without any embarrassment at all.

Not that she isn't a very savvy little girl about the precisely calibrated degrees to which the many adults in her life fit into the larger scheme of things. If you ask her about the members of her "whole" (i.e., extended) family, she will tick off various grandmothers and cousins on her fingers. "Francis [her biological mother's ex-lover and now best friend] is in my family, too," she adds. "But Richard [her father's new boyfriend] isn't *exactly* in my family . . . yet." The adults around her would probably say the same thing, in many more words.

. . . [Sarah's] biological mother, Nancy, had interviewed a dozen potential gay and straight sperm donors before she and Amy met Doug and his then-boyfriend. Unlike many lesbian couples who decide to have a child, Nancy has no particular quarrel with the notion that a parent of each gender is a desirable thing. But in the original scenario, the women weren't necessarily looking for anything much more enduring than a turkey baster deposit. They simply wanted someone they could point to on the day their daughter asked where Daddy was.

This is an edited version of an article that originally appeared in *Ms.,* March/April 1991, pp. 44–47. Reprinted by permission of the author.

But something unexpected happened: a flowering of feeling that turned the American Gothic nuclear family progression on its head. Instead of two people meeting, falling in love, and having a baby, four people met, had a baby, and then became good friends.

In fact, their whole lives became entwined. At the time Nancy got pregnant, all the adults were entering their forties, both Amy and Doug were at career crossroads, and both couples were sick of the expense and hassle of living in New York City. The baby was both a symbol of the changes the adults were ready for and a catalyst to more. . . . The men had moved to the Southwest, where Doug spent his childhood, and the women were talking about following. Although it wasn't part of their original agreement, Doug insisted on helping with Sarah's financial support. . . . Recently, . . . we found Amy, Nancy, Sarah, and their two cats living down the street from Doug in an adobe house with a yard full of mesquite trees. Amy and Doug have pooled their resources and opened a café. He does most of the cooking; she takes care of most of the business end. Nancy meanwhile teaches at a nearby college. All three contribute to Sarah's expenses, although Amy—because she lives with Sarah and has a more flexible schedule than Nancy—is the primary caregiver in terms of time at the moment.

"It confuses the hell out of people," Amy notes cheerfully. "People come into the restaurant, and they see that Doug and I are partners, and then they see this little kid running around after school relating to both of us. Not surprisingly, they assume that Doug and I are married—which, of course, we both hate. Usually, I sit them down and just explain the story." Some people still don't quite get it. "I'm thinking of having palm cards made up," she jokes, "Maybe like, *Good afternoon, you have entered a Strange Other World.*"

Amy, Nancy, and Doug are completely out of the closet in their dealings with the straight community. They grudgingly elected to use pseudonyms in this article only after Nancy's mother asked them to. Nancy's mother has told all her relatives that Sarah was born out of a liaison between Nancy and a married man. "Somehow that's better than being in a happy, committed, lesbian relationship," Nancy sighs.

"I think it behooves us to be out, and even to boast about it, to show that it can work," says Doug. For Sarah's sake, the adults tend to like to deal with the gay issue up front, where it can be defused if need be. "When it came time to get a pediatrician, all three of us marched in—we didn't want some situation later on where the doctor didn't realize that all of us were in on this. It's the same thing now that we've been looking at elementary schools for next year. At interviews, our position is, 'This is our situation, and it's very important that Sarah get support on that if she needs it.'" At one school they considered, they got more than they asked for—several faculty members discreetly came out to them. . . .

Sarah's parents have had some rough times, however. The biggest rupture in their lives occurred when Doug and his longtime boyfriend messily broke up two years ago. Aside from the immediate trauma, the women worried that

Doug might find small-city gay single life intolerable and leave. "For a while he was dating someone here we were not crazy about as stepdaddy material, either," they confide. Then Doug met Richard, an elementary school substitute teacher who loves children. The two men are about to start living together.

"It sounds crass, but part of my getting together with Richard is about Sarah," Doug says. "If I were thirty-six, I probably would have cashed in my chips and left town. But at forty-six, I have different needs." In fact, Richard is now talking seriously with a lesbian woman—a close friend of Amy and Nancy, as it happens—about adding another child to the extended family. . . .

Not surprisingly, the adults in Sarah's life don't always agree. The funniest example was the time that Sarah snookered her father into buying her a Wet 'n' Wild Barbie, only mentioning once they were safely past the checkout counter that the item wouldn't be remotely welcome at her house. The crisis was resolved by keeping Barbie at Daddy's. There have also been many, many jokes about possible Birkenstocks and flannel shirts that one might add to Barbie's wardrobe. Sarah later made all the adults laugh when she bought her father his own Ken doll for his birthday. Of course, now that Doug has Richard, Sarah has Ken. She is not a dumb kid.

Doug and Richard have occasionally hinted that Sarah gets away with too much at Nancy and Amy's house, and the women have occasionally felt a financial pinch when Doug is casual about paying his share of the child support money on time. But the splits are minor, and they're by no means consistently Boys versus Girls. Amy and Doug are currently pushing for Sarah to go to private or Episcopal parochial school next year; Nancy thinks "every justification for sending kids to private school sounds just like what white people in the South historically use as excuses. Okay, maybe the reading scores in the public schools are lower, but maybe it's because a lot of the kids are Mexican Americans who grew up bilingual. It doesn't necessarily mean the education is worse."

Nancy also strenuously objected to the "girls in skirts" dress code required by the school Doug and Amy favor—a rule Amy wasn't thrilled with, either. The three parents brought it up with the administration and ascertained that if Sarah were to wear a nice blouse and a pair of dressy pants instead of a skirt, the school wouldn't object. "But she'll wear a dress anyway, because she likes them," Doug smirks. "She's very femme."

One of the worst parts of parenting for Amy and Nancy is that their schedules leave them very little time to be alone together. Nancy's teaching requires her to be out of the house several nights a week, as well as on Sunday, the one day the café is closed. Doug previously took care of Sarah on a fairly irregular basis, and he unabashedly notes: "I never thought I had to deal with her shitty diapers to bond with her. I wanted the fun parts." But when Nancy and Amy asked him if he would keep Sarah every Sunday night, he was glad to help.

"I told Doug I was asking him this as a personal favor, having nothing to do with his relationship to Sarah," Amy jokes. "I told him that as his friend that he works with, I'll be a lot happier, and therefore he'll be a lot happier. Now when I come in Monday morning, there's lots of leering, and lots of *gee, Sarah and I went to McDonald's last night—what did YOU guys do, hmmmm?*"

But Amy and Nancy are quick to note that almost all their minor difficulties—from scheduled sex to sporadic conflicts about child raising—are typical of those encountered by all parents. "There's almost nothing so far that's wrong because we're gay," says Nancy, "and a lot of what's right is because we're gay." For one thing, there's no ancient sexual bitterness between Sarah's biological mother and father of the sort that mars so much postdivorce parental jockeying.

One gay problem is health insurance: none of them has it. "We've talked about supplying benefits here at the restaurant," says Doug, "but that would only help Amy and me. We have no legal relationship, in the eyes of the insurance companies, with Nancy and Sarah."

"There's also weird stuff you have to think about," says Amy. "Like, when Sarah goes to other kids' houses, sometimes the kids take a bath together. Her friends' parents seem to be cool about us, but it's still the sort of thing I'd think twice about doing, because you just know it would only take one asshole to turn Naked Kids in Lesbian Home into something really sordid and horrible."

But when you ask them all if there's anything they would do over differently, the answer is: not much. "I'm glad I did it with a father that I know, and not a sperm bank," says Nancy. When Sarah was an infant, Nancy did go through a spell of jealousy of Doug's relationship with their child. "I didn't want to share her with him; I hardly knew him," she admits. "Then I told myself to just cool out and think of what was best for Sarah." Nancy adds that she might be less enthusiastic if Doug were an absentee father. "There's this whole Daddy Thing; Daddy gets to be Daddy, and all that that represents, no matter what he does or doesn't do, and kids—all kids—just plug into that. But in fact, Doug *is* lovely with her."

Nancy and Amy have also been lucky in other ways. Seven or eight years ago, when they began their search for a donor, AIDS was an established fact, but it was less discussed than it is now. Despite urgings from their friends, the women thought it would be presumptuously rude to ask Doug to take an HIV test. Recently, Nancy was reading the *New York Times* and happened upon the name of another man she'd asked to be a donor—someone who inexplicably stopped taking her calls. Now there he was on the obit page, dead of AIDS.

Of all the adults in Sarah's life, Amy is the one in the most vulnerable position. She has no legal claim on Sarah if she and Nancy ever break up (although gay civil rights groups are fighting for the rights of nonbiological lesbian mothers who are thus left with no recourse). Nancy's and Doug's wills specify that if they were to die, they would want Amy to have custody, but it's a wish that grandparents or even the state could challenge in court. "It's too devastating to think about," says Amy. "So I don't."

She also finds terminology a problem. "I'll be at the grocery store and some clerk will ask me if Sarah's mine. Well, she is, damn it, even if that's not what they meant. I periodically sit Sarah down to make sure she's okay with this stuff. Like I recently said to her, 'You know, I'm not your mother, but I'm sort of like your parent.' She nodded and said, 'Right. Mommy is my mother. But I *am* your daughter.'"

At the preschool Sarah currently attends, the other kids tend to announce "Your Amy is here to pick you up." There are several other children in Sarah's class who have gay parents, and in one of the more open families, the nonbiological mother also happens to be named Amy. It's becoming a sort of generic honorific: Sarah and her friend Rex both go off after school with their Amys.

Perhaps things will be more awkward when Sarah is older, the adults say. But perhaps they won't be. Or, more likely, they will be, but only because most teenagers find *something* about their parents that's, like, totally gross. So far, so good.

Sarah's only recorded worry about the future is one that she shared with Nancy one day when she was trying to figure out how she could be a doctor and stay home with her own sick child. Nancy assured her that such things were eminently doable; she herself could baby-sit. Sarah sighed with relief, her grownup life secured.

"But," she suddenly asked, "where will I find a Daddy and an Amy?"

20.

I LEFT MY HUSBAND FOR THE WOMAN I LOVE

*Jane Doe**

"Are you going to marry the person you left him for?" she asked.

"The person is a woman," I said.

"How wonderful for you," she said. "But you don't fit the script. No one would know to look at you."

I have heard this many times. Even if nobody else said it, I would know it is true. Neither my appearance nor my "script" betrays that after twenty-five years of family life, I have left my marriage to live with the woman I love.

I wore a pink tutu with sequins when I was nine. At the prom I wore the required crinoline under my white, spaghetti-strapped prom formal. My first love was the captain of the football team, and I could not have been more crazy about him. With him I learned the ways of the body in wild scenes in the sail lockers at the end of the dock near where I lived. I had a typical suburban teenage career "making out" in convertibles.

Then I got married. At the wedding, there were my proud, ambivalent parents, who had protested the marriage, ironically because they had heard that my intended might be homosexual.

Once married, I finished various degrees, made soufflés, learned to use eye makeup, traveled from New York to Nepal, and changed lots of diapers.

Though I was too young to know what mature love was, I did love my husband when I married him. But a few years ago, as we sat eating prawns overlooking the Mediterranean, I wondered what would be left between us when the kids left home. I had known for years that I no longer loved him. My analyst had said, "Couldn't you try?" But how can you *try* to love someone? My eleven-year-old understood right away when I said I had not planned it this way. "No one can change love," he said.

This article originally appeared in *Ms.,* January 1988.

*Jane Doe is a pseudonym.

But most of the time the rapid pace of days took over and obliterated the question of whether love could last and whether it was necessary or important. I never thought that love and marriage were synonymous. For me, as long as there was no lasting outside love, the family came first. There was richness in family life, vitality and interest and fun. I was not looking for escape. I was not angry with my husband or disillusioned about love. Now, though I am not leaving the kids, the pain of breaking apart this family sometimes tears at my gut. I hate to see their sadness.

But when there is no love in marriage, and there *is* a lasting love outside it, everything changes. The center of the family is empty and the children know it. It is no favor to them to live a charade "for their sake." Ultimately, it undermines their sense of emotional truth. What model for a child is a mother who stays to "serve" her children, sacrificing her inner life in a spirit of self-denial for kids she hopes will find their own full lives? I have seen that if you are honest with kids about feelings, though it may not be easy, they will understand even the act of leaving their father for someone of the same sex.

I did not leave, as some think, because I chose women over men. I have never thought that women are better than men, or that men have betrayed me. If I can pinpoint the important lack in my marriage, it is that my particular husband did not have the full range of emotional expression I need. I filled the gap with friends and other loves. I found that I felt things for others I did not feel for him. Until now, I never found one person with all the qualities that mattered to me, but I did find a kind of balance of riches among the people I cared about.

People who knew me as a woman with a twenty-five-year-old marriage and two kids have asked what it is like to love a woman. A male friend said he could understand everything but that part, since he could never love a man. I told him I love certain *people,* men and women, and this woman is the person I love best. I never closed out the idea that women are as interesting and lovable as men. I have known intense, passionate women, and I know that it was not their womanhood but their intensity and passion that attracted me.

The woman I love is the only person I have met with that combination of qualities I want in love. (I cannot answer whether a man could have them, too. Only that I have never met a man who does.) She is gentle and fiery, intelligent and sensitive, imaginative and energetic, wide awake and dreamy, funny and emotional, loving and clear-visioned. When I see her in bed next to me, I wonder by what miracle such a human being, man or woman, exists at all, and exactly how she got in my bed. Real love just is, without reason or motive.

People want to know if *our* sex is different from sex with men. Someone said, "Isn't it like making love to yourself?" To me, in spite of our both being female, we do not seem the same. We both know what it is like to love men and women. We feel the other as different. We listen closely to every nuance. It is not the physical difference from sex with men but the love in every gesture that makes it different. We have seen women couples who assume the roles of nurtured and nurturer, of stronger and weaker, of star and servant. We have no roles. We exchange moments of strength and vulnerability, of giving care and of being cared for. It's rich and sometimes difficult, maybe more difficult than if we had roles, because things are not always clear. Subtleties need attention. But then we both pay attention.

Today my friends and family know about my personal life because I have expressed in public something that previously was there only in private. I find it troublesome when people think I have changed, when all that has happened is that they know more about me.

Although my choice of lover is not a political or public statement but the natural consequence of feeling, the disclosure of it has produced a kind of Rorschach test of possible responses. People ask, "How did you dare to love this woman when it didn't fit with your life?" Among the members of my family of origin I have heard:

"I have trouble thinking of you as a lesbian."

"I have learned a lot of things about you that I might have preferred not to know."

"What kind of people do you socialize with now?"

"I can't imagine your kids with you and another woman. It's not my idea of a family."

A friend of my parents, a famous psychoanalyst I thought was forbidding, said, "You were always a pioneer."

A woman psychiatrist said, "Why do you *need* to carry on this relationship?"

Some friends have understood; others have found it a problem. One said, "I have to call you secretly because my husband cannot deal with your story." Another asked, "Are you getting help?" Still others have said, "You have a lot of guts." "You will get hurt." "If two people can love each other it's a miracle."

I am sitting at lunch with my friend the French professor. She knows my family well. "Have you thought of how your mother was the strong one and your father dresses flamboyantly? Did role switches have anything to do with it?" If there is an influence from childhood, it could as easily be from the intensity of my mother's friendships with women, the feeling I came to recognize as a kind of love, long before I met my lover.

I met her the day she came to rent the apartment in our house. We started talking one day, and now, more than two years later, we have not stopped. In the middle of our first talk, one of my kids called out that he had had a nightmare. She and I spoke of our own adult nightmares. Once I was in the kitchen when she returned from the movies crying, so I asked her to have a cup of tea. We talked about sorrows and loves. When she got up to go, many hours later, we grabbed hands, and then somehow we were hugging. It could have been a hug between friends, but there was so much feeling in it that we were both stunned, as we told each other only later.

A few days later she was reading the paper in our pantry as I came to fix dinner. I said, "Did you have a nice day?" and she said, "No. I ran into a Cadillac on my bicycle." I invited her to have dinner with the family. When the others left the table, she and I practically jumped out of our seats at each other.

"Why do I feel so comfortable with you?" she asked when we were alone.

"Why not?" I said. And we kissed for the first time. And asked each other whether if you touch you risk the rest. Finally, some time later, in a house by the sea, with waves tearing around the rocks, we made love over and over.

Then we started building our own history.

On a vacation on a Caribbean island, a steel band played to the staccato beats of lizards and tree frogs, rousing thumps and tunes, but the middle-aged, middle-American crowd would not budge. We were shy about dancing, but finally we could not resist, so we started on the edge. Soon the rest of the crowd was on the floor, waitresses, barmen, and the stodgy guests. Then two women came on the dance floor and moved together, bumping noses; the hotel manager and, yes, her girlfriend. We started something.

Together we have read Dostoyevsky and Donald Duck. We have been to the Parthenon, Harlem, Paris, Disney World, and we've celebrated New Year's Eve in Times Square.

One summer weekend my friend, my eleven-year-old, my father, and I are eating lobsters at sunset on an island off the New England coast. My son finds a huge yellow moon hanging over the water, opposite the rosy sun. Later my friend and I go to say good night to my father, who is dozing in his bed. He looks at us and smiles. I think they are tears of understanding rolling down his face.

It has not been easy. In the same year, I ended a long marriage and my friend's mother died. I have had family problems, and she has visa problems. We still cannot be sure how much of the year we can be together. When she told a US Embassy official abroad that she had compelling reasons to stay in this country, he quipped, "Then get married."

When my husband learned that I love this woman, he was very angry and said extreme things in front of the kids and my parents and to others. He said, "You are not a mother anymore." He threatened to take the kids from me and drag me to court. Though my younger son found a way to keep out of these scenes, my older son, eighteen, did not. He exploded about my breaking up the family, betraying his father, and loving a woman. Since then, he has not come to our house for more than a few minutes. Although he is beginning to understand, this has been agonizing for me. I can only tell him that I hope he will come to accept my choice and that I love him as much as I always have.

One day he took a photo of the whole family—grandparents, aunts, nieces—from the hallway table and put it in his room, saying, "This was the last time we were a happy family." He wants to keep the family inside him. I try to tell him he will not lose the love, but he feels that my loving another has taken something from him. What happened to change the picture, I try to say, had been there for a long time. Pictures leave things out.

When he got angry, he mostly shouted and stormed. But one night he came home hungry and tired, smelling sweaty from hockey practice. He taunted me about my friend, who happened to call as we were eating dinner. I took my plate to the other room. He followed me with a mouthful of steak and peas. I had not asked him how he felt about my loving someone else, he shouted, starting to cry. I grabbed him, all six feet, and put my arms around him, as he cried his tears of lost innocence and childhood love and peas into my torn jogging jersey and faded sweatpants that used to be his.

"This is the first time I have cried about it," he said, and he cried and cried and hugged me like a child. "How I feel about it is sad."

"Yes," I said, through my own tears.

My eleven-year-old says, "It's hard for me to get used to seeing that you love someone else." Tears drop off his cheeks like beads. We talk about this new claim on my attention, about the sadness of losing a family. I tell him about people who gain strength and wisdom from sadness, about the wise saying that only the wounded physician heals. I tell him a great novelist had a sad childhood.

"Who?" he asks.

"Dickens."

He smiles. One night he asks me to sing a lullaby, and we both start to cry.

He watched a TV show in which two women living together win custody of the son of one of them. He says he is happy it ends that way. He watched it with his father's housekeeper, who said, "I hate that word 'lesbian.'" He does not like her saying this. Sometimes he thrusts himself between my friend and me on the street and holds our hands so we will not hold each other's. But at night when he is going to sleep he seems glad when we both tell him we love him.

So my friend and my younger son and I live together. Two writers, one student. My son has his room, where he lies on the floor making charts of how fruit holds water. At dinner we light candles. Afterward, we read the *Just So Stories* together, about the "great, gray-green, greasy Limpopo River, all set about with fever-trees." There is love in the house; it is the first time my son has lived with grown-ups who love each other. My friend is European, has no kids, and has never been married. It is not easy to blend the two cultures, two very different histories, an unconventional way of life, and one child.

"How do you know it will last?" someone asks. It is hard to answer. My friend and I are not kids; we've had experience, we know about risk. We have looked for oracles and found none. We tell ourselves only this: if anything promises to last forever, we do.

21.

COUNSELING SAME-SEX COUPLES

Douglas Carl

Once coupled, gays and lesbians face myriad problems, some not so unlike those experienced by heterosexual couples, some very different. Needless to say, all couples today face the specter of bleak statistics: 48 percent of all first marriages fail, while 47 percent of all second marriages end in divorce. We have no accurate figures for same-sex couples. However, in these statistics lies an ingrained prejudice or two that we need to explore before we go any further.

We as a culture seem to assume that coupled is best. True happiness, it is written, lies in wending your way down life's highway together. Real fulfillment, popular myth has it, comes from finding the right mate and designing a life that fits the two of you. I remember as a child that my parents had something of a pitying regard for two groups: those unmarried (particularly women, who certainly would not *choose* to remain single) and those who were married but childless (another condition no person would choose willingly).

Attitudes have changed in the last several decades, but most of us still aspire to finding the one *right* relationship that will help make our lives fulfilling. I find no fault in this aspiration per se, but I prefer to believe that, even though coupling will remain the preferred mode of lifestyle in the foreseeable future, we need to look at it as a popular option among several options open to us. In other words, we do ourselves and our clients a disservice with any implicit assumption that coupling is best. It may prove best for some or for most, but marriage-style coupling does not automatically spell happiness. Many single people can and do find real fulfillment in a variety of lifestyles, but we often fail to credit that fact. In addition, there are those who maintain their coupled relationships in less conventional ways that are rewarding to them; from these individuals we can garner ideas that could expand everyone's options. Some of these ideas will emanate from same-sex couples, who need not always be bound by social conventions, even though sometimes unwittingly they are.

The second myth we often buy into is that longevity is best. As a culture we honor and revere long-surviving marriages. I remember taking a genogram from a client whose grandparents had just celebrated their sixtieth wedding anniversary. "That's terrific," I exclaimed. "What's so terrific about it?" he replied. "They haven't talked to each other in twenty years!" Less acceptable and less recognized in our culture are serial relationships—a series of shorter-term relationships that may better fill the needs of individuals as they face the demands of fast-moving, ever-changing lifestyles (something that happens quite often in practice without really being recognized). Childless relationships, without the same issues of consistency and stability for the progeny, could sometimes benefit from this serial orientation.

I do not wish to convey the idea that I am antimarriage or antirelationship, long-term or otherwise. Far from it! Still, I feel that we do clients a disservice by accepting prevailing ideas of what is best in life and not exploring to the fullest what might work best for *them*. Long-term marriage at the end of the twentieth century does not seem to work for large numbers of people. For some, this represents difficulty with commitment or pressures from a rapidly changing world. Perhaps, some feel, the culprit is an erosion of moral/spiritual values. All these things and more merit exploration. Another option is to evaluate conditions as they appear and to think about relationships in terms of how they might fit changing social conditions.

Gays and lesbians approach relationships with the same preconceptions as prevail in the heterosexual world. Most of them have only marriage models as road maps for how their relationships should function, but these maps, based on a different assessment of the landscape, often lead them and their therapists in the wrong direction.

MARRIAGE: RITUAL, BOUNDARIES, ROLES

Just as it is more difficult to function in the world as a gay individual than it is as a straight individual, it is more difficult to function as a same-sex couple than it is as a heterosexual couple. That is simply reality. One major reason for this has to do with marriage and its deeply rooted implications in our culture.

First, there is marriage ritual. In its most elaborate expression, marriage ritual involves family, friends, church or synagogue, the legal system, and a new status. For same-sex couples there usually is none of this. No planning for the big day by friends, family, coworkers, and so on. No parties. No gifts. No introduction of families to each other or to the prospective partner. No ceremony (although a limited number of gay men and women do manage to carry out a ritual ceremony for friends and some family but without any official religious or legal significance). No honeymoon. Often, the joining together just happens gradually, and at some point there is recognition of couple status by the participating individuals through communication about the couple's identity between partners and to others, agreements about sex, and *sometimes* a merging of households. Legally, no state recognizes the union, nor do most official religious institutions (some individual churches will "sanctify" or celebrate the union). There are signs of some small changes in this area. Recently the United Methodist Church voted to accept all members without regard to race, sex, or sexual orientation. And the San Francisco city council passed an ordinance in 1989 that effectively grants spousal equivalency to members of same-sex couples in terms of legal issues of property and employment benefits. Of course, San Francisco is a far cry from the rest of the United States.

More important is what marriage and the surrounding ritual represent. Marriage in our society creates boundaries. It says to family and to the world that there is the beginning of a new nuclear family. Think about traditional ritual: the father of the bride walks her down the aisle, "gives her away" to the bridegroom, and then sits down. Families may sooner or later transgress these boundaries, but "right" is on the side of the married partners to conduct their lives as they see fit. Generally, families back off, give them their space, and see them as a separately functioning unit.

For the same-sex couple, bonding often magnifies the issues of emotional cutoffs. It now becomes more difficult to deny one's homosexuality, unless the couple status remains secret. If so, then emotional cutoffs intensify. Often, coupling signals the need to deal with family and friends. *In fact, gays and lesbians may avoid a real commitment because they cannot face that very issue.*

Generally, same-sex couples do not reap the boundary benefits generated by the married couple. Usually, this happens because of lack of recognition of the legitimacy of their relationship. Sometimes it happens just because friends and family simply have not been informed about the significance of the relationship.

Jennifer and Ione had been together nearly three years when they came into therapy. Jennifer struggled with Ione around closeness. After three years, she expected more from her partner. Ione came from an Italian Catholic family. She had always seen her family as intrusive, and she had worked very hard to fend off what she saw as interfering overtures. In doing so, she had established a pattern she used with her partner, where she defended against closeness that she was afraid would suffocate her.

At my gentle urging, she scheduled a session with her parents. Seeing them together it became clear that the father's motive was to look after his unmarried daughter in his accustomed "old-world" way. He knew nothing of his daughter's relationship with Jennifer. Even if he had, there was some question whether he would have respected the boundary created by their relationship. Clearly, he would have treated the relationship differently than he would a "real" marriage.

(It is possible in working with such families to "legitimize" the relationship in a way that eventually establishes boundaries between the family of origin and the couple.) This represented a major issue between Jennifer and Ione that definitely called for a broader, systemic approach, which would include additional work with family members, either in person or "on paper."

Pete and Larry were friends, not clients. They had recently celebrated eight years together and generally seemed to have a good, supportive relationship, but not one without friction. A major source of that friction (but certainly not directly cause and effect) involved Pete's relationship with his family of origin. His parents were upper-class Bostonians, with the requisite money and social connections. Even after eight years, they did not recognize Pete and Larry's relationship. It was not clear whether they chose not to or whether they were just naive, because when Pete was in college they found out that Pete and Larry were intimate. That was seven years earlier. They threatened to cut off Pete's tuition and expense money unless the two men stopped sharing an apartment and ceased seeing each other. Pete felt that he had no choice but to present the appearance of compliance. Since that incident, seven years before, there had been no discussion about Larry, Pete's sexual orientation, or his social lifestyle.

For Pete and Larry, the issue still lurked behind the scenes. For that next year in college, they kept the relationship as secret as they could. A year after graduation, they again took up residence together, unbeknownst to Pete's parents. Even now, Larry never answered the telephone in his own apartment for fear that it might be Pete's parents. The parents' shadow continued to influence the relationship from a great distance because Pete's inheritance was at stake.

Larry and his family also played a part in the scenario. They knew about the relationship between the two men and, even though they did not openly support it, at least they showed implicit indifference. Larry could at least mention Pete and their vacations, their friends, and their successes. They all avoided anything that smacked of the conflictual.

Both of Larry's parents were over seventy years old. They had both suffered declining health in recent years, and since they lived five hours by car from their son, they felt free to call on him at any time should they require his presence. During a recent summer Larry had spent six weeks at his parents' home tending to their care and their business affairs when his mother was hospitalized. He spent that six weeks apart from Pete, with only two brief visits between them. Larry's married sister, who lived a bit closer with her husband and child, was never asked by her parents to help.

Both men had boundary issues with families of origin that contributed to tension in their relationship. The tension was not likely to dissipate without some sort of systemic intervention. The prevailing myth was that death would eventually resolve the issues in both families. However, too often the prevailing patterns will continue despite the demise of an older generation.

*   *   *

Tony and Rob would have said that their situation differed a lot from that of Pete and Larry. They had coupled five years ago with the full understanding of both families. Tony's father lived a good distance away and his mother was dead. Rob's family lived within a few miles of the two men, who owned a lovely home in a fashionable city neighborhood. Holidays and family gatherings always found Tony included with Rob's family. Rob had an older brother who lived nearby with his wife. The two brothers and their mates socialized fairly frequently.

Then, suddenly, Rob's father developed cancer. In three months he had died. During the illness and in the time following his death, the family called on Rob for endless errands and commitments and energy, not because this had been his previous role in the family, but because he was perceived as being available. On several occasions the message came through loud and clear from his mother, "I would ask your brother to do it, but he has things to take care of for Sally."

Whether or not Tony and Rob would have recognized it, in the final analysis, boundaries held up very much the same in the two different situations. . . .

In the context of marriage and couple relationships, we all carry preconceptions of how roles should and do operate. Gay men and lesbians share the same preconceptions, many of which may not be relevant to their particular contexts: the "supplemental" nature of the woman's income, the male's primary role as "breadwinner," the woman's role as primary manager of the household economy, issues of power and dominance, issues of emotional support, and so on. Although roles in marriage have changed somewhat in the last several decades, there still exist fairly clear-cut guidelines and expectations for how roles sort out in marriage. Sometimes these marital-role expectations cause difficulty for heterosexual couples, such as when spouses decide to reverse the traditional roles.

One such situation was reported to me several years ago. A married couple decided over a several-year period and two children that they would both continue to work, but that she would focus on advancing her career, while he would just work a job and take more responsibility for home and kids. Before too long she had advanced up the corporate ladder and was making more money than he was. One night a neighbor dropped by and in the course of conversation inquired earnestly, "How can you let your wife make more money than you do?"

Gay men and lesbians enter relationships without benefit of clear role expectations because role models remain so invisible. There are advantages and disadvantages to this situation. On the plus side, there is much less likelihood that any well-meaning neighbor will inquire about an income differential. On the minus side, there is the push/shove of reinventing the wheel. Through the years I have found that same-sex couples need some help in negotiating these role issues, *but they do not emerge as stated sources of conflict in most relationships.* In fact, the lack of rigid role delineation often leaves room for creativity in these couples.

There may be one important exception. Sociologists Philip Blumstein and Pepper Schwartz have recently come up with some interesting findings in their research on couples. They studied cohabiting and married heterosexual couples and, as controls because they washed out gender differences, gay and lesbian couples. Basically, their research showed that money equals power, that in heterosexual, lesbian, and gay couples, the person making the lesser amount of money deferred to the person making more. The person with the greater income (and status) interrupted more and, among heterosexuals and lesbians, the person with the smaller income generally supported the ideas and opinions of the greater-status mate ("uh-huh, well said, well done"). However, in gay male couples *no one took the supportive role.* Now, because men make more money than women, they generally have more power, too. But even in the small number of heterosexual couples where the woman made more money, the men took something of a supportive role. This seems to say that men will do the supporting for women, but they will not provide this support for other men. This has interesting implications for working with gay male couples, implications that need to be more fully explored. . . .

Sometimes rigid sexual roles [are] observed in gay and lesbian couples. In my experience, these sexual roles do not necessarily carry over into other parts of the relationship. In other words, the man who is sexually passive in a gay relationship does not necessarily assume more traditional feminine duties in other aspects of the relationship. The same seems true for lesbian couples.

For example, issues of household economy, traditionally a female preserve in marriage, may get attended to by either partner (or both), irrespective of roles he or she plays in bed. What you may see is a struggle between two men or two women who *both* want responsibility in this area. I have seldom seen same-sex couples coming into therapy because they could not sort out who would "play" husband and who would "play" wife. The struggle in the sexual arena represents another matter.

THE ISSUE OF CHILDREN

Another qualitative difference exits between same-sex and opposite-sex couples: one will never produce children together, while in the other it is almost always at least a consideration (discounting age). In fact, the opportunity to produce children is a major reason for religious and legal sanction of marriage and a major reason why the culture glorifies long-term relationships. Even the rules surrounding proper conduct in marriage stem from concerns regarding pregnancy and illegitimacy in the bloodline.

Gay males do not couple with the intent of producing children nor will the decision not to have them constitute a common bond. Neither will the presence of children produced in common produce the guilt and conflict present in many divorce situations—making this aspect of separation easier for gay men.

The circumstances for lesbians are changing. Lesbians do have the option of pregnancy, although obviously not for biologically mutual progeny. However, there are at least opportunities to decide together whether to have children. One couple I heard about recently opted to use donor sperm from the brother of one partner to impregnate the other. Biologically, this is as close as one can get to the process in heterosexual unions; even the family bond with the grandchildren is perpetuated.

Adoption has theoretically always been an option for same-sex couples, but in practice this process is extremely difficult for anyone identified as being homosexual. Adoption, in fact, may prove a tortuous process for qualifying heterosexual couples.

Still, the vast majority of gay and lesbian couples do not make conscious or even subconscious decisions to have children, and this fact means that this bonding factor is unavailable to them.

It is not unusual for one or both partners in gay or lesbian relationships to bring children from a marriage into the same-sex relationship. Such an arrangement brings up two major issues, one common to heterosexual recouplings and one unique to same-sex marriages. The universal-blended family issues present in all recombinations present a force to be reckoned with for homosexuals and heterosexuals alike, but the issue of how and when to deal with children around your sexual orientation represents a distinctly homosexual problem.

Many books have already been written on the challenges and strategies of dealing with blended-family issues. . . . Much less has been explored concerning coming out to the children and all of the implications involved in that process. . . .

As a therapist, I have experienced a much more subtle issue impacting same-sex couples, one that may affect gay males more than lesbians. I have been impressed with a qualitative difference between gay men who have been married, especially those who have been married with children, and those who have never experienced heterosexual marriages. When you think about it, the implications are obvious: those who have been married have experienced firsthand all the supports and role expectations that go with marriage in our culture. So it is not surprising that their expectations in gay relationships come tinged with these feelings and attitudes.

Darryl and Don split up after five years together. The breakup was congenial and could be traced to a number of issues. A major, largely unspoken, issue involved Don's incomprehension of the powerful emotional bond that existed between Darryl and his ex-wife and child. In fact, Darryl, who had maintained a very positive relationship with his ex-wife, admitted that when he visited them in their hometown, he enjoyed the three of them going out as a family, just like in the old days. "Kind of like having your cake and eating it, too," he exclaimed. Don did not resent this bond intellectually, but emotionally it upset him quite a bit. He felt on the outside of a major force in Darryl's life—and, in truth, he was.

Many major cities have support groups or networks for gays and lesbians who have been married, since so often they feel out of sync with never-married gays. "I feel so much better understood around other gay men with kids," Darryl reported. While lesbians may feel just as strongly about this kind of support or lack of it, this has not represented my experience with them. Somehow it *may* be that, since women tend to be more child-focused as a group, there exists more support and understanding in the lesbian culture in general.

DUAL CAREERS

The vast majority of same-sex couples face the issues of dual careers that many heterosexual marriages face. (This is one area where a heterosexual relationship issue, one that has received a good deal of attention in recent years, *does* generalize to the same-sex couple.) Almost always, both participants in a same-sex relationship work at jobs or careers rather than one person staying home as homemaker. Some of the issues confronting any dual-career couple concern where to locate or relocate, coordination of work and time together, and satisfaction from long-term career goals. . . .

In many dual-career marriages, the traditional obstacles of male/female position and status in the marriage plus the demands on one spouse to combine childcare, housework, and career provide fodder for conflict and cry out for resolution. Gay male and lesbian unions do not have to face these concerns. Same-sex couples, though, may experience an obstacle concerning the fruits of their labors, since, because of previous experiences and sociological conditions discussed earlier, there is not necessarily the assumption that "what's mine is ours," as one tends to find in a marriage. In fact, the rampant cynicism concerning lack of permanence in these relationships also contributes to difficulties in sharing resources. However, sometimes the reverse is true: a couple works so hard to stay together just to show that it *can* be done and resources are shared so completely that there is little room for individual use of financial resources (perhaps an extreme embrace of traditional marital values).

Jay, who earned $35,000 per year, complained that he could not even buy a shirt that he might see and want because there was no money left over from the joint budget administered by his lover, Steve, who earned considerably less. These two men adhered strongly to a fairly traditional marital household management philosophy, but there was still resentment caused by the disparity in incomes. The "what's mine is ours" dictum did not work for them, even though they tried to operate like a traditional marriage in many ways.

*   *   *

Another major issue common to dual-career couples is the "whither thou goest" dilemma. Traditionally, families move when the husband gets transferred, but with a more professionally egalitarian arrangement, couples need to prepare to decide when career demands for *either* spouse may dictate a move. Over the years, I have seen a small number of gay male couples split up over this issue: "It was time for us to go our separate ways anyway," Charles said. "We'd been together four years and things were starting to feel stale. We had more time together than most of my friends have had, after all." This couple split when Charles's lover, Phil, took a job across the country. Charles was not willing to give up his job and his friends to make the move. Their expectations regarding impermanence of gay relationships also contributed to the outcome.

This issue may take a slightly different twist for lesbians, since in traditional marriages women most often give in around this issue. Lesbians may struggle with whether they have the *right* to ask a partner to move, while men may assume they have the right implicitly. As was discussed earlier, men also tend to display more open competitiveness around professional accomplishments than their lesbian counterparts, making their actual process around this issue a more vigorous and even hostile one. Coupled men with unequal incomes and potentials will likely experience competition and friction eventually.

THE FUSION ISSUE

[G]ender issues . . . also get played out in relationship styles that are fundamentally different for gay men and for lesbians. We have hinted at some of this operating in other areas, such as dual careers and support for having children. A more basic difference seems to operate in terms of style.

Krestan and Bepko, in a classic 1980 *Family Process* article, present the case for what they call "lesbian fusion." According to the authors, women's socialization tends to make them more homebound, to erode boundaries between them, and to fuse them dysfunctionally under stress. They describe this as a "two against the world" posture. Men, on the other hand, tend to distance under stress, staying away from home, involving themselves in other activities, including sexual ones.

This major difference really is not too surprising when we consider that women in our culture tend to be the ones who hold families together, keeping the home fires burning and providing the lion's share of the emotional support in families. Men are the ones who typically go out to earn a living and to intermingle with a broader world. These differences manifest themselves markedly in therapy. . . .

INTRARELATIONSHIP DIFFERENCES

Several years ago, one of my partners asked me this question: "How come," she said, "most of the heterosexual couples I see come from the same or similar socioeconomic backgrounds, and so many of the gay couples I see come from such unlike backgrounds?" I do not know whether her observations would hold up statistically, but my observations have been somewhat the same. Seemingly, more gays and lesbians come from dissimilar cultural, educational, and economic backgrounds. If this is true, we might attribute it to the fact that the pool of available partners is smaller for gays and lesbians and *as a group gay men and lesbians are thrown together only because they share the same "deviant" sexual orientation.* So the son of a sharecropper from Alabama finds himself in a bar with a corporate attorney's son from New York. They find each other attractive, have sex, and may end up as a couple. Since meeting places for gay men in particular have been limited and reasonably isolated, the selection of partners of unlike backgrounds becomes more likely.

Another observation that may not hold up statistically: I have observed more same-sex relationships with fairly great differences in age than I have in heterosexual relationships. The need for role models in the coming-out process, cutoffs from family, the small pool of eligible partners, and various other reasons may account for this phenomenon. For the therapist, it means another consideration in therapy: different experiences and developmental stages.

Interracial considerations may also play more of a part in therapy. In Atlanta, for example, an organization called Black and White Men Together provides support for a fairly sizable number of interracial couples. Interracial coupling should logically be easier with gays and lesbians, since so many are already cut off from families of origin and having children is usually not a major consideration.

LEGAL ISSUES

There are few legal protections for same-sex couples. Their sexual acts are illegal in most states. They may not file joint income tax returns, claim each other as deductions, qualify as dependents on insurance policies, collect a "spouse's" Social Security, or, in some cases, be named as life insurance beneficiaries. We have mentioned the difficulty with adoption. Gays and lesbians may be barred from visitation with their own biological children, and they experience difficulty gaining custody in divorce proceedings.

Monty, thirty-four, had been married for eight years and divorced over three. He has three children, two sons, nine and seven, and a daughter, four. Since the divorce, his middle child, Alex, has presented problems for his mother. She has remarried and lives 150 miles from her ex-husband. Whenever Alex becomes particularly difficult, his mother sends him to his father to live. Sometimes this has happened with advance notice, sometimes more spontaneously. After several months, she misses Alex, feels guilty about abandoning him to his father, and takes steps to get him back. Since she never has surrendered custody, this gets accomplished with little difficulty. Monty has repeatedly asked for custody, but his ex-wife always puts him off. He is afraid to go to court because the issue of his homosexuality may come up and, in his old hometown, there is some likelihood that the judge would deny visitation altogether. Obviously this situation is detrimental to Alex. It also puts a burden on Monty's relationship with his partner, since the blended-family issues never really get addressed. . . .

AIDS has sharpened the focus on legal protections or rights for spouses. Anecdotal information is replete with examples of a surviving spouse losing everything the two of them had worked for to a deceased lover's next of kin. For most couples, where one partner has contracted AIDS, negotiation around wills, power of attorney, use of life-support measures, and legal issues around death and burial becomes essential in the relationship.

In general, same-sex couples must work at what married couples take for granted as legal rights. Of course, the absence of legal bonds makes it easier for partners to move on with relative legal ease. It may also contribute to the attitude of not really taking the relationship seriously. Some couples may use legal commitments such as joint ownership of property, wills, and life insurance to formalize their bonds.

22.

I HAVE ANGUISHED

Ed Fallon

I have anguished over this [state anti–gay marriage] bill, not because there is any doubt in my mind as to how I should vote, but because I believe strongly that what we are dealing with here is the defining civil rights issue of this decade. Historically, this issue may prove to be the most significant matter we deal with this year, and so I would respectfully ask the body's indulgence and attention during this debate.

My remarks are directed both toward those who sincerely believe that this bill is good and just and toward those who know in their hearts and consciences that this bill is wrong, but in fear of public opinion and of how this issue will be used in campaigns next fall, they are inclined to vote in favor of its passage.

Back in the 1950s, many, many Americans were victimized by relentless, fear-driven red-baiting. There was a Bolshevik lurking in every bathroom, and you never knew, but your neighbor or even your uncle might turn out to be a communist.

In the 1990s, red-baiting is out. But pink-baiting is in. Gay-bashing, generally thought of as a Friday night frolic for inebriated thugs, has its parallel expressions in voting booths, city council halls, and legislative chambers across this country. Today we are witnessing one of those expressions in the form of this bill. By singling out gay and lesbian marriages as a union unacceptable in the eyes of the law, we fuel the fires of ignorance, intolerance, and hatred.

And if anyone here thinks that the positions we embrace, the laws we enact, do not affect the mood of the public, then you have a very low, and I believe, a very inaccurate, view of the powerful influence we here in this body exert over the formation of public opinion. The message we're sending today is that it's okay to discriminate against people of a different sexual orientation, even though for the most part, that's the way they were born and

This address was delivered to the Iowa House of Representatives on February 20, 1996.

there's nothing they can do to change it. And for those who would argue that homosexuality is a choice, I ask you: do you really believe that anyone in their right mind would voluntarily choose to be in a class of people who are constantly made fun of, despised, beaten up and even killed, discriminated against, fired from their jobs, denied housing, and prevented from marrying?

For gay and lesbian people, this array of abuse is par for the course. If you believe that homosexuality is a personal choice, then you have not tried very hard to see this issue from a gay or lesbian person's point of view.

Well, I suppose this is as good a time as any for me to come out of the closet. I can't help the way I was born. It's just who I am. I've never announced this to a group publicly, but I guess it's about time. I am heterosexual. I am absolutely certain in my entire being that I could never be homosexual, no matter how hard I might try. I've never been attracted to another man in my life, and the idea of engaging in a homosexual act is foreign and distasteful to me. But just as I would hope that homosexual men and women could accept me for who I am, I promise to try to accept them for who they are. Why can't you do the same? Why can't we all do the same?

Hatred grows out of fear, and fear grows out of ignorance. Though I've never hated homosexuals, I used to fear them. When I was a kid growing up, the worst name you could call someone was a gay loser. And the stereotype that still pervades the minds of many in this chamber—that of the highly aggressive, promiscuous gay man seeking countless, anonymous relationships—is the stereotype that I grew up with, and the stereotype that contributes to volumes of ignorance and volumes of fear.

Over time, I've come to learn that this stereotype, like most stereotypes, is based on hearsay, not fact. The rogues who may fit the previous description are the exception to the rule, just as there are male heterosexual rogues who are aggressive, promiscuous, and constantly hitting on and harassing women.

In my evolving experience with homosexuals, familiarity has displaced ignorance and dispelled fear. I now count as friends and constituents many same-sex couples. Some have children. Most are in long-term, stable relationships. All are very decent, kind, and normal people. I make no effort to judge the integrity of what they do in their bedrooms, and, to their credit, they've never judged the integrity of what I do in mine.

One lesbian couple I count as friends have two children the same age as my son and daughter. They attend the same elementary school as my children. They play together. They go to the same birthday parties. They swap overnights. These two children are healthy, bright, and courteous, and their parents probably do a better job of parenting than I do.

Though you may have personal, religious reasons why this arrangement seems distasteful to you, there is absolutely no way you could rationally argue that this is not a stable, happy, healthy family. In a pluralistic society that allegedly values the separation of church and state, why can we not simply live and let live? Accept the reality that this couple's religious beliefs on homosexuality are different than yours. Just leave religion out of it, as our founding fathers and mothers saw fit. If the fruit which falls from the tree is good, the tree must also be good.

Indeed, there are many religious groups that openly and lovingly celebrate unions between same-sex couples. For example, Methodists, the United Church of Christ, Congregationalists, Reform Jews, the Metropolitan Community Church, Unitarian Universalists, and Quakers.

There is no shortage of gay or lesbian couples that value and revere marriage. In fact, just last fall I attended the wedding of two women. Their son was present. The wedding was held in a local church. It was conducted by two ministers. And there were 150 family members and friends of the happy couple there to celebrate with them.

Yet, we're told by the bill's supporters that we need legislation to protect ourselves from this kind of marriage? No, ladies and gentlemen, this is not a marriage-protection bill. It is emphatically an antimarriage bill.

This rhetoric used by supporters of HF 2183 may be slick, but it is grossly inaccurate. What are you trying to protect heterosexual marriages from? There isn't a limited amount of love in Iowa. It isn't a nonrenewable resource. If Amy and Barbara or Mike or Steve love each other, it doesn't mean that John and Mary can't.

Marriage licenses aren't distributed on a first-come, first-served basis here in Iowa. Heterosexual couples don't have to rush out and claim marriage licenses now, before they are all snatched up by gay and lesbian couples.

Heterosexual unions are and will continue to be predominant, regardless of what gay and lesbian couples do. To suggest that homosexual couples in any way, shape, or form threaten to undermine the stability of heterosexual unions is patently absurd.

And I know, you'll say: "What about the gay agenda?" Well, just as there turned out to be no Bolsheviks in the bathroom back in the 1950s, there is no gay agenda in the 1990s. There is, however, a strong, well-funded antigay agenda, and we have an example of its efforts here before us today.

All that gay and lesbian people are asking for is, if not understanding, then at least tolerance. All they are asking for is the same basic civil equality that all Americans yearn for and should be entitled to.

To those in this body who know in their hearts and consciences that this bill is wrong, yet are afraid to vote against it, I ask you to consider the powerful message this bill sends to the people of Iowa. It sends the message that discrimination against gays and lesbians is acceptable and officially sanctioned. It sends the message that it's okay to deny civil and equal rights to some minority groups in our society. It sends the message that the gift of marriage is good for some yet forbidden to others. And for those in my own party who plan to vote for this bill, it sends the message that Democrats, who have traditionally stood up for and protected everyone's civil rights, aren't willing to do so in the case of homosexuals.

If you are weighing the political consequences of opposing this bill and find they are too heavy, I'd like you to think about the great moral changes that have occurred in this country over the past two hundred years. Ask yourself when you would have felt safe to speak in favor of the separation of the colonies from Great Britain? When would you have taken a public stand for the abolition of slavery? When would you have spoken in favor of women's suffrage? In the 1960s, when would you have joined Martin Luther King and others in calling for equal rights for African Americans? When would you have spoken out against restrictive marriage laws banning interracial marriages?

While the choice before us today—between a green button or a red one—is a difficult one to make, it is nowhere near as difficult or dangerous as the choices faced by the many freedom fighters who came before us.

We're elected not to follow but to lead. We're elected to cast what might sometimes be a difficult, challenging, and politically inexpedient vote. We're elected to represent our constituents when they're right, and to vote our consciences regardless of whether our constituents are right. And our conscience should be telling us to stand up for civil rights regardless of how unpopular it may appear.

The Reverend Dr. Martin Luther King Jr. once said, "A time comes when silence is betrayal." Such a time is now. With your "no" vote on this bill, you can help break the silence and stand with those who have no one to stand with them.

Part Three.

THE PHILOSOPHICAL ARGUMENTS

23.

THE MORALITY OF HOMOSEXUAL MARRIAGE

Daniel Maguire

For a significant minority of persons in the human community, erotic desire is focused, primarily or exclusively, on persons of the same sex. Psychiatrists are divided on whether to label this de facto variation pathological or not. Similarly, moralists are divided as to whether this orientation is an inclination to moral perversion, or a simple variation in the human quest for intimacy. If it is pathology, medical science should look for a cure; if it is an ingrained tilt toward unconscionable behavior, ethicists must counsel its containment.

The psychiatric or ethical position that sees homosexuality as clinical or moral pathology is blessed with striking simplicity. Clearly, pathologies are not to be encouraged under the specious claim of freedom or self-fulfillment. We find in the human sexual lexicon such manifestly pathological conditions as zoophilia, pedophilia, necrophilia, fetishism, sadistic or masochistic sex, exhibitionism, voyeurism, and rape. If homosexuality fits somewhere in that listing, we need not labor long in discussing its moral or psychological status. We do not speak of a well-adjusted necrophiliac, nor do we consider necrophiliacs as having a moral and civil right to access to corpses. There is no cry for rapist or fetishist liberation. Some things are abnormal and harmful at least to the agent who acts out on them. Is this the case for homosexuality?

Those who say yes face two critical difficulties: (1) they must show that those who act in any way on their homosexual orientation victimize themselves or others and (2) they must show that celibacy is good for all non-heterosexual persons.

First, regarding the harm, it is empty nominalism to name something harmful in the absence of identifiable harm. It is illogical to speak of a moral

This article originally appeared in *A Challenge to Love: Gay and Lesbian Catholics in the Church,* edited by Robert Nugent, and with an introduction by Bishop Walter F. Sullivan (New York: Crossroad Publishing Company, 1983). Reprinted by permission of Daniel Maguire.

or psychological cure for a harmful condition if we cannot show what harm the cure is to address. Illness is known by its symptoms. In the absence of symptoms, we assume persons are well. If psychiatry would label homosexuality a pathology or illness, it must show how it adversely affects persons who express their intimacy-needs homosexually. The delineations of these adverse effects must also show that these are due to the orientation itself and not to the sociocultural effects of seeing the condition as an illness. If a society falsely imputes negative meaning to a sexual orientation, this will adversely affect persons who act out on that orientation, though the fault would be with the social stigmatizing and not with the orientation itself.

Clearly, then, psychiatry and ethics must pass the "show-me" test when they speak of homosexuality as a malady in need of a remedy. The test is not met simply by stating that homosexuality is a "disorder" because it is a minority phenomenon or because anatomy and reproductive needs suggest male-female coitus as the unexceptionable norm. Minority status does not of itself mean objectionable deviance. Indeed, the presence of minority status is the spice of variety and thus of life. But is not anatomy destiny? The penis and the vagina do enjoy a congenial fit, and the species' need for reproduction relies on that. But sex rarely, in any lifetime, has to do with reproduction, and not even heterosexual persons are limited to coitus for sexual fulfillment. Also, the species' need for reproductive sex is being met and often overmet.

In ethics, the term *biologism* refers to the fallacious effort to wring a moral mandate out of raw biological facts. The male-female coital fit and its relationship to reproduction are basic biological facts. The biologistic error would leap from those facts to the moral imperative that all sexual exchange must be male-female coital in kind. The leap could only become likely if you reduce human sexuality to the biological simplicities of the stud farm. Given the infinity of meanings beyond baby making involved in human eroticism and sexuality, such a leap is misdirected and, literally, unreal.

No. If homosexuality is an illness requiring cure, if it is an orientation to sin, it is because it is harmful to persons. If that harm cannot be pinpointed, the charge of sin or illness must be reconsidered.

George Bernard Shaw reminded us that it is the way of barbarians to think of the customs of their tribe as the laws of nature. Is the homosexually oriented quest for intimacy contrary to the laws of nature or simply to the current customs of our tribe? That question is regularly sent to go a-begging. The discussion, however, depends on facing it squarely.

The second question confronting those who see homosexuality as pathology regards celibacy as the only moral option for nonheterosexuals. Moralists of this position say that the condition of being homosexually oriented is not evil in itself since it seems irreversible in many or most instances. (Some deviant Christian fundamentalists see homosexuality as a contumacious and wicked option that can be cast out by prayer and fasting. In the absence of any supportive data, we commend such a position to its own embarrassment.) The evil would be in acting out one's homosexual proclivities. The morally good homosexual, in this view, is the celibate homosexual. This position has inherent contradictions. Implicitly it is reducible to the position of the deviant Christian fundamentalists since it says: You may be homosexual but, with prayer and fasting, you will never have to express it. It insists that there is nothing wrong with being a homosexual as long as you do not act on it. That is too tidy. There is a lot wrong with being a homosexual if all the values that attach to sexual expression are denied you. Sex is more than orgasms; it is an important avenue to many personal values. If the sexual avenue is categorically closed off to gay persons, that is no slight impairment. It makes the condition itself an abridgment of personality.

This "be-but-don't-do" position rests on three errors: (1) a materialistic and narrow view of sex, (2) a stunted epistemology, and (3) a departure from biblical good sense. First, then, it views sex narrowly and materialistically, missing its linkage to such deeply felt human needs as intimacy, trust, and friendship. It would be gratuitous to say that a celibate cannot meet those human needs—that sex is necessary for human fulfillment—but it is equally gratuitous to say that a whole class of persons involving as much as 4 or 5 percent of the human population can be barred morally from the only kind of access to sexuality that attracts them.

1. Erotic desire is deeply interwoven into the human desire and need for closeness and for trusting relationships. The desire for a significant other with whom we are uniquely conjoined is not a heterosexual but a basic human desire. The programmatic exclusion of gay persons from the multiple benefits of erotic attraction, which often opens the way to such a union, is arbitrary, harmful, cruel, and therefore sinful.

Again, I am not saying that marriage or sexual activity are necessary for human fulfillment or psychological normalcy. Voluntary and involuntary celibacy is more common than is generally noted in a time of sexual overemphasis. Celibacy, voluntary or not, does not exclude human fulfillment. Sexually unfulfilled persons may be very fulfilled humanly. However, I stress that the sweeping exclusion of all gay persons from this important access route to meeting intimacy needs could only be based on a narrow and, I must insist, macho-masculine conception of what sex is and how it functions in human personal development.[1]

2. This position also lumps together without distinction all manifestations of homosexuality. Basically, the position is anthropologically naive. Few areas of human life are as variegated as sexual activity. This holds also for homosexuality. Some manifestations of homosexuality are harmful to human personal and social good. A moral argument opposed to homosexual activity in those instances can be made. However, to claim to know, by some encyclopedic intuition, that only celibacy befits homosexuals in any culture, clime, or time is—to say the least—immodest. More accurately, it is epistemologically absurd. It involves a kind of *essentialist* approach to knowing. Thus, even before all the

data is in on what homosexuality is, how it develops, what it means in persons and societies, how it interrelates with other aspects of human relating, and so on—before all of that is known, a formula-panacea has been found that exhausts the moral meaning of homosexuality by prescribing celibacy.

Such essential thinking in ethics has a poor track record. Once we thought we had intuited the nature of money so clearly that we could say that all interest taking was sinful regardless of circumstances. Once we thought that we had so intuited the nature of sex that we could know that all contraceptive sexual exchange was wrong. We also believed that we had so thoroughly plumbed the meaning of speech that even to prevent serious harm such as murder we could not speak untruth. All of these essentialist visions have been humbled. The road to truth is longer and more tortuous than we thought. But now, regarding homosexuality, we are again told that the nature of homosexuality can be so perfectly intuited (especially by heterosexuals) that we can, with majestic calm, make a transcultural judgment that any expression of it anywhere is wrong and dehumanizing. Such arrogance is not the hallmark of truth.

Any position about the complexities of human behavior and development that ignores the witness of experience is suspect. The position that asserts that homosexuality is all right as long as you do not act on it is innocent of and apparently unconcerned with the experience of homosexually oriented persons. The more one looks into that experience and hears sensitive witness from gay persons, the less comfortable one can be with the glib "be-but-don't-do" approach to this human mystery. This approach gratuitously and stubbornly assumes that homosexuality fits with such things as pedophilia and obsessive voyeurism. It assumes with signal cruelty that homoeroticism has no more humanizing possibilities than incest or zoophilia. In this view, homoeroticism is, like all of these demonstrably noxious realities, sick. Since the conclusion of this error is a prescription of universal celibacy for all gays, the burden is clearly upon those who would so prescribe. Instead we receive poor exegesis of religious texts, biologisms, and warmed-over biases in place of argument. Neither ethics nor persons are well served by such careless intuitionism and empirically bereft moralizing.

Jean-Paul Sartre has told us that the greatest evil of which persons are capable is to treat as abstract that which is concrete. That is precisely what the "be-but-don't-do" school does to homosexuality. It takes the infinitely diverse experiences of homosexual persons and classifies them without distinction as evil. Such a globular approach does not commend itself to intelligence.

3. The final error of the "be-but-don't-do" position relates particularly to Christians who should be nourished by the earthy wisdom of the Bible. Facile urgings of celibacy for persons who do not happen to be heterosexual fly in the face of biblical good sense. Saint Paul, in his celebrated First Letter to the Corinthians, talks about the possibility of celibacy. Even though he is writing in a state of high eschatological expectation, and with the expressed conviction that it is better not to have sex (1 Cor. 7:1), he allows that sexual needs are such

that it would be better to marry (7:12). He concedes that persons may lack self-control (7:15), and so even married persons would be better advised not to be sexually abstinent for long. He would prefer all to be celibate but notes that each one has his/her own gift from God (7:17), implying very clearly that not all have the gift of celibacy. Again, he would prefer the unmarried and widowed to stay celibate but, once more, allows for the possible lack of "self-control" and concludes that "it is better to marry than to burn" (7:19).

The "be-but-don't-do" position would certainly allow, with Paul, that it is better for heterosexuals to marry than to burn. But, apparently their message for our homosexual brothers and sisters is: "Burn, burn!" We should not be terribly surprised that gay persons do not see this as "the good news." They can point out that Paul in this passage is reflecting the good sense of Jesus, who also said of voluntary celibacy: "Let him accept it who can" (Matt. 19:12). The Church itself, in the Second Vatican Council, has taken up this sensible idea, describing voluntary celibacy as "a precious gift," not as something indiscriminately given to whole classes of peoples.[2] The council points out that chastity will be very difficult, that it will face "very severe dangers" even for seminarians and religious with all the safeguards built into their lifestyle.[3] Those who would embark on a life of celibacy "should be very carefully trained for this state."[4] The council calls voluntary celibacy a "counsel," not a mandate, "a precious gift of divine grace which the Father gives to *some* persons," but not to all.[5] This gift of "total continence" is seen as worthy of special honor and as something "unique."[6] Celibate chastity "deserves to be esteemed as a surpassing gift of grace . . . which liberates the human heart in a unique way."[7] Persons entering religious orders should be warned in advance that celibacy, even in the sacred confines of religious life, is not easy. Involved in the celibate project are "the deeper inclinations of human nature." Candidates for a celibate religious life should have "a truly adequate testing period" to see if "they have the needed degree of psychological and emotional maturity." They should be warned of "the dangers confronting chastity."[8]

To all of which, our gay brothers and sisters might reply: "If total continence is so difficult for nuns and priests, why is it so easy for us? If it is a counsel for them, why is it a precept for us? These are good questions. If celibacy is so difficult that only some heterosexuals can undertake it—and then with the most extraordinary systems of support—how can we say that all gays have this "unique" talent for self-containment? If celibacy is seen as it is in a religious context as a special charisma, are all gays charismatically blessed with celibate graces? Is this not a radical theological restatement of the position that "gay is good"? It is a traditional axiom of Catholic moral theology that no one is held to the impossible (*nemo ad impossibile tenetur*). Are gays, nevertheless, held to what is impossible for nongays? For nongays, in this view, celibacy is a gifted feat that symbolizes the special, generous presence of the power of God. For gays, it is just a way of life, and the least that they can do. There are problems here that even minimal insight and honesty could see and should admit. The pastoral position resulting from this contorted ethical position is equally strained. The only advice it leaves for gays is this: Pray and repress your erotic tendencies. God does not demand the impossible, and so God will give you the strength to do what moral theology, written by heterosexuals, has decided God wants you to do. If you fall from grace, appeal to God for forgiveness and your pastoral counselor will receive you with kindness and compassion.

Such pastoral advice embodies the theological error of "tempting God." It also harkens back to the medieval "ordeal," which contrived tests and put God on notice to come up with the response dictated by the test. If the fire burned you, you were evil. In this ordeal which we impose on gay persons, ethicists have boxed themselves into an arbitrary theological position which requires total celibacy from all gays and then leaves it up to God to pull off this implausible feat through prayer, sacraments, and pastoral counseling. Poor theology always puts God on the spot.

When we do theological ethics, we are painting a picture of our God. To say that something is good or bad is to say that it is in agreement or disagreement with the perceived will of God. In the position under discussion, we have God asking one thing from gays and considerably less from heterosexuals. If gay persons accept this particular ideological position on the ethics of homosexuality as the mind of God, *and* if they find it in contradiction to their own experience of reality, they have been pushed into the position of having to accept themselves *or* God. It is a position calculated to do precisely what pastoral theology should not do—alienate persons from the experience of God. Even at some risk to their professional situation, pastoral counselors are required not to offer either formal or material cooperations with a position that is so insensitive and religiously devastating.

MARRIAGE AS AN OPTION FOR HOMOSEXUALS

Marriage is the highest form of interpersonal commitment and friendship achievable between sexually attracted persons. Nothing in that definition requires that the sexually attracted persons who are conjoined in committed, conjugal friendship must be heterosexual. Neither is the capacity for having children required. Reproductive fertility is not of the essence of genuine marriage. Even in the Roman Catholic tradition, sterile persons are permitted to marry, and, as a recent celebrated case in the Diocese of Joliet, Illinois, illustrated, even male impotence is no barrier to marriage. This means that the basic sense of the current Catholic position on the relationship of marriage and childbearing is this: If there are to be children, they should be born within the confines of marriage. Yet, even fertile heterosexual persons do not have an obligation to have children. As Pope Pius XII taught, there can be a variety of reasons—social, economic, and genetic—for excluding children from a marriage entirely. Marriage clearly has more goods than the "good of children," the *bonum prolis*. And those other goods, in themselves, are enough to constitute marriage as a fully "human reality and saving mystery."[9]

The Second Vatican Council produced a major statement on the dignity and value of married life. The council Fathers were, of course, speaking of marriage between heterosexual persons. In fact, however, aside from the "good of offspring," which they stress is not essential for a genuine marriage, the goods and values they attach to marriage are not exclusively heterosexual in kind. The needs that marriage fulfills are human needs. The values that marriage enhances are integral to humanity as such and not to humanity as heterosexual. In fact, the *indispensable* goods of marriage are those that do not relate intrinsically to heterosexuality. The *dispensable* good—offspring—is the only good that does relate to heterosexuality.

Let us look to the council's statement on marriage and see what "good news" we might find there for gay persons who seek a humanizing and holy expression of their God-given orientation.

The image that the council gives of marriage is, on the whole, very positive and sensitive to personal needs. Marriage is seen as "an unbreakable compact between persons" of the sort that must "grow and ripen."[10] "Marriage persists as a whole manner and communion of life, and maintains its value and indissolubility, even when offspring are lacking."[11] Married persons should "nourish and develop their wedlock by pure conjugal love and undivided affection."[12] The council continues in a decidedly personalist tone:

> This love is an eminently human one since it is directed from one person to another through an affection of the will. It involves the good of the whole person. Therefore it can enrich the expressions of body and mind with a unique dignity, ennobling these expressions as special ingredients and signs of the friendship distinctive of marriage. This love the Lord has judged worthy of special gifts, healing, perfecting, and exalting gifts of grace and of charity.
>
> Such love, merging the human with the divine, leads the spouses to a free and mutual gift of themselves, a gift proving itself by gentle affection by deed. Such love pervades the whole of their lives. Indeed, by its generous activity it grows better and grows greater. Therefore it far excels mere erotic inclination which, selfishly pursued, soon enough fades wretchedly away.[13]

To make married love prosper, the couple are urged to "painstakingly cultivate and pray for constancy of love, largeheartedness, and the spirit of sacrifice."[14] The married couple are to become no longer two, but one flesh by rendering "mutual help and service to each other through an intimate union of their persons and their actions. Through this union they experience the meaning of their oneness and attain to it with growing perfection day by day." The goal of marriage is "unbreakable oneness."[15] Such "multifaceted love" mirrors the love of God for the Church. It will be marked by "perpetual fidelity through mutual self-bestowal." It should lead to the "mutual sanctification" of the two parties and "hence contribute jointly to the glory of God."[16]

The council does not look on this love as angelic and asexual. In fact, it stresses that this mutually satisfying and sanctifying love "is uniquely expressed and perfected through the marital act."[17] Sexual expression is extolled: "The acts themselves which are proper to conjugal love and which are exercised in accord with genuine human dignity must be honored with great reverence."[18] Again, reflecting the biblical sense of the natural goodness of sexual liturgy and its importance to conjugal love, the council warns that "where the intimacy of married life is broken off, it is not rare for its faithfulness to be imperiled and its quality of fruitfulness ruined."[19] Abstinence from sex, therefore, is viewed cautiously.

All of these texts of the council show a keen sense of the kinds of needs that are met in marital love. Married love will not survive on the thrills of early eroticism. What persons seek in marriage is total acceptance of all aspects of the self, the corrigible and the incorrigible, the lovely and the unlovely, the strong and the weak. Married love is not a selfish investment but an adventure in self-sacrificing, creative love. It is a school of holiness where persons may grow closer to God as they grow closer to one another and where their conjugal love may fuel their passion for justice and love for all people.

By what reasoning should values such as these be reserved for the heterosexual majority and denied to our gay brothers and sisters? By what twisted logic could we assume that gay persons would not experience the advantage of a love that produced such an "unbreakable oneness?" Why would gay persons in love be forbidden to aspire to and pray for "constancy of love, largeheartedness, and the spirit of sacrifice" to sustain their love? If erotic love between heterosexuals "is uniquely expressed and perfected" through sexual language, why would homoerotic love be judged moral only if sexually mute?

TWO OBJECTIONS TO HOMOSEXUAL MARRIAGE

Two immediate objections might be these: (1) gay persons do not display the psychological stability and strength necessary for lifelong commitment in marriage, and (2) the data indicate that gay persons prefer promiscuity to closed one-to-one relationships, showing that marriage is a heterosexual ideal being imperiously imposed on homosexuals.

How stable are gays psychologically? In a recent important study, Profs. Alan Bell and Martin Weinberg bring extensive research to bear on the common stereotypes our society maintains regarding homosexual persons. At the heart of the stereotyping is the belief that homosexuals are "pretty much alike." Accordingly, it is significant that Bell and Weinberg entitle their study *Homosexualities: A Study of Diversity among Men and Women*. According to the stereotype, the homogeneous homosexuals are marked by "irresponsible sexual conduct, a contribution to social decay, and, of course, psychological pain and maladjustment."[20] The study presents strong evidence that "relatively few homosexual men and women conform to the hideous stereotype most people have of them." The authors describe as their "least ambiguous finding" that "homosexuality is not necessarily related to pathology."[21]

Regarding the psychological adjustment of homosexual men, Bell and Weinberg discovered that only one or two of the homosexual subgroups compared adversely to heterosexual men as to psychological adjustment. "The remaining subgroups tended to appear as well adjusted as the heterosexuals or, occasionally, even more so."[22] One quasi-marital subgoup, which the study styles "close-coupled" fared more than well in comparison to heterosexuals. "They felt no more tense, and were even happier than the heterosexual men."[23] Lesbians differed even less than male homosexuals in measures of psychological adjustment. In fact, close-coupled lesbians came out better in some regards than comparably situated heterosexual women.[24]

These findings are remarkable when we consider the stresses gay persons are subjected to in an antihomosexual society. All adolescents are vulnerable in their self-image. They are normally moving out from the nurturing closeness of family life, where their value has been consistently and reliably affirmed. In coping with this the adolescent vacillates between shrillness and bombast and shyness and tears. If, in the delicate move from familial to somewhat broader social endorsement, the young persons discover that a profound aspect of their personality is loathsome to the dominant majority, a painful crisis ensues. The discovery that one is a "queer," a "faggot," and a "pervert" is terrifying news to the delicate emergent ego. The news is so frightening that some self-protectively blind themselves to their own sexual identity in an amazing feat of denial. Others cope, often alone, with little or no solace or support. Even those on whom they have most depended up till now are normally of no help. Parents and siblings usually give clear witness to their detestation of homosexuality. Sexual awareness, then, brings the homosexual adolescent into a terrible loneliness. That so many of them bear this solitary suffering so well and arrive at such high levels of psychological adjustment is a striking tribute to the resilience of the human spirit. Heterosexual youths have their own tensions, but normally nothing comparable to the crushing rejection that greets the young gay person with the onset of puberty.

In view of all this, it is both arrogant and unjust for the heterosexual and dominant majority to perpetuate the myth that gay persons are psychologically unsound when these persons have passed more tests of psychological adjustment than many heterosexuals are ever required to do. There is simply no evidence that the psychological state of gays disqualifies them *as a class* from deeply committed and specifically conjugal relationships. The gratuitous assertion or assumption that they are lamed in this respect constitutes, in terms of traditional Catholic moral theology, a mortal sin of calumny. It is also a sin of injustice requiring restitution. Few of us heterosexuals are without sin in this regard, and so we are required by the virtues of justice and veracity to take the trouble to know better the actual situation of our gay brothers and sisters and to make appropriate reparatory responses to their needs.

The second objection to marital friendship for homosexual persons rests on their alleged preference for promiscuous sexual lifestyles. Again, studies do not support these stereotypes. Lesbians are particularly prone to form lasting marriagelike relationships. Even among male homosexuals, where promiscuity is more common, prolonged "affairs" are common. The Bell-Weinberg study reaches this conclusion:

> Our data indicate that a relatively steady relationship with a love partner is a very meaningful event in the life of a homosexual man or woman. From our respondents' descriptions, these affairs are apt to involve an emotional exchange and commitment similar to the kinds that heterosexuals experience, and most of the homosexual respondents thought that they and their partners had benefited personally from their involvement and were at least somewhat unhappy when it was over. The fact that they generally went on to a subsequent affair with another partner seems to suggest a parallel with heterosexuals' remarriage after divorce rather than any particular emotional immaturity or maladjustment. In any case, most of our homosexual respondents spoke of these special relationships in positive terms and clearly were not content to limit their sexual contacts to impersonal sex.[25]

There is, of course, evidence that homosexual men are more promiscuous than any other group. This fact, however, must be put in context to be evaluated. A major factor is the high availability of sex in the male homosexual world, and homosexual men are men. As the psychologist Dr. C. A. Tripp writes: "The variety of sex the heterosexual male usually longs for in fantasy is frequently realized in practice by the homosexual. . . . There is no indication that homosexual promiscuity is any greater than its heterosexual equivalent would be in the face of equal opportunity."[26] There are other reasons that account for the promiscuous pattern among many male homosexuals. Two men do not have the same social freedom to live together that women enjoy. It often amounts to revelation of one's orientation with all the hazards that entails in a biased society. The prejudice of the community and of traditional Catholic moral theology discourages stable relationships and indirectly opens the way to promiscuity. Homosexual unions also usually lack children. As the Vatican Council noted, "children contribute in their own way to making their parents holy."[27] Part of that holiness is the holiness of fidelity and stable, enduring love. By excluding any serious consideration of mature and stable gay couples adopting children, or of lesbian couples having children by artificial insemination, we block, without due ethical process, this inducement to healthy relationships among gays. Another factor that inclines to promiscuity among gays is the fact that they are more likely to find partners that are more culturally diverse, which makes for greater likelihood of incompatibility on the long haul.

Therefore, we may not simply look from a distance at the statistics of greater male homosexual promiscuity without distinguishing the various groupings of homosexuals and without recognizing the pressures against marital relationships in the life situation of many gays.

THE MARRIAGE OPTION AND SOLIDLY PROBABLE OPINION

Within the confines of Roman Catholicism, there is division on the ethics of homosexual behavior. A number of moralists hold the traditional "be-but-don't-do" position and a number of others are open to humane expressions of gay sexual love. The hierarchical magisterium seems firm on the "be-but-don't-do" position. The theological magisterium is divided. The hierarchical position is admittedly noninfallible and is not an obstacle to open debate as long as there is due account of and study of that position. What tools for such a pluralistic situation did the Roman Catholic tradition provide? The answer is that the tradition provided an excellent moral system known as probabilism for precisely such a situation. The system has been in a state of disuse, and this represents a major loss of a traditional Catholic treasure.

Probabilism, like all good things, was abused, but the theological achievement that it represents was significant and, until we see how it relates to the charismatic theology of Paul and John and to the concept of the moral inspiration of the Holy Spirit in Augustine and Saint Thomas Aquinas, it has not been given its theological due. Another reason for bringing probabilism down from the Catholic attic is that after Vatican II's recognition of the truly ecclesial quality of Protestant Christian churches, neoprobabilism could be the test of ecumenism. Is our ecumenism merely ceremonial or can we really begin to take Protestant moral views into account in discussing liceity in doubtful matters? The older probabilism did not even face such a question.

The triumph of probabilism in the Church was an achievement of many of our long-suffering theological forebears, and we do well to harken back to their work. Let me briefly repeat what probabilism is all about. Probabilism arose, and finally gained prominence over competing systems, as a way of solving practical doubt about the liceity of some kind of behavior. In practice, it confronted a situation in which a rigorous consensus claiming the immorality of certain behavior was challenged. The question was: At what point does the liberty-favoring opinion attain such respectability in the forum of conscience that a person could follow it in good faith? Those who said that even frivolous reasons would justify departure from rigorous orthodoxy were condemned as laxists by Popes Innocent XI and Alexander VII. At the other extreme were the absolute tutiorists who taught that you could never follow the liberal opinion unless it was strictly certain. Even being most probable (*probabilissima*) was not enough. In graph form the situation was like this:

A	/B

A represents the dominant rigorous opinion claiming that certain activity could never be moral. B represents the liberal dissent. Laxism claimed that the most tenuous B would override A. Absolute tutiorism claimed that until B replaced A and was beyond challenge, it could not be followed. The Jansenists found absolute tutiorism attractive, but Alexander VIII did not, and he condemned it on December 7, 1690. Thus between the two banned extremes of laxism and absolute tutiorism, the Catholic debate raged with probabilism gradually becoming dominant.

Probabilism proceeded from the twin insights that a doubtful obligation does not bind as though it were certain, and that where there is doubt there is freedom. It held that a solidly probable opinion could be followed even though more probable opinions existed. To be solidly probable, a liberal opinion had to rest upon cogent though not conclusive reasons (intrinsic probability) or upon reliable authority (extrinsic probability). As Tanquerey puts it in his manual of moral theology, to be probable, an opinion could not be opposed to a "definition of the Church" or to certain reason and should retain its probability when compared with opposing arguments.[28] Since there is no "definition of the Church" regarding homosexuality and since furthermore it is clear that the Church does not have the competence to define such issues infallibly,[29] that condition cannot stand in the way of using probabilism.

Intrinsic probability, where one followed one's own lights to a solidly probable opinion, was not stressed in the history of probabilism, but it was presented as a possibility. Stress fell upon extrinsic probability where one found "five or six" moralists known for their "authority, learning, and prudence." Even one extraordinary preeminent teacher alone could constitute probability. What this meant is that minority B on our graph became solidly probable through private insight or through the insight of five or six learned experts even though the enormous majority of theologians disagreed. Note well that the basis of probabilism is insight—one's own or that of reliable experts. Insight is an achievement of moral intelligence. It cannot be forbidden, neither does it await permission to appear.

Note also that probabilism does not require a consensus or certitude. As Fr. Henry Davis writes, "when I act on the strength of a probable opinion, I am always conscious that though I am morally right in so acting, since I act prudently, nevertheless, the opinion of others who do not agree with me may be the true view of the case."[30] Obviously, the perennial debate will be between those who argue that the defenders of probability in a particular case are actually crypto-laxists and those who argue that the deniers of probability are disguised absolute tutiorists.

Probabilism was a remarkable development, and represents a high point in Catholic moral thought. It recognized that the apparent safety of absolute tutiorism was only apparent. The acceptance of such a rigorous position, as Father Tanquerey explained, would impose an impossible burden on the faithful contrary to the mind of the Gospel, which promises that the yoke will be sweet and the burden light; it would thus increase sins, generate despair, and drive many from the practice of religion.[31] Those reasons and probabilism itself are still relevant today.

To dismiss probabilism as the legalistic bickerings of the sixteenth and seventeenth centuries is theologically shortsighted. In the heyday of the debate, extravagant claims were made. Caramuel, who became known as the "prince of the laxists," taught that Adam and Eve used probabilism successfully to excuse themselves from many sins, until their wits and their probabilism failed them and they did fall. Vigorous efforts were made to trace the formal doctrine of probabilism to Augustine, Jerome, Ambrose, Gregory of Nazianzen, Basil, and Thomas Aquinas. One need not become party to such adventures to insist on and argue how compatible probabilism is with deep Christian traditions. The early Church was remarkably sanguine about the presence of the illumining Spirit in the hearts of the faithful. As Vatican II says:

> The Spirit dwells in the Church and in the hearts of the faithful as in a temple (cf. 1 Cor. 3:16; 6:19). In them He prays and bears witness to the fact that they are adopted sons (cf. Gal. 4:6; Rom. 8:15–16, 26). The Spirit guides the Church into the fullness of truth (cf. John 16:13) and gives her a unity of fellowship and service. He furnishes and directs her with various gifts, both hierarchical and charismatic, and adorns her with the fruits of His grace (cf. Eph. 4:11–12; 1 Cor. 12:4; Gal. 5:22).[32]

The Church has shared the confidence of Saint Paul when he said that the spiritual man "is able to judge the value of everything."[33] Augustine and Thomas manifest in strong theological language this exuberant confidence in the presence in all Christians of the illumining Spirit of God. Augustine asked: "What are the laws of God written by God in our hearts but the very presence of the Holy Spirit?"[34] And Thomas Aquinas, arguing that the new law is not anything written (including the New Testament), cites Jeremiah's promise that in the future testament God will put his law into the minds of his people and inscribe it on their hearts. In its primary meaning, then, the new law for Thomas is not the writings of biblical authors, Church officers, or theologians, all of which are secondary, but the instructive grace of the Holy Spirit.[35]

This, admittedly, is a heady doctrine which called for and did historically elicit a theology of the discernment of the Spirit. One must test one's claimed inspiration against all the witnesses to truth within the community. And yet this heady doctrine, with all of its perils, is not a private preserve of the current charismatic movement in the Church, but is rather bona fide mainstream Catholic thought. It is also, I believe, eminently congenial with the spirit of the debate that led to the championing of probabilism. The debate on probabilism in many ways seems a curious and stilted period piece, but it would be ungrateful and unconservative of us to reject this achievement of the Catholic tradition. And reject it, in effect, we did. Of course, it maintained its presence in the manuals, but in practice it was rendered nugatory. This was done by simply ignoring the genuine possibility of intrinsic probability and by controlling the theological enterprise in such ways that any theologians favoring a liberal opinion that did not square with the contemporary Vatican view were quickly deemed neither learned nor prudent. Thus did extrinsic probability pass. And thus were the doors thrown open to a juridical positivism based on the hierarchical magisterium.

The neoprobabilism for which I call would have to be extended to include Protestant witnesses to moral truth. Vatican II said of Protestant Christians that "in some real way they are joined with us in the Holy Spirit, for to them also He gives his gifts and graces, and is thereby operative among them with His sanctifying power."[36] It becomes unthinkable, therefore, if those words mean anything, that we accept that solid probability could not also be achieved through the witness of Protestant Christians, who are also subjects of the "gifts and graces" of our God. I submit that if that thought is unpalatable, our ecumenism is superficial and insincere.[37]

Obviously, within Protestant and Catholic Christianity, there is considerable support for the possibility of moral, humane, and humanizing sexual expression by gay persons. Extrinsic probability does obtain. Intrinsic probability is within the reaches of mature persons. There is no reason why this traditional tool of Catholic thought should not be used by pastoral counselors. Obviously the acceptance of the ideal of marriage for gay persons is not something that could be celebrated with public liturgy at this point in the history of the Church since such a celebration would imply a general consensus that as yet does not exist. The celebration of private liturgies, however, to conjoin two gays in permanent and committed love would seem commendable, and well within the realm of the principles and spirit of probabilism. The marital good of exclusive, committed, enduring, generous, and faithful love is a human good. We have no moral right to declare it off limits to persons whom God has made gay.

NOTES

    1. On the negative qualities of the macho-masculine, see Daniel C. Maguire, "The Feminization of God and Ethics," *Christianity and Crisis* 42 (March 1983): 59–67.

    2. See Walter M. Abbott, general ed., *The Documents of Vatican II* (New York: Herder and Herder, 1966), p. 447, in the *Decree on Priestly Formation.*

    3. Ibid.

    4. Ibid., p. 446.

    5. Ibid., p. 71, in the *Dogmatic Constitution on the Church.* Emphasis added.

    6. Ibid., pp. 71–72.

    7. Ibid., p. 474, in the *Decree on the Appropriate Renewal of the Religious Life.*

    8. Ibid., p. 475.

    9. The phrase "human reality and saving mystery" is from Edward Schillebeeckx's book *Marriage: Human Reality and Saving Mystery* (New York: Sheed and Ward, 1965).

    10. Abbott, *Documents of Vatican II, The Church Today,* p. 255.

    11. Ibid.

    12. Ibid., p. 252.

    13. Ibid., pp. 252–53.

14. Ibid., p. 253.

15. Ibid., pp. 250–51.

16. Ibid., p. 251.

17. Ibid., p. 253.

18. Ibid., p. 256.

19. Ibid., p. 255.

20. Alan P. Bell and Martin S. Weinberg, *Homosexualities: A Study of Diversity among Men and Women* (New York: Simon & Schuster, 1978), pp. 229–30.

21. Ibid., pp. 230–31

22. Ibid., p. 207.

23. Ibid., p. 208.

24. Ibid., p. 215.

25. Ibid., p. 102.

26. C. A. Tripp, *The Homosexual Matrix* (New York: McGraw, 1975), p. 153.

27. Abbott, *Documents of Vatican II*, p. 252.

28. ". . . ei nec definitio Ecclesiae nec certa ratio adversetur. . . ." See Adolphe Tanquerey, *Theologia moralis fundamentalis: De virtutibus et pracceptis* (Paris: Desclée, 1955), 2: 293.

29. See my "Moral Absolutes and the Magisterium," in which I argued that it is not meaningful to say that the Church is infallible in specific issues of morality, in *Absolutes in Moral Theology?* ed. C. Curran (Washington, DC: Corpus Books, 1968).

30. Henry Davis, *Moral and Pastoral Theology* (London and New York: Sheed and Ward, 1949), 1: 107.

31. See Tanquerey, *Theologia Moralis,* p. 287.

32. Abbott, *Documents of Vatican II,* p. 17.

33. 1 Cor. 2:15.

34. *De spiritu et littera,* C 21, M.L. 44,222.

35. "Ed ideo dicendum est quod principaliter nova lex est lex indita, secundario autem est lex scripta," *Summa Theologica* I–II, q. 106, a. 1, in corp.

36. Abbott, *Documents of Vatican II,* p. 34.

37. See Daniel C. Maguire, *"Human Sexuality*: The Book and the Epiphenomenon," in *Proceedings of the Thirty-third Annual Convention of the Catholic Theological Society of America* (June 1978), ed. Luke Salm, F.S.C., pp. 71–75, from which this description of probabilism is taken.

24.

CONTRA SAME-SEX MARRIAGE

Jeff Jordan

Three models concerning the nature of marriage are discernable in the debate over same-sex marriage.[1] While not exhaustive of possible models of marriage, the three are relevant because they represent the understandings of marriage that inform many of the disputants in the same-sex debate.[2] The first is what we might call the "Sacramental" model of marriage. The characteristic propositions of this model include:

1. God instituted marriage as a lifelong relationship between one man and one woman.
2. Marriage is the proper environment for sexuality, procreation, and the rearing of children.
3. Marriage and the family are basic units of society, and are necessary for social stability.

Clearly enough, the Sacramental model sees marriage as essentially heterosexual and monogamous. Also, clearly enough, the Sacramental model, since it entails that God exists, and that there are certain natural laws built into the fabric of creation, is, we might say, "ontologically thick."[3] Propositions (2) and (3) provide the legal rationale for state recognition and support of marriage. Since marriage is necessary for the good of society, the state has ample justification to accord marriage a prominent legal status, which it denies to other relationships that persons may form or join. The social meaning of marriage—the set of expectations generally shared by the members of the society about the sort of relationship that the couple has[4]—is also shaped by (2) and (3) and includes an expectation of sexual intimacy, cooperation in economic matters,

This is a revised version of an article titled "Is It Wrong to Discriminate on the Basis of Homosexuality?" which appeared in the *Journal of Social Philosophy* 25, no. 1 (Spring 1995).

and a subordination of one's individual interests for the interests of the children and the good of the relationship.

The second model is what we might call the "Communional" model. The characteristic propositions of this model include propositions (2) and (3) and:

4. There is a natural or biological teleology apparent between the male and the female—"a two-in-one-flesh Communion of persons that is consummated and actualized by acts that are reproductive in type, whether or not they are reproductive in effect. . . ."[5]

Germain Grisez describes the "two-in-one flesh" idea:

> Each animal is incomplete, for a male or a female individual is only a potential part of the mated pair, which is the complete organism that is capable of reproducing sexually. This is true also of men and women: as mates who engage in sexual intercourse suited to initiate new life, they complete each other, and become an organic unit. In doing so, it is literally true that "they become one flesh."[6]

The Communional model sees individuals as being, in an important respect, biologically incomplete. Marriage is the civil recognition of the social importance of this two-in-one biological completion. This is reminiscent of Aristophanes' "myth of the hermaphrodite" recounted in Plato's *Symposium*: "and so, gentlemen, we are all like pieces of the coins that children break in half for keepsakes—making two out of one, like the flatfish—and each of us is forever seeking the half that will tally with himself."[7]

The Communional model, unlike the Sacramental model, does not entail the existence of God. While the Communional model fits easily within a theological context, it neither entails nor depends upon theology. One might say that biology replaces theology in this model. Since this model can survive in either a naturalistic or theistic setting, it is "ontologically thin." While many proponents of this model are theists, some are not. David Hume, for instance, can be seen as a proponent of the Communional model since he characterizes marriage as "an engagement entered into by mutual consent, and has for its end the propagation of the species, it is evident, that it must be susceptible of all the variety of conditions, which consent establishes, provided they be not contrary to this end."[8] Hume's variety of conditions, by the way, excludes polygamy and divorce as harmful of the teleology of marriage. Like the Sacramental model, the Communional model is essentially heterosexual and monogamous. And like the first model, this model entails that marriage merits a privileged legal status, in good part because marriage provides benefits to society as a whole. These social benefits include providing the best setting for the rearing of the next generation, and the "civilizing" or taming of young males. Marriage is typically an incentive to maturity.

The third model is what we might call the "Transactional" model of marriage. The essential features posited by this model are social in nature, since it sees marriage as a kind of transaction, recognized and regulated by the state, in much the same way as contractual relationships are treated. Marriage is seen as a legal arrangement akin to a contract, though this model need not see marriage as a contract. As Ralph Wedgwood points out, "Marriage need not strictly speaking be a contract, however. Under US law, for example, the rights and obligations of marriage can be changed by new legislation even without the consent of the spouses themselves."[9] The characteristic propositions of this model include:

5.   Marriage is beneficial to the persons involved.
6.   Marriage is a transaction regulated by the state.

The benefits flowing from marriage to the spouses include legal benefits such as preferential spousal immigration treatment, inheritance rights, and spousal health insurance benefits; and emotional benefits such as long-term commitment and sexual intimacy. Importantly, the Transactional model does not entail that marriage is essentially heterosexual and monogamous. Indeed, as persons explore and desire relationships different from those currently available, marriage law, according to this model, should change to accommodate the desires of the prospective spouses. The first two models understand marriage as a static relationship the parameters of which are determined by theology or biology, with procreation accorded a central place in the social meaning of marriage. Procreation is almost an afterthought in the Transactional model. It sees marriage as a largely plastic arrangement that flexes to social innovation, the basic rationale of which is the benefit of the spouses and not to any children involved. This dismissal of procreation as central to the meaning of marriage is seen in the majority opinion of the Massachusetts Supreme Judicial Court in *Goodridge v. Department of Public Health*, when the majority, in paragraph 48, asserted:

> While it is certainly true that many, perhaps most, married couples have children together (assisted or unassisted), it is the exclusive and permanent commitment of the marriage partners to one another, not the begetting of children, that is the sine qua non of civil marriage.[10]

Much of the current debate over the propriety of same-sex marriage involves a clash of these models. Defenders of traditional marriage typically hold to one or the other of first two models, while those supporting the propriety of same-sex marriage hold to a version of the third model.

In what follows I argue that there is good reason to deny legal marital status to same-sex relationships. In particular, I argue that extending legal marital status to same-sex unions is illiberal. This is a surprising argument but, as we'll see, state recognition of same-sex unions violates two fundamental principles of liberalism. By liberalism I mean the tradition associated historically with Hobbes, Locke, Hume, Kant, and Jefferson, and in our day, with Rawls, Dworkin, and Nagel. Roughly, liberalism regards individuals of a state as free and equal citizens, and requires a constitutional democratic polity, with policies and laws the legitimacy of which require the consent of its citizens.

The argument proceeds via two steps. The first step consists in showing that the most promising argument in support of same-sex marriage, the Equality argument, which contends that equality is violated when the state denies legal status to same-sex marriages, fails.[11] This failure is due to two problems. First, the Equality argument has a false premise. The falsity of this premise will be obvious once we highlight a basic principle of liberalism, "that the state should not promote or justify its actions by appeal to controversial conceptions of the good."[12] And second, even if the soundness of the Equality argument were conceded, it has the absurd result of justifying not only same-sex marriage, but also polygyny, polyandry, and polygynandry.[13] That is, the Equality argument, if successful, disconnects marriage from the traditional requirement of different sexes. But once that uncoupling is done, there's no principled way to maintain the traditional requirement that marriage is limited to a couple. In short, anything goes.

The second step consists in an argument that the case for same-sex marriage requires the state to adopt a controversial model of the nature and value of marriage. In brief, the case for same-sex marriage requires the Transactional model. But the Communional model is just as compatible with liberalism as is the Transactional model. Thus, the extension of legal status to same-sex marriages requires that the state adopt a controversial model of the nature and value of marriage as the correct model of marriage. Once again, the case for same-sex marriage is exposed as illiberal.

Along the way, I also examine two common objections to the denial of legal status to same-sex marriage. One is the claim that homosexuals are uniquely harmed by traditional marriage. The other is the claim that the prohibition contra same-sex marriage is strictly analogous to racist prohibitions against mixed-race marriages. Both objections, as we'll see, come apart under scrutiny.

THE EQUALITY ARGUMENT: PART I

In its most careful version the Equality argument asserts that the essential rational for marriage is found in homosexual couples as well as heterosexual couples. What is this essential rationale? It is simply, argues Ralph Wedgwood, "that many people *want* to be married, where this desire to marry is typically a serious desire that deserves to be respected."[14] A desire is serious just in case it is a desire "of a certain kind, such that there is widespread agreement there are good reasons for the state to support and assist people's attempts to fulfill such desires, and strong reasons for the state not to impede or hinder people's attempts to fulfill such desires."[15] Moreover, "it is strong evidence that a desire is of this kind if the desire is widely and strongly held, and if few people sincerely resent those who succeed in fulfilling the desire."[16] Further, Wedgwood contends, the desire of homosexual couples to wed is every bit as real as that of heterosexual couples, "many same-sex couples have exactly the same desire, to make a mutual commitment of this kind, as opposite-sex couples."[17] One might object that the desire to wed typically found in homosexual couples is not the same as that found in heterosexual couples. Desires are not so coarse as to be describable as just the desire to wed. One desire is a desire to wed someone of the opposite sex, while the other is a desire to wed someone of the same sex. And these are not the same. But let's dismiss this objection, and take the desire to wed to be sui generis.

If the essential rationale of marriage is simply the serious desire to wed, the Equality argument looks like this:

7. The state should support certain serious desires—call the set of serious desires deserving state support, α. And,
8. the desire to marry is an element of α. So,
9. the state should support marriage. And,
10. same-sex desire to wed and opposite-sex desire to wed are such that any public policy toward the one is morally permissible if and only if that same policy toward the other is morally permissible. So,
11. the state should support same-sex marriages.

The Equality argument provides a rationale for state support of marriage as such, and a rationale for state support of same-sex marriages. Again, as Wedgwood puts it:

> So legal marriage really is indispensable for enabling these couples to fulfill this serious desire. If marriage also imposes no serious burdens on anyone else, and violates no principle of justice, then this fact would justify the institution of marriage.[18]

Wedgwood's provision that marriage is justified, given the desire to wed, if it also imposes no serious burdens on anyone else is infelicitously stated. The legal status of marriage may impose a serious burden as long as that burden is morally justified. Eminent domain imposes serious burdens, but some times it is fully justified.

Let's state the obvious: marriage provides legal benefits to those married. Many of the legal benefits involved in marriage are subsidies provided by the state to the spouses, done at the expense of the public. Such public subsidies are not cost free. For example, to expand the class of persons eligible for spousal health insurance increases the cost of the program, or to expand the class of persons eligible for family-leave benefits increases the costs of that program. Or consider taxes: for every tax advantage provided married couples (say the marriage exemption to the federal estate tax), the tax burden of unmarried persons or corporations increases, since this kind of tax relief is not likely to spur economic expansion.[19] For the state to subsidize one group by decreasing its tax burden typically requires an increase of the burden borne by some other group. And this is true also with public subsidies that are not directly financial. Consider legal quotas for immigration. To provide preferential treatment to spouses means that spouses "jump to the head of the line," which implies that another citizen's relative or friend is lower on the queue than she otherwise would have been in the absence of that benefit.

Public subsidies are burdensome. As such they should be carefully rationed to both maximize the good of society at large, and minimize the increased burden on those not receiving the subsidy. Indeed, the liberal principle of distributing public subsidies would require that the practice or arrangement subsidized provide a vital good to society as a whole, including those who bear an increased burden because of the subsidy. More fully, the Legitimacy Principle for Public Subsidies would be:

> A public subsidy of a practice or institution is legitimate if and only if subsidizing that practice or institution is necessary for producing a vital good for society, which good cannot be produced or secured in a less burdensome way.

That the subsidy is beneficial to those who receive it is not sufficient to justify it if someone else, who is not subsidized, is subjected to increased burdens or costs without comparable benefits in return. There must be a benefit flowing to society generally if the state is justified in providing a public subsidy. The principle governing public subsidies is a corollary of the basic liberal principle that the state should not justify its actions by appeal to controversial conceptions of the good. Why is this latter principle basic? Because persons, fully informed and fully rational, could reasonably reject state actions justified on the basis of controversial conceptions of the good.[20] What's meant by fully informed and fully rational? Roughly, we can say that someone is fully informed as long as she is aware of all the facts and arguments relevant to the issue at hand; and we can say that someone is fully rational as long as his deliberation employing those facts and arguments is not skewed or biased by considerations immaterial to the issue at hand. While the notion of a fully informed and fully rational deliberator is an idealization, it is useful, since political legitimacy requires principles that reflect the fact that citizens are free and equal, and should be subject only to rules and principles that, from the point of view of being fully informed and fully rational, no one could reasonably reject. If someone fully informed and fully rational could reasonably reject a principle, then that principle is illegitimate. Persons, fully informed and fully rational, could reasonably reject burdensome public subsidies that benefit only those who are subsidized. Public subsidies that provide a vital good to society, however, are such that no one, fully informed and fully rational, could reasonably reject them.

Recognizing this point requires a fine-tuning of the Equality argument:

7'. The state should *subsidize* the satisfaction of certain serious desires—call the set of serious desires satisfaction of which deserve state subsidy, α.[21] And,

8. the desire to marry is an element of α. So,

9'. the state should *subsidize* marriage. And,

10. same-sex desire to wed and opposite-sex desire to wed are such that any public policy toward the one is morally permissible if and only if that same policy toward the other is morally permissible. So,

11'. the state should *subsidize* same-sex marriages.

Let's grant (7'). The Legitimacy Principle for Public Subsidies however conditions our grant. Membership in α is predicated upon legal recognition of the desire providing a vital good to society as a whole, including those who will bear an increased burden because of the subsidy. Proposition (8) seems obvious enough since two vital benefits flowing to society from marriage are that of procreation and rearing of the next generation within a two-parent family, and the protection of children.[22] And given (7') and (8), (9') follows.

But what about (10)? Here the Equality argument breaks down. Homosexual relationships do not, indeed cannot, provide the vital goods to society that heterosexual ones provide. Apart from artificial insemination homosexual couples cannot procreate, and thereby generate the next generation. Moreover, consisting of the same sex, it is far from clear that homosexual couples can provide the gender-differentiated parenting important for human development.[23] Marriage of a man and a woman, however, provides a father and a mother for any child produced or adopted.[24] Even an aged heterosexual couple can provide a father and mother for any child adopted. In addition, same-sex marriage would not provide the protection of children associated with traditional marriage. Heterosexuals present a high risk of producing out-of-wedlock children. This risk can be dramatically lowered if fidelity is maintained among married heterosexuals. Even infertile married heterosexual couples probably provide this protection, since it is rare that an infertile couple consists of both spouses being infertile. As long as the fertile spouse remains faithful, there is no risk of an out-of-wedlock child.[25] Homosexuals, however, whether faithful or not, present almost no risk of producing out-of-wedlock children. So, again, there is no comparable social good gained from same-sex marriages.

Wedgwood suggests that there may be social goods associated with marriage in addition to procreation and the protection of children: "Single people are more likely to commit suicide, to suffer from poor health, to become dependent on public assistance, and so on."[26] The idea is that empirical studies show that the emotional benefits generated by marriage result in lower incidences of social pathologies, and these lower incidences translate into lower public costs. So, perhaps, there are social goods provided by same-sex marriage, such that same-sex marriage deserves the same public subsidies enjoyed by heterosexual marriage.

Wedgwood's claim is problematic, since the cited studies and the populations surveyed would have understood marriage as traditionally understood. There are no studies showing that legal same-sex marriages provide the benefits, emotional or social, that heterosexual ones provide.[27] And without question same-sex marriages cannot provide the vital social goods of procreation and protection for children that heterosexual marriages typically provide.

Since heterosexual marriages provide vital social goods not provided by homosexual relationships, (10) is false. It is not true that there is a moral equivalence between state recognition of homosexual and heterosexual desires to marry. The latter provides vital social goods that the former does not. Hence, state subsidy of the one but not the other accords with the liberal principle governing public subsidies. For a state to extend legal marital status to same-sex couples, would be illiberal, since the state would be granting a burdensome public subsidy without receiving any compensating social benefit.

THE EQUALITY ARGUMENT: PART II

The second problem with the Equality argument is that, if sound, we find ourselves with an embarrassment of matrimonial riches, since the reasoning involved in the Equality argument supports a parallel argument justifying poly-marriages, whether polygyny, polyandry, or polygynandry. Groups of people can enter into transactions just as couples do. Indeed, if the essential rationale of marriage is simply the serious desire to wed, it seems arbitrary to hold that two people can have that serious desire, but three could not. In other words, of the two primary restrictions imposed on traditional marriage—heterosexuality and monogamy—the Equality argument seeks to lift the former restriction, but, if successful, a parallel argument can be used equally well to lift the latter. This embarrassment of matrimonial riches is what we might call the "Anything Goes" problem. In short, if the Equality argument is sound, then anything goes. Since the concern of this paper is the propriety of same-sex marriage and not poly-marriage, I assume without argument that the latter is problematic.[28]

The proponent of the Equality argument has to produce a stopper to prevent the Anything Goes problem. Wedgwood, to his credit, admits there's a problem:

> It would be presumptuous to deny that anyone could have a serious desire to have more than one marriage at the same time. It seems perfectly possible for someone to have the most serious religious or personal reasons for wanting this. So, offhand, my version of the fundamental argument for same-sex marriage seems to support a parallel argument for polygamy.[29]

Wedgwood's stopper consists of two claims: there is little demand for polygamy, and "there is a serious concern that polygamy would have uncontroversial harmful effects, especially for women."[30] Wedgwood's stopper is remarkably porous. First, it is very likely that were matrimonial law revised to accommodate same-sex marriage, fundamentalist Mormons and Muslims will seek to have their desires for polygamous marriages accommodated by matrimonial law as well. Second, consider the concern that polygamy (or more narrowly, polygyny) may be harmful to women, keeping in mind that marriage is a voluntary arrangement among consenting adults. Even if it were the case that polygamy is a net harm to the consenting participants, it is far from clear that that is a good reason to deny legal status. Paternalism does not sit well with liberalism. Moreover, whatever historical evidence there may be that polygamy has been harmful to the participants is irrelevant. There are no cases of legal polygamous marriage in a liberal state, with all the protections of modern property laws, so there is no relevant historical evidence that polygamy is a net harm to the participants. Wedgwood's stopper stops nothing.

What's needed is a reason to think that the lifting of the quantity restriction would either harm society, or that the public subsidy involved in legal recognition is not warranted because poly-marriages provide no vital good to society. Jonathan Rauch, in his 2004 book, *Gay Marriage*, takes on the Anything Goes problem.[31] Rauch argues that polygyny would harm society, since it would violate an important legal concern. Rauch first asserts "as a mathematical necessity (given that polyandry is extremely rare), for one man to have two wives means that some other man will have none. Moreover, the higher the man's status, the more wives he gets."[32] This would result in a shortage of available women, and in a population of low-status unmarried men. Polygyny would result in a skewed market in which the supply of available women is diminished. A high sex ratio—when there are many more men than women—is a recipe, Rauch claims, for social problems. So, the state has a good reason to deny legal status to poly-marriages: "The law's interest is only in making sure that, in a world full of romantic disappointment, we can all find plenty of other candidates if our first choice falls through."[33] "Everyone," Rauch claims, "should have a reasonable chance of marrying somebody, as opposed to nobody, or everybody, or anybody."[34]

This is a remarkable assertion; so let's dub it "Rauch's principle":

The state has a legitimate role in ensuring that everyone has an opportunity of marriage.

Rauch's principle is the foundation upon which he erects his contention that legal poly-marriages would be harmful to society. But how plausible is Rauch's principle?

It is just about as implausible as it could be. For one thing, is it at all plausible that the force of law should be employed to advance the matrimonial prospects of individuals? For another, it erroneously assumes that the pool of marriage candidates is constituted only by the subject's preferences. It neglects that the preferences of others also play a crucial role in whether one has any real opportunity of marriage. That is, Jones may be attracted to Smith, but Smith may not be attracted to Jones. It's conceivable that no one finds Jones an attractive marriage partner. Hence his pool is empty. And there is nothing that the state could or should do to remedy this misfortune.

Indeed Rauch's principle may inadvertently support poly-marriages. Imagine a society with twenty adult females, and twenty-one adult males, all of whom are heterosexual and desire to marry. Clearly, if Rauch's principle was true, polyandry or polygynandry would be legally necessitated in our imagined society, otherwise the odd man out would have no marriage prospects at all.

Moreover, Rauch's claim that a high sex ratio is a ready recipe for social problems is dubious. There's good evidence that with a high sex ratio—many more men than women—marriage is commonplace and cohabitation is rare, divorce is infrequent, and children are more often raised in two-parent homes, with women playing the more traditional roles.[35] With a high sex ratio "women have a lot of bargaining power and so find it easier to get men to marry and stay with them. . . ."[36] In the absence of evidence that the social ills produced by a high sex ratio outweigh the social benefits associated with it, Rauch's claim is best rejected.

Although I have provided no proof that there is no stopper to the Anything Goes problem, I have provided good reason to think that two prominent attempts to blunt the problem are abject failures. It is safe to conclude that the Equality argument, if sound, has the absurd result of justifying poly-marriages as well as same-sex ones. The Anything Goes problem is a bane to the Equality argument.

CONDEMNED TO LONELINESS?

Rauch presents a clever wrinkle to the appeal to equality that's worth considering. Gays are uniquely harmed, he contends, by limiting legal marriage to unions that are heterosexual and monogamous:

> If, therefore, the rule is that the law should give everyone a realistic hope of marrying somebody he loves—not zero people, not two people, not three people, but one person—there is no other group in the country whose situation is comparable to homosexuals', because only homosexuals are barred, by law, from marrying anybody they love. The gay situation is unique. It is not that gays have to settle for their second or third choice. It is that gay people's set of choices is the null set.[37]

Hence equality requires that gays be treated as everyone else and not exposed to a singular harm. David Boonin makes a similar point when he claims:

> A law forbidding same-sex marriage . . . says that a heterosexual man can marry
> any member of the sex he is attracted to while a homosexual man can marry any
> member of the sex he is *not* attracted to, and that a heterosexual man is forbid-
> den to marry any member of the sex he is not attracted to while a homosexual
> man is forbidden to marry any member of the sex that he is attracted *to*.[38]

I suspect that Boonin does not really mean what he says. No law anywhere has
ever granted anyone a license to marry "any member of the sex he is attracted
to." Marriages under such a legal regime would be "nasty, brutish, and short."
Boonin's point, like Rauch's, is that limiting legal marriage to heterosexual
unions singularly harms gays.

Does limiting legal marriage to unions that are monogamous and heterosexual uniquely harm gays? There's reason to think not. Since the claim that it does
presupposes Rauch's principle, it suffers from "implausibility by association."
More important, someone desiring a poly-marriage is not settling for his second
or third choice if he is legally allowed to marry only one wife. The poly person's
desires are frustrated by the monogamy restriction every bit as much as the gay
person's desires are by the heterosexual restriction. Does this mean that marital
nonconformists—whether gay or poly—are condemned to loneliness? No. In a
society in which cohabitation is legally possible, same-sex cohabitation is possible, as is group cohabitation. Persons with no desire to marry have other options.

THE BASIC PRINCIPLE OF LIBERALISM
AND MODELS OF MARRIAGE

Liberalism's basic raison d'être is the principle that the state should not promote or justify its actions by appeal to controversial conceptions of the good.
Expressed a bit differently, the state should be neutral between competing conceptions of the good. Now, of course, this principle, the Basic Principle, we
might call it, is itself a moral principle, and is itself controversial. Still, a sub-
scription to liberalism implies an acceptance of the Basic Principle. What follows for state recognition of marriage, given a commitment to liberalism?
Clearly enough, the state ought to be neutral regarding the nature of marriage.
The Basic Principle requires that the state forswear ontologically thick models and restrict itself to models that are ontologically thin. For this reason, the
Sacramental model is a nonstarter for the liberal as a justification for state
action, since the Sacramental model implies that God exists. While the Communional model and the Transactional model present competing views of the
nature of marriage, they are both ontologically thin. Hence, the Basic Principle of liberalism requires the state to be neutral between the Communional
model and the Transactional model of marriage.

Notice however that legal recognition of same-sex marriage is compatible with the Transactional model (but not required by it), while it is incom-

patible with the Communional model. Proposition (4) presents an insurmountable obstacle to same-sex marriage. Proposition (4) implies that a union is a valid marriage only if it is a member of the kind whose characteristic actions are reproductive in type, even if not in effect. Hence (4) is compatible with infertile heterosexual unions, but not with same-sex unions. The latter is not a kind of union that can in principle be procreative, while infertile heterosexual marriages are a kind of union that in principle could be procreative. Proposition (4) accommodates the one but not the other.

The case for same-sex marriage is at home only within the Transactional model. For the state to recognize same-sex marriage, then, requires an appeal to a controversial view of marriage as a justification for that state action. By recognizing same-sex marriage the state would, in effect, declare that the Transactional model is correct, and that the Communional model is incorrect. In this way the state would be violating its desirable neutrality regarding controversial views of the nature of marriage. Once again, the push for same-sex marriage is exposed as illiberal.

One might object that by not extending legal recognition the state would, in effect, declare that the Communional model is correct and that the Transactional model is incorrect. The desirable neutrality of liberalism, that is, is illusory when it comes to same-sex marriage.

This objection neglects a crucial asymmetry. The Transactional model is compatible with same-sex marriage; it is also compatible with legal recognition not extended to homosexual unions. The Communional model, however, is incompatible with the extension of legal recognition to homosexual unions. The Transactional model does not entail legal recognition; while the Communional model does entail no legal recognition. Thus, for a liberal state to not extend legal recognition is consistent with the desirable neutrality between the competing models, but to extend legal recognition is inconsistent with liberal neutrality.

AS BAD AS ANTIMISCEGENATION?

A common objection to the refusal to extend legal status to same-sex marriage is that it is morally equivalent to laws precluding mixed-race marriages:

> People today forget how the language now being used against same-sex couples' equal marriage rights not so long ago was used against interracial couples—denying people's equal human dignity and freedom to share in the rights and responsibilities of marriage.[39]

The idea here is that arguments contra same-sex marriage are in the same boat as the laws and arguments contra mixed-race marriage that were prevalent in the United States decades ago. Since the latter were morally reprehensible, so too are the former.

This is serious indictment, if true. Is it? There's conclusive reason to think not. For one thing, it's a breathtaking claim that ignores the historical context of antimiscegenation laws. Antimiscegenation laws were just one part of a regime designed to oppress blacks. Whether education, or employment, or public accommodations, or housing, or politics, a society-wide system was in place that violated the civil rights of blacks. This violation was punctuated by legally tolerated violence as a way of ensuring compliance. To claim that the denial of legal recognition of same-sex marriage is akin to the reign of Jim Crow is astonishingly inaccurate, and belittles the sacrifices made in the long struggle against racial injustice.

Every argument supporting antimiscegenation was in historical fact either motivated by racist attitudes or intended to harm blacks.[40] The reasons for supporting antimiscegenation were inextricably linked to racism. But there is nothing like this with reasons or arguments contra same-sex marriage. Arguments contra same-sex marriage need not be motivated by animus toward gays, nor intended to harm gays. Let me briefly sketch six arguments contra same-sex marriage, any one of which are acceptable without moral blemish. By sketching these arguments I suggest nothing about their soundness or cogency, only that one could endorse any of them, without having done anything immoral.

A. The argument from the Communional model. If one believes that this model best represents marriage, then she will naturally favor public policies that exclude same-sex marriage and poly-marriages.

B. The argument from analyticity. One might hold that it is analytically true that a marriage consists of a husband and a wife, and that, necessarily, husbands are male, while wives are female. If one accepts the analyticity of these terms, then one will favoring reserving the term "marriage" for heterosexual unions.

C. The argument from religious doctrine. Traditional Catholicism, many denominations of Protestantism, the Orthodox branch of Judaism, and traditional or Orthodox Islam all assert that homosexual activity is immoral. Hence a "marriage" predicated on that activity is sinful according to the doctrines of these religions. So, a proponent of one of these religious traditions will favor public policies that exclude same-sex marriage.

D. The argument from the freedom of the conscience. Understanding the argument from religious doctrine, and knowing that there are many sincere adherents of religious traditions that assert that homosexual behavior is immoral, one could hold that state endorsement of same-sex marriage unduly tramples the freedom of conscience and religious liberty of those religious believers. Since state recognition is a de facto endorsement, the state, by extending legal recognition, would be declaring that a certain theology was incorrect. While there are theo-

logical disputes in which the state cannot in principle avoid involvement, this is one dispute in which it can and should avoid involvement.

E. The argument from public disagreement. One could hold that deep
social controversies should generally be settled in a liberal society via
legislation, and not by judicial intervention. The latter is permissible
only when fundamental rights are at issue, and one could hold that
there is no fundamental right to same-sex marriage. Both polls and
referendums (witness the popular referendums in two of the more
politically progressive American states—Hawaii in 1998, California
in 2000—both of which passed by substantial majorities laws precluding same-sex marriage) provide sufficient evidence that a substantial majority of Americans disagree with same-sex marriage, and
hence should be excluded. Knowing this, one would naturally favor
public policies that exclude same-sex marriage, as this respects and
reflects the majority will.

F. The cumulative case argument. One could adopt any combination of
(A) through (E).

Excepting the argument from religious doctrine, a liberal could invoke any of
these as acceptable arguments in the public square. No such list of arguments
in support of antimiscegenation is possible. There are no arguments or reasons
supporting antimiscegenation laws that one could accept without having done
anything wrong. But obviously there are reasons or arguments supporting traditional marriage that one can accept without having done anything wrong.

Could an argument that's neither motivated by animus toward gays nor
intended to harm gays still be akin to antimiscegenation arguments if it in fact
harms gays? One might argue that the legal exclusion of gays from legal marriage frustrates the desire to wed that some gays have, and that frustration is
harm. So, even though an argument contra same-sex marriage is neither motivated by animus toward gays, nor intended to harm gays, its effect—providing justification for a public policy excluding same-sex marriage—is harmful,
and hence morally problematic.

This will not do. The causation of harm is not always immoral or a matter calling for compensation or redress. Revisit our imaginary society popu-
lated with twenty adult females and twenty-one adult males. Suppose twenty
monogamous marriages occur. One man desiring to wed has that desire frustrated. Indeed, suppose in our imagined society that poly-marriages are illegal,
so that man's desire is legally frustrated. While it may be true that the unwed
man is harmed, it is also clear that his misfortune is due no legal redress or
compensation, and that the forty who married, and in doing so brought about
the harm, did nothing wrong. Just because harm occurs does not imply that an
immoral action has occurred, or that a right was violated, or that legal redress
is appropriate.

Policies or practices that have a disparate impact on some group may require a heightened legal or moral scrutiny but clearly such policies or practices are sometimes morally and legally permissible, even morally mandatory. For instance, if we were casting for *Othello*, our casting call for particular parts would have a disparate impact on various racial groups. Even so, we do nothing wrong in adhering to a practice that enhances the employment prospects of one racial group and diminishes the prospects of another. Generally speaking, if the policy or practice, which produces the disparate impact, is itself necessary for a socially desirable outcome—a color-blind casting would diminish the value of viewing *Othello*—then the policy or practice is justified.

The upshot is this: Arguments and reasons employed in support of antimiscegenation policies were always morally problematic or factually misguided, since it is hard to imagine such an argument or reason that was neither motivated by animus toward blacks, nor intended to harm blacks. Arguments or reasons employed in support of traditional marriage are crucially and relevantly different. It is obvious that such arguments and reasons can be advanced without any antigay motivation or intent to harm gays. This is a significant disanalogy, which demonstrates that the common charge that arguments in support of traditional marriage are close relatives to racist arguments is false. Why then is it commonly leveled? Probably because it is an attempt to piggyback on the moral stature of the civil rights movement in the United States, thereby gaining the moral high ground in the public debate over same-sex marriage. It is always advantageous in combat to control the high ground, and one way to gain an advantage in a debate over public policy is to cast your opponents and their proposals as hopelessly immoral. If this diagnosis is correct, then it is likely that the charge is nothing more than overheated rhetoric masking the lack of argumentative support, and obscuring the relevant issues.

LIBERALISM AND SAME-SEX MARRIAGE

Liberalism does not require legal recognition of same-sex marriage.[41] In fact, it cannot, since legal recognition is incompatible with at least two principles of liberalism—the Legitimacy Principle for Public Subsidies and the Basic Principle of liberalism. The push for legal recognition of same-sex marriage, though often packaged as being motivated or required by liberal reasons, is in fact illiberal. As has been so often the case with the illiberal, the push for legal recognition is also Orwellian in its means, as the ballot box is disregarded in favor of judicial fiat. Litigation replaces legislation. In any case, it is now clear that even if marriage is seen as nothing but a transaction, same-sex marriages are not justified within a liberal society.[42]

NOTES

1. By marriage I mean the civil arrangement found in England, and other Western countries, since at least the thirteenth century. This arrangement, recognized by the state, is formed by mutual consent and, traditionally, restricted to monogamous and heterosexual unions. See James Q. Wilson, *The Marriage Problem: How Our Culture Weakens Families* (New York: HarperCollins, 2002), pp. 65–105. All three of the models I discuss see marriage as satisfying this minimal characterization.

2. James Witte examines five prominent models of marriage, from the Catholic model of the mid-twelfth century to the contemporary contractual model, in western Europe and the United States. See his *From Sacrament to Contract: Marriage, Religion, and Law in the Western Tradition* (Louisville, KY: Westminster John Knox Press, 1997).

3. Typically proponents of the Sacramental model hold that God has created humans with certain psychological traits and propensities, such that conforming to the divine design facilitates human well-being.

4. On the notion of the social meaning of marriage see Ralph Wedgwood, "The Fundamental Argument for Same-Sex Marriage," *Journal of Political Philosophy* 7, no. 3 (1999): 229.

5. Robert P. George, "'Same-Sex' Marriage and 'Moral Neutrality,'" in *The Clash of Orthodoxies: Law, Religion, and Morality in Crisis* (Wilmington, DE: ISI Books, 2001), p. 77, and see his *In Defense of Natural Law* (Oxford: Clarendon Press, 1999), pp. 139–83, 213–18. See also Gerard Bradley, "Same-Sex Marriage: Our Final Answer?" *Notre Dame Journal of Law, Ethics & Public Policy* 14, no. 2 (2000): 729–52.

6. Germain Grisez, *The Way of the Lord Jesus*, vol. 2, *Living a Christian Life* (Quincy, IL: Franciscan Press, 1993), p. 570.

7. Plato, *Symposium*, trans. Michael Joyce (London: Everyman's Library, 1935), p. 191d.

8. David Hume, "Of Polygamy and Divorce," in *Essays: Moral, Political, and Literary* (1742; reprint, London: Longmans, Green, 1882), p. 231. By "propagation of the species" I take Hume to mean procreation.

9. Wedgwood, "The Fundamental Argument for Same-Sex Marriage," p. 231.

10. *Goodridge v. Department of Public Health*, 440 Mass. 309 (2003).

11. I take Wedgwood's 1999 article, "The Fundamental Argument for Same-Sex Marriage," as a guide to the Equality argument.

12. Wedgwood, "The Fundamental Argument for Same-Sex Marriage," p. 225.

13. I understand polygyny as one husband with several wives, polyandry as one wife with several husbands, polygynandry as group marriage, whether same-sex or opposite-sex, and polygamy as marriages taking the form of either polygyny or polygynandry. I will use the term "poly-marriages" as a general term for either polygamous marriages or polygynandry.

14. Wedgwood, "The Fundamental Argument for Same-Sex Marriage," p. 235.

15. Ibid.

16. Ibid.

17. Ibid., p. 240.

18. Ibid., p. 236.

19. Notoriously, under the US income tax code married couples often face higher rates of taxation than they would if single. This "marriage penalty" has of late been reduced.

20. For more on legitimizing rules and laws within a liberal state, see Thomas Nagel, *Equality and Partiality* (New York: Oxford University Press, 1991), pp. 33–40; John Rawls, *Justice As Fairness: A Restatement*, ed. Erin Kelly (Cambridge, MA: Harvard University Press, 2001), pp. 40–41, 89–92; and Rawls's *Political Liberalism* (New York: Columbia University Press, 1993), lectures IV and V.

21. Wedgwood suggests that the legal benefits associated with state recognition are not essential to the institution of marriage and so "a justification of marriage need not by itself

involve a justification of these additional benefits. Instead, there should be a separate justification for attaching these benefits to marriage."

See Wedgwood, "The Fundamental Argument for Same-Sex Marriage," pp. 231–32. Two points in response: the case for same-sex marriage is often in part an appeal to access to the legal benefits associated with civil marriage. Second, legal recognition itself is a benefit and is inextricably linked with various other legal benefits, so to counsel separation as Wedgwood does is impracticable.

22. See, for instance, David Popenoe, *Life without Father: Compelling New Evidence That Fatherhood and Marriage Are Indispensable for the Good of Children and Society* (New York: Free Press, 1996); Judith Wallerstein, Julia Lewis, and Sandra Blakeslee, *The Unexpected Legacy of Divorce: A 25-Year Landmark Study* (New York: Hyperion, 2000); and Barbara Dafoe Whitehead, "Dan Quayle Was Right: The Social-Science Evidence Is In—Though It May Benefit the Adults Involved. The Dissolution of Intact Two-Parent Families Is Harmful to Large Numbers of Children," *Atlantic Monthly* (April 1993), and her *The Divorce Culture* (New York: Alfred A. Knopf, 1997). Each of these works presents strong evidence that an intact, two-parent home is generally the best environment for the rearing of children.

23. Even if a homosexual couple provides gender-differentiated parenting, via a kind of role-playing, it is questionable whether that's sufficient for full human development. See Popenoe, *Life without Father*, p. 146.

24. I owe this point to Maggie Gallagher, "What Marriage Is For: Children Need Mothers and Fathers" *Weekly Standard* 8, no. 45 (2003): 25.

25. Ibid.

26. Wedgwood, "The Fundamental Argument for Same-Sex Marriage," p. 235.

27. Of course, same-sex marriages may provide the same emotional benefits as heterosexual marriages demonstratively do. We just do not know. In any case, I assume without argument that it is very likely that any social benefit associated with the legal recognition of same-sex marriage would be significantly outweighed by the harm produced by the Anything Goes problem, introduced in the next section.

28. For an argument against poly-marriages, one might begin with Hume, "Of Polygamy and Divorce."

29. Wedgwood, "The Fundamental Argument for Same-Sex Marriage," p. 242.

30. Ibid.

31. Jonathan Rauch, *Gay Marriage: Why It Is Good for Gays, Good for Straights, and Good for America* (New York: Times Books, 2004), pp. 123–37.

32. Ibid., p. 129.

33. Ibid., pp. 126–27.

34. Ibid., p. 136.

35. Marcia Guttentag and Paul F. Secord, *Too Many Women? The Sex Ratio Question* (Newbury Park, CA: Sage Publications, 1983), pp. 19–33, 43–49, 153–71.

36. Wilson, *The Marriage Problem*, p. 47.

37. Rauch, *Gay Marriage*, p. 127.

38. David Boonin, "Same-Sex Marriage and the Argument from Public Disagreement," *Journal of Social Philosophy* 30, no. 2 (1999): 256.

39. Evan Wolfson, "Why We Should Fight for the Freedom to Marry," in *Same-Sex Marriage: Pro and Con*, ed. Andrew Sullivan (New York: Vintage Books, 1997), p. 131.

40. Were there arguments in support of antimiscegenation that were not predicated on racism? Perhaps some supporters of antimiscegenation based their views on arguments gleaned from science or theology. But these arguments were factually misguided, and the propensity to entertain them was, I suspect, largely facilitated by racism.

41. A note on Federalism: Some proponents of same-sex marriage in the United States suggest that the states should be used as social laboratories, with some legalizing it and others precluding it, and we can then observe whether same-sex marriage is socially pernicious, beneficial,

or benign. The problem with this proposal is illustrated by a similar "experiment" done with "no-fault" divorce laws, which are now generally seen as socially pernicious, but were adopted by nearly all the states less than twenty years after adoption by one state. The effects of a social policy can take decades to reveal themselves, but once the proverbial camel has its nose under the tent, it may be too late to keep it out.

42. I thank Robin Andreasen, Bob Baird, Joel Pust, Mike Rea, Kate Rogers, and David Silver for their generous comments. Problems that remain are mine alone.

25.

HOMOSEXUALITY AND MARRIAGE

John B. Cobb Jr.

There is [a] segment of society whose sexual explorations have not been . . . readily accepted. I refer to those whose sexual desires are directed to persons of their own sex. Millions of parents who are quite content for their children to be living in heterosexual partnerships, even when they are not sanctioned by marriage, would be shocked and appalled if they found that the partners were of the same sex.

There are many reasons for this shock. First, most people in this society, even those with homosexual inclinations, are "homophobic." That is, their self-understanding as sexual beings is challenged and disturbed by the encounter with homosexuality, both in themselves and in others, and they react with fear. This is true of many Christian parents. But even if homophobia is overcome, there are still reasons for shock. Most parents want not only children, but grandchildren as well. To learn that the sexual practice of one's child will not lead in that direction is disappointing. Perhaps more important, parents want their children to have lives that are as easy and happy as possible in an inevitably difficult world. Any realistic appraisal of this society indicates that homosexuals have enormous handicaps imposed on them. The hostility of parents is often one of these handicaps, but even when parents are supportive, the obstacles are still immense.

The church's teaching is one source of the social hostility that causes so much of the suffering of homosexuals. The question today is whether the church should continue the teaching that contributes so massively to this suffering or should recognize that homosexuals also have the right to love.

The church's unfortunate tendency to legalism has come to the fore on this topic more than on any other. Indeed, the quality of the discussion in recent

Reprinted from *Matters of Life and Death.* Used by permission from Westminster John Knox Press.

years has been distressing. It seems that many people have simply assumed that homosexual practice is totally unacceptable and that therefore it must be forbidden in the Bible. When challenged, they have surveyed the entire literature to find every negative reference, actual or imagined. Whereas the Levitical code has generally been supposed to represent the kind of law set aside in the new covenant, its condemnation of homosexuals is often cited as evidence that homosexuality is not an acceptable practice among Christians. Most of those who use Leviticus against homosexuals do not take so seriously its much more central call for a year of jubilee, in which property rights are to revert to the original owner. Paul's scattered and unsystematic comments are turned into a set of ethical rules and principles on this issue in a way that they are not on other topics.

It is particularly ironic that many Christians are prepared to set aside the direct and explicit teaching by Jesus on divorce but cling rigidly to obscure and questionable sources as justification for condemning homosexuality. There is nothing "biblical" or responsibly theological about such practice. The question to be asked is why so many Christians are searching so hard for biblical condemnation of homosexuality as opposed to the question of whether some biblical authors objected to it. That is why the study of homophobia is so important and appropriate today.

If the irrational fear and hostility that homosexuality arouses were overcome, the problem of acceptance would still not be easily solved. The question remains, What ideals should the church hold up before those who find themselves sexually attracted primarily to members of their own sex?

[The classic Christian ideal is] of a man and a woman who have only one sexual partner in their lives and whose sexual intercourse is exclusively within marriage. As mutual fulfillment of the partners was more fully recognized as essential to the ideal marriage, divorce and remarriage came to be accepted. The next step is for Christians to recognize that, as long as society encourages the delay of marriage far beyond the time of sexual maturation, it needs to approve temporary and provisional bondings that involve real mutual commitment and love.

The ideal of marriage, whether permanent or serial, has been deeply associated with the raising of children. For many homosexuals this is not a practical option. Some features of the classic Christian ideal are closed to them, so that even in a wholly unprejudiced society they will be in some measure deprived. On the other hand, many heterosexuals choose not to have children of their own or find that they are unable to do so. And, in an unprejudiced society, homosexuals are able to adopt children or even to bring up their own children. There are limitations built into the situation of the homosexual with respect to what has traditionally been sought in marriage; in a supportive society, however, these need not be extensive.

But even if some of the most meaningful possibilities of life for the heterosexual are denied the homosexual, this certainly need not mean that additional burdens and restrictions should be imposed! It seems, rather, that the church's task is to help the homosexual envision positive scenarios for a happy future, scenarios that order the sexual life to wider purposes without simply denying or repressing it.

In a wholly unprejudiced society it would be pointless to mention any disadvantage of homosexuality if the division between heterosexuals and homosexuals were an absolutely clear and fixed one. But it is not. There are many people who have sexual attraction toward some members of both sexes. Today, sexual fulfillment has become for many people an end, even *the* end, in itself, encouraging bisexuals to act out both aspects of their feelings. But if sexuality is viewed in a wider context, then other matters besides desire should be considered in deciding on how to express one's sexuality. The potential joy of being a parent and of bringing up the child together with the other parent should be factored in. Furthermore, in this highly prejudiced society, there are obviously other reasons for expressing only one's heterosexual feelings!

Factoring these considerations into the decision, however, should not involve social pressure toward marriage without regard to real feelings. The mere capability of having intercourse with a member of the opposite sex does not suffice to favor a heterosexual lifestyle over a homosexual one. If sexual desire for members of the same sex is clearly stronger, a heterosexual marriage will fall far short of the ideal. Often homosexually inclined spouses will be unfaithful, and even if they are faithful in act, important elements will be lacking in the marriage. The ideal includes a depth and warmth of personal relations that extend far beyond sexual intercourse but that are also hardly separable from sexual passion. Mere "performance" is not enough. The fulfillment of both partners will be truncated.

It is important to realize that this consideration is a relatively recent one. Through most of history, in most societies, procreation and property played the central roles in marriage, not mutual fulfillment. Death rates, especially among children, were high, and the replenishment or expansion of the population taking into account this high death rate took priority for the community as a whole over personal feelings. Raising a family was not an optional pleasure or privilege, but one's central duty to society. Although women other than prostitutes were strictly forbidden sexual activity outside of marriage, many societies had little objection to men seeking sexual pleasure with women other than their wives, or even with men, as long as they fulfilled their social duties of raising a family. Marriage itself was not, for most women or men, one option among others. Same-sex preferences were not seen as a reason for abstaining from marriage.

The global situation has now changed. Most countries, and the world as a whole, have more reason to be concerned about too many births than about too few. This is chiefly because modern medicine keeps alive many of the babies who in past ages would have died. This is a great gain in itself, but when it is not accompanied by other changes in cultural habits, the result is a terrible curse. Population growth rates point toward catastrophe!

In this context, the disinclination of a portion of the population to propagate the species is no longer something socially negative. Indeed, it relieves pressures, allowing those who do want to give birth to children more space in which to do so. Society as a whole, therefore, has no reason to push unwilling homosexuals to act as if they were heterosexual on this ground.

To sum up, there are two reasons for not continuing to pressure homosexually inclined men and women into heterosexual marriage, as society still does. First, the marriages are unlikely to meet the needs of either partner. Second, the traditional social reasons for urging marriage on the disinclined no longer apply.

If this reasoning is correct, it is time the church ceased to function as a religious support of social pressure toward undesirable heterosexual marriages. Instead, it should become the place to which troubled youth can turn for understanding and counsel. That cannot happen as long as legalism and homophobia prevail.

For those whose homosexual orientation is too strong to be denied, what is the best way to order their lives? For a few, perhaps, total celibacy is best. But surely for most, in a society that recognizes so clearly the positive value of sexual experience, this is not best. Their "burning" is unlikely to be redemptive either for themselves or for others. Also, the fragmentation of community leaves those who live alone peculiarly isolated and lonely. Even the church fails to include them readily and naturally. On the other hand, the too-often-selected alternative of promiscuity and casual sex also has marked disadvantages. The best choice for most is bonding, taking mutual responsibility for each other.

For homosexuals, as for heterosexuals, one ideal is that all sexual activity be with one partner in the context of lifelong commitment. But it is no more certain that the first such partnership can endure throughout life than in the case of heterosexual pairing. Nevertheless, to look toward lifelong mutual commitment as the goal is not misguided. Even in a society in which pressures are exerted more against such mutual commitments of homosexual couples than for them, many have succeeded. Today the agony of many a gay man dying of AIDS is eased by the faithful ministration of a partner who stays with him and ministers to him until death does them part. If the church threw the full weight of its moral support behind this ideal, more of these partnerships would succeed.

Perhaps most homosexual bondings will be more like the premarital bondings of heterosexuals than like marriages. But this is not necessarily the case. Homosexuals, like heterosexuals, do bond for life, and the church's role should be to encourage this.

Does this mean that homosexual couples ready to make this lifelong commitment should be married? The answer depends on which of the elements in marriage is emphasized.

If marriage is seen as primarily the context for raising children, then most of these homosexual bondings would not be marriages, although even by this criterion some would be. But if other aspects of marriage are emphasized—

permanence, social support, the bonding of families—then in principle marriage is open to homosexual couples as much as to heterosexual ones. Whether the word "marriage" is the best to use for permanent homosexual pairing is, in any case, not the crucial question. Temporary and permanent bondings should be distinguished, and the latter should be especially celebrated by the church, whatever name is chosen. It should have the same legal, moral, and religious status as heterosexual marriage.

THE CURRENT DEBATE

This approach to homosexuality is still seen by many Christians as failing to deal with Paul's picture of certain homosexual practices as degrading. But there is no inconsistency. Paul is surely correct that there are degrading homosexual practices. For example, the type he seems to have in mind in the famous Romans passage appears to be the ultimate in self-indulgence. But there are also degrading heterosexual practices. The issue should not be heterosexual versus homosexual, but humanizing versus degrading. How can this distinction be effectively made? This is an important question for Christians.

The sexual revolution has led to the widespread view that the only sexual acts that are objectionable are those in which one partner participates unwillingly or is not old enough to make a responsible decision. A second level of restriction can be made around faithfulness to covenants. If two people agree to an exclusive relationship, then sexual acts that break the covenant can be condemned. But Paul's point involves something else. Is it possible, despite the basic affirmation of sexual enjoyment, still to distinguish on other grounds between humanizing and degrading expressions?

Yes, such a distinction is possible and important, and can be formulated in such a way as to make sense of Paul's outburst. The needed distinction has to do with how sexuality is related to the rest of life. One trend in the sexual revolution celebrates the separation of sexuality from its immersion in the whole pattern of human relationships. Some think that the most complete sexual abandon is attained when the partners are merely physical objects for one another. There is an element in the male psyche that idealizes this completely impersonal sex, often associated with aggression and even sadism. It involves revolt against all social and societal restraints.

The pursuit of new pleasurable sensations involving the depersonalization of the partner can be imposed on an unwilling partner or on one who is made willing only by payment of money. Many proponents of the sexual revolution oppose this. But what if one partner, most often the woman, agrees to cooperate in sexual experimentation that is dehumanizing to her for fear that otherwise her husband will seek another woman or simply out of the desire to do her duty as wife? Does this kind of willingness render such sex acceptable? Emphatically not. Once sexual experience is sought for its own sake, rather than as a means of mutual enjoyment and of deepening personal relations, it can easily become degrading rather than humanizing.

But how is this related to Paul's reference to homosexual practices as illustrating sexual degradation? Once the quest for sexual experiences becomes an end in itself, rejecting all social and personal considerations, even primarily heterosexual men can extend their experimentation in ways that deny not only their social roles but even their dominant natural inclinations. They may want to add to their experience even what it is like to be a woman. As the extreme limit of turning the restricted good of sexual enjoyment into the absolute good to which all else is subordinated, these homosexual acts illustrate the gross idolatry against which Paul inveighs. This has nothing to do with sexual expressions of mutual affection between two women or two men who are personally committed to each other.

The goodness of sexuality does not mean that the pursuit of sexual sensations without regard for human relations and larger purposes is good. On the contrary. The righteous life is one in which sexual enjoyment is subordinated to other ends. We do not live in order to savor delicate tastes, to have emotional highs, or to enjoy sexual or religious ecstasies. These may come to us in the course of working with others toward the upbuilding of human community in anticipation of God's reign. If so, we have cause for gratitude. If we seek God's reign first, much else may be added to us. But this does not justify seeking first these other goods.

To affirm committed homosexual relationships is not, therefore, to condone what Paul depicted as the final outcome of idolatry. Instead, it is calling for a high level of personal discipline and commitment. What is wrong with the church's present stance is that by making no distinction between utterly self-indulgent and irresponsible pleasure seeking and lifelong commitments, often made in the face of social contempt, it contributes to immorality among homosexuals. If every homosexual act is equally condemned, why adopt the more demanding lifestyle?

Furthermore, much of the least responsible behavior of homosexuals is engendered by low self-esteem. For this, too, the church shares major responsibility. To care for homosexuals, as the church professes to do, is to love and affirm them as homosexual persons, not despite their homosexuality. It is to ask of them just as much self-denial and self discipline as it asks of heterosexuals, while offering as much sexual fulfillment and human happiness as they are capable of attaining in a context that is oriented primarily to the service of God through the service of human beings.

Some Christians who would agree with much of the above are still convinced that homosexuality is not morally acceptable, that it is against God's intentions for human beings, that it violates something fundamental in the nature of things. These Christians may want to support individual homosexuals in any way they can and to avoid self-righteous and moralistic condemnation. But they are not prepared to support any affirmation by the church that there is a legitimate homosexual lifestyle. In their view, the only options for those who are homosexually inclined are transformation to heterosexuality or complete self-denial.

This deep-seated sense that homosexual activity violates something basic in the nature of things must be considered openly and fairly. It can be supported from the importance of heterosexuality in the evolutionary process; homosexuality has played no analogous role. In theological terms it appeals to the story of the Creation. God created man and woman. God created them for one another. That is what sexuality is all about. The mating of male and female fulfills the intent of creation. There is no analogous place for the mating of male with male or female with female. Even though there are no clear condemnations of all homosexual behavior in the Bible, all discussions of sexuality assume that the mating of male and female is normative.

It would probably be more accurate to say that the biblical accounts are reflections of the same deep-seated sensibility in their authors that is felt by such readers than that the accounts are the reason for this attitude among Christians. Nevertheless, the point is well taken. Although it is seriously misleading to say that the Bible condemns homosexuality, it is accurate to say that it looks on heterosexuality as normal and normative.

The question before Christians today is: What conclusions should we draw about present teaching from this historical fact? Does the way the Bible describes the creation of male and female tell us something about God's intentions for the church's dealings with homosexuals now? If so, what?

The mode of thinking that draws the conclusion that the church cannot condone any form of homosexual activity is similar to that of Roman Catholic natural-law thinking. . . . One discerns in the dominant patterns a purpose which is then understood absolutistically as applying to all. One judges that because men and women are made for each other, analogous relations between men or between women are precluded.

It is important to see that a slightly different conclusion could be drawn. One could decide that because men and women are made for each other, celibacy is precluded. Jews have tended to draw this conclusion, but most Christians have not. The fact that both Jesus and Paul seem to have been celibate has encouraged Christians to think of celibacy as a noble estate to which some Christians are called.

Since an exception is made here to the general pattern derived from the story of the Creation, the question is whether other such exceptions cannot be made, specifically in favor of homosexual bondings. The refusal to do this seems to reflect the assumption that these bondings fall below the established norm. It is difficult not to conclude that the difference in judgment expresses deep-seated feelings that in fact have little to do with biblical authority.

There are other difficulties with drawing too many conclusions about sexual relations from the story of the Creation. Although the story in the first chapter of Genesis is almost gender neutral, the story in the second chapter is patriarchal to the core. The subordination of the wife to the husband is a far clearer implication of the Creation story than any rejection of homosexuality. Furthermore, this subordination of the wife is even more pervasive of biblical texts than is the norm of heterosexuality.

If, today, Christians are prepared to repent of millennia-long patriarchal sexism, deeply rooted in scripture, why should they cling to millennia-long patriarchal homophobia, much less explicitly supported in the Bible? Surely the answer must be found in personal feelings rather than in the Bible!

26.

THE MARRIAGE AMENDMENT

The Editors, First Things

Marriage in the United States shall consist only of the union of a man and a woman. Neither this Constitution or the constitution of any state, nor state or federal law, shall be construed to require that marital status or the legal incidents thereof be conferred on unmarried couples or groups.

That is the proposed amendment to the Constitution that is now gathering powerful support in the Congress and in several states. Prudent citizens are reluctant to amend the Constitution unless persuaded that it is necessary. What would become the twenty-eighth amendment is necessary because the courts are moving toward a de facto amendment of the Constitution that mandates the radical redefinition of marriage and family. The question before us is how the Constitution will be amended: by judicial fiat or by "We the People of the United States" employing the means established by the Constitution. Entailed in that question is whether change will serve to advance a social revolution unsought and unwanted by the American people or will serve to secure an institution essential to the well-being of our society. The Constitution will be amended, either by constitutional means or by activist judges practicing what is aptly described as the judicial usurpation of politics.

The proposed marriage amendment has been carefully crafted by leading constitutional scholars. The first sentence means that no legislature or court may confer the name of marriage on same-sex unions or recognize a same-sex marriage contracted in another country, such as Canada or the Netherlands. The second sentence is aimed more specifically at activist courts, both state and federal, preventing them from imposing same-sex marriage or its equivalent. The question of adopting arrangements other than marriage, such as civil

Reprinted from "The Marriage Amendment," by the editors of *First Things*, October 2003, pp. 14–17.

unions, is left to the determination of the people through the democratic process in the several states. Where the people have had the opportunity to decide the question of same-sex marriage—in Hawaii and Alaska, for instance—they have decided against it, and have done so decisively.

A proper devotion to the principles of federalism has led some to question the amendment because, they say, it would "nationalize" marriage law. The nationalizing of marriage law, however, is precisely what the activists pressing for same-sex unions are on the edge of achieving. They hope that in the next few years same-sex marriage will be decreed by the Supreme Court. In addition, same-sex couples will travel to any state that allows them to marry or enter civil unions, and will then demand that their home states give "full faith and credit" to the judgment that recognizes their status. The great majority of same-sex couples contracting civil unions in Vermont, for instance, do not live in Vermont. They will be suing for recognition of their status in the courts of their home states. An additional and declared strategy is to attack the constitutionality of the federal Defense of Marriage Act, overwhelmingly adopted by Congress in 1996. One way or another, federalism is compromised. The marriage amendment will establish a general rule against same-sex marriage while leaving the matter of contractual unions and other nonmarital arrangements to the states.

We have been brought to the present circumstance by the astonishing success of the homosexual movement over the past three decades. Traditionally, sodomy was viewed as an act, and was condemned as unnatural and deviant. A hundred years ago, homosexuality was viewed as a condition afflicting people who are prone to engaging in such unnatural and deviant acts. Today "gay" signifies not so much an act or condition as the identity of people who say that they most essentially *are* what they do and want to do sexually. The rhetorical and conceptual movement has been from act to condition to identity; bringing us to the demand for same-sex marriage. About 2 percent of the combined teenage and adult male population, and considerably less of the female, are said to be a minority deprived of their rights. In particular, they claim to be discriminated against in that they are "excluded" from the institution of marriage. They are not asking for tolerance of their private sexual practices and of the gay subculture constituted by such practices. They are demanding, rather, public acceptance and approval. That is the whole point of focusing on the status of marriage, which is a quintessentially public institution.

It is by no means evident that most, or even many, gays are interested in entering into a legally recognized union. Until recently, more radical activists and proponents of "queer theory" vigorously opposed the movement for same-sex unions, arguing that gays should not surrender their erotic freedom to the constraints associated with the "bourgeois" institution of marriage. More recently, the radicals have lined up in support of same-sex marriage, joining the proponents of polygamy and "polyamory" who are now so influential, if not dominant, in the academic field of marriage and family law. We do not

have to speculate about their aims. They have by now produced a large literature in support of what they themselves describe as a social revolution that
would replace traditional marriage and family with a wide array of "family"
arrangements constructed on the basis of expressive individualism and the
maximizing of erotic options. A quarter century ago, President Jimmy Carter
convened the White House Conference on the Family. Under pressure from
such radical ideologues, the name was changed to the White House Conference on Families, in the plural. The hour of the ideologues has now arrived,
and they have rallied to the battle for same-sex marriage.

There are a few gays who express admiration for traditional marriage and
say they simply want to be included in its benefits. They claim they are now
excluded. And they are right. They are not excluded by others; they are
excluded by their identity as gays. To be homosexual is a condition; to be gay
is a decision. Some say no other decision is available to them, but that is not
true. Sexual temptations, like other temptations, can be resisted. In many
cases, sexual orientation can be changed. Human frailties notwithstanding,
chastity is a possibility for all. Yet we are faced with a not-insignificant number of people who say that gay is who they are, whether by choice or by fate,
and that they are unfairly excluded from the companionship, stability, and
other goods of marriage. Were the Supreme Court to do their bidding tomorrow, however, they would still be excluded from marriage. Throughout history
and in all major cultures, marriage is a union between a man and a woman.
That is what marriage is. A man and a man or a woman and a woman may have
an intense but chaste friendship, including shared living arrangements. It is not
the business of the state to certify or regulate friendships. As for those who
choose a sexual relationship, we may well understand their yearning for public approval of their choice. But same-sex marriage is not marriage. It is at
most a simulacrum of marriage, a poignant attempt to create a semblance of
some features of marriage, a pretending to be something like the relationship
between husband and wife that is marriage. The reality is not changed if the
state collaborates in the pretense and calls it marriage.

To which some respond that it is a harmless pretense. If a very small
minority so desperately want to be legally designated as married, even though
everybody knows that their relationship is not really a marriage, why not let
them? It seems the generous thing to do. It is further argued that such state-
sanctioned unions would reduce the typically wild promiscuity that is characteristic of the gay lifestyle. Nobody can know whether same-sex marriage
would, in fact, help domesticate the gay subculture. We do know, however, that
it would radically change the customs, laws, and moral expectations embedded in millennia of human experience. Marriage and family law reflects the
historically cumulative complexities of necessarily public concerns about
property; inheritance, legal liability, and the legitimacy of children—the latter entailing a host of responsibilities for which parents, and especially men,
can be held accountable. One of the most fundamental prerequisites of social

order, it has been almost universally recognized, is the containment of the otherwise unbridled sexual activity of the human male, and marriage is—among the many other things that marriage is—the primary instrument of that necessary discipline.

Marriage and family law is, above all, about children. Same-sex couples cannot from their sexual acts procreate children. Gay activists contend that that only makes their circumstance identical with that of a marriage in which the woman is beyond the childbearing years. But that, too, is not true. A marriage between an older man and woman does not contradict the definition of marriage as a union between a man and a woman. In addition, such a marriage aims at preventing the man from having children by other women, which is, obviously, not a consideration in same-sex relations. The activists respond that gays can adopt children, which is legal in some jurisdictions. Here again the concern for children becomes paramount. After decades of experiments with single-parent families, "open marriages," and easy divorce, the evidence is in, and there is today near-unanimous agreement on what should always have been obvious: judged by every index of well-being, there is no more important factor in the lives of children than having a mother and father in the home. Lesbians and gays in same-sex unions cannot be mothers and fathers, except in the poignant simulacrum of pretended sex roles. Given the ambiguities, uncertainties, and curiosities of children in coming to understand their sexuality; the Vatican's Congregation for the Doctrine of the Faith is surely right when it says in its recent statement that denying the child the experience of having a mother and father is a cruel deprivation.

Many oppose same-sex unions and the consequent revolution in marriage and family law because they believe homosexuality is a disorder and homosexual acts are morally wrong. That is not a private prejudice. It is not, as the Supreme Court has claimed, an "irrational animus." It is a considered and very public moral judgment grounded in clear reason and historical experience, and supported by the authority of the biblical tradition. Nobody should apologize for publicly advocating a position informed by the foundational moral truths of Western civilization. Of course, those who do so will be accused of "homophobia." Homophobia is a term of recent coinage intended to serve as a conversation stopper. Its power to intimidate is rapidly diminishing. Support for the civilizational tradition in this regard is not a phobia; it is not an irrational fear. Concern about the legal establishment and normalization of sexual deviance is fully warranted. What is called homophobia is more accurately understood as a positive judgment regarding the common good and, most particularly, the well-being of children. It should not be, but it still is, necessary to add that hatred of gays or denial of their human or civil rights is evil and must be unequivocally condemned. Moreover, it must be candidly acknowledged that gay demands and agitations today are not unrelated to patterns of sexual hedonism in the general culture.

The debate is now underway as to whether civil rights include the right of gays to have their relationships legally designated as marriage. There are many factors in the debate not addressed here. It is claimed, for instance, that a gay right to marriage is on a moral and legal continuum with extending rights to blacks and women. That convenient but simplistic comparison does not bear close examination. Discrimination against blacks and women was recognized, albeit too slowly, as contradicting the foundational values and institutions of our society. Those values were vindicated and those institutions strengthened by including people who had been unjustly excluded. The just demand of blacks and women was for full participation in the opportunities and responsibilities of the social order. The demand for gay marriage, by way of sharpest contrast, is premised upon the recognition that gays cannot participate in that order's most basic institution, and it is therefore aimed not at their inclusion but at the institution's deconstruction by redefinition. The humpty-dumpty logic is that, if you cannot do something you want to do, you redefine that something, turning it into something you can do. When such word games are translated into law, the public meaning of the something that most people can and want to do is radically changed. The public meaning of marriage and family—in law, and more gradually, in social customs and expectations—is changed for everybody. Gay activists can try but we do not think they will succeed in persuading most Americans that their marriages and families are the same thing that gays can and want to do.

One factor that has been neglected to date is that, according to the reasoning of the recent *Lawrence* decision of the Supreme Court, homosexuality will be viewed as a suspect category that, as in the case of race, will trigger a vast array of laws and regulations associated with the antidiscrimination regime. With respect to affirmative action, quota systems, rules about "hate speech," and much else, attitudes and actions relating to gays will be subject to, in the language of the courts, "strict scrutiny." Minimally, this will mean that homosexuality and heterosexuality, marriage and the gay semblance of marriage, will in the public schools be presented on the basis of scrupulous equality. Since almost no parents want their children to be homosexual or gay, this prospect is likely to generate powerful resistance.

Without the marriage amendment, the debate that is now underway may well be short-circuited by the courts. One way or another, the Constitution will be amended. If it is amended by the judiciary, as the Supreme Court did in its 1973 invention of an unlimited abortion license, we will almost certainly enter upon a severe intensification of what is rightfully called the culture war. Lincoln forcefully stated in his first inaugural address that the American people are not prepared to surrender their right to self-government to even the most eminent tribunal. Whether that is still true of the American people is once again being put to the test.

Just government is derived from the consent of the governed, says the

Declaration of Independence. In this democracy, consent means popular deliberation, debate, and decision through the representative polity established by the Constitution. In the *Lawrence* decision, Justice Anthony Kennedy, writing for the majority, invoked what Justice Antonin Scalia calls the "sweet mystery of life" passage from the 1992 *Casey* decision that affirmed the infamous *Roe* ruling on abortion: "At the heart of liberty is the right to define one's own concept of meaning, of the universe, and of the mystery of human life." In that way of thinking, the dominant, if not exclusive, purpose of the Constitution in dealing with rights is to serve the autonomous self as construed by the foundationless philosophy of expressive individualism. The moral, social, political, and legal order must bend to the individual definition of truth, no matter how willful or arbitrary. In support of that logic, the *Lawrence* opinion cites the authority of the above-mentioned ideologues and even of like-minded jurists in the European Union.

It appears that the Supreme Court has quite forgotten the purpose and source of authority set forth by the Constitution. That purpose and source of authority is clearly stated in the Preamble: "We the people of the United States, in order to form a more perfect union, establish justice, insure domestic tranquility, provide for the common defense, promote the general welfare, and secure the blessings of liberty to ourselves and our posterity; do ordain and establish this Constitution for the United States of America."

We are now engaged in a great debate about whether same-sex marriage and the criminalizing of opposition to homosexuality and the gay agenda will serve to establish justice, ensure domestic tranquility, and promote the general welfare. (Provision for the common defense is, of course, relevant to the inclusion of gays in the military, which the logic of *Lawrence* would make mandatory.) Of crucial importance is the securing of liberty understood as what the founders called the "ordered liberty" of a blessing bestowed, as distinct from the unbridled license of expressive individualism and the quest for the satisfaction of insatiable desire.

The marriage amendment might finally fail, but its passage by Congress and submission to the states for ratification can ensure that "We the People" will not be excluded from the deliberation and decisions that will determine the future of marriage and family, the most necessary of institutions in the right ordering of this or any society.

27.

SAME-SEX MARRIAGE
The Theologies Can Vary

Dudley Rose

As people well beyond the borders of Massachusetts are aware, the state's Supreme Judicial Court (SJC), in a split decision, has ruled that it is unconstitutional to withhold the right of marriage from same-sex couples.[1] What was already a heated debate has, and will, become hotter as opponents seek constitutional means to reverse the effect of the SJC's decision.

Opponents of the decision make both civil and religious arguments, and very vocally so. Using the former, these opponents suggest that "activist" judges have no business foisting their will upon society, that instead the people and the Massachusetts legislature should control the definition and regulation of marriage. With the latter, the opponents turn to biblical and other theological bases to condemn homosexuality and same-sex marriage as evil. (In many respects, these two arguments are difficult to separate, because they are often meshed into one line of reasoning.)

I want to argue here briefly for a theological approach to the issue of same-sex marriage that is more credible than many of those being advanced. Furthermore, I want to point out that the majority in *Goodrich* followed an approach in the civil arena that makes for interesting comparison.

Paul Tillich claimed that true theology walked the ground between what he called the kerygmatic and the apologetic. Roughly, he characterized the kerygmatic as the uncritical application of supposed eternal religious truth to a current situation, and the apologetic as the uncritical identification of current societal norms with eternal truth. Tillich understood the untenability of both poles and opted instead for what he called a "method of correlation," which put the questions of the day and, in his case, the Christian message[2] into interdependent conversation.

Reprinted from the *Harvard Divinity Bulletin* (Winter/Spring 2004).

Tillich said that kerygmatic theology understood eternal truth to be unambiguously available in the Christian message. Kerygmatic theology, he said, simply imported answers, unrelated to the questions being asked and, indeed, often hostile toward the questions of contemporary society. Tillich argued that true theology should, in contrast, find within the Christian message truths that inform and converse with the questions of the day. But he took the questions of the day as just that, questions, which were also inappropriately decided by the simple application of current opinion.

In the interdependent conversation Tillich envisioned, it becomes obvious that whatever truths the Christian message contains, its tradition and scripture bear the marks of their own historical situation, and that separating eternal truth from contemporary noneternal norms and influences is thus as much a historical project as a contemporary one. Tillich understood that our ultimate concern was what was at stake and that kerygmatic theology missed it as easily as the apologetic. Tillich's process would call us, through this conversation between the questions of the day and the Christian message, to find relevant truths that depend, as much as is possible to know it, on eternal or ultimate truth.

The religious arguments against *Goodrich* have largely been, in Tillich's terms, kerygmatic and purportedly biblical. The Bible, say the religious opponents, condemns homosexuality and gives no evidence of sanctioned same-sex marriages. But readers and interpreters of the Bible who have grappled with separating the Bible's noneternal norms from its more enduring truths have largely found little support for a reading against homosexuality.[3] Indeed, many of the opponents of same-sex marriage and homosexuality seem to recognize the thin ice on which they are skating when they go to great lengths to argue that homosexuality is different from race. Sensitive to the fact that some of the very people arguing against homosexuality today used the Bible yesterday to argue against civil rights and interracial marriage, they are eager to confess their earlier sin but also to say that homosexuality and race are two entirely different issues.

One such argument goes like this: We were wrong to believe in racial discrimination and oppose miscegenation. We were wrong because we said that race was an essential characteristic, but we now understand that race is a constructed category. On the other hand, it is clear that gender difference truly is essential; race is a constructed category, but gender is not.[4]

Today many recognize that to posit gender difference as essential rather than constructed is as risky as to consider racial difference to be essential. And it is, indeed, sad to hear the same biblical arguments being made against same-sex marriage as were successfully made against interracial marriage until late in the twentieth century. Something akin to Tillich's "method of correlation" ought to help us arrive at better foundational ingredients for marriage than considerations of either race or gender.

Interestingly, the Massachusetts SJC, from the civil side, seems to have reached similar conclusions. The court has declared that societal norms and proclivities cannot stand in the way of fundamental human rights. The court's opponents brand the lack of resemblance between its decision and popular opinion to be the result of the judges' being "activist." (That is actually a misuse of the legal term, but what they mean is that the court is not representing popular opinion.) Quite clearly, however, the court's duty is not to mirror public opinion; it is to put the constitutional framework into conversation with the questions of the day, to bring enduring and fundamental truths to bear on the questions of the day in much the same way the theologian does from a religious perspective.

Historically the courts have appropriately led the nation, even when public opinion would have prevented them. It was the California SJC that in 1948 became the first in the country to overturn a state's laws against miscegenation. It was the United States Supreme Court that finally, in 1967, overturned these laws throughout the land.

In these and in many other decisions, courts have gone against the grain of popular opinion. And doing so is far from inappropriate—it is the court's obligation. One imagines that churches and people of faith have at least as much obligation to bring good theological method and argument to bear on the important questions that face humankind.

NOTES

1. November 18, 2003, in *Goodridge v. Department of Public Health*, and February 4, 2004, in an SJC clarification.

2. While Tillich himself insisted on the supremacy of the Christian message (at least until late in his life), his method of correlation does not depend on that supremacy. However, for the sake of not putting words in Tillich's mouth, I use his language when referring to his argument.

3. These arguments are well made among many biblical interpreters. Peter Gomes in *The Good Book* (Boston: Compass Press, 1997) summarizes the arguments quite well.

4. This argument has been made by members of the Coalition for Marriage and the Massachusetts Family Institute, among others.

28

A MORE PERFECT UNION
Reservations about Gay Marriage

Dennis O'Brien

We have a bumper sticker on our car: "Keep Vermont Civil." The sticker is a bit tattered, since it goes back to the controversy about "civil unions"—the Vermont law passed in 2000 establishing various legal equivalencies to marital rights for gay and lesbian couples. The legislature had been forced to take action following the 1999 ruling of the Vermont Supreme Court holding that denial of marital rights to such unions violated the Vermont Constitution's "common benefits" clause.

In a neat bit of Solomonic judgment, the court both rejected the gay and lesbian plaintiffs' claim that they were entitled to marriage licenses and declared that they were entitled to the benefits "incident on the marital relation." The court ruled that those benefits could be established by granting a marriage license, but that there might be other legislative means to assure proper benefits. The matter of specific statute was handed over to the legislature. The result was "civil unions."

A ruling in November 2003 by the Supreme Judicial Court of Massachusetts similarly affirmed "marital" rights for gay and lesbian couples and handed the matter on to the legislature of the commonwealth. The tone of the 4-to-3 decision of the Massachusetts court appears, however, to push toward an unequivocal affirmation of "gay marriage." That would seem to be the hope and expectation of gay activists. Perhaps "gay marriage" will finally emerge as the statutory provision as it has in Canada and in various European jurisdictions. The heavens will not fall, the republic will not totter if that is the direction of public policy, but I am not enthusiastic about such a result. I prefer the "civil unions" approach.

Anyone who writes on this topic must do so with something akin to despair. Rationality is not on broad display in our discussion about sexuality, from homosexuality to abortion rights and back again. Advocates on all sides misstate their opponents' views and overstate their own to the point where careful discourse disappears. Nevertheless, I think it is worth trying to explicate some of the central claims and key issues that swirl around the discussion of gay marriage. I choose four topics—nature, education, culture, and law— as relevant to framing moral concerns and public policy.

First, nature: One of the dominant views both within and without the gay community is that sexual orientation is a given, a natural determinant—perhaps the expression of a "gay gene." In his judicious exposition of the arguments for gay marriage, Bruce Bawer states the point succinctly:

> One can approve or disapprove of somebody's actions or opinions, beliefs; but it is meaningless to speak of approving or disapproving of another's innate characteristics. To say that someone approves or disapproves of somebody's homosexuality is like saying that one approves or disapproves of somebody's baldness or tallness.

I think that the gay community puts all too much weight on the notion of natural sexual orientation. In the first place, it just may not be true. If one were to assess sexual orientation by behavior rather than biology, one would be more inclined to Freud's view that our sexuality is polymorphous: heterosexual and homosexual and what all, through a fascinating range of fact and fantasy. Unipolar sexuality may be a strange outlier, not the rule.

The second problem with the idea of a "gay gene" is that it simply bypasses the value of homosexuality. How do we decide that the gay gene is not a defective gene like the gene for sickle-cell anemia? Given access to abortion or gene therapy, the decision could be made to eliminate this fault of nature. Indian villagers have traditionally sought abortions for female fetuses; perhaps parents and societies will seek to abort fetuses with a gay gene. Gene therapy may lead to "designer children" who are handsomely tall, definitely not bald—and certainly not gay! If one believes, as I certainly do, that it is immoral to abort gay and female fetuses, that must be because there is some value in the expression of such a sexuality or such a gender. It would be much better for the gay community to argue that homosexuality enriches the range of human values in a way that being bald does not.

The third problem with resting the case on natural sexual orientation is that it needs a middle term to justify sexual behavior. This is as true of heterosexual behavior as of homosexual. The human gene pool is full of behavioral urges that may or may not be worthy of expression. Priests who choose celibacy or couples who choose an active sexual life claim that certain values are being expressed in their abstention from or participation in sexuality.

The standard Catholic position on homosexuality does not condemn homosexual orientation; it does condemn homosexual behavior. Thomas Aquinas is correct, I think, when he says that all human acts are moral acts. Sexual acts and behavior are distinctly human acts in that we can choose to engage in them or not. Not engaging in them may be difficult, but so is checking my anger and all too many other urges. We do not act sexually by automation, as animals do when biologically triggered. The gay community has been so exercised to deny that homosexual orientation is chosen that it runs the danger of draining homosexual behavior of its human dimension as a chosen act or life.

The real issues about sexuality are choice, lifestyle, and cultural value. On the basis of genes or Freudian polymorphous sex, sexuality in many forms is a fact. The question is, How should society assess and shape various sexual expressions? Is America now more morally sensitive, more well structured in its laws and practices insofar as it accepts publicly avowed homosexual behavior; constructs laws that protect homosexuals from the criminal penalties formally attached to homosexual acts; and allows for civil unions or even gay marriages? On the whole, I am inclined to say that getting gay sex out of the closet and legally protected is a moral and political advance. But that is not because homosexuality is natural but because something of value emerges from it.

Education: If one holds that sexual orientation may be polymorphous, one should then face the problem of the sexual education of children and young adults. Admittedly, educating for sexual direction is somewhere between unclear and utter mystery, but to whatever extent parents and educators can give advice and cues for sexual orientation and behavior, one must ask: Are some kinds of sexual lives to be preferred?

Having worked with late adolescents most of my career, I am inclined to think that sexual confusion is as much a fact of life as sexual determination. One of the reasons to be concerned with the notion of natural, genetically determined sexual orientation is that it assumes that inclination is destiny. If a young person flirts with homosexuality, sexual-orientation-by-nature confirms gay identity. Maybe not.

What then should a parent, educator, or society in general say to a young person caught in a mixed stew of sexual inclinations? Would it be proper to advise a confused teenager that heterosexuality is a preferred sexual life? And if so, what are the grounds for such advice? Difficult and complex as assessing various sexual lives may be, I want to resist the notion that it is a matter of indifference. "I don't care. Any sexual life—heterosexual, homosexual, bisexual—is OK. It's all the same. You choose whatever you want."

I am not denying that there can be deep determinations toward differing sexual lives. Though I am skeptical that sexual orientation is genetic, it certainly can emerge as "second nature": a pattern of desire, circumstance, and culture that is virtually ineradicable. And so I am equally skeptical about the possibility (or morality) of persuading or treating mature homosexuals in order to change their sexual direction.

The issue is not with the mature, stable homosexual (or heterosexual); it is with the immature, whose sexual orientation may well be relatively open.

202   Part Three. The Philosophical Arguments

Is it legitimate morally, politically, or spiritually to commend one or the other sexual orientation? I don't necessarily want to prejudice the question toward heterosexuality; I can imagine a sensitive male homosexual commending the unusually close bonding and intense sexuality of that relationship as the preferred life choice. The educational problem I want to raise is whether any conversation commending this or that sexual life pattern is legitimate.

Culture: One of the confusions in the sexual polemics of the day is the blurring of the line between natural orientation and chosen behavior. If you have the orientation, then of course behavior should follow and is fully morally legitimate. Sexual libertarians argue that the repression of sexual urges of whatever sort is psychologically disastrous and culturally stultifying. I like this argument because it shifts to issues of moral choice and social values. Repression is bad for you and your society!

Just how far should the value of nonrepression be taken? One of the by-products of the sexual revolution has been the emergence of bisexuality—presumably a natural given. Advocates of marriage, heterosexual or gay, would both have to agree that bisexual orientation must be repressed in the interests of marital fidelity: one cannot be faithful to a sexual partner if one is having sex with someone of a different sex. Gay marriage advocates are, as they often say, conservatives on the issue of sexual fidelity.

Returning to my sexually confused adolescent: If I am in favor of the spiritual and moral value of sexual fidelity, then I am going to commend traditional marriage. A bisexual life or an "open" marriage is judged as an unacceptable choice, natural inclination to the contrary notwithstanding.

Of course, one can then go on and question the value of sexual fidelity both for partners and for the social good. The least negative comment I would make here about "open" sexuality is that while it may be compatible with a large range of other social goods like justice and friendship, it is not clearly conducive to those broader social values. (I credit the distinction to the late Victor Preller.)

Can one go any farther in advising the young about sexual life choices? If there is genuine sexual polyvalence and confusion, I would be inclined to commend heterosexuality. Why? Given the drift of this essay, it would have to be because the moral and spiritual values that can be realized in heterosexual life are either impossible or difficult to realize or sustain in homosexual life. At this point, any gay friend will ask how I know about the values of gay life since I haven't lived it!

To be sure, I grant the argument and reinforce it. I suspect that there are deep values that can emerge in certain homosexual lives which are unique to that life and which cannot be replicated in content or depth in heterosexual life. A commitment to heterosexuality obviously attenuates male-male relations from the wilder, deeper passions and revelations of mutual sexuality. That is the price one pays for heterosexual life choice.

Any argument for heterosexuality as a preferred sexual choice does not rest on how this or that heterosexual life works out. Heterosexual marriage can be a human disaster—the divorce statistics attest to that! Homosexual bonding may be deeply valuable and, as noted, reach ranges of the human heart that heterosexuality cannot. Any argument for heterosexuality must deal with broad cultural and spiritual realities.

Having said that, it is obvious that constructing the case for heterosexuality must be as complex and nuanced as the cultural and spiritual trajectories of the human spirit. To short-circuit that long argument, I would say that it comes down to the ancient belief that men and women are different. Luce Irigary puts it well in *An Ethics of Sexual Difference*: "Man and woman, woman and man are always meeting as though for the first time because they cannot be substituted for one another."

Why heterosexuality? Because the human spirit can expand as it moves toward the different. It can; it may not. Certainly some homosexual (or celibate) life choices arise from a fear of the different in women (or men). On the other hand, in a society that devalues heterosexuality and marriage through a mix of sentimentality and sexual titillation, the choice of homosexuality may be the choice of the different which is revelatory. So be it. But the final fact is that the bodily, biological difference between men and women is the urtext of the heterosexual narrative. Writing that sexual script is inherently difficult— that is the reason that sentimentality and fantasy are so popular: they conceal the pain of difference and the lessons of loving across that pain.

Law: One might well conclude that commending heterosexuality as a preferred sexual life is educationally legitimate, and then ask: But what about the law? Just because one may commend one life choice over another—being a social worker over being a stockbroker—does not mean the preference needs to be legally enforced (there is no law against being a stockbroker). Perhaps the issue of gay or heterosexual direction should be left to the subtleties of parental or church guidance. Whether that is the find conclusion or not will depend on how one views the role of law.

For classical philosophers law had an educational function; it was set up to structure individual and communal life in order to produce certain human virtues. In Aristotle's work, the *Nichomachean Ethics* and the *Politics* are mutually supporting. One needs certain virtues like courage, temperance, and justice in order to realize human good, but those virtues are also necessary to be a good citizen. The state, in turn, is bound through the enactment and enforcement of proper laws to educate for virtue both for its own sake and for human prospering.

The educational role of law is at best recessive in the American understanding of law. We tend to view law not as aimed at creating individual or common good but as a means of mediating dispute and keeping civil peace. In so far as that is the dominant view of law in America, "gay marriage" says nothing about the morality of homosexuality one way or the other, it simply guarantees that all "domestic partnerships" (an alternative term considered for "civil unions") are treated equally. All well and good. But I am not certain that one can ever completely erase the educational effect of law.

The law may not deliberately create culture, but it certainly becomes a sign within the culture. Giving legal status to gay marriage does appear to suggest that the difference between gay and heterosexual partnerships is a matter of irrelevance. It will surely make it more difficult for parents or the churches to argue a preference for heterosexual marriage (which I hope they will wish to do). Thus I remain in favor of "civil union" as a concept more in keeping with our restrained sense of law and less tilted toward the equating of gay and heterosexual unions.

29.

VIRTUALLY NORMAL

Andrew Sullivan

The centerpiece of [the] new [homosexual] politics . . . is equal access to civil marriage. . . .

This is a question of formal public discrimination, since only the state can grant and recognize marriage. If the military ban deals with the heart of what it means to be a citizen, marriage does even more so, since, in peace and war, it affects everyone. Marriage is not simply a private contract; it is a social and public recognition of a private commitment. As such, it is the highest public recognition of personal integrity. Denying it to homosexuals is the most public affront possible to their public equality.

This point may be the hardest for many heterosexuals to accept. Even those tolerant of homosexuals may find this institution so wedded to the notion of heterosexual commitment that to extend it would be to undo its very essence. And there may be religious reasons for resisting this that, within certain traditions, are unanswerable. But I am not here discussing what churches do in their private affairs. I am discussing what the allegedly neutral liberal state should do in public matters. For liberals, the case for homosexual marriage is overwhelming. As a classic public institution, it should be available to any two citizens.

Some might argue that marriage is by definition between a man and a woman; and it is difficult to argue with a definition. But if marriage is articulated beyond this circular fiat, then the argument for its exclusivity to one man and one woman disappears. The center of the public contract is an emotional, financial, and psychological bond between two people; in this respect, heterosexuals and homosexuals are identical. The heterosexuality of marriage is intrinsic only if it is understood to be intrinsically procreative; but that definition has long been abandoned in Western society. No civil marriage license is granted on the condition that the couple bear children; and the marriage is no less legal and no less defensible if it remains childless. In the contemporary West, marriage has become a way in which the state recognizes an emotional commitment by two people to each other for life. And within that definition, there is no public way, if one believes in equal rights under the law, in which it should legally be denied homosexuals.

Of course, no public sanctioning of a contract should be given to people who cannot actually fulfill it. The state rightly, for example, withholds marriage from minors, or from one adult and a minor, since at least one party is unable to understand or live up to the contract. And the state has also rightly barred close family relatives from marriage because familial emotional ties are too strong and powerful to enable a marriage contract to be entered into freely by two autonomous, independent individuals; and because incest poses a uniquely dangerous threat to the trust and responsibility that the family needs to survive. But do homosexuals fall into a similar category? History and experience strongly suggest they don't. Of course, marriage is characterized by a kind of commitment that is rare—and perhaps declining—even among heterosexuals. But it isn't necessary to prove that homosexuals or lesbians are less—or more— able to form long-term relationships than straights for it to be clear that at least some are. Moreover, giving these people an equal right to affirm their commitment doesn't reduce the incentive for heterosexuals to do the same.

In some ways, the marriage issue is exactly parallel to the issue of the military. Few people deny that many homosexuals are capable of the sacrifice, the commitment, and the responsibilities of marriage. And indeed, for many homosexuals and lesbians, these responsibilities are already enjoined—as they have been enjoined for centuries. The issue is whether these identical relationships should be denied equal legal standing, not by virtue of anything to do with the relationships themselves but by virtue of the internal, involuntary nature of the homosexuals involved. Clearly, for liberals, the answer to this is clear. Such a denial is a classic case of unequal protection of the laws.

But perhaps surprisingly, . . . one of the strongest arguments for gay marriage is a conservative one. It's perhaps best illustrated by a comparison with the alternative often offered by liberals and liberationists to legal gay marriage, the concept of "domestic partnership." Several cities in the United States have domestic partnership laws, which allow relationships that do not fit into the category of heterosexual marriage to be registered with the city and qualify for benefits that had previously been reserved for heterosexual married couples. In these cities, a variety of interpersonal arrangements qualify for health insurance, bereavement leave, insurance, annuity and pension rights, housing rights (such as rent-control apartments), adoption, and inheritance rights. Eventually, the aim is to include federal income tax and veterans' benefits as well. Homosexuals are not the only beneficiaries; heterosexual "live-togethers" also qualify.

The conservative's worries start with the ease of the relationship. To be sure, potential domestic partners have to prove financial interdependence, shared living arrangements, and a commitment to mutual caring. But they don't need to have a sexual relationship or even closely mirror old-style marriage. In principle, an elderly woman and her live-in nurse could qualify, or a pair of frat buddies. Left as it is, the concept of domestic partnership could open a Pandora's box of litigation and subjective judicial decision making about who qualifies. You either are or you're not married; it's not a complex question. Whether you are in a domestic partnership is not so clear.

More important for conservatives, the concept of domestic partnership chips away at the prestige of traditional relationships and undermines the priority we give them. Society, after all, has good reasons to extend legal advantages to heterosexuals who choose the formal sanction of marriage over simply living together. They make a deeper commitment to one another and to society; in exchange, society extends certain benefits to them. Marriage provides an anchor, if an arbitrary and often weak one, in the maelstrom of sex and relationships to which we are all prone. It provides a mechanism for emotional stability and economic security. We rig the law in its favor not because we disparage all forms of relationship other than the nuclear family, but because we recognize that not to promote marriage would be to ask too much of human virtue.

For conservatives, these are vital concerns. There are virtually no conservative arguments either for preferring no social incentives for gay relationships or for preferring a second-class relationship, such as domestic partnership, which really does provide an incentive for the decline of traditional marriage. Nor, if conservatives are concerned by the collapse of stable family life, should they be dismayed by the possibility of gay parents. There is no evidence that shows any deleterious impact on a child brought up by two homosexual parents; and considerable evidence that such a parental structure is clearly preferable to single parents (gay or straight) or no effective parents at all, which, alas, is the choice many children now face. Conservatives should not balk at the apparent radicalism of the change involved, either. The introduction of gay marriage would not be some sort of leap in the dark, a massive societal risk. Homosexual marriages have always existed, in a variety of forms; they have just been euphemized. Increasingly they exist in every sense but the legal one. As it has become more acceptable for homosexuals to acknowledge their loves and commitments publicly, more and more have committed themselves to one another for life in full view of their families and friends. A law institutionalizing gay marriage would merely reinforce a healthy trend. Burkean conservatives should warm to the idea.

It would also be an unqualified social good for homosexuals. It provides role models for young gay people, who, after the exhilaration of coming out, can easily lapse into short-term relationships and insecurity with no tangible goal in sight. My own guess is that most homosexuals would embrace such a goal with as much (if not more) commitment as heterosexuals. Even in our society as it is, many lesbian and gay male relationships are virtual textbooks of monogamous commitment; and for many, "in sickness and in health" has become a vocation rather than a vow. Legal gay marriage could also help bridge the gulf often found between homosexuals and their parents. It could bring the essence of gay life—a gay couple—into the heart of the traditional family in a way the family can most understand and the gay offspring can most easily acknowledge. It could do more to heal the gay-straight rift than any amount of gay rights legislation.

More important, perhaps, as gay marriage sank into the subtle background consciousness of a culture, its influence would be felt quietly but deeply among gay children. For them, at last, there would be some kind of future; some older faces to apply to their unfolding lives, some language in which their identity could be properly discussed, some rubric by which it could be explained—not in terms of sex, or sexual practices, or bars, or subterranean activity, but in terms of their future life stories, their potential loves, their eventual chance at some kind of constructive happiness. They would be able to feel by the intimation of a myriad examples that in this respect their emotional orientation was not merely about pleasure, or sin, or shame, or otherness (although it might always be involved in many of those things), but about the ability to love and be loved as complete, imperfect human beings. Until gay marriage is legalized, this fundamental element of personal dignity will be denied a whole segment of humanity. No other change can achieve it.

Any heterosexual man who takes a few moments to consider what his life would be like if he were never allowed a formal institution to cement his relationships will see the truth of what I am saying. Imagine life without a recognized family; imagine dating without even the possibility of marriage. Any heterosexual woman who can imagine being told at a young age that her attraction to men was wrong, that her loves and crushes were illicit, that her destiny was singlehood and shame, will also appreciate the point. Gay marriage is not a radical step; it is a profoundly humanizing, traditionalizing step. It is the first step in any resolution of the homosexual question—more important than any other institution, since it is the most central institution to the nature of the problem, which is to say, the emotional and sexual bond between one human being and another. If nothing else were done at all, and gay marriage were legalized, 90 percent of the political work necessary to achieve gay and lesbian equality would have been achieved. It is ultimately the only reform that truly matters.

So long as conservatives recognize, as they do, that homosexuals exist and that they have equivalent emotional needs and temptations as heterosexuals, then there is no conservative reason to oppose homosexual marriage and many conservative reasons to support it. So long as liberals recognize, as they do, that citizens deserve equal treatment under the law, then there is no liberal reason to oppose it and many liberal reasons to be in favor of it. So long as intelligent people understand that homosexuals are emotionally and sexually attracted to the same sex as heterosexuals are to the other sex, then there is no human reason on earth why it should be granted to one group and not the other. . . .

[L]ifting the marriage bar [is] simple, direct, and require[s] no change in heterosexual behavior and no sacrifice from heterosexuals. [It would] represent a politics that tackles the heart of prejudice against homosexuals while leaving bigots their freedom. This politics marries the clarity of liberalism with the intuition of conservatism. It allows homosexuals to define their own future and their own identity and does not place it in the hands of the other. It makes a clear, public statement of equality while leaving all the inequalities of emotion and passion to the private sphere, where they belong. It does not legislate private tolerance; it declares public equality. It banishes the paradigm of victimology and replaces it with one of integrity. . . .

It has become a truism that in the field of emotional development, homosexuals have much to learn from the heterosexual culture. The values of commitment, of monogamy, of marriage, of stability are all posited as models for homosexual existence. And, indeed, of course, they are. Without an architectonic institution like that of marriage, it is difficult to create the conditions for nurturing such virtues, but that doesn't belie their importance.

It is also true, however, that homosexual relationships, even in their current, somewhat eclectic form, may contain features that could nourish the broader society as well. Precisely because there is no institutional model, gay relationships are often sustained more powerfully by genuine commitment. The mutual nurturing and sexual expressiveness of many lesbian relationships, the solidity and space of many adult gay male relationships, are qualities sometimes lacking in more rote, heterosexual couplings. Same-sex unions often incorporate the virtues of friendship more effectively than traditional marriages; and at times, among gay male relationships, the openness of the contract makes it more likely to survive than many heterosexual bonds. Some of this is unavailable to the male-female union: there is more likely to be greater understanding of the need for extramarital outlets between two men than between a man and a woman; and again, the lack of children gives gay couples greater freedom. Their failures entail fewer consequences for others. But something of the gay relationship's necessary honesty, its flexibility, and its equality could undoubtedly help strengthen and inform many heterosexual bonds.

In my own sometimes comic, sometimes passionate attempts to construct relationships, I learned something of the foibles of a simple heterosexual model. I saw how the network of gay friendship was often as good an emotional nourishment as a single relationship, that sexual candor was not always the same as sexual license, that the kind of supportive community that bolsters many gay relationships is something many isolated straight marriages could benefit from. I also learned how the subcultural fact of gay life rendered it remarkably democratic: in gay bars, there was far less socioeconomic stratification than in heterosexual bars. The shared experience of same-sex desire cut through class and race; it provided a humbling experience, which allowed many of us to risk our hearts and our friendships with people we otherwise might never have met. It loosened us up and gave us a keener sense, perhaps, that people were often difficult to understand, let alone judge, from appearances. My heterosexual peers, through no fault of their own, were often denied these experiences. But they might gain from understanding them a little better, and not simply from a position of condescension.

As I've just argued, I believe strongly that marriage should be made available to everyone, in a politics of strict public neutrality. But within this model, there is plenty of scope for cultural difference. There is something baleful about the attempt of some gay conservatives to educate homosexuals and lesbians into an uncritical acceptance of a stifling model of heterosexual normality. The truth is, homosexuals are not entirely normal; and to flatten their varied and complicated lives into a single, moralistic model is to miss what is essential and exhilarating about their otherness.

This need not mean, as some have historically claimed, that homosexuals have no stake in the sustenance of a society, but rather that their role is somewhat different; they may be involved in procreation in a less literal sense: in a society's cultural regeneration, its entrepreneurial or intellectual rejuvenation, its religious ministry, or its professional education. Unencumbered by children, they may be able to press the limits of the culture or the business infrastructure, or the boundaries of intellectual life, in a way that heterosexuals, by dint of a different type of calling, cannot. Of course, many heterosexuals perform similar roles; and many homosexuals prefer domesticity to public performance; but the inevitable way of life of the homosexual provides an opportunity that many intuitively seem to grasp and understand.

Or perhaps their role is to have no role at all. Perhaps it is the experience of rebellion that prompts homosexual culture to be peculiarly resistant to attempts to guide it to be useful or instructive or productive. Go to any march for gay rights and you will see the impossibility of organizing it into a coherent lobby: such attempts are always undermined by irony, or exhibitionism, or irresponsibility. It is as if homosexuals have learned something about life that makes them immune to the puritanical and flattening demands of modern politics. It is as if they have learned that life is fickle; that there are parts of it that cannot be understood, let alone solved; that some things lead nowhere and mean nothing; that the ultimate exercise of freedom is not a programmatic journey but a spontaneous one. Perhaps it requires seeing one's life as the end of a biological chain, or seeing one's deepest emotions as the object of detestation, that provides this insight. But the seeds of homosexual wisdom are the seeds of human wisdom. They contain the truth that order is in fact a euphemism for disorder; that problems are often more sanely enjoyed than solved; that there is reason in mystery; that there is beauty in the wild flowers that grow randomly among our wheat.

30.

THE MARRYING KIND

Elizabeth Kristol

What would life be like if we were not allowed to marry? That is the question at the heart of Andrew Sullivan's first book, *Virtually Normal*. In a sharp departure from the brash tone of the *New Republic,* the political weekly he edits, Sullivan here takes a sober look at the public debate over homosexuality and offers a moving, often lyrical, plea for the legalization of same-sex marriage.

Virtually Normal should be of special interest to conservatives. For one thing, Sullivan has occasionally described himself as such. Second, he is a Roman Catholic who has always taken matters of faith and the teachings of his Church seriously. Finally, Sullivan's thesis hinges on the claim that legalizing homosexual marriage would have a conservatizing influence on society as a whole.

Sullivan begins his book with a poignant memoir of growing up gay. He describes the pain and embarrassment he experienced in his struggles to come to terms with his homosexuality; his determination, once his desires became undeniable, to remain celibate in accordance with his faith; the explosive mix of joy and confusion he experienced when he had his first homosexual experience at age twenty-three.

From this autobiographical opening, Sullivan turns to what he considers the four prevailing attitudes toward homosexuality. These range from the authoritarian "prohibitionists," who consider homosexuality an abomination warranting legal punishment, to the anarchistic "liberationists," who reject the very distinction between homosexuality and heterosexuality as merely semantics. In between lie the "conservatives," who combine private tolerance of homosexuals with public disapproval of homosexuality, and the "liberals," who speak a language of victimhood and look to the state to enforce private tolerance.

This review of Andrew Sullivan, *Virtually Normal: An Argument about Homosexuality* (see chapter 29) originally appeared in *First Things: A Monthly Journal of Religion and Public Life* 59 (January 1996). Reprinted by permission of the publisher.

Sullivan analyzes each of these attitudes and concludes that they have all proven ineffective in developing a workable public position on homosexuality. Instead, he offers a political remedy that he claims will transcend the divisiveness. His solution is unique, Sullivan explains, in focusing exclusively on the actions of the "public neutral state." The state—but only the state—would have to treat homosexuals and heterosexuals with perfect equality. This would mean repealing antisodomy laws, permitting homosexuals to serve in the military on the same terms as heterosexuals, including lessons about homosexuality in public school sex-education programs, and legalizing homosexual marriage and divorce.

Sullivan claims that, since he does not seek to bar discrimination against homosexuals in the private sector, there would be "no cures or reeducation, no wrenching private litigation, no political imposition of tolerance; merely a political attempt to enshrine formal public equality, whatever happens in the culture and society at large." This solution, he adds, has the virtue of respecting religion; as part of the "private sector," churches can take whatever positions they like on homosexuality.

Is there such a thing as a purely "public" solution to the question of homosexuality that leaves the "private" realm untouched? We know Sullivan does not really believe this, because his entire argument in favor of legalized homosexual marriage hinges on the recognition that public law is the most powerful tool for shaping individual attitudes. The core assumption of *Virtually Normal*—and a compelling one, too—is that the *absence* of public laws granting homosexuals full equality has helped create a culture in which homosexuality is considered dirty or sinful, and in which homosexuals are deemed incapable of loving each other with dignity and commitment. As Sullivan rightly observes, the surest way to reverse the trickle-down effect of this message would be to stand the current law on its head. Far from being a simple matter of what the "neutral liberal state should do in public matters," then, public law is for Sullivan the crucial tool of social transformation.

Thus Sullivan notes that the existence of gay marriage would be an "unqualified social good" for homosexuals in providing role models for children coming to terms with their sexuality. As gay marriage

sank into the subtle background consciousness of a culture, its influence would be felt quietly but deeply among gay children. For them, at last, there would be some kind of future; some older faces to apply to their unfolding lives, some language in which their identity could be properly discussed, some rubric by which it could be explained—not in terms of sex, or sexual practices, or bars, or subterranean activity, but in terms of their future life stories, their potential loves, their eventual chance at some kind of constructive happiness.

The influence of gay marriage, Sullivan believes, would not only make it easier to grow up gay, but would actually change how adult homosexuals conduct their lives. He acknowledges that many homosexual men are self-centered and promiscuous. According to Sullivan, though, "there is nothing inevitable at all about a homosexual leading a depraved life." Homosexuals simply lack the proper "social incentives" not to be depraved. Once same-sex marriage is the law, Sullivan predicts, most homosexuals would enter into marriage "with as much (if not more) commitment as heterosexuals."

But is that really true? Sullivan does not address the fact that most lesbians, who grow up facing the same stigmas and the same lack of role models as male homosexuals, live conventional lives and form long-term monogamous relationships. Why, with gay men, are quasi marriages the exception to the rule? On this key point, Sullivan sends us a mixed message.

On the one hand, *Virtually Normal* presents a very sanitized picture of male homosexual life; there are no details of the gay subculture to repel heterosexual readers and make them less amenable to Sullivan's political proposals. Even Sullivan's chapter on "The Liberationists" does not include those we have come to associate with that term (the strident gay-rights activists or flamboyant gay liberationists) but focuses instead on a ragtag group of theoreticians influenced by French philosophy. Sullivan makes every effort to portray homosexuals as sharing the same emotions, longings, and dreams as heterosexuals.

Yet in the closing pages of his book, Sullivan undermines his own argument. In the final chapter he returns to the opening chapter's personal tone and reflects on some of the strengths he sees in the contemporary homosexual community. He asserts that "homosexual relationships, even in their current, somewhat eclectic form, may contain features that could nourish the broader society as well." The "solidity and space" of gay relationships "are qualities sometimes lacking in more rote, heterosexual couplings." Moreover, the "openness of the contract makes it more likely to survive than many heterosexual bonds." As Sullivan puts it, there is "more likely to be a greater understanding of the need for extramarital outlets between two men than between a man and a woman; and again, the lack of children gives gay couples greater freedom."

Sullivan suggests that gay marriage would do well to retain some of this "openness":

> I believe strongly that marriage should be made available to everyone, in a politics of strict public neutrality. But within this model, there is plenty of scope for cultural difference. There is something baleful about the attempt of some gay conservatives to educate homosexuals and lesbians into an uncritical acceptance of a stifling model of heterosexual normality. The truth is, homosexuals are not entirely normal; and to flatten their varied and complicated lives into a single, moralistic model is to miss what is essential and exhilarating about their otherness.

Rote? Stifling? Moralistic? These are strange epithets to come upon in the final pages of a book whose goal is to convince readers that homosexuals want to marry and deserve to marry; that homosexual love is as dignified as heterosexual love; that it is inhumane not to allow the dignity of this love to find fruition in marriage; that marriage is so venerable an institution that it is single-handedly capable of leading men out of lives of empty promiscuity into unions of commitment and fidelity. Suddenly we learn, almost as an afterthought, that the institution of marriage may have to change to accommodate the special needs of homosexuals.

At first glance, it seems odd that Sullivan would be so eager to support an institution for which he seems to have serious reservations. But Sullivan is more interested in marriage as a symbol than as an institution. On its most fundamental level, *Virtually Normal* is not about politics or ideas, but about emotions: Sullivan's overwhelming priority is to spare future generations the suffering he experienced. His argument for gay marriage is memorable, not as a cry for equal access to the covenant of marriage, but as a fervent hope that someday the stigma may be removed from homosexuality.

Sullivan is probably right that his proposals would make it easier for young homosexuals to accept themselves. But it could make adolescence a rougher time for everyone: children confronted with two equally legitimate images of adult sexual roles would be rudderless for many years, and no one knows what personal or social toll would result from this prolonged period of sexual confusion.

Nor does Sullivan take seriously the question of how children would be raised by same-sex parents, and what long-term effects this upbringing might have on their emotional and sexual development. Sullivan addresses only one sentence to this complicated subject: "There is no evidence that shows any deleterious impact on a child brought up by two homosexual parents." He does not discuss the practical implications of his reform for foster care, adoption, child-custody suits, and the like.

And while Sullivan would presumably not consider this a social "cost," policymakers would have to grapple with the fact that legalizing gay marriage would probably increase the number of homosexuals overall. Any societal influence that is strong enough to be "felt deeply" by children who are destined to become homosexual is also going to be felt by children whose sexual orientation is less certain. Even if Sullivan is correct in guessing that an individual's sexual orientation is firmly established by the age of five or six (a debatable point), this would hardly mean that sexual orientation is immune from social influence.

Finally, as many of Sullivan's "conservative" thinkers point out, placing gay marriage on an equal footing with heterosexual marriage might end up weakening marriage as an institution. Sullivan offers a particularly unsatisfying response to this concern. Because homosexuals "have no choice but to be homosexual," he declares, "they are not choosing that option over heterosexual marriage; and so they are not sending any social signals that heterosexual family life should be denigrated."

This answer misses the point of the pro-family argument. Conservatives do not fear that legalizing gay marriage would send heterosexuals the message that they are settling for second best. Conservatives are concerned that the more society broadens the definition of "marriage"—and some would argue that the definition has already been stretched to the breaking point—the less seriously it will be taken by everyone.

If *Virtually Normal* is any indication, this fear is warranted. When all is said and done, Sullivan is not just interested in admitting a new group of people to marriage (although that would be revolutionary enough). He wants to redefine marriage to accommodate a particular lifestyle. Sullivan's willingness to jettison the monogamous aspect of marriage (and what more important aspect is there?), and his suggestion that heterosexuals should rethink their own "moralistic" and "stifling" notions of marriage: these are the "social signals" that worry conservatives. In short, Sullivan's book beautifully engages our sympathy for the difficulties homosexuals encounter in our society, but it is unpersuasive in its argument that gay marriage would be a conservatizing force.

31.

EMBODIMENT, CARE ETHICS, AND THE SAME-SEX MARRIAGE CONTROVERSY

Maurice Hamington

In his critically acclaimed and controversial theater production *Corpus Christi*, Tony Award–winning playwright Terrence McNally offers an alternative rendering of the Christian gospel story. Near the conclusion of the play, Joshua, the Christ figure, sanctions the marriage of two of his disciples:

> James: Bartholomew and I had wanted our union blessed for a long time—some acknowledgement of what we were to each other.
>
> Bartholomew: We asked, Josh. They said it was against the law and the priests said it was forbidden by scripture.
>
> James: "If a man lies with a man as with a woman, both of them have committed an abomination; they shall be put to death, their blood is upon them."

Joshua recognizes that the Christian bible is a rich and complex text with many possible points of reference for moral insight. He offers an alternative selection.

> Joshua: Why would you memorize such a terrible passage? "And God saw everything that He had made, and behold it was very good." I can quote Scripture as well as the next man. God loves us most when we love each other. We accept you and bless you. Who's got a ring?

Bartholomew and James are astonished that Joshua is willing to officiate their wedding and furthermore, he wishes to do so in public where critics might observe. After obtaining rings, Joshua performs the simple ceremony.

> Joshua: It is good when two men love as James and Bartholomew do and we recognize their union. No giggling back there! Now, take each other's hand. Love

217

each other in sickness and health. Respect the divinity in your partner, Bartholomew. Cherish the little things in him, James, exalt in the great. May the first face you see each morning and the last at night always be his. I bless this marriage in Your name, Father. Amen. Now let's all get very, very drunk.

McNally has written a passion play, not a philosophical treatment of the arguments surrounding same-sex marriage, but, as Martha Nussbaum has suggested, "literary works typically invite their readers to put themselves in the place of people of many different kinds to take on their experiences."[1] Accordingly, in his preface to the published version of the play, McNally indicates that plays provide "new insight into the human condition." In this instance, Joshua has also given us insight into the workings of moral deliberation. He replaces one moral statement with another he believes is superior. Many Christians will be unhappy with McNally's interpretation. Attempts to assert the priority of one isolated passage of scripture over another are common although not entirely satisfying because the impression remains that yet another passage might trump the current victor and that perhaps such one-upmanship could go on for some time. Reconciling moral claims in this competitive manner is a vexing and often head-spinning proposition. Perhaps the old wineskins of moral argumentation cannot entirely contain the new wine of today's social concerns.

In this essay I suggest that Western philosophic tradition has overlooked the role of care as well as the significance of the body in moral theory. Current debates over same-sex marriage reflect an approach to morality overly focused on adjudication within a competitive style of moral deliberation. Whose rights are greater? What consequences are worst or best? Whose interpretation of history is superior? Or in the case of "religions of the book," which passage supercedes the other? These questions underpin many of the lines of argument currently utilized to address same-sex marriage. *While adjudication is an important part of ethical theorizing, it does not represent the entirety of morality.* Decisions do have to be made but they represent only particular moments in time. As social beings we exist in a web of relationships that extend beyond individual moral crises. The approach to moral understanding that I call *embodied care* integrates feminist care ethics with philosopher Maurice Merleau-Ponty's phenomenology of the body to suggest that our bodies are built for care.[2] In this essay I review traditional approaches used to evaluate the morality of same-sex marriage, and I offer the idea of embodied care as a means to an ethical position about this issue, but not at the expense of the flesh-and-blood human beings whose opinions differ.

EMBODIED CARE

The development of an ethic of care is one of the most significant innovations in moral philosophy of the latter part of the twentieth century. Although receiving mixed reactions, care ethics galvanized a groundswell of research and writing by feminist theorists in a number of disciplines around the notion that rules and consequences do not exhaust the content of morality. Care is a relational approach to ethics that emphasizes personal connection, context, and affective responses. Since the 1980s, when the term "care ethics" was first coined, there has been a tidal wave of books and articles that clarify and extend this nascent moral trajectory. Although feminist philosophers have led this charge, there has been an ironic lack of attention paid to the embodied aspect of care ethics. The irony exists because of the widespread feminist critique of disembodied modernist moral theory and the extensive work that feminists have offered in returning attention to the body in other disciplines such as epistemology and sociology.

Feminist scholars Carol Gilligan, Nel Noddings, Rita Manning, Joan Tronto, Sara Ruddick, Susan Hekman, and others have contributed significant elaborations and extensions of care ethics. Today, no discussion of ethics from a feminist perspective is complete without some mention of care. While feminist care ethicists have employed divergent methodologies, assumptions, and conclusions, they share a concern for connection and particularity over universality and abstraction. Although emotive and affective responses have been stressed, little specific treatment of the embodied dimension of care has been developed. In other words, while many feminists have clearly rejected the disembodied, abstract understanding of modern moral theory, few have explored how care pervades the experience of lived bodies.

Elsewhere I extrapolate Merleau-Ponty's philosophically dense notions of the flesh and its reversibility to suggest that our bodies are built for caring.[3] Our bodies are not incidental to morality as they have been treated by the Western tradition of philosophy. Our bodies are our entrée into the world and our relationships with others. Here I am not addressing bodies as separate from minds but as integrated wholes—bodies and minds. Human bodies know how to care as exhibited in habits of care reflected in gestures, vocalizations, facial expressions, posture, and so on. One does not explain caring to a child separate from action in order to teach him or her how to care. Caring cannot be fully captured by articulation. There is an unspoken implicit dimension to caring. One learns care from observing and mimicking behaviors of the body. Nevertheless, caring is so basic to human relations that it is easy to overlook its significance in the morality of our daily lives.

TRADITIONAL APPROACHES APPLIED TO SAME-SEX MARRIAGE

For the sake of brevity, we can organize the arguments for and against same-sex marriage into the classic moral categories of deontology and teleology. Deontological arguments employ some rule for adjudication. The rule may be

historical, legal, rights-based, semantic, or otherwise characterized, but ultimately it is a moral rule. Teleological arguments utilize ends, consequences,
or results. People may make a variety of arguments but the majority of positions on same-sex marriage fit into one of these perspectives. What most
moral arguments have in common is that they operate as competitive games
with combatants searching for victory through superiority given the rational
parameters of engagement. I now explore a few deontological and teleological arguments.

One principled approach to the issue of same-sex marriage is the semantic argument that focuses on the definition of marriage. Some make the claim
that because "marriage" is defined as a particular kind of relationship—
between a man and a woman—therefore, a gay marriage is a true oxymoron.[4]
This linguistic argument equates definitional authority with moral authority.
For example, *Webster's Encyclopedic Unabridged Dictionary of the English
Language*'s first definition of marriage is "the social institution under which
a man and woman establish their decision to live as husband and wife by legal
commitments, religious ceremonies, etc."[5] Brian Harradine employs a definitional approach to same-sex marriage: "Moving away from this shared community standard [the system of marriage between a man and a woman] would
become just one in a list of relationship options. It would lose its meaning.[6]
The diffusion or loss of meaning is presumed rationally unacceptable. Of
course, semantic arguments can be countered by the observation that defini-
tions can and do evolve. Historians point out that understandings of marriage
have changed over time. Different cultures and eras have defined marriage in
a variety of ways. Some recent Western changes in the definition of marriage
include viewing women as equal partners, recognizing marriage between
those of different races and religions, and the notion that marriage can be legitimately dissolved.

Another principled approach to same-sex marriage is to frame the arguments in terms of rights. Is the denial of same-sex marriage a violation of a
right, and, if so, is it a legal right or a human right being abrogated? Most of
the current arguments address legal rights. For example, William Eskridge Jr.
dedicates a chapter of his book *The Case for Same-Sex Marriage* to making
constitutional arguments for legalizing same-sex marriage including applications of the right to privacy and equal rights. The moral discussion takes place
over the hierarchy of rights. For example, "In light of the Supreme Court's
precedents, a state's refusal to recognize same-sex marriage would seem to be
both the denial of fundamental liberty and discrimination in the allocation of
a fundamental right."[7] Robert Goss suggests that heterosexuals and homosexuals alike have the positive right "to create family forms that fits his or her
needs to realize the human potential for love in nonoppressive relationships."[8]
Opponents claim that no such right exists and granting such a right runs
counter to the intention of the framers of the Constitution.

Sometimes the arguments surrounding rights address the unequal application of these rights. For example, M. D. A. Freeman argues that criminals such as "murderers and rapists" are allowed to marry so why are homosexuals not allowed to marry? Furthermore, he points out that no one is asked to prove their sexual orientation when they marry so when men and women present themselves it is assumed that they are heterosexual, which may not be accurate.[9] Another legal strategy is to claim that homosexuals occupy a position similar to oppressed ethnic groups or "suspect class" in legal terms, and therefore deserve similar protection under the law.[10] Kevin Moss argues that the discrimination and stereotypes directed at homosexuals is one indication that they deserve status as a separate class.[11] However, there has been strong legal and popular opposition to such a classification.

Deontological arguments demonstrate how the discussion surrounding same-sex marriage may be framed around principled approaches to morality. *The aim is to seek an authoritative right or principle that supports a position.* Accordingly, as in legal arguments, the opposition can attempt to find a counterprinciple to trump the original one or question the legitimacy of claims. Principles play an important role in morality, and embodied care is not antithetical to rule-based morality. However, embodied care recognizes that an abstract formulaic approach to ethics does not capture the whole of human morality. Abstract moral principles also imply that they are somehow "value free" and disinterested; this is not so because fallible human beings with their own biases must apply these principles. As Christine Pierce observes, "Until current sentiments in our society are changed, lesbians and gay men will not be able to expect that ethical (and legal) principles will be applied fairly to them."[12] Valuing embodied care involves asking questions that recenter the debate on the individuals involved, including their affections, their relationships, and their context. What are their emotions and why are they so strong? How do various positions impact ongoing relationships? How do various positions affect the interconnectedness of society?

Not all the current arguments surrounding gay marriage depend on principles. Many arguments are consequentialist or outcome based. President George W. Bush employed a consequentialist argument in his 2004 statement of support for a constitutional amendment limiting marriage to a union between a man and a woman: "The union of a man and woman is the most enduring human institution, honoring—honored and encouraged in all cultures and by every religious faith. Ages of experience have taught humanity that the commitment of a husband and wife to love and to serve one another promotes the welfare of children and the stability of society."[13] Accordingly, the consequences of legitimizing same-sex marriage will be to damage children and create instability. Advocates of same-sex marriage contend that the consequences of not legitimizing it are hazardous to the children of gay parents financially and emotionally if their relationship is not legally recognized.[14]

One sticky entanglement with abstract calculations of good is that they can be devised to support any number of positions depending upon what slice of reality is employed. For example, social conservatives equate marriage with a social good. The stability of society depends upon these committed relationships. Taken at face value, more marriage equates with greater overall good. Therefore, allowing homosexuals to marry would result in more marriages and thus more good. Of course, many have great reservations in universally equating marriage with social good, but again, the limitation of consequentialist argument is apparent.

While deontological arguments are abstract and often cite textual evidence for support, consequentialist arguments tend to cite empirical data and experience. For example, Craig Benson, a pastor in the Cambridge United Church, claims that legalizing same-sex marriage is akin to supporting the idea that "motherless and fatherless families will not have an adverse effect on children. . . . [T]hat, from a developmental-psychology point of view is a lie."[15] Benson claims that scientific data supports his concern for the negative consequences to children. Often children are a bellwether for social issues because of their vulnerable status. However, supporters of same-sex marriage can also cite recent research on children in homosexual families that reveals no significant harmful impact as compared to children raised in heterosexual families. Both sides of the issue have evidence to support their consequentialist perspective. Some who favor same-sex marriage might even grant some negative results from legitimizing gay marriage; they think, however, that the good effects outweigh the bad. Andrew Sullivan proclaims that same-sex marriage is simply "good for gays. It provides role models for young gay people . . . help[s] bridge the gulf often found between gays and their parents. . . . It could do much to heal the gay-straight rift."[16] Consequentialist arguments center on producing the most good in society. Debate in this area then centers on who has the most compelling evidence for their outcomes and, applying the happiness principle, which outcomes provide the greatest good for the most people.

Through the above examples of the deployment of deontological and teleological arguments I intend not to debate the merits of their claims but to show how approving same-sex marriage can be just as rational as disapproving it. These are not unimportant discussions. Rights, principles, and consequences have significant implications that merit consideration. However, framing the discussion in rational terms leaves out the affective, emotive dimension. The fundamental notion of human continuity is absent. In other words, embodied care is not at the fore of traditional approaches. How can opponents in the same-sex controversy reflect care? If context and affective knowledge were more highly valued, the arguments would be concerned less with winning and concerned more with maintaining the interconnectedness of the social fabric.

Debates over the consequences of same-sex marriage reveal that the controversy is more about the legitimacy of homosexuality than about the institution of marriage. For example, arguments that legalizing same-sex marriage have negative consequences for all marriages are difficult to support because the cause-and-effect relationships are impossible to demonstrate. How can two same-sex individuals marrying hurt any particular heterosexual marriage? The damage cannot be material other than in some socially constructed manner. Similarly, if consequences were the only object of those favoring same-sex marriage then civil unions that granted equal protection under state and federal law would provide equal results. Of course, the debate goes much deeper than the form rituals of union take. The issue of marriage is to some extent a referendum on homosexual existence. Christine Pierce contends that homosexuals have been inappropriately viewed only as individuals and not as in relationship: "Gay marriage needs to be on the political agenda for the sake of gaining a certain level of social awareness and acceptance of serious lesbian and gay relationships."[17] This concern is significant if we accept that humans are essentially social beings. Denying the committed relationships of homosexuals in a sense denies part of their humanity. The emotions on both sides of this issue run too deep for the strategies arguments of traditional moral philosophy to address fully.

APPLYING EMBODIED CARE
TO THE ISSUE OF SAME-SEX MARRIAGE

Embodied care begins not with an abstract theory of right and wrong, but with the concrete reality of human embodiment: *Same-sex marriage is a controversial issue that involves members of the same species.* This seems like an absurdly obvious statement to begin the discussion, but as Merleau-Ponty has explained, human embodiment is vital. Merleau-Ponty describes humans as "intercorporeal beings" whose embodied experiences—touch, sight, and so on—undergo a "propagation of these exchanges to all the bodies of the same type" resulting in a "transivity from one body to another."[18] The body's ability to perceive, and focus, as well as its continuity with the world, allows it to capture movements in habits. These habits give us not only the means for being in the world, but also they provide a basis for understanding and caring for others. Bodies are built for care. However, bodies are confronted with obstacles of time, space, and socially constructed differences that make caring difficult. These obstacles can be overcome by a caring imagination informed by knowledge we hold in our bodies.

Sexual orientation has become just such an obstacle for caring. Labels such as "gay" and "straight" are so politically charged that it appears as if two completely different species are being addressed. For example, Richard D. Mohr describes one persistent stereotype of gay men as "child molester, and more generally as a sex-crazed maniac."[19] The persistence of such stereotypes allows homosexuals to be treated as dangerous others, and perhaps as less-than-human predators. Those fighting for gay rights have also been marginalized through persistent labels. US Supreme Court Justice Antonin Scalia perpetuated such stereotypes in his dissent to the landmark decision in *Lawrence v. Texas* that upheld a homosexual's right to liberty that the state may not intrude upon. Scalia held that this ruling would call into question state laws against "bigamy, same-sex marriage, adult incest, prostitution, masturbation, adultery, fornication, bestiality, and obscenity."[20] Note how same-sex marriage is implied to be on par with incest, bestiality, and obscenity. Jonathon Goldberg-Hiller describes popular "stories about extensive gay and lesbian political agendas, outrageous queer direct action, poor hygiene and AIDS, pedophilia and the threat of youth 'recruitment,'" as causing a reactionary retrenchment to romanticized notions of family and marriage.[21] Beginning with the obvious, but commonly ignored, idea that all the agents involved in the same-sex marriage debate are humans who share an embodied nature produces a baseline of understanding from which to work. Homosexual persons and heterosexual persons share much more of experienced existence than they do not. Although social discourse has helped leverage differences in sexual orientation into central aspects of identity, the continuity of embodied experience significantly segments potential resources for understanding across sexual orientation.

Consistent with a phenomenological reduction, embodied care attends to the idea that at its core, the same-sex marriage debate is about human beings and their relations. Empathy among humans transcends rational argument. This affective knowledge does not resolve the issue, but it does provide an important starting point that insists on basic human continuity.

The affective knowledge in our body also offers a foundation for imagination. I may not know what it is to be romantically in love with someone of the same sex nor to desire to demonstrate commitment through marriage, but I may know what it is to be in love. Imagination plays a crucial role in embodied care. As Debra Shogun points out, "If I am to identify with another's situation I must . . . be able to imagine subjectively what this person's world is like."[22] If I allow my caring imagination to take flight, I can recall the feelings and affections of falling in love, having that relationship grow, and perhaps wanting to reify that feeling by getting married. I can also recall how important marriage was for me, or for family and friends, and how emotions run high at such events. For many, the marriage ceremony and subsequent celebration are the highlight of their lives marked by overwhelming joy, crying, hugs, kisses, and so on.[23] Perhaps the biggest imaginative leap is to extrapolate the feelings I have had, or observed in relationships, to a man who loves another man, or a woman who loves another woman. What makes this such an enormous leap is that homosexuality is such a tremendous social taboo and a powerful counternarrative to social norms. Adrienne Rich and others describe the prevalence of "compulsory heterosexuality" in our society, which has made heterosexuality not a choice but a social mandate.[24] For some, heterosexuality is such an ingrained expectation that imagination hits an impasse. Personal identification becomes difficult because for many heterosexuals, homosexuals are social outcasts. However, if, in the spirit of Merleau-Ponty's phenomenology of the body, one focuses on human continuity, then one sees sexual expression is only one part of human life. All the feelings of emotion in a mutual experience of love should be available for embodied beings to project onto others even if they have a different sexual orientation.

The more experiences we have with people considered "others," the more apparent is the continuity of embodied existence. In the case of sexual orientation, the more acquaintances, friends, coworkers, family members, or even fictional characters that we come to know who are gay (and more than just caricatures or stereotypes), the greater the chance that such knowledge will break down the mystery and distrust of the unknown other. However, we must make the effort to experience a variety of other people. The explicit or implicit discovery will be that "in many ways, *they* are just like me."[25] This interpersonal understanding does not guarantee that minds will be changed, but it reminds us that morality is more than just winning an argument, being right, or celebrating moral superiority. Moral deliberation involves real people who are very much like us.

An example of an interpersonal connection came in the Vermont state legislature that passed a historic civil union bill. One of the legislators who voted in favor of the bill (it passed by only an eleven-vote majority) was eighty-four-year-old Rep. William Fry, a Republican from a conservative working-class town. Given his background, Fry would not appear to be a social liberal who might favor same-sex marriage. When asked why he voted for the bill, Fry answered, ". . . there were two ladies who were my next door neighbors. . . . (sobbing) They were treated terrible. I'm just glad I could do something to help."[26] He made a connection between the treatment of fellow human beings and the impact of political policy. One can read principles or consequences into Fry's actions, but he acted on more than propositional knowledge; he acted out of care based on his ability to empathize with a lesbian couple that he knew.

What about the rules, standards, and norms of my society? Do I ignore them? While empathy is a crucial aspect of the caring imagination, there is also a recognition that we do not exist in a vacuum and a consideration of the rules, norms, and values of our society comes into play. Pearl Oliner and Samuel Oliner express this recognition in their vision of a caring society: "A caring society, as we conceive it, is one in which care penetrates all major social institutions, including the family, schools, the workplace, and religious institutions. Penetrating means to be present in some important degree, but it does not mean expunging or replacing all other modes of social relationships or goals."[27] Given embodied care as we have described it, such social standards are recognized, but they do not trump our capacity to care.

CONCLUSIONS AND INCONCLUSIONS

Embodied care shifts the analysis of same-sex marriage from making arguments strictly from rules or consequences to attending to the voices, passions, relationships, and context of those involved in the debate. What resources of embodied knowledge help me use habits of caring imagination to understand relational, affective dimensions of this issue? When one practices habits of active listening, what does one learn from the people of each side of the issue? These activities exhibit care grounded in a body; they do not enable an easy or formulaic response. Sarah Hoagland describes rules and principles as attractive because they are "certain and secure."[28] Embodied care does not offer the security of a belief that same-sex marriage is absolutely right or wrong. However, embodied care brings into focus the affective knowledge that may contribute to a more holistic understanding of this moral dilemma.

Embodied care attends to and develops certain habits of the body. As these habits develop, normative responses become clearer. My affective knowledge of the importance of committed relationships to the social animals that are human beings does not deny opportunities for development. Human relationships are challenging enough without prejudice from society. The promotion of growth and flourishing warrant removing unnecessary social constraints. Given the practices, values, and commitments discussed, an approach consistent with embodied care points to the legitimacy of same-sex marriage. From what I know in my body about feelings for loved ones, from what I learn through listening to others, same-sex marriage allows many relationships to flourish in this socially ritualized relationship. There are outcomes and rules that support this conclusion, but most of all this endorsement expresses care and concern for fellow human beings. It is difficult to genuinely care for a class of people such as "homosexuals" but I can care for concrete individual people that I have known who are gay. As I think about them and their humanity—they are always presented to me as faces and bodies with joys and sorrows like my own—how can I deny them a ritual commitment that is so important in our society? My humanity compels me to want for them the opportunity to marry if they desire it just as I have this opportunity. Arguments against same-sex marriage are ultimately too steeped in justice approaches that are external to the human condition.

What about the concern that same-sex marriage is a veritable "line in the sand" and those on both sides of the issue view it as a watershed for the future of our society? So be it. Care ethics is not easy. It cannot rest on principles or consequences but must continually respond to context and relationships. If caring is indeed important, then legitimizing same-sex marriage is a form of caring. At the beginning of this millennium, same-sex marriage is a vexing civil rights issue, but if caring is truly the heart of morality, then socially constructed barriers to gay marriage—religious, legal, and political—must be permeated by our fundamental connections to one another.

What about those who oppose same-sex marriage? Does a decision to support same-sex marriage mean that care is unidirectional in this case? Just because embodied care as I have described it appears to support gay marriage, it does not mean that those who oppose gay marriage should be stigmatized as evil. The goal is not to find further evidence to "win" the debate, but to understand those who have the opposing position because they are human beings who share with me an embodied existence as well. The feelings that underlie the oppositions to same-sex marriage are just as legitimate as any feelings and cannot be summarily discounted. One expression of care should not create another barrier to care. Without compromising the belief that same-sex couples ought to be allowed to express themselves through marriage, those who oppose same-sex marriage should continue to be listened to and cared for. The morality of embodied care calls us from the depth of our shared embodied existence to be vigilant in our ongoing efforts to understand one another.

NOTES

1. Martha Nussbaum, *Poetic Justice: The Literary Imagination and Public Life* (Boston: Beacon Press, 1995), p. 5.

2. For a more comprehensive explanation of the term "embodied care" see *Embodied Care: Jane Addams, Maurice-Merleau Ponty, and Feminist Ethics* (Urbana: University of Illinois Press, 2004).

3. Ibid., chap. 2.

4. Igor Primoratz, *Ethics and Sex* (London: Routledge, 1999), p. 129.

5. *Webster's Encyclopedia Unabridged Dictionary* (New York: Portland House, 1989), p. 879.

6. Brian Harradine, "Redefine Wedlock at Children's Peril," *Australian,* March 9, 2004, Features Section, p. 13.

7. William N. Eskridge Jr., *The Case for Same-Sex Marriage* (New York: Free Press, 1996), p. 130.

8. Quoted in Jeffrey Weeks, Brian Heaphy, and Catherine Donovan, *Same-Sex Intimacies: Families of Choice and Other Experiments* (London: Routledge, 2001), p. 9.

9. Jonathon Goldberg-Hiller, *The Limits to Union: Same-Sex Marriage and the Politics of Civil Rights* (Ann Arbor: University of Michigan Press, 2002), pp. 6–7.

10. Joshua Gamson, "Must Identity Movements Self-Destruct?" *Social Problems* 42 (1995): 396.

11. Kevin Moss, "Legitimizing Same-Sex Marriage," *Peace Review* 14 (2002).

12. Christine Pierce, "Gay Marriage," *Journal of Social Philosophy* 26, no. 2 (Fall 1995): 13.

13. "President Calls for Constitutional Amendment Protecting Marriage," February 24, 2004, http://www.whitehouse.gov/news/releases/2004/02/20040224-2.html.

14. Charlene Gomes, "The Need for Full Recognition of Same-Sex Marriage," *Humanist* 63, no. 5 (September/October 2003): 6.

15. David Goodman, "A More Civil Union," *Mother Jones* (July/August 2000).

16. Andrew Sullivan, "Here Comes the Groom: A Conservative Case for Gay Marriage," *New Republic,* August 28, 1989.

17. Pierce, "Gay Marriage," p. 14.

18. Maurice Merleau-Ponty, *The Visible and the Invisible* (Evanston, IL: Northwestern Universty Press, 1968), p. 143.

19. Richard D. Mohr, *A More Perfect Union: Why Straight America Must Stand Up for Gay Rights* (Boston: Beacon Press, 1994), p. 2.

20. Gomes, "The Need for Full Recognition of Same-Sex Marriage," p. 8.

21. Goldberg-Hiller, *The Limits to Union,* p. 45.

22. Debra Shogun, *Care and Moral Motivation* (Toronto: Ontario Institute for Studies in Education, 1988), p. 69.

23. I recognize that fully half of all marriages end in divorce and many people get married under circumstances that preclude celebration, but marriage remains a joyfully evocative event in the public imagination.

24. Adrienne Rich, "Compulsory Heterosexuality and Lesbian Existence," in *Powers of Desire* (New York: Monthly Review Press, 1973).

25. For example, there is no evidence that homosexuals have a higher rate of sexual predation than heterosexuals, but scientific studies will not overcome stereotypes to the same degree that the confirmation of interpersonal experience will. Mohr, *A More Perfect Union*, p. 2.

26. Goodman, "A More Civil Union," p. 56.

27. Pearl Oliner and Samuel Oliner, *Toward a Caring Society: Ideas into Action* (Westport, CT: Praeger, 1995), p. 2.

28. Sarah Hoagland, *Lesbian Ethics: Toward New Value* (Palo Alto: Institute of Lesbian Studies, 1988), p. 11.

32.

GAY MARRIAGE—AND MARRIAGE

Sam Schulman

The feeling seems to be growing that gay marriage is inevitably coming our way in the United States, perhaps through a combination of judicial fiat and legislation in individual states. Growing, too, is the sense of a shift in the climate of opinion. The American public seems to be in the process of changing its mind—not actually in favor of gay marriage, but toward a position of slightly revolted tolerance for the idea. Survey results suggest that people have forgotten why they were so opposed to the notion even as recently as a few years ago.

It is curious that this has happened so quickly. With honorable exceptions, most of those who are passionately on the side of the traditional understanding of marriage appear to be at a loss for words to justify their passion; as for the rest, many seem to wish gay marriage had never been proposed in the first place, but also to have resigned themselves to whatever happens. In this respect, the gay-marriage debate is very different from the abortion debate, in which few with an opinion on either side have been so disengaged.

I think I understand why this is the case: as someone passionately and instinctively opposed to the idea of homosexual marriage, I have found myself disappointed by the arguments I have seen advanced against it. The strongest of these arguments predict measurable harm to the family and to our arrangements for the upbringing and well-being of children. I do not doubt the accuracy of those arguments.* But they do not seem to get at the heart of the matter.

To me, what is at stake in this debate is not only the potential unhappiness of children, grave as that is; it is our ability to maintain the most basic components of our humanity. I believe, in fact, that we are at an "Antigone

---

Reprinted from *Commentary*, November 2003, by permission; all rights reserved.

*For a summary of the scant research on children raised in homes with same-sex parents as of six or seven years ago, see James Q. Wilson, "Against Homosexual Marriage," *Commentary* (March 1996).

moment." Some of our fellow citizens wish to impose a radically new understanding upon laws and institutions that are both very old and fundamental to our organization as individuals and as a society. As Antigone said to Creon, we are being asked to tamper with "unwritten and unfailing laws, not of now, nor of yesterday; they always live, and no one knows their origin in time." I suspect, moreover, that everyone knows this is the case, and that, paradoxically, this very awareness of just how much is at stake is what may have induced, in defenders of those same "unwritten and unfailing laws," a kind of paralysis.

Admittedly, it is very difficult to defend that which is both ancient and "unwritten"—the arguments do not resolve themselves into a neat parade of documentary evidence, research results, or citations from the legal literature. Admittedly, too, proponents of this radical new understanding have been uncommonly effective in presenting their program as something that is not radical at all but as requiring merely a slight and painless adjustment in our customary arrangements. Finally, we have all learned to practice a certain deference to the pleas of minorities with a grievance, and in recent years no group has benefited more from this society-wide dispensation than homosexuals. Nevertheless, in the somewhat fragmentary notes that follow, I hope to rearticulate what I am persuaded everyone knows to be the case about marriage, and perhaps thereby encourage others with stronger arguments than mine to help break the general paralysis.

Let us begin by admiring the case *for* gay marriage. Unlike the case for completely unrestricted abortion, which has come to be something of an embarrassment even to those who advance it, the case for gay marriage enjoys the decided advantage of appealing to our better moral natures as well as to our reason. It deploys two arguments. The first centers on principles of justice and fairness and may be thought of as the civil rights argument. The second is at once more personal and more utilitarian, emphasizing the degradation and unhappiness attendant upon the denial of gay marriage and, conversely, the human and social happiness that will flow from its legal establishment.

Both arguments have been set forth most persuasively by two gifted writers, Bruce Bawer and Andrew Sullivan, each of whom describes himself as a social conservative. In their separate ways, they have been campaigning for gay marriage for over a decade. Bawer's take on the subject is succinctly summarized in his 1993 book, *A Place at the Table*; Sullivan has held forth on the desirability of legalizing gay marriage in numerous articles, on his Web site (andrewsullivan.com), and in an influential book, *Virtually Normal* (1995).

The civil rights argument goes like this. Marriage is a legal state conferring real, tangible benefits on those who participate in it: specifically, tax breaks as well as other advantages when it comes to inheritance, property ownership, and employment benefits. But family law, since it limits marriage to heterosexual couples over the age of consent, clearly discriminates against a segment of the population. It is thus a matter of simple justice that, in Sullivan's words, "all public (as opposed to private) discrimination against homosexuals be ended and that every right and responsibility that heterosexuals enjoy as public citizens be extended to those who grow up and find themselves emotionally different." Not to grant such rights, Sullivan maintains, is to impose on homosexuals a civil deprivation akin to that suffered by black Americans under Jim Crow.

The utilitarian argument is more subtle; just as the rights argument seems aimed mainly at liberals, this one seems mostly to have in mind the concerns of conservatives. In light of the disruptive, anarchic, violence-prone behavior of many homosexuals (the argument runs), why should we not encourage the formation of stable, long-term, monogamous relationships that will redound to the health of society as a whole? In the apt words of a letter writer in *Commentary* in 1996:

[H]omosexual marriage . . . preserves and promotes a set of moral values that are essential to civilized society. Like heterosexual marriage, it sanctions loyalty, unselfishness, and sexual fidelity; it rejects the promiscuous, the self-serving, the transitory relationship. Given the choice between building family units and preventing them, any conservative should favor the former.

Bawer, for his part, has come close to saying that the inability of many male homosexuals to remain faithful in long-term relationships is a consequence of the lack of marriage rights—a burning sign of the more general stigma under which gays labor in our society and which can be redressed by changes in law. As it happens, though, this particular line of argument is already somewhat out of date and is gradually being phased out of the discussion. The toleration of gay styles of life has come about on its own in American society, without the help of legal sanctions, and protecting gay couples from the contempt of bigots is not the emergency Bawer has depicted. Quite the contrary: with increasing numbers of gay partners committing themselves to each other for life, in full and approving view of their families and friends, advocates of gay marriage need no longer call upon the law to light (or force) the way; they need only ask it to ratify a trend.

In brief, legalizing gay marriage would, in Andrew Sullivan's summary formulation,

offer homosexuals the same deal society now offers heterosexuals: general social approval and specific legal advantages in exchange for a deeper and harder-to-extract-yourself-from commitment to another human being. Like straight marriage, it would foster social cohesion, emotional security, and economic prudence.

The case is elegant, and it is compelling. But it is not unanswerable. And answers have indeed been forthcoming, even if, as I indicated at the outset, many of them have tended to be couched somewhat defensively. Thus, rather than repudiating the very idea of an abstract "right" to marry, many upholders of the traditional definition of marriage tacitly concede such a right, only going on to suggest that denying it to a minority amounts to a lesser hurt than conferring it would impose on the majority, and especially on children, the weakest members of our society.

Others, to be sure, have attacked the Bawer/Sullivan line more forthrightly. In a September 2000 article in *Commentary*, "What Is Wrong with Gay Marriage," Stanley Kurtz challenged the central contention that marriage would do for gay men what it does for straights—that is, "domesticate" their natural male impulse to promiscuity. Citing a number of academic "queer theorists" and radical gays, Kurtz wrote:

> In contrast to moderates and "conservatives" like Andrew Sullivan, who consistently play down [the] difference [between gays and straights] in order to promote their vision of gays as monogamists-in-the-making, radical gays have argued— more knowledgeably, more powerfully, and more vocally than any opponent of same-sex marriage would dare to do—that homosexuality, and particularly male homosexuality, is by its very nature incompatible with the norms of traditional monogamous marriage.

True, Kurtz went on, such radical gays nevertheless support same-sex marriage. But what motivates them is the hope of "eventually undoing the institution [of marriage] altogether," by delegitimizing age-old understandings of the family and thus (in the words of one such radical) "striking at the heart of the organization of Western culture and societies."

Nor are radical gays the only ones to entertain such destructive ambitions. Queuing up behind them, Kurtz warned, are the proponents of polygamy, polyandry, and polyamorism, all ready to argue that their threesomes, foursomes, and other "nontraditional" arrangements are entitled to the same rights as everyone else's. In a recent piece in the *Weekly Standard*, Kurtz has written that the "bottom" of this particular slippery slope is "visible from where we stand":

> Advocacy of legalized polygamy is growing. A network of grassroots organizations seeking legal recognition for group marriage already exists. The cause of legalized group marriage is championed by a powerful faction of family-law specialists. Influential legal bodies in both the United States and Canada have presented radical programs of marital reform, . . . [even] the abolition of marriage. The ideas behind this movement have already achieved surprising influence with a prominent American politician [Al Gore].

Like other critics of same-sex marriage, Kurtz has himself been vigorously criticized, especially by Sullivan. But he is almost certainly correct as to political and legal realities. If we grant rights to one group because they have demanded it—which is, practically, how legalized gay marriage will come to pass—we will find it exceedingly awkward to deny similar rights to others ready with their own dossiers of "victimization." In time, restricting marriage rights to couples, whether straight or gay, can be made to seem no less arbitrary than the practice of restricting marriage rights to one man and one woman. Ultimately, the same must go for incestuous relationships between consenting adults—a theme to which I will return.

A different defense of heterosexual marriage has proceeded by circling the wagons around the institution itself. According to this school of thought, ably represented by the columnist Maggie Gallagher, the essential purpose of that institution is to create stable families:

> Most men and women are powerfully drawn to perform a sexual act that can and does generate life. Marriage is our attempt to reconcile and harmonize the erotic, social, sexual, and financial needs of men and women with the needs of their partner and their children.

Even childless marriages protect this purpose, writes Gallagher, by ensuring that, as long as the marriage exists, neither the childless husband nor the childless wife is likely to father or mother children outside of wedlock.

Gallagher is especially strong on the larger, social meaning of heterosexual marriage, which she calls "inherently normative":

> The laws of marriage do not create marriage, but in societies ruled by law they help trace the boundaries and sustain the public meanings of marriage. . . . Without this shared, public aspect, perpetuated generation after generation, marriage becomes what its critics say it is: a mere contract, a vessel with no particular content, one of a menu of sexual lifestyles, of no fundamental importance to anyone outside a given relationship.

Human relationships are by nature difficult enough, Gallagher reminds us, which is why communities must do all they can to strengthen and not to weaken those institutions that keep us up to a mark we may not be able to achieve through our own efforts. The consequences of not doing so will be an intensification of all the other woes of which we have so far had only a taste in our society and which are reflected in the galloping statistics of illegitimacy, cohabitation, divorce, and fatherlessness. For Gallagher, the modest request of gay-marriage advocates for "a place at the table" is thus profoundly selfish as well as utterly destructive—for gay marriage "would require society at large to gut marriage of its central presumptions about family in order to accommodate a few adults' desires."

James Q. Wilson, Maggie Gallagher, Stanley Kurtz, and others—including William J. Bennett in *The Broken Hearth* (2001)—are right to point to the deleterious private and public consequences of instituting gay marriage. Why, then, do their arguments fail to satisfy completely? Partly, no doubt, it is because the damage they describe is largely prospective and to that degree hypothetical; partly, as I remarked early on, the defensive tone that invariably enters into these polemics may rob them of the force they would otherwise have. I hardly mean to deprecate that tone: anyone with homosexual friends or relatives, especially those participating in longstanding romantic relationships, must feel abashed to find himself saying, in effect, "You gentlemen, you ladies, are at one and the same time a fine example of fidelity and mutual attachment—and the thin edge of the wedge." Nevertheless, in demanding the right to marry, that is exactly what they are.

To grasp what is at the other edge of that wedge—that is, what stands to be undone by gay marriage—we have to distinguish marriage itself from a variety of other goods and values with which it is regularly associated by its defenders and its aspirants alike. Those values—love and monogamous sex and establishing a home, fidelity, childbearing and childrearing, stability, inheritance, tax breaks, and all the rest—are not the same as marriage. True, a good marriage generally contains them, a bad marriage is generally deficient in them, and in law, religion, and custom, even under the strictest of moral regimes, their absence can be grounds for ending the union. But the essence of marriage resides elsewhere, and those who seek to arrange a kind of marriage for the inherently unmarriageable are looking for those things in the wrong place.

The largest fallacy of all arises from the emphasis on romantic love. In a book published last year, Tipper and Al Gore defined a family as those who are "joined at the heart"—"getting beyond words, legal formalities, and even blood ties." The distinction the Gores draw in this sentimental and offhand way is crucial, but they utterly misconstrue it. Hearts can indeed love, and stop loving. But what exactly does this have to do with marriage, which can follow, precede, or remain wholly independent of that condition?

It is a truism that many married people feel little sexual or romantic attraction to each other—perhaps because they have been married too long, or perhaps, as some men have always claimed, because the death of sexual desire is coincident with the wedding ceremony. ("All comedies are ended by a marriage," Byron wittily and sadly remarked.) Many people—in ages past, certainly most people—have married for reasons other than sexual or romantic attraction. So what? I could marry a woman I did not love, a woman I did not feel sexually attracted to or want to sleep with, and our marriage would still be a marriage, not just legally but in its essence.

The truth is banal, circular, but finally unavoidable: by definition, the essence of marriage is to sanction and solemnize that connection of opposites which alone creates new life. (Whether or not a given married couple does in fact create new life is immaterial.) Men and women *can* marry only because they belong to different, opposite sexes. In marriage, they surrender those separate and different sexual allegiances, coming together to form a new entity. Their union is not a formalizing of romantic love but represents a certain idea—a construction, an abstract thought—about how best to formalize the human condition. This thought, embodied in a promise or a contract, is what holds marriage together, and the creation of this idea of marriage marks a key moment in the history of human development, a triumph over the alternative idea, which is concubinage.

Let me try to be more precise. Marriage can only concern my connection to a woman (and not to a man) because, as my reference to concubinage suggests, marriage is an institution that is built around female sexuality and female procreativity. (The very word "marriage" comes from the Latin word for mother, *mater.*) It exists for the gathering-in of a woman's sexuality under the protective net of the human or divine order, or both. This was so in the past and it is so even now, in our supposedly liberated times, when a woman who is in a sexual relationship without being married is, and is perceived to be, in a different state of being (not just a different legal state) from a woman who is married.

Circumstances have, admittedly, changed. Thanks to contraception, the decision to marry no longer precedes sexual intercourse as commonly as it did fifty years ago, when, for most people, a fully sexual relationship could begin only with marriage (and, when, as my mother constantly reminds me, one married *for* sex). Now the decision can come later; but come it almost certainly must. Even with contraception, even with feminism and women's liberation, the feeling would appear to be nearly as strong as ever that, for a woman, a sexual relationship must either end in marriage, or end.

This is surely understandable, for marriage benefits women, again not just in law but essentially. A woman can control who is the father of her children only insofar as there is a civil and private order that protects her from rape; marriage is the bulwark of that order. The 1960s feminists had the right idea: the essential thing for a woman is to control her own body. But they were wrong that this is what abortion is for; it is, rather, what marriage is for. It is humanity's way of enabling a woman to control her own body and to know (if she cares to) who is the father of her children.

Yes, marriage tends to regulate or channel the sexual appetite of men, and this is undoubtedly a good thing for women. But it is not the ultimate good. A husband, no matter how unfaithful, cannot introduce a child who is not his wife's own into a marriage without her knowledge; she alone has the power to do such a thing. For a woman, the fundamental advantage of marriage is thus not to regulate her husband but to empower herself—to regulate who has access to her person, and to marshal the resources of her husband and of the wider community to help her raise her children.

Every human relationship can be described as an enslavement, but for women the alternative to marriage is a much worse enslavement—which is why marriage, for women, is often associated as much with sexual freedom as with sexual constraint. In the traditional Roman Catholic cultures of the Mediterranean and South America, where virginity is fiercely protected and adolescent girls are hardly permitted to "date," marriage gives a woman the double luxury of controlling her sexuality and, if she wishes, extending it.

For men, by contrast, the same phenomenon—needing to be married in order to feel safe and free in a sexual relationship—simply does not exist. Men may wish to marry, but for more particular reasons: because they want to have children, or because they want to make a woman they love happy, or because they fear they will otherwise lose the woman they love. But it is rare for a man to feel essentially incomplete, or unprotected, in a sexual relationship that has not been solemnized by marriage. In fact, a man desperate to marry is often considered to have something wrong with him—to be unusually controlling or needy.

Because marriage is an arrangement built around female sexuality, because the institution has to do with women far more than it has to do with men, women will be the victims of its destruction. Those analysts who have focused on how children will suffer from the legalization of gay marriage are undoubtedly correct—but this will not be the first time that social developments perceived as advances for one group or another have harmed children. After all, the two most important (if effortless) achievements of the women's movement of the late 1960s were the right to abort and the right—in some social classes, the commandment—to join the professional workforce, both manifestly harmful to the interests of children.

But with the success of the gay liberation movement, it is women themselves, all women, who will be hurt. The reason is that gay marriage takes something that belongs essentially to women, is crucial to their very freedom, and empties it of meaning.

Why should I not be able to marry a man? The question addresses a class of human phenomena that can be described in sentences but nonetheless cannot be. However much I might wish to, I cannot be a father to a pebble—I cannot be a brother to a puppy—I cannot make my horse my consul. Just so, I cannot, and should not be able to, marry a man. If I want to be a brother to a puppy, are you abridging my rights by not permitting it? I may say what I please; saying it does not mean that it can be.

In a gay marriage, one of two men must play the woman, or one of two women must play the man. "Play" here means travesty—burlesque. Not that their love is a travesty; but their participation in a ceremony that apes the marriage bond, with all that goes into it, is a travesty. Their taking over of the form of this crucial and fragile connection of opposites is a travesty of marriage's purpose of protecting, actually and symbolically, the woman who enters into marriage with a man. To burlesque that purpose weakens those protections, and is essentially and profoundly antifemale.

Radical feminists were right, to an extent, in insisting that men's and women's sexuality is so different as to be inimical. Catharine MacKinnon has proclaimed that in a "patriarchal" society, all sexual intercourse is rape. Repellent as her view is, it is formed around a kernel of truth. There is something inherently violative about sexual intercourse—and there is something dangerous about being a woman in a sexual relationship with a man to whom she is not yet married. Among the now-aging feminists of my generation, no less than among their mothers, such a woman is commonly thought to be a victim.

Marriage is a sign that the ever-so-slight violation that is involved in a heterosexual relationship has been sanctioned by some recognized authority. That sanction is also what makes divorce a scandal—for divorce cannot truly undo the sanction of sexual intercourse, which is to say the sanction to create life, with one's original partner. Even in the Jewish tradition, which regards marriage (but not love) in a completely unsacralized way, divorce, though perfectly legal, does not erase the ontological status of the earlier marriage. (The Talmud records that God weeps when a man puts aside his first wife.) This sanction does not exist for homosexual couples. They are not opposites; they are the same. They live in a world of innocence, and neither their union nor their disunion partakes of the act of creation.

This brings us back to the incest ban, with which marriage is intimately and intricately connected. Indeed, marriage exists for the same reason that incest must not: because in our darker, inhuman moments we are driven toward that which is the same as ourselves and away from that which is fundamentally different from ourselves. Therefore we are enjoined from committing incest, negatively, and commanded to join with our opposite, positively—so that humanity may endure.

Homosexuals are, of course, free to avoid the latter commandment—and those who choose to do so are assuredly capable of leading rich and satisfying lives. The same goes for all those nonhomosexuals who have decided or been advised not to marry in certain circumstances—for example, if they wish to be members of celibate religious communities, or ascetic soldiers in a cause, or geniuses (as Cyril Connolly warned, "there is no more somber enemy of good art than the pram in the hall"). Men and women alike now spend more time as sexually mature adults outside of marriage than ever before, and some number of them live together in unreal or mock marriages of one kind or another. The social status of homosexuals is no better and no worse than that of anyone else who lives in an unmarried condition.

What of simple compassion? What do we owe to our fellow beings who wish, as they might put it, to achieve a happiness they see we are entitled to but which we deny to them? From those of us who oppose gay marriage, Andrew Sullivan demands *some* "reference to gay people's lives or relationships or needs." But the truth is that many people have many needs that are not provided for by law, by government, or by society at large—and for good reason.

Insofar as I care for my homosexual friend as a friend, I am required to say to him that, if a lifelong monogamous relationship is what you want, I wish you that felicity, just as I hope you would wish me the same. But insofar as our lives as citizens are concerned, or even as human beings, your monogamy and the durability of your relationship are, to be blunt about it, matters of complete indifference. They are of as little concern to our collective life as if you were to smoke cigars or build model railroads in your basement or hang glide, and of less concern to society than the safety of your property when you leave your house or your right not to be overcharged by the phone company.

That is not because you are gay. It is because, in choosing to conduct your life as you have every right to do, you have stepped out of the area of shared social concern—in the same sense as has anyone, of whatever sexuality, who chooses not to marry. There are millions of lonely people, of whom it is safe to say that the majority are in heterosexual marriages. But marriage, though it may help meet the needs of the lonely, does not exist because it is an answer to those needs; it is an arrangement that has to do with empowering women to avoid even greater unhappiness, and with sustaining the future history of the species.

Marriage, to say it for the last time, is what connects us with our nature and with our animal origins, with how all of us, heterosexual and homosexual alike, came to be. It exists not because of custom, or because of a conspiracy (whether patriarchal or matriarchal), but because, through marriage, the *world* exists. Marriage is how we are connected backward in time, through the generations, to our creator (or, if you insist, to the primal soup), and forward to the future beyond the scope of our own lifespan. It is, to say the least, bigger than two hearts beating as one.

Severing this connection by defining it out of existence—cutting it down to size, transforming it into a mere contract between chums—sunders the natural laws that prevent concubinage and incest. Unless we resist, we will find ourselves entering on the path to the abolition of the human. The gods move very fast when they bring ruin on misguided men.

33.

BLESS THE TIE THAT BINDS
A Puritan-Covenant Case
for Same-Sex Marriage

Dwight J. Penas

INTRODUCTION

An increasing number of legal scholars and students, practicing attorneys, lobbyists and legislators, and private individuals are calling for the legal recognition of gay and lesbian marriages. Those writers claim that the denial of legal status for such marriages violates basic legal and moral guarantees of American law. They also argue that full legal recognition of same-sex marriage would be good for society as a whole. The commentators advance various rationales for their arguments. Absent, however, from their analyses is attention to one significant authority. That overlooked authority is Puritan[1] ideology[2]—specifically, the concept of *covenant* in Puritan theology and social thought. As ironic as it may seem, Puritan values—and especially those embodied in the notion of covenant—encourage reversal of the hostility which contemporary marriage law manifests toward same-sex couples.

The Puritans were a principal influence on American thought and polity during America's formative decades. Puritan concepts and metaphors guided those who led the War for Independence and who designed the political structures of the nascent republic. According to one scholar, "The remarkable coherence of the American revolutionary movement and its successful conclusion in the constitution of a new civil order are due in considerable part to the convergence of the Puritan covenant pattern [of thought] and the Montesquieuan republican pattern."[3] Another scholar has said, "Without some understanding of Puritanism, . . . there is no understanding of America."[4]

A critical component in legal analysis is a sense of history. "We find our visions of good and evil . . . in the experience of the past, in our tradition. . . ."[5]

This is an edited form of an article that originally appeared in *Law and Inequality* 8, no. 3 (July 1990). Reprinted by permission of the publisher.

That is not to suggest that the past determines the present and the future—in law any more than in psychology or history. But it does point out that in legal analysis it is necessary to account for both written sources of law (e.g., the Constitution) and ideologies that lie behind those texts. As Justice Holmes explained:

> The law embodies the story of a nation's development through many centuries.
> . . . In order to know what it is, we must know what it has been, and what it tends
> to become. We must alternately consult history and existing theories of legislation. But the most difficult labor will be to understand the combination of the two
> into new products at every stage.[6]

Such a "pragmatic" approach is not enslaved to history, but it recognizes the importance of history. That courts—most notably the United States Supreme Court—take history into account is clear. Any effort to explain, justify, or change current legal positions must comprehend historical events, doctrines, and developments. The appreciation of history implicates historically important social theories.

Puritan ideology is one of the essential sources of American law, and as such it is a valuable and authoritative source of insight for resolving difficult legal issues. Puritan thought provides a historical balance to other theoretical arguments—for example, "original intentionalism" or majoritarian rule or "neutral principles"—that claim historical authority. Puritan-covenant ideology complements and corrects interpretive frameworks that root in other social-political theories so that legal analysis is grounded in a more complete understanding of the historical and intellectual milieu which produced American law.

This article argues that the implications of Puritan-covenant ideology encourage the legal recognition of marriage between gays or lesbians. It is meant to complement—and certainly not to contradict—trenchant legal arguments for the recognition of gay/lesbian marriage. It begins with a brief sketch of the history and theology of the Puritan movement in America, to demonstrate the authority of Puritanism for American law and to set forth Puritanism's basic themes. The article goes on to infer basic jurisprudential principles, or values, from that Puritan thought. It then analyzes how those principles encourage the legal recognition of same-sex marriage.

THE PURITAN UNDERSTANDING OF LIFE AND SOCIETY

Historical Importance of the Puritans

The Puritans and their ideology were essential elements in the development of American self-understanding and of American law. Puritan influence was felt early in American history, since Puritans were among the earliest white settlers in America. The Pilgrims who landed at Plymouth in 1620 were Puritans. The members of the Massachusetts Bay Colony, who arrived in 1629, were Puritans. Rhode Island, Connecticut, New Jersey, Maryland, and Pennsylvania also began as Puritan enclaves.

Once established, Puritan colonies thrived and grew, and all sections of the "New World"—not just "New England"—eventually felt the Puritan influence. In the original thirteen colonies, for example, an estimated 85 percent of the churches were Puritan congregations. That religious dominance greatly influenced the development of American social and political attitudes.

Puritan theology was a major intellectual force behind the development of American "tradition, culture, institutions, and nationality."[7] Puritan thought about the nature of life and of society encouraged and contributed to the formation of American republican polity. Puritan theology inspired political doctrines about human equality, participatory government, and concern for the common good. Puritan influence is apparent from the history of the formulation of the Declaration of Independence and the Constitution of the United States. Even the fundamental image of the United States as a "federation" or a "federal union" roots in Puritan thought. M. Susan Power analyzed the political writings of three early American Puritan leaders and found in them the early expression of essential themes of American constitutional government.[8]

Puritan themes pervaded early American thought and were especially prominent in the struggle to shape the polity of the new nation. Winthrop Hudson summarizes the importance of Puritanism in America:

> [D]emocracy as we understand it in America was derived from the three [Puritan] theological doctrines of the sovereignty of God, human bondage to sin, and a particular understanding of the way in which the implications of revelation are made known and confirmed. From these three doctrines, in turn, were derived an insistence upon fundamental law, limitation of power, and the efficacy of discussion and persuasion.[9]

Hudson understands those three political doctrines—fundamental law, limitation of power, and the freedom of speech—as the core values around which America was "constituted."[10]

The Theological Foundation of Puritan Social Thought

To urge renewed appreciation for the Puritans is not to suggest the adoption of their particular theological or religious stance. Even in the early days the peculiarly religious character of Puritanism was rapidly displaced, even among strict Puritan groups, by the secular concerns of settling the new nation, including government, law, trade, and war. What began as a theological movement was transformed into a more generalized social theory. Nevertheless, Puritanism was religious in its origins, and some sense of Puritan theology is necessary in order to understand secularized Puritan social theory.

Puritans understood themselves to be agents of God on earth, entrusted with responsibility for subjecting all aspects of life to God's rule. They were convinced that they had special duties in the world. All of life was infused with a potential for ministry.

At the heart of Puritan thought about religion and life—as Perry Miller has called it, the "marrow of puritan divinity"[11]—was the notion of *covenant*. A covenant is a mutually beneficial relationship formed when two parties pledge absolute faithfulness to each other. A covenant shares some of the features of a contract, in that each party can hold the other accountable for the terms of the arrangement—an arrangement to which both parties freely assent. It is, however, a broader concept than contract, one more akin to romantic notions of marriage: each party commits, as an integral aspect of the agreement, to remain bound by the agreement even in the event of the other's breach. The Puritans structured their entire theological system around the notions of a covenant between God and humanity and of human covenants that reflected the divine-human covenant. Covenant became the central motif in the exposition of Puritan thought about both religion and society.

For the Puritans, the history of the human race was suffused with covenants. At the creation of the world, God had established a covenant with humanity. In general terms, God promised to care for and protect the human race; humans for their part were to live according to God's will and to care for and protect one another. Eventually, humanity failed to fulfill its covenantal responsibilities, but God did not abandon humanity. Instead, God established a new covenant with humanity through Jesus—who fulfilled the original covenant vicariously for humanity.

Though the second covenant—or "covenant of grace"—was built on faith, it nevertheless incorporated some aspects of the earlier covenant, the so-called covenant of works. The covenant of grace "repeat[ed] and embellish[ed] for sinful [humans] the terms of the old covenant. . . . Both required that the faithful believer lead his [*sic*] life in devotion, service, and praise of God—not as a condition of salvation, but as an expression of gratitude for God's grace and mercy."[12] Within this scheme, every believer had a contribution to make. Each person was created with a unique combination of traits and talents which she was expected to employ in the service of God.

The Puritans understood both covenants to require service to one's neighbor. The covenant between God and humankind had its correlate in the believer's covenant with her neighbors and with the physical universe. The Puritans understood life to be a vital and exuberant—if sober and responsible—embrace of the world as the place where one expressed her devotion and service to God. Care for and service to one's neighbor were a part of worship, on a par with singing psalms and preaching sermons.

Covenant theology impressed on Puritans that human life is essentially communal. Human being is defined in terms of relationships with others. Every human event and relationship (covenant) is a reflection of the covenant between God and the human race, and each is invested with divine significance.

Puritan notions of covenantal relationship are clearly manifested in the Puritan doctrine of marriage, which Puritans understood to be a covenant between a man and a woman.[13] Puritans played down the Anglican view of marriage as "an expression of the natural requirements of procreation."[14] Instead, Puritans emphasized the partnership of marriage: Puritan sermons on marriage emphasized mutual help, affection, and respect. Puritans married with an open-eyed understanding that in marriage they undertook serious obligations toward their spouses. For that reason, there was an emphasis on a person's freedom to choose whether or not and whom to marry. In addition, marriage served an iconic function, exemplifying in microcosm the love and cooperation, service and care that the city, state, and nation were to practice. . . .

But the Puritan doctrine of covenant embraced realms wider than the family: the emphasis on covenantal service led Puritans to emphasize the believer's duty to contribute to the "common good." "Living in covenant [meant] regarding persons and events with an unselfish eye, with a view to the whole rather than to a partial [individual] interest."[15] The Puritans were by no means communitarians. But they were conscious that those well-off should help those less-well-off. By employing its God-given intelligence, humanity would address human problems in such a way that everyone was better off.

The "common good" encompassed community and nation as well as personal relationships. Puritans understood their individual destinies to be wrapped up with the political subdivisions in which they lived. For example, before landing in Massachusetts, John Winthrop exhorted his fellow travelers to form the kind of closely knit and care-filled society that would fulfill God's covenantal requirements and assure the Puritan community's success in the New World:

> [W]ee must be knit together in this worke as one man [*sic*], wee must entertaine each other in brotherly [*sic*] Affeccion, wee must be willing to abridge ourselves of our superfluities, for the supply of others necessities . . . wee must . . . make others Condicions our owne, rejoyce together, mourne together, labor and suffer together. . . .[16]

Winthrop's sermon indicates the interrelatedness of all spheres of life in Puritan ideology. Community and nation were religious concerns as much as church and home.

Whether at the level of the community or at the level of the nation, political covenants, like personal covenants, were "triparty agreement[s among] God, the civil ruler, and the people."[17] Civil rulers were to be accorded great respect because they represented God's authority to the society and guided the society in living according to God's will. Such respect did not require absolute obedience, however. If the ruler violated God's will, it was the people's responsibility to replace the unsatisfactory ruler with one faithful to the ways of God.

Puritans' concern for their righteousness before God led them to profound concern for the orders of society. Since all aspects of life were integrated under the rule of God, politics and law were as much dimensions of religion as was worship. Even after Puritan theological zeal waned, the religious-like dedication to political and legal matters had been planted too firmly in American soil to be dislodged.

Puritans and Same-Sex Marriage

There is no suggestion that the Puritans would have sanctioned same-sex marriage. The historical Puritans were people of their times. Official abhorrence of "sodomy" or "unnatural acts" was a part of their milieu. In their denunciations of homosexuality, Puritans were scarcely distinguishable from their counterparts. Puritans did not always follow their ideology to its logical implications. For example, while Puritans were remarkably ahead of their times in affording equality and dignity to women in society, they did not extend the right to vote to women. As another example, slavery was the subject of divisive concern for the Puritans at the founding of this country, but their treatment of the question—while radical in some quarters in their day—is unenlightened by modern standards. It is, therefore, neither surprising nor contradictory to suggest that, while the Puritans themselves would not have advocated legal status for same-sex marriage, Puritan ideology planted the seeds which would blossom into just such a stance.

The Puritans are important to contemporary legal analysis because of their importance to the formation of American law; their importance does not derive from their particular structures of society or from their solutions to social problems. The history-bound forms of their society are less important in modern times than are the values that informed their social structure and what they contributed to the American mix:

> A political Puritan paradigm of covenant adequate to contemporary needs cannot be provided by simple resuscitation of some Puritan commonwealth in old or New England. . . . What we want to recover from the Puritan commonwealth is, not its constitution, but the basic normative guidelines that follow from its covenant structure of freedom and accountability.[18]

The Puritan-Covenant Case for Same-Sex Marriage

There exists no systematic Puritan jurisprudence. The earliest Puritans did not develop one and modern advocates of covenant theory have not yet undertaken the task. Even though law and the ordering of society were of vital concern to Puritans, Puritans did not isolate jurisprudential concerns from the rest of their reflections on how to structure their lives in faithfulness to their covenant with God. Still, it is possible to identify a set of basic jurisprudential principles—or "values"—implicit in Puritan ideology.

After an analysis of the "problem" posed by same-sex marriage, this section of the article articulates major principles of Puritan jurisprudence. It relates those principles to modern expressions of legal philosophy. Finally, it demonstrates that each of those principles contributes to the substantial case for the legal recognition of same-sex marriage. Legal recognition is not only permissible under modern articulations of Puritan jurisprudence; it is compelled.

Costs of the Denial of Legal Status to Same-Sex Marriage

Marriage between partners of the same sex is illegal in every state. Despite legal prohibitions, however, gay men and lesbians continue to form committed relationships, marriage-like in all aspects except legal status.

The denial of legal status to the relationships does not have merely incidental repercussions. The costs to a gay or lesbian couple of being denied legal status for their relationship are enormous. The denial of marriage to couples exposes them to discrimination from employers, landlords, and institutions offering facilities to the public. Unmarried couples face discrimination in housing. Gay and lesbian partners are generally barred from spousal benefits under workers' compensation laws, since they are not legal spouses. Married couples receive benefits from the federal government which are denied to gay and lesbian partners, such as special tax treatment and Social Security benefits.

Not only does denial of legal recognition deprive same-sex couples of entitlements accorded "married" couples, but the lack of legal marital status limits the causes of action available in tort to gay and lesbian partners. For example, a California court held that an unmarried partner could not collect damages for negligent infliction of emotional distress or loss of consortium. Another court held that an intimate homosexual relationship does not fall within the "close relationship" standard for negligent infliction of emotional distress.

Domestic relationship law is a field in which gay and lesbian partners face definite hardship. The legal difficulties associated with child custody and visitation, and with conceiving and adopting children, are manifold. There are no rights of inheritance for a gay or lesbian partner in the event of the death of the other partner. Since the famous *Marvin v. Marvin* decision there may be grounds, at least in California, for an unmarried heterosexual partner to get support from the other partner—so-called palimony. In the event that a gay or lesbian relationship breaks up, however, there is no precedent for the award of such support as is available to unmarried heterosexual partners. The experience of one lesbian couple in Minnesota demonstrates that the lack of legal status for their relationship has adverse implications even for one partner's right to visit her disabled lover.

The denial of legal recognition for same-sex marriage takes a toll beyond the economic and legal costs. Richard Mohr has written passionately of the intertwined legal and emotional burdens that he and his "lover and husband" must bear as a result of the lack of legal sanction for their relationship:

[I]n the eyes of the law we are necessarily strangers to each other, people who had as well never met. In Illinois, [where Mohr and his lover live] one cannot will one's body. By statute, it goes to next of kin. That which was most one's own—the substrate for personality—which was most one's own for another—that in which and by which one loved and made love—is, for gays, not one's own at all. The lover is barred from the lover's funeral. The compulsory intervention of heterosexuality at death is the final degradation worked by The People on gay people.[19]

Numerous rationales have been offered to justify denial of legal status to gay and lesbian marriage. Friedman identified and evaluated several of the most common of those rationales. In every case, she found the rationale inadequate to justify the practice.

States claim an interest in encouraging procreation, but such an interest cannot withstand scrutiny: certainly, there is little reason to fear the extinction of the human race from underpopulation. Neither do Supreme Court rulings with respect to birth control and abortion support the assertion that the state has an overriding interest in encouraging procreation.

Concern for the well-being of children conceived within or brought into a marriage is a legitimate state interest. But there is no empirical evidence that the legalization of same-sex marriage represents a threat to children of the marriage. Children are no more likely to be molested by gay or lesbian parents than by heterosexual parents. If the concern is to discourage development of homosexual identity in children, there is no evidence that children develop homosexual identities because of their families' makeup. Children of gay or lesbian partners are no more apt to be stigmatized if the partners are married than if they are merely living together. There is thus little support for the claim that children would be more "at risk" in gay- or lesbian-parent families than they are in heterosexual-parent families.

Another claim advanced by those who oppose same-sex marriage is that the denial of marriage to same-sex couples discourages illegal homosexual activity. They argue that the state has an interest in discouraging illicit sexual activity so as to encourage fidelity, responsible sexual activity, and public health. By legalizing same-sex marriage, however, the state does not give up authority to regulate extramarital sexual activity. (Arguably a state would have to decriminalize intramarital homosexual activity. Still, in *Bowers v. Hardwick,* the Supreme Court held that while the right to privacy protects marriage, procreation, and family decisions, it does not necessarily protect all sexual practices in marriage. Thus the legalization of marriage between gays or lesbians would not necessarily prevent a state with a sense of the ironic from prohibiting certain sexual practices—as Georgia's sodomy statute does.)

Another common objection to same-sex marriage is that it represents a challenge to the "traditional" family, but how same-sex marriage would undermine the values associated with family life is vaguely defined. The institution of same-sex marriage would foster the same values as does heterosexual marriage: same-sex marriage would foster commitment, loyalty, and intimacy, just as does heterosexual marriage. There is no evidence that gay men and lesbian women in committed relationships are any less committed to the permanency of their relationships than are heterosexual partners. If, on the other hand, the fear is that legalization of same-sex marriage would lessen the appeal of opposite-sex marriage, the answer is obvious: people do not choose their sexual orientation; neither, then, for the vast majority of people, is the gender of a potential marriage partner a matter of choice.

Courts have given permission for the majority culture to promote and impose its cultural and moral norms, and some justify legal hostility toward gay and lesbian couples by recourse to a history of disfavor of homosexuality. But under the Constitution there are limits to majority rule:

> Majority rule is simply not the same thing as constitutionalism, as that concept was classically defined. One cannot understand the notion of a constitution, at least prior to twentieth-century thought, without including its role of placing limits on the ability of majorities (or other rulers) to do whatever they wish in regard to minorities who lose out in political struggles.[20]

The issue of the rights of gay and lesbian people—and in particular the right to legal recognition of their committed relationships—will not go away. The issue is of vital concern, not only to gay and lesbian Americans, but also to heterosexual Americans. Puritan-covenant analysis reveals that what is at stake is fidelity not just to the letter of American law, but also to its "spirit" or its "heart." Puritan-covenant analysis reveals both what is at stake in the argument and how to resolve the problem.

Special Protection for Relationships

As a first principle, covenant theory "both in affirmations of its ideals and [in] lamentations over its failure, reminds us that relations between persons in . . . society carry a special weight."[21] That is, because of their importance in the overall scheme of life, personal relationships are due special attention and protection. The fundamental premise of covenant theory is that human life is communal, interpersonal, social: "[O]ur lives . . . are caught up with each other. They cannot be lived in splendid isolation, each pursuing an independent pathway. . . ."[22] Covenanting with others—individuals and collectivities—is of the essence of human being.

Among covenants, marriage is special. Marriage is a covenant between two independent people and the most basic expression of the communal nature of human being. The marriage bond embodies, in covenant terms, a community of mutual "love and service, cooperation and care." It is the basic level of social involvement. The Puritan view suggests that marriage is due special care and protection. Marriage is fundamentally important to the people involved, of the utmost importance to them. As such, it is also of utmost importance to society. As an institution, marriage contributes to the common good of society.

Such high respect for the covenant between two people is neither unique to the Puritan view nor lost to the past. Time and again, the US Supreme Court has recognized—at least implicitly—that one-to-one relationships are of vital importance to the fulfillment of liberty. Thus, for example, it has severely restricted the power of states to interfere with an individual's decisions about whether and whom to marry, birth control, with whom to live, child care and education, and whether to carry a fetus to term. The Court has had to struggle, however, to articulate a rationale for such protection. Most decisions propound an individualistic, social-contract doctrine of "privacy" or "fundamental" rights. For example, Justice [William O.] Douglas, writing for the majority in *Griswold* [*v. Connecticut*], identified a "penumbra of privacy" among the rights guaranteed by the Bill of Rights. The argument is that the Bill of Rights is not a limited specific list of rights aside from which there are no others guaranteed. Rather, the Bill of Rights describes a field of rights from which it is possible to extrapolate specific applications. The Bill of Rights establishes a zone of individual autonomy which the government may not invade or violate.

Covenant theory reinforces "privacy theory" while also transcending it. It builds on the view that not all of the "rights" of members of society are articulated in specific passages of the Constitution. In the case of marriage, protection does not depend solely on "penumbral" guarantees of individual liberty located within the interstices of constitutional amendments. It is grounded in the "morality" of the Constitution's framers, which morality can be "translate[d] . . . into . . . rule[s] to cover unforeseen circumstances."[24]

Marriage is a fundamental right[25]—whether considered from the standpoint of "privacy" doctrine or from covenant theory. States must have a substantial reason for interfering with or denying marriage to heterosexual couples.[26] There is insufficient reason to deny its benefits to couples who are of the same sex. Covenant ideology asserts that committing to a relationship is a basic expression of being human. Such commitment is no less fundamental for gay men and lesbian women than it is for heterosexual couples. The need to connect with another is felt as keenly by homosexual people as by heterosexual people.

There is no valid reason to distinguish between homosexual and heterosexual couples in matters regarding the right to marry; studies suggest that homosexual couples are virtually indistinguishable from heterosexual couples. In many cases, gays and lesbians already live in de facto marriages. Many have formalized and publicized their commitment through rituals, even though those rituals do not have legal effect.

Richard Mohr suggests the positive consequences of legalizing gay and lesbian marriage: "[I]f current discrimination, which drives gays into hiding and into anonymous relations, was lifted . . . one would see gays forming [families]. Virtually all gays express a desire to have a permanent lover. . . . In general, when afforded the opportunity, gays have shown an amazing tendency to nest."[27] The legal recognition of gay and lesbian marriages would afford all people, regardless of their sexual nature, the opportunity to fulfill this aspect of their human nature. From a covenantal perspective, no less can be demanded of a social order. No one suggests that all gay or lesbian couples would choose to marry. To deny the option to those who would marry, however, is to deny them a basic guarantee of the Constitution as Puritans would understand that document.

Equality for All

The heart of covenant theory is the affirmation of the equality of all people. In Puritan thought, even the covenant between God and humanity involved God's treatment of humanity as an equal. The centrality of personhood and the dignity with which each person was to be treated were and are hallmarks of covenant thought.

Covenant equality is equality of participation in society and in the apparatus by which decisions about that society are made. Covenant affords a dynamic model of relationships in which covenant partners "sustain one another, contribute to one another, and constitute a creative center for the ongoing life of the community."[28] Participation is an end in itself; it is not simply a means to some other end, such as peace in society.

Participation is more than equality "before law"—that is, equality in some procedural sense. The concept of equality of participation includes equality of opportunity and of access to the "benefits" of society. Through their participation, people share in the benefits of the whole society, and they learn to gear their individual and group contributions to the "common good" of the society. It is incumbent on a legal system to remove any and all barriers to full and equal participation by all people.

The dual qualities of equality and participation categorically forbid the suppression of or discrimination against minorities. It is a radical denial of covenant for a majority of the members of society to draw lines of participation in the society in such a way as to exclude others. To do so is to deny the humanity of those excluded, effectively denying them both a voice in their own destiny and an opportunity to contribute to the common good.

The society which is faithful to covenant, therefore, must be an open society. A society cannot be accounted free if it closes the door on members—any members. If it does so, it is not a covenant community, for it has thereby institutionalized inequality and barred certain would-be members from the society. Society, if it is to be faithful to the covenant model, must be amenable to change. It must be willing to allow participation by all the members of society to bring about change. An open society is one equally respectful of tradition, contemporary communication, and creativity. Neither the stability of the past nor the innovations of the future can be easily ignored. Both must be tested, however, against the ideal of full participation by all persons in society.

The importance of equality in covenant theory "requires a method something like . . . 'strict scrutiny' of any deviation from a standard of equality. . . ."[29] Unless the state can demonstrate a compelling reason for discrimination, discrimination must be abandoned. Any less is the society's breaking faith with those who are the objects of discrimination. Social change to eliminate discrimination has priority over other frequently expressed concerns for cautious development or pragmatic deliberation. "The covenantal idea of equality overrules the usual objections of prudence to tampering with social systems that seem to be working efficiently, if not altogether fairly."[30]

The Constitution already provides for such equality, but without the emphasis of covenant theory the radicality of the Constitution's guarantees is often ignored. The Equal Protection Clause mandates that the government act to end discrimination against disadvantaged groups, regardless of the depth or history of social contempt for the group.[31] Built into the Constitution's structure is a means for "look[ing] forward, serving to invalidate practices that were widespread at the time of [the Constitution's] ratification and that were expected to endure."[32] Where due process guarantees fail to protect substantive rights, the Equal Protection Clause may be invoked to protect "fundamental rights."[33] The Equal Protection Clause allows the Constitution to transcend "common law," "status quo baselines," and "Anglo-American conventions" in favor of a much broader principle of equality.[34]

The Supreme Court has acknowledged that the Constitution requires treating people equally with respect to the right to marry. In *Loving v. Virginia,*[35] the Court struck down a Virginia law that prohibited interracial marriages. The law, which classified potential marriage partners on the basis of race, violated the Fourteenth Amendment and was "subversive of the principle of equality at the heart of the Fourteenth Amendment. . . ."[36] Since the freedom to marry is "vital" and "essential to the orderly pursuit of happiness by free men [*sic*],"[37] legal obstacles can only be justified by compelling state interest effectuated by narrowly tailored means.

From a covenant perspective, the equal-protection case for same-sex marriage is even stronger than the due process argument discussed above. The fundamental assumption of covenant ideology is that all members of society are to be treated with fundamental equality. Coupled with the in-place radical constitutional guarantee of equal protection, that assumption argues vigorously against the denial of marriage to gay and lesbian couples. To deny them the right to marry is to foreclose their enjoying the "benefits" of marriage—benefits which are legal, economic, and emotional. Denial of the right to marry thus excludes them from full participation in the life of the society. It relegates them to the margins of society and isolates them from the processes of government by which they were banished to the periphery.

To deny marriage to same-sex couples violates an essential aspect of government, as Puritan-covenant theory understands government. It violates the basic human dignity of gay and lesbian people by treating them as inferiors and excluding them from the society. The fact that no suggested state interest withstands scrutiny compounds the outrage.

The Common Good

A third major strain in covenant thought concerns what is called "the common good." Politics, according to covenant theory, has as its raison d'être and its goal the service of society. Its purpose is to serve the public good. That public good, however, is not divorced from the good of the individual; it does not have a significance beyond or transcending the individual:

> [P]ublic good is the good of the public. It is the good of the open society itself. It is the good of the relationships through which the members of the community sustain one another, contribute to one another, and constitute a creative center for the ongoing life of the community. To act in the public good is not to deny the individuality of persons of associations, but it is to reject the indifference to others of individualism.[38]

The function of the legal process is "to pursue ways and means of improving [the] quality [of living together]. It is to create and to sustain those relationships in which the actions of each enhance the life of all."[39] Both individuals and the society itself are duty-bound to work toward the well-being of all individuals.

Covenant theory recognizes that there is no "public life" separate from the individual and collective existences of the individuals. Conversely, the life of each individual is wrapped up with the lives of others. Service to the well-being of the individual and service to society are inextricably linked. If one person is harmed, all people suffer. If one individual harms another, the entire web of social relationships—which is to say, the society—is assaulted. If public action harms an individual, the greater society is also thereby harmed. That harm, furthermore, is not some idealistic imperfection; it is a real and palpable harm. For the stability of a society is in direct proportion to the extent to which it "invites and ultimately requires" citizens to achieve "full citizenship" in the society and "places them in reciprocal relationship to each other."[40] The legitimacy of a social order is integrally related to the well-being of the individuals within society. By assuring the well-being of individuals, a social order serves the good of all. A society is not merely "less good" because it treats some people inhumanely; it is no society at all. A society which breaches the public or common good reverts to lawlessness and threatens to destroy itself.

Society, to the extent that it has an existence independent of those people whom it comprises, benefits when it serves all those who constitute society. Thus,

> civil liberties do not fulfill a function only for the individual. In principle, they fulfill a critical function for the political association as well, indeed, for the entire community of being. Civil liberties are a means for effective participation in communal decisions. They are a means to press for reform and to introduce novel patterns of relationship. They constitute a structure within which and through which persons and groups may contribute alternative modes of thought and styles of life to the ongoing community.[41]

By drawing persons into the social matrix, the society elicits their loyalty and their effort in behalf of the well-being of the society. It accomplishes the integration of society—that is, the integrity, unity, and wholeness of the community.

By denying legal recognition to same-sex marriage, American society denies itself the loyalty and integration of a segment of its population. Not only does it disserve those people, but it also disserves itself. By recognizing same-sex marriage, society could channel the personal and political energy of gay and lesbian couples into the society and not away from it. By including them, instead of excluding them, the society establishes its authority with them in such a way as to encourage them to "make an 'internal' commitment to covenant"[42]—commitment to each other and to the society.

A function of covenant society is to assist the members of society to adjust their desires from self-interest toward the good of the larger community. It can only do so if it brings those members into commerce with the wider society. If it blocks the participation in society by some, it fractures the unity of the society and destroys the community by and through which individual desires or interests are socialized. That much should be clear from the African American civil rights movement.

Richard Mohr implies that the legal recognition of same-sex marriage would be good for America beyond its good to individual Americans:

> [I]n extending to gays the rights and benefits it has reserved for its dominant culture and extended selectively to others, America would confirm its deeply held, nearly religious vision of itself as a morally progressing nation, a nation itself advancing and serving as a beacon for others—especially with regard to human rights. . . . Ours is a nation given to a prophetic political rhetoric which acknowledges that morality is not arbitrary and that justice is not merely the expression of the current collective will.[43]

The legal recognition of same-sex marriage would confirm America's commitment to full justice for all people. It would thereby strengthen America's claim to "legitimacy." It would justify society's claim of authority over one segment of the population that currently experiences that authority as repression.

CONCLUSION

Legal analysis of complex and troubling social problems is a sophisticated enterprise. It calls for the contributions of a range of thinkers, not just legal scholars, legislators, and judges. Legal decision making is "contextual"—that is, it implicates sources of learning outside of case reporters and hornbooks. Values, history, and interpretive frameworks influence how law is made. Legal decisions "must be defended as flowing from a coherent and uncompromised vision of fairness and justice, because that, in the last analysis, is what the rule of law really means."[44]

The treatment of same-sex marriage by the American legal establishment raises profound questions about "the fairness and justice" of that treatment. Gay and lesbian couples are denied the full benefit of their citizenship by laws that refuse legal sanction for same-sex marriages. That legal posture can and should be changed.

Supporting a change in the law is the strain of social thought which this paper calls "Puritan-covenant thought." Originating in the sixteenth- and seventeenth-century religious movement, Puritan social thought transcended both its religious origins and its sphere of influence in New England. Puritanism was a dominant intellectual strain which contributed to the development of the new land that became the United States. The importance of that strain of thought should be rerecognized and its themes resuscitated to inform legal and political decisions.

Puritan-covenant thought buttresses the arguments which come from many different perspective in favor of the legal recognition of gay and lesbian marriages. The decision to legalize such marriages would afford gays and lesbians the kind of support for their committed relationships which the society rightly offers heterosexual marriages. It would be a step toward the full participation of gays and lesbians in American society, recalling them from the margins of society where they have been forced by legalized discrimination. American society itself would benefit from the decision. It would be able more reasonably to count on the loyalty of those whom it would newly include among its full citizens; it would be truer to its declared ideals; and it would be a more complete incarnation of the just and equitable commonwealth its founders envisioned.

NOTES

1. There is no single, commonly accepted definition of "Puritan." In general, however, the Puritans were British Calvinists who were zealous in their efforts to reform religion and society. Edmund Morgan has suggested a useful, nontechnical definition of Puritan:

> The Puritans were English Protestants who thought the Church of England as established under Henry VIII and Elizabeth retained too many vestiges of Rom[an Catholicism]. In the 1640's [*sic*] and 1650's [*sic*] they reorganized not only the church but also the government of England and for eleven years ran the country without a king. When the monarchy was restored in 1660, Puritans were disgraced, but their work could not be wholly undone. Moreover, in the 1630's [*sic*] they had carried their ideas to the New World, where the king could not undo them.

Edmund S. Morgan, introduction to *Puritan Political Ideas 1558–1794*, ed. Edmund S. Morgan (Indianapolis: Bobbs-Merrill, 1965). See also John Witte Jr., "Blest Be the Ties That Bind—Covenant and Community in Puritan Thought," *Emory Law Journal* 36 (1987): 579; Goldwin Smith, *The United States: An Outline of a Political History 1492–1871* (1893), p. 4.

Not all scholars define the Puritan movement so inclusively. Margo Todd, for example, stresses that Puritans "were a self-conscious community of [Calvinist] protestant zealots committed to purging the Church of England *from within* of its remaining Romish 'superstitions,' ceremonies, vestments and liturgy, and to establishing a biblical discipline on the larger society, primarily through the preached word." Margo Todd, *Christian Humanism and the Puritan Social Order* (New York: Cambridge University Press, 1987), p. 14 (emphasis added). She thus distinguishes Separatists (such as the Plymouth Pilgrims) from other Puritans, even though the two groups shared common theological and social points of view. Ibid. See also Allan Nevins and Henry Steele Commager, *A Short History of the United States*, 5th ed. (New York: Alfred A. Knopf, 1966), pp. 8–16.

The term "Puritan" was, originally, a term of opprobrium, highlighting a kind of "holier-than-thou" attitude within the reformist party. Leon Howard, *Essays on Puritans and Puritanism* (Albuquerque: University of New Mexico Press, 1986), p. 41. By the end of the sixteenth century, however, Puritan persistence "had rescued the term from contempt and given it a definable meaning with reference to church government and morality." Ibid., p. 3. There remains in the modern, colloquial use of the term some of the earlier connotations of excessive strictness and sobriety. Throughout this paper, however, the term is used with no overtones of disfavor. "Puritan" denotes the biologic or ideologic heirs of the British reformers who came to the New World to escape scorn and persecution in England and were instrumental in shaping what became the United States.

2. "Ideology" is used to include both theological and nontheological reflection and is used with no pejorative connotation.

3. Robert Bellah, *The Broken Covenant* (New York: Seabury Press, 1975), p. 27.

4. Perry Miller, "The Puritan Way of Life," in *The Puritans*, ed. Perry Miller and Thomas H. Johnson (New York and Cincinnati: American Book Company, 1938), p. 1.

5. Alexander Bickel, *The Morality of Consent* (New Haven: Yale University Press, 1975), p. 24.

6. Oliver Wendell Holmes, *The Common Law*, ed. Mark DeWolfe Howe (Cambridge, MA: Belknap Press of Harvard University Press, 1963), p. 5.

7. Ralph Barton Perry, *Puritanism and Democracy* (New York: Vanguard Press, 1944), p. 34.

8. M. Susan Power, *Before the Convention: Religion and the Founders* (Lanham, MD: University Press of America, 1984).

9. Winthrop Hudson, "Theological Convictions and Democratic Government," in *Puritanism and the American Experience*, ed. Michael McGittert (Reading, MA: Addison Wesley, 1969), p. 227.

10. Ibid., p. 226.

11. Perry Miller, "The Marrow of Puritan Divinity," in *Errand into the Wilderness*, ed. Perry Miller (Cambridge, MA: Belknap Press of Harvard University Press, 1956), p. 48.

12. Witte, "Blest Be the Ties That Bind," p. 583.

13. Puritans held marriage in high regard as a state ordained by God. Nevertheless, they desacralized marriage and made marriage a civil matter. For several years they considered weddings which occurred in church to be illegal. Christopher Durston, *The Family in the English Revolution* (New York: Basil Blackwell, 1989), p. 16.

14. Robin W. Lovin, "Covenantal Relationships and Political Legitimacy," *Journal of Religion* 60 (1980): 5.

15. Ibid., p. 6.

16. Bellah, *The Broken Covenant*, p. 14 (quoting John Winthrop).

17. Witte, "Blest Be the Ties That Bind," p. 592.

18. Lovin, "Covental Relationships and Political Legitimacy," p. 1.

19. Richard Mohr, *Gays/Justice: A Study of Ethics, Society, and Law* (New York: Columbia University Press, 1988), p. 18.

20. Sanford Levinson, *Constitutional Faith* (Princeton, NJ: Princeton University Press, 1988), p. 70. See also *Bowers v. Hardwick*, 478 US at 210 (Justice Brennan dissenting) ("I cannot agree that either the length of time a majority has held its convictions or the passion with

which it defends them can withdraw legislation from this Court's scrutiny."). Such a view echoes the Puritan emphasis on personal dignity and has significant implications for the majority's interference with interpersonal relationships. Constitutional rights cannot be abridged by majoritarian moral beliefs. Furthermore, there is little reason for the majority to do so.

21. Lovin, "Covental Relationships and Political Legitimacy," p. 1.

22. Douglas Sturm, *Community and Alienation: Essays on Process Thought and Public Life* (Notre Dame, IN: University of Notre Dame Press, 1988), p. 61.

23. Witte, "Blest Be the Ties That Bind," pp. 594–95.

24. Levinson, *Constitutional Faith,* p. 81 (quoting Robert Bork).

25. *Loving v. Virginia,* 388 US 1, 12 (1967) ("The freedom to marry has long been recognized as one of the vital personal rights essential to the orderly pursuit of happiness by free men [*sic*]. . . . Marriage is one of the basic civil rights . . ."). Courts have consistently rejected strict scrutiny of marriage laws that distinguish between heterosexual and homosexual orientation. The United States Supreme Court, for example, dismissed the appeal from *Baker v. Nelson,* 291 Minn. 310, 191 N.W.2d 185 (1971) "for want of substantial federal question." 409 US 810 (1971). Courts and legislatures need not remain bound, however, to a past that gives short shrift to fundamental rights not heretofore recognized. See *Loving's* rejection of the rationale in *Pace v. Alabama,* 106 US 583 (1883), as "represent[ing] a limited view of the Equal Protection Clause which has not withstood analysis in subsequent decisions of this court." *Loving,* 388 US at 10. Both courts and legislatures should be confronted with the covenant case for same-sex marriage and convinced to reverse that part of legal tradition which denies recognition to same-sex marriage.

26. *Loving,* 388 US at 9.

27. Mohr, *Gays/Justice,* p. 44. Mohr goes on to suggest that the social and legal hostility to homosexuality makes the development of committed relationships difficult: "[A] life of hiding is a tense and pressured existence not easily shared with another." Ibid.

28. Sturm, *Community and Alienation,* p. 85.

29. Lovin, "Covental Relationships and Political Legitimacy," pp. 14–15.

30. Ibid., p. 15.

31. Cass Sunstein, "Sexual Orientation and the Constitution: A Note on the Relationship between Due Process and Equal Protection," *University of Chicago Law Review* 55 (1988): 1161, 1163. Sunstein understands the Due Process Clause to be much less "activist" than the Equal Protection Clause:

> From its inception, the Due Process Clause has been interpreted largely . . . to protect traditional practices against short-run departures. . . . [It] often looks backward; it is highly relevant to the Due Process issue whether an existing or time-honored convention, described at the proper level of generality, is violated by the practice under attack.

The Equal Protection Clause, in marked contrast, has been employed in much more radical ways to eliminate discrimination, "however deeply engrained and longstanding." Ibid.

32. Ibid.

33. Ibid., pp. 1169–70.

34. Ibid., p. 1174.

35. 388 US 1 (1967).

36. Ibid., p. 12 (discussing the denial of due process as a ground additional to equal protection for invalidating Virginia's law).

37. Ibid.

38. Sturm, *Community and Alienation,* p. 85.

39. Ibid., p. 21.

40. Reinhold Niebuhr, "The Idea of Covenant and American Democracy," *Church History* (1954): 132.

41. Sturm, *Community and Alienation,* p. 86.

42. Lovin, "Covental Relationships and Political Legitimacy," p. 13.

43. Mohr, *Gays/Justice*, pp. 44–45.

44. Ronald Dworkin, *A Matter of Principle* (Cambridge, MA: Harvard University Press, 1985), p. 2.

34.

SINCE WHEN IS MARRIAGE A PATH TO LIBERATION?

Paula L. Ettelbrick

"Marriage is a great institution. If you like living in institutions," according to a bit of T-shirt philosophy I saw recently. Certainly, marriage is an institution. It is one of the most venerable, impenetrable institutions in modern society. Marriage provides the ultimate form of acceptance for personal, intimate relationships in our society, and gives those who marry an insider status of the most powerful kind.

Steeped in a patriarchal system that looks to ownership, property, and dominance of men over women as its basis, the institution of marriage has long been the focus of radical-feminist revulsion. Marriage defines certain relationships as more valid than all others. Lesbian and gay relationships, being neither legally sanctioned nor commingled by blood, are always at the bottom of the heap of social acceptance and importance.

Given the imprimatur of social and personal approval that marriage provides, it is not surprising that some lesbians and gay men among us would look to legal marriage for self-affirmation. After all, those who marry can be instantaneously transformed from "outsiders" to "insiders," and we have a desperate need to become insiders.

It could make us feel okay about ourselves, perhaps even relieve some of the internalized homophobia that we all know so well. Society will then celebrate the birth of our children and mourn the death of our spouses. It would be easier to get health insurance for our spouses, family memberships to the local museum, and a right to inherit our spouse's cherished collection of lesbian mystery novels even if she failed to draft a will. Never again would we have to go to a family reunion and debate about the correct term for introduc-

This is an edited version of an article that originally appeared in *OUT/LOOK National Gay and Lesbian Quarterly* 6 (Fall 1989).

ing our lover/partner/significant other to Aunt Flora. Everything would be quite easy and very nice.

So why does this unlikely event so deeply disturb me? For two major reasons. First, marriage will not liberate us as lesbians and gay men. In fact, it will constrain us, make us more invisible, force our assimilation into the mainstream, and undermine the goals of gay liberation. Second, attaining the right to marry will not transform our society from one that makes narrow, but dramatic, distinctions between those who are married and those who are not married to one that respects and encourages choice of relationships and family diversity. Marriage runs contrary to two of the primary goals of the lesbian and gay movement: the affirmation of gay identity and culture and the validation of many forms of relationships.

When analyzed from the standpoint of civil rights, certainly lesbians and gay men should have a right to marry. But obtaining a right does not always result in justice. White male firefighters in Birmingham, Alabama, have been fighting for their "rights" to retain their jobs by overturning the city's affirmative-action guidelines. If their "rights" prevail, the courts will have failed in rendering justice. The "right" fought for by the white male firefighters, as well as those who advocate strongly for the "rights" to legal marriage for gay people, will result, at best, in limited or narrowed "justice" for those closest to power at the expense of those who have been historically marginalized.

The fight for justice has as its goal the realignment of power imbalances among individuals and classes of people in society. A pure "rights" analysis often fails to incorporate a broader understanding of the underlying inequities that operate to deny justice to a fuller range of people and groups. In setting our priorities as a community, we must combine the concepts of both rights and justice. At this point in time, making legal marriage for lesbian and gay couples a priority would set an agenda of gaining rights for a few, but would do nothing to correct the power imbalances between those who are married (whether gay or straight) and those who are not. Thus, justice would not be gained.

Justice for gay men and lesbians will be achieved only when we are accepted and supported in this society despite our differences from the dominant culture and the choices we make regarding our relationships. Being queer is more than setting up house, sleeping with a person of the same gender, and seeking state approval for doing so. It is an identity, a culture with many variations. It is a way of dealing with the world by diminishing the constraints of gender roles that have for so long kept women and gay people oppressed and invisible. Being queer means pushing the parameters of sex, sexuality, and family, and in the process transforming the very fabric of our society. Gay liberation is inexorably linked to women's liberation. Each is essential to the other.

The moment we argue, as some among us insist on doing, that we should be treated as equals because we are really just like married couples and hold the same values to be true, we undermine the very purpose of our movement and begin the dangerous process of silencing our different voices. As a lesbian,

I am fundamentally different from nonlesbian women. That's the point. Marriage, as it exists today, is antithetical to my liberation as a lesbian and as a woman because it mainstreams my life and voice. I do not want to be known as "Mrs. Attached-to-Somebody-Else." Nor do I want to give the state the power to regulate my primary relationship.

Yet, the concept of equality in our legal system does not support differences. It only supports sameness. The very standard for equal protection is that people who are similarly situated must be treated equally. To make an argument for equal protection, we will be required to claim that gay and lesbian relationships are the same as straight relationships. To gain the right, we must compare ourselves to married couples. The law looks to the insiders as the norm, regardless of how flawed or unjust their institutions, and requires that those seeking the law's equal protection situate themselves in a similar posture to those who are already protected. In arguing for the right to legal marriage, lesbians and gay men would be forced to claim that we are just like heterosexual couples, have the same goals and purposes, and vow to structure our lives similarly. The law provides no room to argue that we are different but are nonetheless entitled to equal protection.

The thought of emphasizing our sameness to married heterosexuals in order to claim this "right" terrifies me. It rips away the very heart and soul of what I believe it is to be a lesbian in this world. It robs me of the opportunity to make a difference. We end up mimicking all that is bad about the institution of marriage in our effort to appear to be the same as straight couples.

By looking to our sameness and deemphasizing our differences, we do not even place ourselves in a position of power that would allow us to transform marriage from an institution that emphasizes property and state regulation of relationships to an institution that recognizes one of many types of valid and respected relationships. Until the Constitution is interpreted to respect and encourage differences, pursuing the legalization of same-sex marriage would be leading our movement into a trap; we would be demanding access to the very institution that, in its current form, would undermine our movement to recognize many different kinds of relationships. We would be perpetuating the elevation of married relationships and of "couples" in general, and further eclipsing other relationships of choice.

Ironically, gay marriage, instead of liberating gay sex and sexuality, would further outlaw all gay and lesbian sex that is not performed in a marital context. Just as sexually active nonmarried women face stigma and double standards around sex and sexual activity, so, too, would nonmarried gay people. The only legitimate gay sex would be that which is cloaked in and regulated by marriage. Its legitimacy would stem not from an acceptance of gay sexuality but because the Supreme Court and society in general fiercely protect the privacy of marital relationships. Lesbians and gay men who do not seek the state's stamp of approval would clearly face increased sexual oppression.

Undoubtedly, whether we admit it or not, we all need to be accepted by the broader society. That motivation fuels our work to eliminate discrimination in the workplace and elsewhere, fight for custody of our children, create our own families, and so on. The growing discussion about the right to marry may be explained in part by this need for acceptance. Those closer to the norm or to power in this country are most likely to see marriage as a principle of freedom and equality. Those who are acceptable to the mainstream because of race, gender, and economic status are more likely to want the right to marry. It is the final acceptance, the ultimate affirmation of identity.

On the other hand, more marginal members of the lesbian and gay community (women, people of color, working class, and poor) are less likely to see marriage as having relevance to our struggles for survival. After all, what good is the affirmation of our relationships (that is, marital relationships) if we are rejected as women, people of color, or working class?

The path to acceptance is much more complicated for many of us. For instance, if we choose legal marriage, we may enjoy the right to add our spouse to our health insurance policy at work, since most employment policies are defined by one's marital status, not family relationship. However, that choice assumes that we have a job and that our employer provides us with health benefits. For women, particularly women of color who tend to occupy the low-paying jobs that do not provide health-care benefits at all, it will not matter one bit if they are able to marry their woman partners. The opportunity to marry will neither get them the health benefits nor transform them from outsider to insider.

Of course, a white man who marries another white man who has a full-time job with benefits will certainly be able to share in those benefits and overcome the only obstacle left to full societal assimilation—the goal of many in his class. In other words, gay marriage will not topple the system that allows only the privileged few to obtain decent health care. Nor will it close the privilege gap between those who are married and those who are not.

Marriage creates a two-tier system that allows the state to regulate relationships. It has become a facile mechanism for employers to dole out benefits, for businesses to provide special deals and incentives, and for the law to make distinctions in distributing meager public funds. None of these entities bothers to consider the relationship among people; the love, respect, and need to protect that exists among all kinds of family members. Rather, a simple certificate of the state, regardless of whether the spouses love, respect, or even see each other on a regular basis, dominates and is supported. None of this dynamic will change if gay men and lesbians are given the option of marriage.

Gay marriage will not help us address the systemic abuses inherent in a society that does not provide decent health care to all of its citizens, a right that should not depend on whether the individual (1) has sufficient resources to afford health care or health insurance, (2) is working and receives health insurance as part of compensation, or (3) is married to a partner who is working and has health coverage that is extended to spouses. It will not address the underlying unfairness that allows businesses to provide discounted services or goods to families and couples, who are defined to include straight, married people and their children, but not domestic partners.

Nor will it address the pain and anguish of the unmarried lesbian who receives word of her partner's accident, rushes to the hospital, and is prohibited from entering the intensive care unit or obtaining information about her condition solely because she is not a spouse or family member. Likewise, marriage will not help the gay victim of domestic violence who, because he chose not to marry, finds no protection under the law to keep his violent lover away.

If the laws changed tomorrow and lesbians and gay men were allowed to marry, where would we find the incentive to continue the progressive movement we have started that is pushing for societal and legal recognition of all kinds of family relationships? To create other options and alternatives? To find a place in the law for the elderly couple who, for companionship and economic reasons, live together but do not marry? To recognize the right of a longtime, but unmarried, gay partner to stay in his rent-controlled apartment after the death of his lover, the only named tenant on the lease? To recognize the family relationship of the lesbian couple and the two gay men who are jointly sharing child-raising responsibilities? To get the law to acknowledge that we may have more than one relationship worthy of legal protection?

The lesbian and gay community has laid the groundwork for revolutionizing society's views of family. The domestic-partnership movement has been an important part of this progress insofar as it validates nonmarital relationships. Because it is not limited to sexual or romantic relationships, domestic partnership provides an important opportunity for many who are not related by blood or marriage to claim certain minimal protections.

It is crucial, though, that we avoid the pitfall of framing the push for legal recognition of domestic partners (those who share a primary residence and financial responsibilities for each other) as a stepping-stone to marriage. We must keep our eyes on the goals of providing true alternatives to marriage and of radically reordering society's view of family.

The goals of lesbian and gay liberation must simply be broader than the right to marry. Gay and lesbian marriages may minimally transform the institution of marriage by diluting its traditional patriarchal dynamic, but they will not transform society. They will not demolish the two-tier system of the "haves" and the "have nots." We most not fool ourselves into believing that marriage will make it acceptable to be gay or lesbian. We will be liberated only when we are respected and accepted for our differences and the diversity we provide to this society. Marriage is not a path to that liberation.

35.

THE LIBERTARIAN QUESTION
Incest, Homosexuality, and Adultery

Stanley Kurtz

There is a mystery at the heart of the gay marriage debate. I call it the "libertarian question." The libertarian question (really a series of questions) goes like this: Why should any form of adult consensual sex be illegal? What rational or compelling interest does the state have in regulating consensual adult sex? More specifically, how does the marriage of two gay men undermine my marriage? Will the fact that two married gay men live next door make me leave my wife? Hardly. So how, then, does gay marriage undermine heterosexual marriage? Why not get the state out of such matters altogether?

The libertarian question is mysterious because, in modern society, we find it difficult to understand the continuing necessity of shared moral standards—and of collective taboos against actions that violate those standards. Traditional societies depend on shared moral sentiments and collective taboos. Modern democracies, for the most part, have rejected these forms of collective morality in favor of an emphasis on personal freedom. Yet the truth is, although their workings are mysterious to us, shared moral codes (and a structure of taboos that guards those codes) can never be entirely dispensed with.

INCEST

Let's approach the libertarian question about gay marriage from a new angle. The flap over Sen. Rick Santorum's remarks has raised the question of incest. If homosexual sex is declared private, why won't consensual adult incest fall under the same sort of protection? (In raising this question, Senator Santorum was simply echoing Justice Byron White's decision in *Bowers v. Hardwick*.)

Reprinted from the *National Review Online*, April 30, 2003.

In his very useful exploration of the consensual incest problem (See "Incest Repellent?" and "Incest Repellent, Continued."), William Saletan points to a case of incest in which a woman was drawn into a sexual relationship with her uncle while she was still a minor, but continued that relationship as an adult. The woman was found guilty of incest and sentenced to supervised probation. After violating probation (presumably to return to her uncle) she was sentenced to five years in jail. Why should this woman have been jailed?

The prevalence of consensual adult incest is difficult to judge. It may be relatively rare. The deeper problem, of course, is the sexual abuse of children by older family members. The impossibility of real consent, as well as the potential psychological damage in cases of incestuous child abuse, is a matter of very serious concern. But incestuous child abuse can obviously be made illegal. What is wrong with consensual adult incest?

Let's return to the libertarian question. *If a man happens to walk around town arm and arm with his adult niece, is that going to make me abuse my teenaged niece?* In most cases, probably not. Clearly, however, there is a connection. Our collective horror at incest—even adult incest—acts as a protective barrier against the temptation to incest with minors. The very real dangers of child abuse within families shows us that a significant number of people are potentially susceptible to sexual interest in the children under their control. Our collective taboo on incest, as expressed in our laws, helps to offset that potential temptation.

The mechanism here is embodied in the law, but goes well beyond the mere mechanical workings of the law. The real mechanism is collective and psychological. The law on incest expresses a shared moral value. It is a collective statement. As such, it reinforces a sense of disgust that helps to ward off temptation.

To see the mechanism of our incest taboo at work, imagine a world in which consensual adult incest was legal. Once we see or hear of couples—even a relatively small number—who engage in legal, consensual, adult incestuous relationships, the whole idea of incest with minors becomes thinkable. Preventing incest with minors from becoming thinkable is the purpose of the taboo.

The reason we need an incest taboo is that there is no effective way for the state to protect children from sexual abuse by family members. Children are essentially at the mercy of the adults who care for them. So only by building into adults a psychological mechanism of disgust and horror at incest can society protect children from the psychological harm of abuse by close relatives. The taboo runs deeper than the law itself. Yet the law embodies and reinforces the taboo. Were the law to be eliminated—even for consenting adults only—the taboo on incest with minors would be weakened, or break down—maybe not in all families, or even most, but for far too many.

HOMOSEXUALITY

The taboo against homosexuality works in a similar fashion. But what, exactly, does the taboo on homosexuality protect? There is more than one way to approach that question, but the short answer is: The taboo on homosexuality protects marriage. Or, to look at the same problem from a slightly different angle, the institution of Western marriage, in its most traditional form, has been protected by a many-sided taboo against all sexuality outside of its confines—and against nonprocreative sexuality within it. Just as the taboo on incest reduces the temptation to child abuse, the taboo on nonmarital and nonreproductive sexuality helps to cement marital unions, and helps prevent acts of adultery that would tear those unions apart.

As an ultimate symbol of sexuality for the sake of pleasure (rather than reproduction) homosexuality has traditionally been taboo. That taboo was embodied and expressed in sodomy laws. Rigorous enforcement of these laws was secondary—and in any case, next to impossible. The important thing was the statement of collective values made by the laws against sodomy. By making homosexuality taboo, the law reinforced the idea that the highest and proper purpose of sexuality itself was to bind and energize families.

Of course, over the last thirty years, the taboo on homosexuality, like the broader taboo on a purely pleasure-seeking sexuality inside and outside the confines of marriage, has substantially broken down. And it's not surprising that, as a consequence of our changed understanding of sexuality, the rates of divorce and out-of-wedlock birth have dramatically risen. Of course, at the same time as the divorce rate has risen, the weakening of the old taboos has substantially increased our personal freedom. And our new sexual freedom has benefited no one more than homosexuals, who no longer serve, in nearly the degree they once did, as ultimate symbols of forbidden sexuality.

On balance, I think we as a society have gained much from the weakening of the old sexual taboos, although it is important to keep in mind that we are in fact dealing with a trade-off here. Traditional sexual taboos protect marriage, and their weakening cannot help but weaken marriage—even as they increase personal freedom. But again, on balance, I believe that at least some of the weakening in the old sexual system has been worth the trade-off.

ADULTERY

What we need to understand—but do not—is that gay marriage will undermine the structure of taboos that continue to protect heterosexual marriage—and will do so far more profoundly than either the elimination of sodomy laws or the general sexual loosening of the past thirty years. Above all, marriage is protected by the ethos of monogamy—and by the associated taboo against adultery. The real danger of gay marriage is that it will undermine the taboo on adultery, thereby destroying the final bastion protecting marriage: the ethos of monogamy.

Gay marriage threatens monogamy in two ways. First, gay marriage threatens monogamy because homosexual couples—particularly male homosexual couples—tend to see monogamy as nonessential, even to the most loyal and committed relationships. Of course, advocates argue that legal gay marriage will change all that—that marriage will make gays more monogamous. But it is just as likely (indeed, far more likely) that the effect will go in the other direction—openly nonmonogamous married gay couples will break the connection between marriage and monogamy. (For more on this, see the NRO Gay-Marriage Debate, particularly my "Point of No Return.")

Even more powerfully, gay marriage threatens monogamy through its tendency to lead, on a slippery slope, to the legalization of polygamy and polyamory. (For more on this, see my *Commentary* article, "What Is Wrong with Gay Marriage.")

It's important to understand what the danger of openly nonmonogamous gay marriages, and of legalized polygamy and polyamory, really is. The key problem here is not, say, that polygamous marriages are unfair or exploitative to women. (That is a legitimate concern, of course, but it is not the greatest social danger posed by legalized polygamy.) The real problem is the effect of openly nonmonogamous gay unions, and of legalized polygamy and polyamory, on the ethos of monogamy.

Even in the wake of the sexual-cultural changes of the sixties, there is still a strong consensus in our society that marriage means monogamy. That consensus is expressed in the taboo on adultery. Legal recognition for group marriage, and for openly nonmonogamous gay unions, would effectively destroy the taboo on adultery. That doesn't mean that everyone would instantly go out and commit adultery—any more than everyone exposed to legal incestuous unions between consenting adults would engage in child abuse. But there would be a significant social effect—and it would be over and above the weakening of marriage that has already occurred in the wake of the changes since the sixties.

The libertarian asks, Just because two married gay men live next door, is that going to make me leave my wife? In a way, the answer is yes. For one thing, as a new generation grows up exposed to gay couples who openly define their marriages in nonmonogamous terms, the concept of marriage itself will gradually change. No doubt, movies and television in a post-gay-marriage world will be filled with stories of the "cutting edge" understandings of open marriage being pioneered by the new gay couples, even if the actual number of such married gay couples is relatively small.

A large segment of the gay community looks forward to gay marriage for precisely this reason. Many thoughtful gay activists see same-sex marriage as a chance to redefine marriage itself—stripping marriage of what they see as its outdated and constricting connection to monogamy. And of course, even more powerfully than openly nonmonogamous gay marriages, legalized group marriage would destroy the taboo against adultery. (Lot's of potential for movies and TV there.)

Still, the libertarian asks, Would the group marriage next door really make me leave my wife? Maybe not. Of course, the married commune next door might invite the two of you over for some fun, with potentially problematic results for your marriage. But even that is not the real problem. The deeper difficulty is simply the breaking of the taboo on adultery. Sodomy laws were barely enforced, yet they made a collective statement about social attitudes toward nonmarital and nonreproductive sexuality. Similarly, incest laws are rarely invoked. Yet their existence reinforces the horror of incest and helps prevent the sort of violations that make incestuous temptation thinkable.

So the mere social statement that marriage does not mean monogamy is where the real danger of legalized gay marriage and polyamory lie. And the collapse of consensus about shared social institutions really does affect us as individuals. Once we as a society no longer take it for granted that marriage means monogamy, you may not decide to leave your wife. But you may be more likely to give in to the temptation of an affair. And that could mean the end of your marriage, whether that's what you wanted going into the affair or not. (For another way of looking at this problem, see my "Code of Honor," where I compare the operation of the taboo against adultery to the working of a college's anticheating honor code.)

As with the taboos on incest and sodomy, society can't enforce the taboo on adultery with laws. Laws on matters of sexual conduct do make a difference, but less as enforcement mechanisms than as embodiments of common values. Precisely because the state cannot monitor and prosecute adultery, society writes a taboo against the practice into our hearts. The laws of marriage as currently constituted embody and express that taboo. Transform those laws, and the taboo will disappear.

The ongoing need for shared social understandings on matters pertaining to the family and sexuality does not fit neatly into the libertarian playbook. Social and sexual taboos are the stuff of traditional societies. But the truth is, so long as we live, not merely as isolated individuals, but in families together, we shall be in need of social and sexual taboos.

If the controversy over Sen. Rick Santorum's remarks has made it possible to openly discuss the real basis of our shared social and sexual understandings, then it will have done some good. Unlike Senator Santorum, I would rather accept some disruption in family stability than go back to the days when homosexuality itself was deeply tabooed. The increase in freedom and fairness is worth it. Yet there has been a terrible social cost for the changes of the sixties. We need to mitigate those costs. And we certainly do not need to risk the destruction of an already weakened family system by radically undermining the ethos of monogamy.

Gay marriage would set in motion a series of threats to the ethos of monogamy from which the institution of marriage may never recover. Yet up to now, our society has been unable to face the real costs and consequences of the proposed change. That is partly because of an understandable sympathy for the gay rights movement. But it also reflects the sheer inability of modern folk to grasp the operation, necessity—or even the existence—of the system of moral consensus and prohibition upon which society itself depends.

36.

MAKING THE
FAMILY FUNCTIONAL
The Case for Same-Sex Marriage

Larry A. Hickman

I

Several years ago, when I was a regular columnist for the *Bryan-College Station* (Texas) *Eagle,* I wrote a piece in which I suggested that Americans need to rethink their notion of the family.[1] I argued that we would all benefit from thinking of the family as a functional unit rather than as something with a fixed and finished essence. I urged my readers to entertain the idea that if a particular social arrangement *functions* like a family, then we should *count* it as a functioning family. The philosophical idea behind my column was this: hard-line essentialism often bars the way to the solution of pressing social problems. We need to pay more attention to how things work than to their purported "essences."

Few if any of us would admit to being antifamily, so there should be widespread agreement that our society needs more functioning families. But most of us know of nontraditional social units that perform precisely the same functions that traditional families perform. So why should we not count them as families? Why should we not afford them the same kind of legal protection that is given to traditional families?

A consequence of this way of thinking, I argued, is that we as a society should begin to offer legal recognition to marriages between gay men, between lesbians, among certain polygamous and polyandrous groups, and even among small associations of elderly men and women insofar as those small associations perform certain functions.

Here is a quotation from one of the angry letters printed in response to my suggestion: "The *American Heritage Dictionary* definition of a family is 'the

---

Since 1997, when this essay was published in the first edition, much has changed in terms of public perceptions of what counts as a family. Nevertheless, I offer it again at this time with only minor revisions.

most instinctive, fundamental social or mating group in man and animal, especially the union of man and woman through marriage and their offspring;
parents and their children; persons related by blood. . . .' You tell me: What
does homosexuality have to do with a family?"

My respondent continued: "Can you imagine the havoc the legal system and
the insurance system would suffer if, as [Hickman] suggests, America began to
recognize and accept his nontraditional family units? Shame on you . . . for
allowing this man to continue to publicly promote a homosexual lifestyle."[2]

There you have it in a nutshell: a traditional definition of the family, as
enshrined in the *American Heritage Dictionary,* relying on hard-line essentialist criteria. There is in nature a biological union in which a male and a
female come together in order to procreate and to nurture their offspring.[3]
What makes this view hard-line essentialist is that it says that there is a fixed
and finished essence of "family" which we must recognize and honor if we are
to know, to act appropriately, and to flourish in the world. Put a bit differently,
the claim is that if we do not recognize and acquiesce to this fixed and finished
essence, then we can expect havoc.

For those who suspect that I have constructed a straw argument, let me
assure you that this is a quotation from an actual letter, written by an actual person to an actual newspaper. I am confident that most of us would not have to leave
our own towns or cities in order to find people who hold a similar point of view.[4]

Now the author of the response to my column did not elaborate on or justify her claim that she had articulated the essence of the family. Except for her
vague warning about the havoc that would result from following my suggestion, she did not appeal to anything beyond the *American Heritage Dictionary.*
So let's consider how she might have justified her claim.

She might have appealed to a supernatural ordering of things, such as one
finds in certain theological treatises on the family. Or she might have appealed
to certain naturalist criteria, thus extrapolating from the larger biological order
of which human beings are a part. Finally, she might have appealed to a somewhat weaker form of essentialism, namely, that human societies have worked
out over several centuries a satisfactory set of rules for establishing the essence
of what it means to be a family and that the time has now come to stop inquiry
into the matter because all the work of defining the family has been done.

In fact, all three of these responses, which I will call the *supernaturalist,*
the *naturalist,* and the *historical-cultural* strategies, would be an appeal to
work already done, either by a god, nature, or culture, and therefore not in need
of any further revision.

I suggest that this is one of the main problems of hard-line essentialist
views in general: they are static or backward-looking and thus do not take into
sufficient account the fact that we live forward in time, that we must take
changing circumstances into account if we are to act intelligently, and that
foresight and experimental problem solving are required wherever human
beings expect to continue to flourish.

But what, more specifically, are the problems with the hard-line essentialist notion of the family? In the remainder of this essay I will point out and discuss several of those problems. Then I will indicate some of the ways in which a pragmatic or functional understanding of the family can be more productive of both proximate and long-term good. In order to do this, I will have to explain what goods I hope to gain by such a functional understanding of the family, that is, what is to be gained by making the family functional.

II

The first problem with essentialist views as I have described them is that they suffer from a type of historical dislocation that we might call antiquation: they do not begin where we *are* but where we have *been*. Like the notorious generals who send their troops into battle to fight the previous war, essentialists busily prescribe goals and plans of action for societies and cultures that have ceased to exist.

I will pass rather briefly over the types of antiquation involved in the supernaturalist and naturalist claims advanced by the essentialist in order to get to what I take to be the more important cultural claim.

Regarding the supernaturalist claim, it is clear that theological doctrines and organized religions, like other types of institutions, either change and develop as their environing conditions alter or else they become at best irrelevant and at worst extinct. Some progressive mainstream religious groups in the United States are beginning to recognize this fact and are now moving—some slowly, others more rapidly—toward acceptance of the idea that homosexuals should not be discriminated against on the basis of their homosexuality alone.

On the other hand, religionists of the literalist-fundamentalist stripe tend to claim (even against the testimony of their own sacred texts) that their theology involves a fixed essence and that changing conditions must therefore measure up to their theology. It is on such grounds that they oppose the legalization of homosexual marriage. It is they who have mounted most of the anti-gay initiatives in cities and states across our nation.

But their position is historically dislocated in a double sense. In the first sense, it fails to take into account the historical facts that militancy with respect to theological views has a history of failure, that the source of most of the major conflicts in the world today are due to such religious intransigency, and that much of the success of contemporary social and political arrangements has been built upon compromise and understanding, not on the basis of drawing lines in the sand.

In the second sense, their position fails to take into account the historical fact that American society is increasingly secular and to an even greater extent increasingly multicultural, with all that that entails. In character and outlook, American society is no longer predominantly Christian, or for that matter even predominantly Judeo-Christian. What is called for at the present time is therefore not narrow secularism, but what John Dewey termed "a common faith," a faith that can resolve rather than engender strife, and a faith that can unite individuals and groups in their quest for shared goals and social amelioration.

In addition to their supernaturalist strategy, hard-line essentialists sometimes employ naturalist strategies. These also suffer from antiquation. By arguing from "nature" that families must by definition be heterosexual and reproductive, the hard-line essentialist is arguing that what has in fact occurred in terms of the developmental history of nonhuman and human biology ought to be the pattern for what should be held as valuable, now and in the future, as components of human cultural practice.

Ironically, the same type of argument is sometimes advanced by proponents of legalized homosexual behavior. This is the claim that such behavior is acceptable because it occurs among nonhuman animals: "lesbian" sea gulls and "gay" dolphins were at one time favorite cases. But the argument from "nature," whether marshaled by pro- or antihomosexual partisans, is flawed. It suffers not only from a missing premise, but one which probably cannot be supplied, namely, that the behavior of nonhuman animals constitutes the grounds for the justification of human behavior.

Regarding the third, and to my mind the most important, strategy open to the essentialist in this regard, namely, the historical-cultural strategy, the functionalist is compelled to make the following admission. There are good indications that there have been times in the history of humankind during which infant mortality rates were high, disease and famine were rampant, and the population of tribal groups was regularly decimated by warfare. These factors made it highly desirable that high levels of reproduction should have been maintained. The various prohibitions in the Hebrew Bible, especially in the book of Leviticus, against same-sex copulation and masturbation have their roots in a culture that suffered all of these adversities. It is probable that when these proscriptions were articulated they had a high level of pragmatic value.

But the world of the ancient Hebrews is not the world in which we in industrialized countries now live. If we have a problem associated with our population, it is certainly not that it is too small.[5] Furthermore, the means of eradicating disease and hunger are now within our grasp, even if the expenditure of funds to combat these problems is not always a high priority among our elected representatives. A moment's reflection indicates, too, that tribal warfare in industrialized countries—with the possible exception of Northern Ireland—is now minimal.

It is telling, then, that one of the most frequently utilized arguments against the acceptance of homosexual family units is that such units do not allow for procreation. A heterosexual couple can procreate, or so the argument goes, and so they are a family. A homosexual couple cannot procreate, so they are not a family.

This argument is unacceptable on at least three counts. As I have already indicated, its first fault is that it is historically antiquated: it does not take into account the current need within industrialized societies—and other societies as well—to manage population growth. In short, it rests on an empirical error. Its second fault is that it rests on a second empirical error: not all heterosexual couples can procreate. Should they thereby be denied the legal protection afforded to other families? The third empirical error committed by this argument is its failure to recognize that homosexuals as a group are as capable of procreation as are heterosexuals as a group. Many homosexuals do in fact have children: some are the products of former heterosexual marriages, and others are the result of various methods such as sperm donorship. I mention in this regard the famous technique known among lesbian couples as the "turkey baster" method of insemination.

From the functionalist's point of view, then, the essentialist is at fault because she has divided up the world in the wrong place. On one side, the side on which she places things and practices that are acceptable to her, she puts the kinds of things that are ordained by a god or gods, by nonhuman nature, or by cultures historically prior to our own. On the other side she places everything else as either neutral or unacceptable.

The functionalist, on the other hand, divides up the world in a quite different manner. He attempts to determine what problems are currently being experienced, and he attempts by experimental means to find ways of solving those problems. He understands, for example, that there now exist enormous pressures on the family as a result of increased geographic mobility, the technological pull toward ever-more-complex and rapid-paced lifestyles, the increased use of debilitating and life-threatening drugs, unemployment, and so on. He also understands that the family, creatively understood and restructured, can function as a bulwark against these pressures.

Because of this, he thinks it appropriate to divide up matters differently. On one side of the dividing line he places what works or what might work out in the sense that it promises solutions to these problems and should therefore be tried out. On the other side he places what he knows does not work because it has been tried out and has failed.

With respect to the question at hand, then, what we ought to count as a family, his different method leads the functionalist to place on one side of his dividing line small associations of mutual support, usually involving individuals living together under one roof, and who exhibit unconditional love, financial cooperation, and long-term commitment. Again with respect to the question at hand, he places on the other side of the dividing line groups that do not function in this way.

To put matters succinctly, the functionalist's sorting criterion is pragmatic. He divides not on the basis of heterosexuality and the capacity for reproduction on one side and everything else an the other, but rather on the basis of what well-functioning families do, on the one side, and what groups that do not function as families do, on the other. Furthermore, the functionalist is not afraid to try out nontraditional, experimental candidates as solutions to problematic situations. He takes into account empirical data that indicate that under the proper circumstances homosexual domestic partnerships not only function well but also tend to stabilize their environing social institutions. And this is ground enough for him to count a homosexual domestic partnership as a family.[6]

The first problem with the hard-line essentialist's definition of the family, then, is that it tends to be historically antiquated: it does not take into account where we are, speaking historically, but where we have been.

A second problem with the hard-line essentialist's definition of the family, and one that is intertwined with her tendency to appeal to antiquated ideas and practices, is that her view is reductionistic. By this I mean that the hard-line essentialist isolates a small number of the functions of well-functioning families at the expense of other functions, some of which are at least as important as the ones that she isolates and holds as valued. It is certainly true that one of the functions of a family may be reproduction and nurturing of offspring. This may take place in a variety of ways: it may occur "naturally," which is to say without the intervention of much technological apparatus (although this is now less and less the case) or it may take place by highly artificial means, such as in vitro fertilization. When we look at the possibilities now impinging just on the "reproduction" part of the hard-line essentialist's definition, however, we can say that her desire to reduce the many diverse functions of the family to one or two simple ones is thwarted.

The "reproductive" component of the essentialist's definition of the family turns out to be much more complex than she has been willing to admit. This complexity has the effect of pushing her central concern back step after step until it becomes a different issue entirely, namely, one that concerns the ethics of reproductive technology.

The functionalist, on the other hand, is quite willing to take on both problems. He is willing to work out an experimental, functional account of the family, and he is also willing to address the complex issues surrounding the technology of human reproduction. But he insists that these issues be kept separate wherever there is no good reason for mingling them. He insists even more emphatically that one issue should not be reduced to the other. (And of course he challenges the hard-line essentialist to give such good reasons if she insists on such a reduction.)

What I as a pragmatist and functionalist am suggesting, then, is that we ought to characterize families in terms of what families do when they function well. Now my hard-line essentialist opponent might at this point shift her argument somewhat, claiming that it is now just a matter of my values against hers and that she at least has cultural tradition, perhaps "the Judeo-Christian tradition," on her side. This, of course, is a weaker form of the cultural-historical argument that she has already advanced. But she may think that it nevertheless strengthens her hand at this point in our discussion, since her implicit claim is that she and I will just have to continue to disagree, that she at least has historical-cultural support on her side, and that she can now abandon the discussion with a slight advantage.

In an attempt to bring her back to the discussion, I would then offer her my working characterization of a family, the one that I have already sketched, and which I here repeat in order to refresh your memory, which would be a small association of mutual support, usually involving individuals living together under one roof and who exhibit unconditional love, financial cooperation, and long-term commitment. My attendant claim would be that when you encounter such a situation then you have found a more or less well-functioning family and that there is no reason to deny a group its proper status, even though the group may incidentally be an association of partners of the same sex or perhaps a polygamous or polyandrous association. In order to make my point, to establish the relevance of my argument, all I have to do is to present one case in each category of association that functions well as a family. And such cases are not hard to find.

Once I have reframed my argument in this way, my opponent is faced with a dilemma. She may respond either that such a group, functioning as I have indicated, is not functioning well, or that it is in fact functioning well but as something other than a family. If she takes the latter tack, then she must retreat into a reductionistic position that accepts heterosexual associations and rejects other types on that basis alone, and so her argument becomes circular. A family would be defined only as a heterosexual couple and their offspring, and nothing else would count as a family. A homosexual union could not, by that very fact, be counted as a family. Her reductionistic argument would then miss the point of what families in our society do, as opposed to how they are defined in her view or as a part of some other dogmatic position.

If she were to take the former tack, however, and tell me that a loving, monogamous relationship of two decades between two gay men that meets the functional definition I have advanced does not in fact function as a family, then she would be obligated to tell me why this is so. She might choose one of several strategies. She might return to her argument that such a unit cannot procreate, and is therefore not a family. This would have the unfortunate consequence of also committing her to the view that heterosexual unions in which one or more of the partners is sterile, or heterosexual unions in which one of the partners is past the age of childbearing, are not families for that reason and thus by her definition.

Of course the hard-line essentialist might shift the argument somewhat at this point and say that she is not talking about actual reproductive capacities, but "natural sexual attraction," or perhaps more strongly, "natural sexual attraction that could, under normal circumstances, product offspring." But a functionalist would have a series of ready replies to this argument.

First, neither the strong nor the weak version of her argument would disallow heterosexual associations that are polygamous or polyandrous. Second, the weak form of her argument does not take into account the well-documented innate, which is to say "natural," attraction between gay men and between lesbians. Third, the strong form of her argument relies on the very reductionistic move that she sought to avoid by shifting her argument in the first place. Under at least one interpretation of this argument, marriage between heterosexuals where one or both is sterile or past the age of reproduction would be disallowed. Her argument therefore remains faulty because she has too closely identified sexual attraction with reproductive capacities. In short, her strong argument is so strong that it becomes circular, excluding from its premise any but heterosexual unions. It could even be read as excluding some of those unions as well.

Alternatively, she might argue that acceptance of legalized marriage between two gay men would lead children in our society to conclude, erroneously, that such an arrangement was acceptable. But of course this merely pushes the argument back one step, because she would then be required to provide reasons why the homosexual family *should not* be presented to children as acceptable. She might appeal to one or more of the standard arguments against accepting homosexual sexual behavior as moral behavior, such as are found in fundamentalist-literalist or other traditionalist accounts. But then the functionalist might ask "What reasons can you give us for accepting your theology or your tradition over others?" This question would have the effect of pushing the debate into another territory—perhaps into the study of anthropology or comparative religion—where the essentialist's footing is even less secure.

As a part of the essentialist's move to reduce the function of the family to sexual behavior, or at the very least to make sexual behavior central to its definition, she might argue that the sex act is a uniquely apt symbol of the marriage union and that it is a medium of communication without which a marriage is "defective." But there are several difficulties that vitiate this line of argumentation. First, in the absence of some additional premise, sex between gay males or lesbians might also be considered a uniquely apt symbol of the marriage union and as a medium of communication without which a marriage is defective. If the hard-line essentialist wishes to deny this parity between heterosexual and homosexual sex, then she must either provide a missing premise or risk begging the question. A second difficulty with this line of argumentation is that it is reductionistic. As I have already argued, given the complex and multifarious ways in which families do in fact function in our society, to isolate sex as a defining characteristic would constitute a form of reductionism that is both empirically false and tactically absurd.

Here is a third point: the hard-line essentialist's position with respect to the family is overly exclusive. Its exclusivity follows from its reductionism. It first reduces the notion of the many and varied functions of the family to a few representative ones, a kind of synecdochical move in which sexual behavior is taken as standing for a whole complex of functions. It then follows up by utilizing the reductionist thesis to warrant exclusion of well-functioning social units that do the same type of work that heterosexual families do when they function at their best, and it does so only on those reductionistic grounds.

The fact is that recent (1993) census bureau figures indicate that there are some 3.5 million households of unmarried couples in the United States.[7] Using even a conservative estimate of 3 percent, over one hundred thousand of these households probably comprise gay men or lesbians. (Figures from the 2000 census indicate that my earlier estimate was quite conservative: the Department of Commerce reports that about 11 percent of unmarried households are now self-reporting as same-sex partnerships.)[8] My hard-line essentialist opponent thus seems to want to deny that there are among this sizable contingent of our population any well-functioning families. She wants to do so without the slightest empirical inquiry into whether there are among this population any viable and ongoing relationships of the sort I have described, and she wants to do this on the basis of an essentialist definition that I have claimed is indefensible.

Finally, the hard-line essentialist position is wasteful. In a time of the notorious "breakdown" of the family, including the instability that is consequent to divorce, the rise in the number of single parents who live below the poverty line, and the technological pressures on family units (such as job loss and geographic mobility), the hard-line essentialist's insistence on her reductionistic and exclusive position regarding what counts as a family is to a certain extent self-fulfilling. As long as her position is held as the social norm, it serves to create stresses on alternative family associations that tend to render them more fragile than they would otherwise be. This is wasteful because family associations that would otherwise function so as to strengthen the social fabric are weakened as a result of the enforcement of the norms she is defending.

Her argument that the acceptance of gay marriages would wreak havoc on the legal system is absurd to the point of undermining her general claim. I know of no one who has advanced the position that there should be fewer heterosexual marriages because of their burden on the legal system, although it is certainly possible to argue that current levels of divorce among heterosexual unions do place a burden on the court system. What we generally say in this regard is that this is a price we as a society are willing to pay in order to sanction associations that benefit society. If the essentialist is willing to admit, as I expect that she is, that heterosexual marriages benefit society, then she is obligated to explain (in a noncircular manner) why homosexual marriages do not and cannot provide the same or similar benefits.

Her concern about burdening the insurance system is likewise a red herring. If we hold the view that it strengthens our society to extend rights of inheritance, rights of next of kin in medical emergencies, survivor's benefits, and other such rights to heterosexual couples, then one is just left wondering at her claim that society would be harmed if those same rights were extended to homosexual couples. Would homosexuals carry more, or less, insurance as a result of participating in legalized marriage? And whatever they did, is it clear that insurance companies would suffer as a result? It is at least conceivable that homosexuals who were accepted as members of legal, functional families would experience less stress and therefore be less prone to physical and psychological disorders than they are under the current arrangement. In the absence of evidence to the contrary, then, it is reasonable to expect that legalized homosexual marriages would have very little impact on the insurance industry. Even if there were some modest impact on that industry, it is perhaps more reasonable to conclude that it would be beneficial than to conclude that it would be detrimental.

III

At this point I want to recall a suggestion made over a hundred years ago by the American pragmatist William James. He wrote that "*the only meaning of essence is teleological and . . . classification and conception are purely teleological weapons of the mind.* The essence of a thing is that one of its properties which is so *important for my interests* that in comparison with it I may neglect the rest."[9]

I believe that James has here given us a key to effecting social amelioration with respect to the problem at hand. Notice that the pragmatic functionalist does not give up essences entirely, but merely functionalizes them by making them contextual, that is, by choosing them in a way that renders them appropriate to a specific process of deliberation.

Perhaps the reason that the hard-line essentialist and the pragmatic functionalist remain at an impasse is that they are in fact asking different sorts of questions, that is, they have different ends in view. Perhaps the problem that the hard-line essentialist is working on is this one: "How can I maintain a world in which I am not threatened by what is foreign to me and unknown in its consequences?" Or put another way, perhaps the hard-line essentialist holds that her prescription has worked in the past and would work again if only we returned to those conditions. On the other hand, the problem that the pragmatic functionalist is working on is this one: "How can I find a solution to a serious social problem by means of active and controlled experimentation?" Or put another way, the functionalist holds that what the hard-line essentialist prescribes either never really worked or has ceased to function, so that something needs to be done to fix an unsatisfactory situation.

If this is true, then it may be the case that no amount of discussion will serve to bring the two sides to a common ground. It may be that the hard-line essentialist will change her mind only when she begins to achieve some level of familiarity with the types of alternative family associations I have described, and as they consequently become less threatening to her.

It may even be that the solution to the problem here under consideration does not ultimately lie with the type of activity I am undertaking in this essay, namely, the articulation and analysis of the arguments on both sides of the issue. It may be that the solution lies rather in members of alternative family units working through social and political means to establish themselves as nonthreatening and credible—in a word, as functional. But, to add a word in defense of the exercise I have just undertaken, it may also be that the kind of analysis I have just done will be of some help to members of alternative family units as they seek to establish themselves through judicial and legislative action.

NOTES

1. Larry A. Hickman, "American Family Must Be Nurtured," *Bryan-College Station Eagle*, October 22, 1991, p. 6A.

2. Letter to the editor, "Gays Cannot Be a Family," *Bryan-College Station Eagle*, November 7, 1991, p. 4A.

3. I should note that the person who responded to my column cited the second edition of the *American Heritage Dictionary*. The third edition, published since I wrote my column, contains a definition that is similar to the one to which my critic objected. The *b* definition is now: "Two or more people who share goals and values, have long-term commitments to one another, and reside usually in the same dwelling place." The fourth edition, published in 2000, retains this definition.

4. This paper was first presented in Colorado in 1993. Voters in that state had registered just such an opinion.

5. The writer of a letter to the editor of the *New York Times* (March 12, 2004, p. A20) is nevertheless still concerned with precisely this matter, which he relates to the future of Social Security. His argument, of course, fails to take into account the considerable immigration that the United States currently enjoys, as well as the ability of homosexuals as a group to procreate.

6. Here is an example of the counterproductive effects of accepting the hard-line essentialist's position as reported in the *New York Times*, January 1, 1994. It involves a woman, Megan Lucas, who gave up parental rights to her child in 1992. "But she says she was twenty-one years old then and at a low point in her life, abusing drugs and alcohol. She had a history of trouble with the law and had abandoned the boy when he was five months old." Her son was "moved around, spending time in at least six foster homes until, in September, he was placed with a new couple, Ross and Louis Lopton, two gay men. This time Mrs. Lucas, who says she is now devoutly Christian, objected. Since learning of the Loptons' homosexuality, Mrs. Lucas has been fighting in court to get her son back. First she contended that she had been coerced by social workers into giving up permanent parental rights to the state. But a Whatcom County Superior Court judge rejected that argument." Her husband, Mr. Lucas, who is thirty, "has had his own run-ins with the law. On February 24 he was given a suspended one-year jail sentence and ordered to perform 240 hours of community service for stealing a vacuum cleaner from his employer."

The *Times* reported in the same article that "two conservatives in the Washington legislature, Val Stevens, a Republican, and Thomas Campbell, a Democrat, plan to introduce a bill that would prohibit adoptions in the state except by married, heterosexual couples."

The argument put forward by Mrs. Lucas, her attorney, and the antigay Rutherford Institute, a conservative think tank in Charlottesville, Virginia, which has helped sponsor her case, is remarkable. Its explicit claim is that a married heterosexual couple, at least one of whom has a recent felony conviction and one of whom has a history of drug abuse and child abandonment, would make better parents than a homosexual couple, neither of whom has been shown to possess a criminal record and neither of whom has had questions raised concerning his character, except for his admitted homosexuality. In other words, the Rutherford Institute is claiming that the felonious Mr. Lucas and the child-abandoning Mrs. Lucas are a functioning family because they are heterosexual and married, whereas the law-abiding Loptons, because they are homosexual, are not a functioning family.

This is only one of many such cases. On February 3, 1996 (p. 4A), the *Southern Illinoisan* reported that "a killer who won custody of his eleven-year-old daughter because his former wife is a lesbian said Friday he can give the girl a better home. John A. Ward, who murdered his first wife, won custody of his daughter in August from a judge who wanted to give the girl a chance to live in 'a nonlesbian world.' " In this case, the judge seems to have concluded that it was worse to be a lesbian than to be a convicted wife murderer!

7. *Statistical Abstract of the United States 1994* (Washington, DC: US Department of Commerce, 1994), p. 56.

8. Recent census figures (2000) indicate that about one in nine, or 11 percent (594,000) of, unmarried-partner households had partners of the same sex. US Department of Commerce, "Census 2000 Special Reports: Married-Couple and Unmarried-Partner Households: 2000," February 2003, p. 1.

9. William James, *The Principles of Psychology* (New York: Holt, 1890; reprint, Cambridge, MA: Harvard University Press, 1981), p. 961.

37.

A CHRISTIAN CASE
FOR SAME-SEX MARRIAGE

Jack McKinney

In June of 1958, Mildred Jeter and Richard Loving were married in Washington, DC. Upon their return to Virginia to take up residence there, they were promptly arrested, convicted of a felony, and sentenced to a year in jail. What great crime had Mildred and Richard committed that would bring the force of the law down on them so swiftly and severely? Mildred was black and Richard was white. The trial judge suspended the sentence as long as the couple promised to leave the state and not to return for a minimum of twenty-five years. At the sentencing of the couple, the judge gave his rationale for upholding Virginia's statutes forbidding interracial marriage:

> Almighty God created the races white, black, yellow, and red, and he placed them on separate continents. And but for the interference with his arrangement there would be no cause for such marriages. The fact that he separated the races shows that he did not intend for the races to mix.[1]

Eight years later, when the United States Supreme Court finally took up Mildred and Richard's case, the justices did not quite agree with the remarkable theology of the Virginia judge. In fact, Chief Justice Earl Warren, in stating the Court's rationale for dismantling interracial marriage bans across the country, made this sweeping statement about marriage:

> Marriage is one of the "basic civil rights of [humanity]," fundamental to our very existence and survival. To deny this fundamental freedom on so unsupportable a basis as the racial classifications embodied in these statutes, classifications so directly subversive of the principle of equality at the heart of the Fourteenth Amendment, is sure to deprive all the State's citizens of liberty without due

...rocess of law. The Fourteenth Amendment requires that the freedom of choice to marry not be restricted by invidious racial discriminations. Under our Constitution, the freedom to marry, or not marry, a person of another race resides with the individual and cannot be infringed by the State.[2]

I wonder if we took Chief Justice Warren's statement, and altered the context from interracial marriage to same-sex marriage, if it would still stand up? Hear the statement again with that one alteration:

Marriage is one of the "basic civil rights of [humanity]," fundamental to our very existence and survival. To deny this fundamental freedom on so unsupportable a basis as the "sexual" classifications embodied in these statutes, classifications so directly subversive of the principle of equality at the heart of the Fourteenth Amendment, is sure to deprive all the State's citizens of liberty without due process of law. The Fourteenth Amendment requires that the freedom of choice to marry not be restricted by invidious "sexual" discriminations. Under our Constitution, the freedom to marry, or not marry, a person of "the same sex" resides with the individual and cannot be infringed by the State.

I think the statement is true whether we are talking about racial discrimination or the discrimination against sexual minorities. The freedom to marry, or not marry, resides with individuals and should not be infringed by the state.

And so I begin this sermon titled "The Christian Case for Gay Marriage" with the clear belief that the highest court in the land has already articulated why people of the same sex should be allowed to marry. Marriage is such a basic civil right that no state is justified in denying this right to people based on discriminatory classifications, classifications "directly subversive of the principle of equality." But, of course, the states are doing just that. Thirty-seven states have already adopted statutes preventing people of the same sex from having the right to marry. The president threatened in his State of the Union address to sign a constitutional amendment banning same-sex marriage if the states begin granting this basic civil right to gay and lesbian couples. And it all makes you wonder if we are not back in a Virginia courtroom in 1958 hearing a judge rant about God's plan to keep the races separate.

How can this be? How can states so easily deny one of our most basic civil rights to millions of citizens? The short answer is that it is the church's fault. The church, just as it did for centuries with women and people of color, has provided the cover for our leaders to deny gay, lesbian, bisexual, and transgendered citizens the right to marry whomever they choose. Laws are not created in vacuums of justice untouched by the cultural values around them. The law is just as impressionable as other institutions in our society. And when the dominant religious power in our country, the Christian church, states that gay citizens are deviant and must not be allowed to marry, the law tends to be influenced by such majoritarian thinking.

Which is why I believe it is critical for the church to repent and begin to understand how its own teachings and traditions provide a natural rationale to support same-sex marriage. I am not naive about the obstacles in the way of that happening. The reality is that not only are most heterosexuals opposed to the concept of gay marriage, but many people in the gay community are not convinced this is a battle worth fighting. And who can blame them? Why would gay citizens be excited about entering into an institution that has been used to oppress people for much of history and has not always been the panacea for social ills that heterosexuals claim. (See Britney Spears's recent marriage fiasco for more evidence of why gays and lesbians should think twice about jumping into this quagmire with the rest of us.) Therefore, let me make clear, while I believe the church has an interest in supporting the right to marry for gays and lesbians, that is not to say marriage is the answer for all people.

So where do we begin in searching for a Christian defense of gay marriage? I think our scripture readings for the morning make an excellent starting place. In Luke 4 Jesus begins his public ministry by returning to his hometown, entering into the synagogue, and making something of a mission statement:

> The Spirit of God is upon me, because God has anointed me to bring good news to the poor. God has sent me to proclaim release to the captives and recovery of sight to the blind, to let the oppressed go free, to proclaim the year of God's favor. (Luke 4:18–19)

For his mission statement Jesus reaches for the language of the prophet Isaiah (61:1–2). He is calling to mind the period in Jewish history when the exile had rendered the people powerless. Like the prophet centuries before him, Jesus is saying that one of the most fundamental religious tasks is to stand with those who have been excluded and marginalized. Those with no power because of their social status, their physical status, or because of the way they were born are the focus of Jesus' ministry from day one. He is determined to stand with them, to name them beloved of God, and to dedicate his life to seeing them empowered.

Paul's letter to the Corinthians takes this idea of empowering the powerless in another direction by tearing down the social hierarchy that threatened the early church. In a congregation that was divided by social class, ethnic background, and gender status, Paul writes these remarkable words:

> For just as the body is one and has many members, and all the members of the body, though many, are one body, so it is with Christ. For in the one Spirit we were all baptized into one body—Jews or Greeks, slaves or free, male or female—and we were all made to drink of one Spirit. (1 Cor. 12:12–13; also see Gal. 3:27–29)

What a revolutionary statement that was. In a world where men had all the power and women had none, Paul says that through baptism we are all the same. In a world where your religious and cultural heritage gave you all the power, or none,

Paul says that all people are equal by the power of the Spirit. Do we understand that these were not just sweet words about how God loves all of us the same? This is a radical egalitarian vision that states all the hierarchical divisions that demean and demoralize people have no standing in Christ's church.

And so, in constructing a Christian case for gay marriage, I reach for this original vision of Jesus' ministry, and Paul's early vision of the church, and note that what they have in common is a significant reordering of the balance of power. Jesus and Paul are naming all the ways power has been held by certain members of society to the exclusion of others—and they are naming it sin. The founder of the church, Jesus of Nazareth, and the first theologian of the church, Paul, are convinced that God's purpose is fulfilled when power is shared and abusive hierarchical distinctions are abolished.

And let's not kid ourselves. The debate over gay marriage in our society is a power struggle. Like all other justice struggles, the majority is rarely willing to give up its sense of privilege easily. But you may be thinking that's not fair. That's not why people are opposed to the concept of gay marriage. Maybe you are persuaded by those who say it is wrong to change the definition of marriage that has been so firmly in place for thousands of years. But I ask you, Which definition of marriage would that be? Is it the definition of marriage that allowed men complete control over women until the last century, or is it the definition of marriage that criminalized Mildred Jeter and Richard Loving's marriage because their skin color was different? To say marriage has been a static institution that never changed or evolved is to ignore the historical facts.

Or maybe you are persuaded by those who say there is a basic immorality to people of the same sex entering into marriage. But since when has it been immoral for two people to commit themselves to a relationship of mutual love and caring? No, the true immorality around gay marriage rests with the heterosexual majority that denies gays and lesbians more than one thousand federal rights that come with marriage. As Anna Quindlen has written, laws such as the Defense of Marriage Act are immoral because they "exist purely for the purpose of codifying and justifying bigotry."[3]

And of course there is the moderate position that says gays and lesbians are entitled to reasonable alternatives, such as civil unions, but they should not expect our society to grant them full marital rights. But even if the effect of such alternatives is to grant more power to gay couples than they currently have, didn't we learn anything during the civil rights struggle? Separate but equal never equates to equality. Reasonable alternatives are just another way for the majority to grasp its privileged position even as it seeks ways to ease its conscience.

The heterosexual majority in this country can state these various objections all it wishes, but in the end it comes back to power. Straight people have it and are not giving it up easily. Jesus and Paul remind Christians that we can dress that up any way we choose, but in the end it is nothing more than sin.

Twelve years ago this church took a courageous stance when it not only opened its doors formally to sexual minorities, but it also decided to do something even more explicitly Christian: bless the unions of gay men and lesbians. Remembering that it is in the truest teachings of the church to encourage people to live in covenant relationships, and knowing that such relationships promote the social welfare of our entire society, Pullen embarked on a sacred journey into the unknown. Since that time we have been privileged to witness many gay couples take solemn vows in this sanctuary. Every time we do a holy union here there are tears of joy. But for many of us there are also tears of sorrow. For unlike the marriage ceremonies that take place in this room that not only include the church's blessing, but also the full legal support of the state, the couples who have a holy union derive no particular benefit outside of this space. Even though the couple is married in our eyes, and in the eyes of God, they are just as powerless as before in the eyes of the state. Which means we still have work to do. For it is not enough to say we have done all we can inside the walls of this church; we must commit ourselves to the larger struggle for justice taking place in our society. Every generation of the church must take up Jesus' mission statement and find those places where people without power are being abused and marginalized. In previous generations the struggle was for women and people of color. In our generation the struggle is to support our gay brothers and sisters as they seek full equality.

I end with a pop quiz. Which of the following are not allowed to marry in this country: (1) violent criminals in maximum security prisons; (2) deadbeat parents who marry and divorce repeatedly leaving a trail of children uncared for; or (3) a gay couple that has lived together for years in a mutually supportive and loving relationship? Of course the answer is number three. You can commit any crime on the books and our society will respect your right to marry. You can marry and divorce a dozen times over, leaving all kinds of pain and suffering in your past, and our society will respect your right to marry. But if you happen to love a person of the same sex because that is how God has created and blessed you, you cannot exercise that basic human right. If that doesn't tell us this is a struggle about power then nothing will. Let's join with Jesus in declaring this the year of God's favor and let's declare it on behalf of our gay and lesbian friends who are only asking for what is rightfully theirs.[4]

NOTES

1. *Loving v. Virginia*, 388 US 1 (1967).
2. Ibid.
3. Anna Quindten, "Getting Rid of the Sex Police," *Newsweek*, January 13, 2003, p. 72.
4. Marvin Ellison's excellent book, *Same-Sex Marriage?: A Christian Ethical Analysis* (Cleveland, OH: Pilgrim Press, 2004) was a major resource for this sermon.

APPENDIXES

Appendix 1.

THE TEXT OF THE DEFENSE OF MARRIAGE ACT

ONE HUNDRED FOURTH CONGRESS
SECOND SESSION
JANUARY 3, 1996

Be it enacted by the Senate and House Representatives of the United States of America in Congress assembled,

Section 1. Short Title

This act may be cited as the 'Defense of Marriage Act'.

Sec. 2. Powers Reserved to the States

(a) IN GENERAL—Chapter 115 of title 28, United States Code, is amended by adding after section 1738B the following:

Sec. 1738C. Certain acts, records, and proceedings and the effect thereof

No State, territory, or possession of the United States, or Indian tribe, shall be required to give effect to any public act, record, or judicial proceeding of any other State, territory, possession, or tribe respecting a relationship between persons of the same sex that is treated as a marriage under the laws of such other State, territory, possession, or tribe, or a right or claim arising from such relationship. . . .

Sec. 3. Definition of Marriage

(a) IN GENERAL—Chapter 1 of title 1, United States Code, is amended by adding at the end the following:

Sec. 7. Definition of 'marriage' and 'spouse'

In determining the meaning of any Act of Congress, or of any ruling, regulation, or interpretation of the various administrative bureaus and agencies of the United States, the word 'marriage' means only a legal union between one man and one woman as husband and wife, and the word 'spouse' refers only to a person of the opposite sex who is a husband or a wife.

Appendix 2.

GAY MARRIAGES IN SAN FRANCISCO
Mayor Gavin Newsom's Letter to the County Clerk

February 10, 2004

Nancy Alfaro
San Francisco County Clerk
City Hall, Room 168
1 Dr. Carlton B. Goodlett Place
San Francisco, CA 94102

Dear Ms. Alfaro,

Upon taking the Oath of Office, becoming the Mayor of the City and County of San Francisco, I swore to uphold the Constitution of the State of California. Article I, Section 7, subdivision (a) of the California Constitution provides that "[a] person may not be . . . denied equal protection of the laws." The California courts have interpreted the equal protection clause of the California Constitution to apply to lesbians and gay men and have suggested that laws that treat homosexuals differently from heterosexuals are suspect. The California courts have also stated that discrimination against gay men and lesbians is invidious. The California courts have held that gender discrimination is suspect and invidious as well. The Supreme Courts in other states have held that equal protection provisions in their state constitutions prohibit discrimination against gay men and lesbians with respect to the rights and obligations flowing from marriage. It is my belief that these decisions are persuasive and that the California Constitution similarly prohibits such discrimination.

Pursuant to my sworn duty to uphold the California Constitution, including specifically its equal protection clause, I request that you determine what changes should be made to the forms and documents used to apply for and issue marriage licenses in order to provide marriage licenses on a nondiscriminatory basis, without regard to gender or sexual orientation.

Respectfully,

Mayor Gavin Newsom

Appendix 3.

BAEHR V. LEWIN
An Edited Version of the 1993 Hawaii Supreme Court Decision

Ninia BAEHR, Genora Dancel, Tammy Rodrigues, Antoinette Pregil,
Pat Lagon, Joseph Melilio, Plaintiffs-Appellants,

v.

John C. LEWIN, in his official capacity as Director of the Department of
Health, State of Hawaii, Defendant-Appellee.

No. 15689.

Supreme Court of Hawaii.

May 5, 1993.

Opinion Granting in Part and Denying in Part
Clarification and Reconsideration May 27, 1993. . . .

I. BACKGROUND

On May 1, 1991, the plaintiffs filed a complaint for injunctive and declaratory
relief in the Circuit Court of the First Circuit, State of Hawaii, seeking, inter alia:
(1) a declaration that Hawaii Revised Statutes (HRS) § 572-1 (1985)—the section of the Hawaii Marriage Law enumerating the [r]equisites of [a] valid marriage contract"—is unconstitutional insofar as it is construed and applied by the
DOH to justify refusing to issue a marriage license on the sole basis that the applicant couple is of the same sex; and (2) preliminary and permanent injunctions prohibiting the future withholding of marriage licenses on that sole basis. . . .

The plaintiffs' complaint avers that: (1) the DOH's interpretation and application of HRS § 572-1 to deny same-sex couples access to marriage licenses violates the plaintiffs' right to privacy, as guaranteed by article I, section 6 of the Hawaii Constitution, as well as to the equal protection of the laws and due process of law, as guaranteed by article I, section 5 of the Hawaii Constitution; (2) the plaintiffs have no plain, adequate, or complete remedy at law to redress their alleged injuries; and (3) the plaintiffs are presently suffering and will continue to suffer irreparable injury from the DOH's acts, policies, and practices in the absence of declaratory and injunctive relief.

On June 7, 1991, Lewin filed an amended answer to the plaintiffs' complaint. . . .

On July 9, 1991, Lewin filed his motion for judgment on the pleadings, pursuant to Hawaii Rules of Civil Procedure and to dismiss the plaintiffs' complaint. . . .

In his memorandum, Lewin urged that the plaintiffs' complaint failed to state a claim upon which relief could be granted for the following reasons: (1) the state's marriage laws "contemplate marriage as a union between a man and a woman"; (2) because the only legally recognized right to marry "is the right to enter a heterosexual marriage, [the] plaintiffs do not have a cognizable right, fundamental or otherwise, to enter into state-licensed homosexual marriages"; (3) the state's marriage laws do not "burden, penalize, infringe, or interfere in any way with the [plaintiffs'] private relationships"; (4) the state is under no obligation "to take affirmative steps to provide homosexual unions with its official approval"; (5) the state's marriage laws "protect and foster and may help to perpetuate the basic family unit, regarded as vital to society, that provides status and a nurturing environment to children born to married persons" and, in addition, "constitute a statement of the moral values of the community in a manner that is not burdensome to [the] plaintiffs"; (6) assuming the plaintiffs are homosexuals (a fact not pleaded in the plaintiffs' complaint), they "are neither a suspect nor a quasi-suspect class and do not require heightened judicial solicitude"; and (7) even if heightened judicial solicitude is warranted, the state's marriage laws "are so removed from penalizing, burdening, harming, or otherwise interfering with [the] plaintiffs and their relationships and perform such a critical function in society that they must be sustained." . . .

The circuit court heard Lewin's motion on September 3, 1991, and, on October 1, 1991, filed its order granting Lewin's motion for judgment on the pleadings on the basis that Lewin was "entitled to judgment in his favor as a matter of law" and dismissing the plaintiffs' complaint with prejudice. The plaintiffs' timely appeal followed.

II. JUDGMENT ON THE PLEADINGS WAS ERRONEOUSLY GRANTED

. . . We conclude that the circuit court's order runs aground on the shoals of the Hawaii Constitution's equal protection clause and that, on the record before us, unresolved factual questions preclude entry of judgment, as a matter of law, in favor of Lewin and against the plaintiffs. Before we address the plaintiffs' equal protection claim, however, it is necessary as a threshold matter to consider their allegations regarding the right to privacy. . . . *The right to privacy does not include a fundamental right to same-sex marriage.*

It is now well established that "'a right to personal privacy, or a guarantee of certain areas or zones of privacy,' is implicit in the United States Constitution." And article I, section 6 of the Hawaii Constitution expressly states that "[t]he right of the people to privacy is recognized and shall not be infringed without the showing of a compelling state interest." . . .

Accordingly, there is no doubt that, at a minimum, article I, section 6 of the Hawaii Constitution encompasses all of the fundamental rights expressly recognized as being subsumed within the privacy protections of the United States Constitution. In this connection, the United States Supreme Court has declared that "the right to marry is part of the fundamental 'right of privacy' implicit in the Fourteenth Amendment's Due Process Clause." *Zablocki v. Redhail* (1978).

The issue in the present case is, therefore, whether the "right to marry" protected by article I, section 6 of the Hawaii Constitution extends to same-sex couples. Because article I, section 6 was expressly derived from the general right to privacy under the United States Constitution and because there are no Hawaii cases that have delineated the fundamental right to marry, this court . . . looks to federal cases for guidance.

The United States Supreme Court first characterized the right of marriage as fundamental in *Skinner v. Oklahoma* (1942). In *Skinner,* the right to marry was inextricably linked to the right of procreation. . . . Whether the Court viewed marriage and procreation as a single indivisible right, the least that can be said is that it was obviously contemplating unions between men and women when it ruled that the right to marry was fundamental. This is hardly surprising inasmuch as none of the United States sanctioned any other marriage configuration at the time.

The United States Supreme Court has set forth its most detailed discussion of the fundamental right to marry in *Zablocki*, which involved a Wisconsin statute that prohibited any resident of the state with minor children "not in his custody and which he is under obligation to support" from obtaining a marriage license until the resident demonstrated to a court that he was in compliance with his child support obligations. . . . In so doing, the *Zablocki* court delineated its view of the evolution of the federally recognized fundamental right of marriage. . . .

Implicit in the *Zablocki* court's link between the right to marry, on the one hand, and the fundamental rights of procreation, childbirth, abortion, and child rearing, on the other, is the assumption that the one is simply the logical predicate of the others.

The foregoing case law demonstrates that the federal construct of the fundamental right to marry—subsumed within the right to privacy implicitly protected by the United States Constitution—presently contemplates unions between men and women. (Once again, this is hardly surprising inasmuch as such unions are the only state-sanctioned marriages currently acknowledged in this country.)

Therefore, the precise question facing this court is whether we will extend the present boundaries of the fundamental right of marriage to include same-sex couples, or, put another way, whether we will hold that same-sex couples possess a fundamental right to marry. In effect, as the applicant couples frankly admit, we are being asked to recognize a new fundamental right. . . . However, we have also held that the privacy right found in article I, section 6 is similar to the federal right and that no "purpose to lend talismanic effect" to abstract phrases such as "intimate decision" or "personal autonomy" can "be inferred from [article I, section 6], any more than . . . from the federal decisions." . . .

Applying the foregoing standards to the present case, we do not believe that a right to same-sex marriage is so rooted in the traditions and collective conscience of our people that failure to recognize it would violate the fundamental principles of liberty and justice that lie at the base of all our civil and political institutions. Neither do we believe that a right to same-sex marriage is implicit in the concept of ordered liberty, such that neither liberty nor justice would exist if it were sacrificed. Accordingly, we hold that the applicant couples do not have a fundamental constitutional right to same-sex marriage arising out of the right to privacy or otherwise.

Our holding, however, does not leave the applicant couples without a potential remedy in this case. As we will discuss below, the applicant couples are free to press their equal protection claim. If they are successful, the state of Hawaii will no longer be permitted to refuse marriage licenses to couples merely on the basis that they are of the same sex. But there is no fundamental right to marriage for same-sex couples under article 1, section 6 of the Hawaii Constitution.

Inasmuch as the applicant couples claim that the express terms of HRS § 572-1, which discriminates against same-sex marriages, violate their rights under the equal protection clause of the Hawaii Constitution, the applicant couples are entitled to an evidentiary hearing to determine whether Lewin can demonstrate that HRS § 572-1 furthers compelling state interests and is narrowly drawn to avoid unnecessary abridgments of constitutional rights.

In addition to the alleged violation of their constitutional rights to privacy and due process of law, the applicant couples contend that they have been denied the equal protection of the laws as guaranteed by article I, section 5 of the Hawaii Constitution. On appeal, the plaintiffs urge and, on the state of the bare record before us, we agree that the circuit court erred when it concluded, as a matter of law, that: (1) homosexuals do not constitute a "suspect class" for purposes of equal protection analysis under article I, section 5 of the Hawaii Constitution; (2) the classification created by HRS § 572-1 is not subject to "strict scrutiny," but must satisfy only the "rational relationship" test; and (3) HRS § 572-1 satisfies the rational relationship test because the legislature "obviously designed [it] to promote the general welfare interests of the community by sanctioning traditional man-woman family units and procreation." . . .

The applicant couples correctly contend that the DOH's refusal to allow them to marry on the basis that they are members of the same sex deprives them of access to a multiplicity of rights and benefits that are contingent upon that status. Although it is unnecessary in this opinion to engage in an encyclopedic recitation of all of them, a number of the most salient marital rights and benefits are worthy of note. They include: (1) a variety of state income tax advantages, including deductions, credits, rates, exemptions, and estimates; (2) public assistance from and exemptions relating to the Department of Human Services; (3) control, division, acquisition, and disposition of community property; (4) rights relating to dower, curtesy, and inheritance; (5) rights to notice, protection, benefits, and inheritance; (6) award of child custody and support payments in divorce proceedings; (7) the right to spousal support; (8) the right to enter into premarital agreements; (9) the right to change of name; (10) the right to file a nonsupport action; (11) postdivorce rights relating to support and property division; (12) the benefit of the spousal privilege and confidential marital communications; (13) the benefit of the exemption of real property from attachment or execution; and (14) the right to bring a wrongful death action. For present purposes, it is not disputed that the applicant couples would be entitled to all of these marital rights and benefits, but for the fact that they are denied access to the state-conferred legal status of marriage.

Notwithstanding the state's acknowledged stewardship over the institution of marriage, the extent of permissible state regulation of the right of access to the marital relationship is subject to constitutional limitations or constraints.

The equal protection clauses of the United States and Hawaii Constitutions are not mirror images of one another. The Fourteenth Amendment to the United States Constitution somewhat concisely provides, in relevant part, that a state may not "deny to any person within its jurisdiction the equal protection of the laws." Hawaii's counterpart is more elaborate. Article I, section 5 of the Hawaii Constitution provides in relevant part that "[n]o person shall . . . be denied the equal protection of the laws, nor be denied the enjoyment of the person's civil rights or be discriminated against in the exercise thereof because of *race, religion, sex, or ancestry*" (emphasis added). Thus, by its plain language, the Hawaii Constitution prohibits state-sanctioned discrimination against any person in the exercise of his or her civil rights on the basis of sex. . . .

In a landmark decision, the United States Supreme Court, through Chief Justice Warren, struck down the Virginia miscegenation laws on both equal protection and due process grounds. The Court's holding as to the former is pertinent for present purposes:

[T]he Equal Protection Clause requires the consideration of whether the classifications drawn by any statute constitute an arbitrary and invidious discrimination. . . .

There can be no question but that Virginia's miscegenation statutes rest solely upon distinctions drawn according to race. The statutes proscribe generally accepted conduct if engaged in by members of different races. . . . At the very least, the Equal Protection Clause demands that racial classifications . . . be subjected to the "most rigid scrutiny," . . . and, if they are ever to be upheld, they must be shown to be necessary to the accomplishment of some permissible state objective, independent of the racial discrimination which it was the object of the Fourteenth Amendment to eliminate. . . .

There is patently no legitimate overriding purpose independent of invidious discrimination which justifies this classification. . . . We have consistently denied the constitutionality of measures which restrict the rights of citizens on account of race. There can be no doubt that restricting the freedom to marry solely because of racial classifications violates the central meaning of the Equal Protection Clause.

. . . We hold that sex is a "suspect category" for purposes of equal protection analysis under article I, section 5 of the Hawaii Constitution and that HRS § 572-1 is subject to the "strict scrutiny" test. It therefore follows, and we so hold, that (1) HRS § 572-1 is presumed to be unconstitutional (2) unless Lewin, as an agent of the state of Hawaii, can show that (a) the statute's sex-based classification is justified by compelling state interests and (b) the statute is narrowly drawn to avoid unnecessary abridgements of the applicant couples' constitutional rights. . . .

III. CONCLUSION

Because, for the reasons stated in this opinion, the circuit court erroneously granted Lewin's motion for judgment on the pleadings and dismissed the plaintiffs' complaint, we vacate the circuit court's order and judgment and remand this matter for further proceedings consistent with this opinion. On remand, in accordance with the "strict scrutiny" standard, the burden will rest on Lewin to overcome the presumption that HRS § 572-1 is unconstitutional by demonstrating that it furthers compelling state interests and is narrowly drawn to avoid unnecessary abridgements of constitutional rights.

Vacated and remanded.

REPORT OF THE HAWAII COMMISSION ON SEXUAL ORIENTATION AND THE LAW

Thomas P. Gill, Chair
Morgan Britt
L. Ku'umeaaloha Gomes
Lloyd James Hochberg, Jr.
Nanci Kreidman
Marie A. "Toni" Sheldon
Bob Stauffer

December 8, 1995

PREFACE

This report is submitted by the Commission on Sexual Orientation and the Law to the Eighteenth Legislature as requested by Act 5, Session Laws of Hawaii 1995.

I. BACKGROUND AND AUTHORITY

The Commission on Sexual Orientation and the Law was convened by the legislature to address some of the issues that have arisen in the case of *Baehr v. Lewin,* 74 Haw.530, (1993).

This edited version includes the minority report and the majority response.

A. *BAEHR V. LEWIN* : AN OVERVIEW

A lawsuit filed in May 1991 by three same-gender couples against the state of Hawaii, specifically against John Lewin, in his capacity as the Director of Health, complained of an unconstitutional marriage law that prohibited same-gender couples from obtaining marriage licenses. The complaint alleged a violation of the couples' right to privacy and equal protection under the Constitution of the State of Hawaii. The trial court dismissed the case on the pleadings and the couples appealed to the Supreme Court of Hawaii.

In May 1993 the Supreme Court reversed the trial court and remanded the case back for trial. Although the Supreme Court found that there is no fundamental right to same-sex marriage under the right to privacy, the court did conclude that the marriage law does deny the same-gender couples equal protection rights in violation of article 1, Section 5 of the Hawaii Constitution. The Hawaii Supreme Court held that the discrimination is based on the "gender" of an individual and is a "suspect category." Therefore, for purposes of the equal protection analysis, the marriage law is subject to a "strict scrutiny" test. This places the burden on the state to show that the statute's gender-based classification is justified by compelling state interests and the statute is narrowly drawn to avoid unnecessary abridgments of the applicant couples' constitutional rights.

B. LEGISLATIVE ACTION

The legislature reacted to the Supreme Court's decision in *Baehr v. Lewin* by holding public hearings throughout the state in September and October of 1993. At the next legislative session the legislature proceeded to pass Act 217, Session Laws of Hawaii 1994. Act 217 accomplished several things. First, Act 217 provided a venue in its purpose section for the legislature to express its position. The purpose section of Act 217 has been interpreted to create legislative history after the fact while at the same time telling the Supreme Court not to interpret the law in a different fashion. Second, Act 217 also amended the marriage law to specifically require a man and a woman to be eligible for a marriage license, but it did not prohibit the private solemnization of any ceremony. Third, Act 217 created the prior Commission on Sexual Orientation and the Law. . . .

SEXUAL ORIENTATION AND THE LAW COMMITTEE REPORT

FINDINGS AND RECOMMENDATIONS

I. Findings

1. The commission finds that the conferring of a marriage certificate can bestow benefits in other jurisdictions. While those may be beyond the scope of this commission, the ability of the state to extend those benefits by providing a marriage certificate to individuals is significant.

2. The commission finds that major legal and economic benefits conferred by the marriage certificate through the Hawaii Revised Statutes include intangible, substantial-quantifiable, and general benefits.

3. The commission finds there are substantial public policy reasons to extend those benefits in total to same-sex couples. Those public policy reasons include:

   a. Article 1, sections 2, 3, and 5 of the Constitution of the State of Hawaii clearly states that all persons in Hawaii are entitled to equal protection under the law, including the right to enjoy their inherent and inalienable rights to life, liberty, and pursuit of happiness, and be free from illegal discrimination or the denial of basic rights on the basis of gender.

      The commission finds that the denial of the benefits of marriage to same-gender couples, purely on the basis of their gender, is a violation of those basic constitutional rights.

   b. In the case which gave rise to the establishment of this commission, *Baehr v. Lewin,* 74 Haw. 530 (1993), the Supreme Court of Hawaii recognized the relevance of the United States Supreme Court's 1967 decision to strike down a Virginia statute which prohibited miscegenation, or interracial marriage, *Loving v. Virginia,* 388 US 1 (1967). The Hawaii Supreme Court has found that denial of same-gender marriage was presumed to be a violation of equal protection of the law unless the state could show a "compelling state interest" for such denial. The commission finds that the various reasons advanced for denying same-gender marriages, including religious, moral, and public health and safety, are similar to the *Loving* case and do not constitute a "compelling state interest" and, as a matter of public policy, should not be used to deny equal rights under the law to same-gender couples.

   c. The argument that same-sex marriage should be barred because it cannot lead to procreation is invalid, inconsistent, and discriminatory. Public policy should not deny same-sex couples the right to marriage and the right to raise a family if they wish to do so, on the excuse that they, between themselves, cannot procreate, when this reason is not applied to opposite-gender couples. State law does not require that opposite-sex couples prove that they are capable of procreation before they can be married, and many are obviously not, because of age, medical, or other reasons. Individuals in a same-gender marriage may have children from a prior opposite-gender marriage, or can adopt children if they desire a family.

   d. Under our constitutional government the fact that some religions or churches condemn same-gender marriages does not mean that those religious beliefs can be imposed on others. Our separation of church and state prevents religious enforcement through state institutions, such as the Department of Health. Furthermore, the Constitution prohibits any religious group from having to perform the marriage of a couple that is not recognized by that religion.

4. The commission finds that, based on the major legal and economic benefits and the substantial public policy, the only logical conclusion is to recommend that same-gender couples be allowed to marry under chapter 572, Hawaii Revised Statutes. The commission also acknowledges that the extension of marriage to same-gender couples may not be a legislative alternative at this time.

5. In the event that same-gender marriage under chapter 572, Hawaii Revised Statutes, is not a legislative alternative, the commission recommends a universal comprehensive domestic partnership act that confers all the possible benefits and obligations of marriage for two people regardless of gender.

II. Recommendations

Based on the findings stated above, the commission first recommends the legislature amend chapter 572 to allow two people to marry, regardless of their gender. The commission also recommends the legislature adopt a universal comprehensive domestic partnership act that confers all the possible benefits and obligations of marriage for two people, regardless of gender.

MINORITY OPINION

The irony of this "minority" opinion is that its conclusions actually reflect the view of a majority of Hawaii's residents. According to the most recent poll taken by SMS Research, the *Honolulu Advertiser,* and KHON, July 19–29, 1994, more than two-thirds of the respondents stated that Hawaii should not allow people of the same sex to marry. The public response to the Draft Final Report of this commission confirms this as well. Of 1,033 written comments received, 455 were in favor and 578 were opposed to homosexual marriage. At the December

6, 1995, meeting, where public comment was received, of 103 who testified, 22 were in favor and 81 were opposed to homosexual marriage. . . .

Opposition to changing the definition of marriage is also consistent with the policy in Hawaii prohibiting "common law marriage." The state of Hawaii has protected traditional marriage and has narrowly circumscribed marriage rights since 1920.

So zealously has this court guarded the state's role as the exclusive progenitor of the marital partnership that it declared, over seventy years ago, that "common law marriages"—i.e., "marital" unions existing in the absence of a state-issued license and not performed by a person or society possessing governmental authority to solemnize marriages—would no longer be recognized in the territory of Hawaii. . . .

I. INTRODUCTION

A. Reason for Minority Opinion

Due to the five-member majority of commission members who vigorously support homosexual rights, the debate needed for serious analysis did not occur. The Governor's Commission on Sexual Orientation and the Law failed in its effort to seriously analyze the issues presented. . . .

This opinion of a minority of the Governor's Commission on Sexual Orientation and the Law is written because the two-member minority disagreed with the substance of the majority's analysis and because the process employed by the majority to reach their conclusions is faulty. Instead of looking to Act 5, 1995 Session Laws, for guidance, the majority of the commission saw its role as validating favorable portions of the court opinion in *Baehr v. Lewin* even though in Act 217, 1994 Session Laws, the legislature roundly criticized the court opinion in *Baehr*. As a result, during the actual commission meetings, the majority of commissioners refused to examine the major legal and economic benefits reserved for married couples, but instead simply reached their conclusions. In addition, the majority refused to examine substantial public policy reasons not to extend these benefits in part or in whole to homosexual couples. The overwhelming credible evidence available to the commission requires that the state of Hawaii not recognize homosexual unions as equivalent to traditional, heterosexual marriage.

B. Recommendations

The minority of the commission recommends that no action be taken to extend any legal or economic marital benefits to homosexual couples that they do not already enjoy. . . . The minority also strongly recommends that the legislature undertake to amend the Constitution of the State of Hawaii to reserve marriage and marital rights to unions between one man and one woman. If any marital rights are granted to homosexual couples, the minority vigorously recommends that the legislation contain a sweeping religious exemption. Finally, the minority recommends that the legislature consider reviewing Hawaii laws to determine whether it should enlarge the definition of "family" in some statutes in order to protect legitimate "family" needs for unmarried people. In evaluating which, if any, statutes should be changed in this regard, the minority also strongly recommends that the legislature evaluate the cost to the state from such change.

C. Summary

This report presents information received from persons who testified before the commission as well as material included in the commission's bibliography. This modern literature concerns legal, economic, and social policy analysis of marriage and marital rights, family and child rearing, the attributes of homosexuality and the effects of homosexuality on the community. Many people testified that they were opposed to homosexual marital rights on economic, religious, historical, medical, and psychological grounds. Of critical importance to many people who testified was the protection of children. The majority report simply rejects all these bases of opposition to homosexual marital rights. The majority's argument relies on the tenuous assumption that the present legal status of gay marriages parallels the laws against interracial marriages in the 1960s. The minority opinion addresses some of the reasons why this is a false assumption. Race and gender are immutable characteristics. Clearly, sexual orientation is not in the same category—sexual orientation is known to change and is, to a large extent, behavioral. The argument that homosexuality is genetically determined and so in the same category as race or gender has no valid scientific support. There are many elements of behavior, such as the propensity to violence, for which a genetic determinant has been found. This does not mean that such a behavior should be elevated to the status of the most favored in the state. Homosexual marital rights are simply not civil rights. . . . Homosexuality is not immutable but is caused by disturbed family environment and interaction between the parents and their children.

Regardless of any person's philosophy that homosexuality is either deviant or an acceptable alternative lifestyle, the issue of homosexual marital rights must be resolved on the basis of what is good for society. While the majority were not interested in discussion of reasons not to extend the benefits of marriage to homosexual couples, this minority opinion identifies the following major reasons why there should not be a drastic revision of the marriage law. The minority refutes the assumption that legalizing same-sex marriage will be of any benefit at all to Hawaii's economy. On the contrary, it is more likely that Hawaii's major industry, tourism, will be negatively affected, as the image of Hawaii deteriorates from the Aloha State to the gay honeymoon and wedding destination of the world.

The minority is seriously concerned about the adverse effect legalizing homosexual marriage will have on the social, sexual, and psychological development of children. The majority did manage to find some "expert" to testify that being raised in a homosexual household had no detrimental effects on children, but the vast body of work done on the issue suggests the opposite.

The minority believes that the ramifications on the education system would be far-reaching, touching all elements of the curriculum. Parents are protective and concerned about their children's education. . . . The rights of parents must be favored over the rights of the homosexual community.

Every person's review of this report should focus on resolving the issue of homosexual marital rights in such a manner as to protect and preserve society, both in Hawaii and the United States. Clearly, this issue will affect everyone in the state. It will affect the entire country, since other states will be forced to deal with whether their states must accept any homosexual marital rights granted on a statewide basis in Hawaii. There is even a home page on the Internet where homosexual activists freely discuss this issue across the country.

The majority supports its position by arguing that withholding marital rights constitutes discrimination against homosexuals. However, even the Hawaii Supreme Court in *Baehr* held that there is no fundamental right to homosexual marriage:

> Applying the foregoing standards to the present case, we do not believe that a right to same-sex marriage is so rooted in the traditions and collective conscience of our people that failure to recognize it would violate the fundamental principles of liberty and justice that lie at the base of all our civil and political institutions. Neither do we believe that a right to same-sex marriage is implicit in the concept of ordered liberty, such that neither liberty nor justice would exist if it were sacrificed. Accordingly, we hold that the applicant couples do not have a fundamental constitutional right to same-sex marriage arising out of the right to privacy or otherwise.

Therefore, the resolution of this issue cannot be analyzed solely on the basis of the value of autonomous freedom for homosexuals, or an assumption of improper discrimination. Permissible discrimination occurs in many ways on a daily basis.

Not all forms of discrimination are inappropriate, and one should not jump to the conclusion that opposition to endorsing homosexuality constitutes inappropriate discrimination. Discrimination (approval or disapproval of a person or group) based on judgments in the absence of evidence is inappropriate. However, certain distinctions can reflect prudent judgment based on evidence. Therefore, the commission should have first examined the evidence of the attributes of homosexuality and the effects those attributes have on children, family, and society. Although the majority of the commission did not even consider such information important, only with that information can one take a rational position regarding the extent to which the state of Hawaii should endorse—and by its endorsement encourage—homosexual practices. The majority's recommendations actually constitute prejudiced discrimination against those whose prudent judgment, based on the evidence, does not equate homosexuality and heterosexuality. . . .

The majority of the commission failed to consider whether homosexuality and heterosexuality are so distinctly different that the two cannot be equivalents. However, significant evidence of that fact was available to the commission, but ignored. The interests of society in marriage and family have justified substantial regulation of marriage throughout history. Aristotle taught that it was the first duty of legislators to establish rules regulating entrance into marriage. Throughout history societies have given unique and special preference to heterosexual marriage because of the benefits that those relationships provide for society in general, and for individual women, men, and children.

To justify giving similar preferred legal protection to same-sex couples, it is necessary to consider the social purposes of marriage, and to compare heterosexual unions with same-sex unions in terms of how each relationship furthers those purposes.

It is important to not oversimplify and distort the heterosexual-marriage position. We acknowledge that two men or two women may share a deep, meaningful personal relationship with each other (usually called "friendship"), support each other, develop and pursue mutually fulfilling, socially beneficial common interests, make strong commitments to each other, and in many ways be as good citizens as persons in heterosexual marriages. However, we believe that same-sex unions simply do not equate with heterosexual union of husband and wife in terms of the purposes of marriage.

We believe that the majority's Commission Report denies and devalues the unique strengths and social contributions of heterosexual marriage, and that legalization of same-sex marriage or domestic partnership would put the state in the position of presenting a false image of both marriage and of same-sex unions. We agree with Gov. Pete Wilson of California who said, when he vetoed a much narrower, much more modest domestic partnership proposal last year: "Government policy ought not to discourage marriage by offering a substitute relationship that demands much less—and provides much less than is needed by the children . . . and ultimately much less than is needed by society."

He also stated that government has an obligation to "encourage and reward marriage and the formation of strong families." He added: "A society that devalues marriages, and which accepts illegitimacy as commonplace, encourages the explosion of teenage out-of-wedlock births that California has in fact experienced."

There are numerous social purposes of marriage as to which heterosexual marriages provide tremendous benefits to society that are unequaled by homosexual unions. They are: (1) protecting safe sexual relations, (2) social concerns regarding procreation and child rearing, (3) protecting the status of women, (4) fostering marital stability, (5) promoting economic security for parents and children, (6) providing for recognition of Hawaii marriages in other jurisdictions, and (7) protecting the foundations of self-government. Clearly, the marriage statute itself regulates who may marry in order to prevent incest (HRS 572-1[1]), to protect children (HRS 572-1[2] and 572-2), to prevent the spread of venereal disease on public health grounds (HRS 572-1[5]), and to prevent bigamy (HRS 572-1[3]).

First, sexual behavior is a central concern in marriage and marriage regulation. Same-sex marriage is, by definition, homosexual marriage because sexual relations between the spouses is an integral part of marriage. Thus, it is disingenuous (and simply erroneous) to suggest, as a plurality of the Hawaii Supreme Court did in *Baehr v. Lewin,* that not all same-sex marriages will be homosexual marriages. If, however, homosexual marital rights are extended to all unmarried people, then marriage would be stripped of all of its value to society and simply reduced to a vehicle for obtaining benefits from government without contributing to society those benefits which were historically given by marriage to society. Moreover, in these days of sex-saturated entertainment, when the exploitation of children in pornography is such a severe problem that Congress has had to pass laws to try to restrain it, when incidents of forcible rape and "date rape" are skyrocketing, when American servicemen incite an international incident bringing dishonor on the nation they serve because of their callous rape of a preteen girl in another nation in which they were guests, when children are receiving less sex-education in the home and more on the street, when rates of adolescent sexuality, pregnancy, and even abortion are at near-disaster levels, it would be an act of unforgivable irresponsibility to brush aside the tremendous social interest in regulating sexual behavior.

Moreover, it is the very nature and acts of homosexual behavior that are the core and identifying feature of homosexual relations. It is not friendship between persons of the same gender or mere cohabitation of persons of the same gender that creates social concern, but the acts of homosexual sexual relations that is at the core of the moral concern. Thus, to try to evade that issue, to refuse (as the majority) to investigate it or even to listen to witnesses discuss it, is to evade a critical dimension of the marriage issue.

Second, marriage has long been favored because it is the most favorable setting in which to bring children into the world and to raise them. If anything is clear in social science, it is that conventional male-female marriage provides the best environment for the nurture, care, training, education, and responsible socialization of children. It is equally clear that children suffer most from the creative "alternative" relationships that adults sometimes pursue for their own adult self-interest. Children are the most numerous (and most innocent) victims of the disintegration of marriage. The impoverishment of children has been shown repeatedly and irrefutably to be a direct result of the change in family structure in the past three decades. Yet, incredibly, the majority of the commission blithely ignores the suffering of children and proposes yet another radical destructuring of marriage. Why must Hawaii's children pay and suffer for the faddish social experimentation of same-sex marriage or domestic partnership?

The concern for our children is not limited to specific children living with specific parents. Undoubtedly, one can find conscientious and devoted adults caring for children under any kind of family structure. Rather, the greater concern is that children generally will suffer from the message that homosexual marital rights send to all prospective parents, the message that a mother and a father are not both optimally necessary for the raising of children. In a time when fathers are abandoning their children's lives in record numbers, it would be irresponsible to adopt a marriage or domestic partnership reform that sent the false message that same-sex marriage and domestic partnership clearly convey about the disposability of two-gender parenting. A state and society that cares for its children and its future will not be so reckless when the interests, futures, and lives of its children are at risk. The law should emphatically model, support, and encourage two-parent, mother-father parenting rather than create yet another ill-considered alternative to that institution that will impose untold misery on yet another generation of Hawaii's children.

Third, studies repeatedly have shown that wives and mothers make the greatest investment in marriage and children, and suffer the greater economic disadvantage when marriage is undermined. Marriage is the one institution which historically has recognized the indispensable equality of women because a man could not have a marriage without a woman. It is the oldest equal rights relationship in law and society. Since male homosexuals outnumber female homosexuals, even this new domestic institution will become just another male-dominated institution. How many mothers in Hawaii will lose custody to their "gay" former husband and his same-sex partner if same-sex marriage or domestic partnership is legalized? The message of same-sex marriage and domestic partnership trivializes the contributions of tens of thousands of Hawaii wives and mothers and says to them, "your contributions to your children, your family, and our society are no different, no better than those of a homosexual partner."

Fourth, fostering marital stability is a great concern of the state. Given the indisputable evidence (summarized elsewhere in the Minority Opinion) of the unavoidably promiscuous, fleeting nature of most same-sex relationships, it is facetious to compare the stability of same-sex marriage with conventional male-female marriage—even in these days of high divorce rates marriages are as solid as the Rock of Gibraltar compared to same-sex liaisons. While one might shrug and say it is up to the adults to choose for themselves whether they want one stable relationship or many temporary relationships, that is simply irresponsible when one is talking about marriage, the basic unit of society. Male-female relations are complementary in ways that same-sex relations are not. The law should not pretend otherwise and send false messages about reality simply because that happens to be the popular political fashion of the day. And, again, the people who suffer the most from unstable families are children. Their interest must not be sacrificed to the instability of same-sex relationships.

Fifth, marriage has been repeatedly shown to promote economic security for parents and children. Marital instability is associated with poverty for women and children. Again, the concern is not so much for particular couples because undoubtedly exceptional cases can be found in any family form. The greater concern is for the impact on society and the children of society generally if the law presents unstable unions as the equivalent of and as socially as valuable as real heterosexual marriage. The law should not engage in false advertising. Equating same-sex unions with conventional male-female marriage would clearly send a false message which would hurt untold thousands of individuals and their families when the bitter realities of the instability of same-sex unions set in. Not only are unstable marriages impoverishing for the individuals involved, but they impose heavy costs on society, ranging from the costs to the state (for the agencies typically involved in dealing with family instability—courts, social work agencies, domestic violence, welfare, etc.) but also many great indirect costs resulting from lowered productivity of the individuals involved in the unstable relationship, stress, emotional problems, etc.

Sixth, Hawaii, like all states, has an important interest in providing for recognition of Hawaii marriages in other jurisdictions. Hawaii has an interest in not creating a form of marriage that will not be recognized elsewhere. Indeed, if Hawaii legalizes same-sex marriage or domestic partnership and that new institution is not recognized, persons who rely on the legality of the marriage in Hawaii may find that their rights in other jurisdictions are severely curtailed or rejected. Again, this would do a great disservice to many people. Rights derived from lawful marriages (including inheritance rights, insurance rights, pension rights, property rights, etc.) may be denied in other states and other nations. Spouses and children of a person who once entered into a same-sex marriage and later entered into a conventional marriage could find their marriage-derivative rights were challenged or not recognized in other jurisdictions.

Seventh, the state has a profound interest in preserving society from disintegration. Dr. Socarides opined in 1994:

> As regards the creation of a new psychosexual institution (i.e., homosexual "marriage") alongside that of heterosexual marriage, I submit the following. The institutions of heterosexuality and heterosexual marriage are created for family structure. To introduce homosexuality as a valid psychosexual institution is to destroy the function of heterosexuality as the last place in our society where affectivity can still be cultivated. Homosexuals cannot make a society, nor keep ours going for very long. It operates against the cohesive elements of society in the name of a fictitious freedom. It drives the opposite sex in a similar direction and no society can long endure when the child is neglected or when the sexes war upon each other.
>
> The adoption of children by homosexual couples is a serious issue. A child should be brought up with a mother and a father, in order to develop appropriate gender-defined self identity. If he does not do so, severe individual problems will occur. The matter should be approached with great caution for the child has no

voice in this matter and he may be unfortunately consigned to a pathological family setting from which he cannot escape without serious psychological damage.
. . . The negative effect on children who are adopted into homosexual "family" structure can be profound. I believe that:

1. a normal environment provides a child with the opportunity to utilize his capacities in order to further the promotion of a sense of autonomy and identity, to enhance and affirm ego-boundaries between himself and other family members, and to promote a healthy self-esteem as a member of his own sex;
2. the parents' function is to promote the child's separation from the mother into an independent entity, all the while supplying physical and emotional security needs;
3. both mother and father are models for identification toward the assumption of appropriate sexual identity and sexual role in accordance with anatomy;
4. the alleviation of conflicts, especially those involving distortion of roles during the earliest years, help the child to channel his drives, energy, and role-learning in the proper direction. . . .

The families of homosexual patients I have treated are markedly deficient in carrying out many of the functions necessary for the development of an integrated heterosexual child. Distorting influences are very profound in families in which the child is not helped to develop the appropriate gender-identity. . . . The disturbance in gender-defined self-identity sets the stage for the development of all sexual deviations and many of the neurotic conditions.

Not all marriages and families "work," but it is unwise to let pathology and failure, rather than a vision of what is normative and ideal, guide us in the development of social policy. . . .

The majority of commissioners refused to discuss the necessity for a very broad religious freedom exemption covering religious institutions and individuals who have religiously motivated objections to accepting homosexual couples as marriage-equivalent.

Many of the people who testified before the commission expressed opposition to homosexual marital rights on the basis of their religious beliefs. The majority dismisses all of these arguments based on an extreme view of the doctrine of separation of church and state. This view has, as recently as 1986, been rejected by the US Supreme Court. In upholding criminal punishment for sodomy in Georgia, the Supreme Court relied on "the millennia of moral teaching" in opposition to homosexuality. Clearly, in Hawaii, our common law restricting same-sex couples from marrying reflects that same moral teaching. In addition, looking to the sometimes-cited ancient Hawaiian cultural view of homosexuality in reference to the Alkane and the Mahu cannot support same-sex marriage in light of the fact that before going to war, the Hawaiians would purge all the Mahus, including in many instances, killing them. Abandoning such Hawaiian traditions was a great improvement in Hawaiian society.

The majority also find that no one should "impose" his religious or moral views on others. Yet, that is precisely what the majority seeks to do with homosexual marital rights to more than two-thirds of the Hawaii population for the benefit of some portion of 2 percent of the population. The majority goes so far as to report . . . that the religious groups opposed to homosexual marriage will be able to refuse to solemnize homosexual marriages, but that the pressure which will be exerted on these traditional religious people and their churches will force them to abandon their religious objections to homosexuality. It is for exactly these reasons that the religious exemption must be as broad and sweeping as possible.

Richard Duncan, Esq., Constitutional Law Professor, University of Nebraska, College of Law, desired to discuss the critical need for a religious exemption via telephone with the commission. He was not permitted; however, he did send written suggestions to adopt a very broad religious exemption. Even Dan Foley, Esq., the lawyer for the plaintiffs in *Baehr,* supports a religious exemption.

If homosexual marital rights are recognized in Hawaii, either in the form of domestic partnership, homosexual marriage, or otherwise, a very broad religious exemption is necessary for many reasons. Parents of public school students, teachers in the public schools, people who are licensed to solemnize marriages, owners of rental housing, and employers who object to homosexual marriage rights on religious grounds should be protected from government-forced acknowledgment of homosexual marriage rights.

One of the serious consequences of including homosexual coupling in the marital partnership will occur in the public school setting. If homosexual coupling is acknowledged on the same level with heterosexual marriage, the public schools will be forced to teach children that homosexual coupling is equivalent to marriage. Since as many as two-thirds of the people polled in Hawaii do not support homosexual marriage rights, it is safe to assume that a great majority of parents and teachers also do not agree with homosexual marriage rights.

Public anxiety about homosexuality is preeminently a concern about the vulnerabilities of the young. This, we are persuaded, is a legitimate and urgent public concern.

Indeed, we do not think it a bad thing that people should experience a reflexive recoil from what is wrong. To achieve such a recoil is precisely the point of moral education of the young.

Those parents who on religious grounds object to the school teaching their children that homosexual coupling is equivalent to heterosexual marriage must be given the express statutory right to remove their children from such school lessons. However, the difficulty in enforcing such a right counsels the legislature to prohibit such teaching in any public school by teachers or invited speakers. . . .

Teachers who, for religious reasons, do not desire to teach that homosexual coupling is on par with heterosexual marriage must be protected by express statutory provisions as well. Their religious freedom must be protected by specifically creating in the homosexual marriage rights legislation their freedom to oppose the teaching of homosexual marriage rights as equivalent to heterosexual marriage. At least one of the commissioners, Morgan Britt, desires to ensure that schools are forced to teach, and children forced to learn, that homosexuality and heterosexuality are equivalent.

Any legislation creating homosexual marriage rights must expressly state that no person shall be subject to fine, loss of license, liability for damages, or other punishment or penalty for rejecting homosexual marriage rights on religious grounds.

In addition, religious people who are authorized to solemnize marriages based upon licensing from the State Health Department must not be required to solemnize homosexual couples, and must not be in any manner punished for refusing to do so. The legislation creating homosexual marriage rights must expressly state that no person licensed to solemnize marriages in Hawaii shall be subject to fine, loss of license, liability for damages, or other punishment or penalty for rejecting homosexual marriage rights on religious grounds.

Furthermore, people who on grounds of religious belief oppose homosexual coupling must not in any manner be forced to acknowledge homosexual coupling, either as a landlord renting a house or apartment, as an employer extending spousal benefits, or otherwise. The legislation creating homosexual marriage rights must expressly state that no person shall be subject to fine, liability for damages, or other punishment or penalty for rejecting homosexual marriage rights on religious grounds.

The religious freedom of the US Constitution and the Constitution of the State of Hawaii must be fully protected in the event homosexual couples are extended any marriage benefits. . . .

MAJORITY RESPONSE TO MINORITY OPINION

Many minority witnesses, and their testimony made it clear, consider homosexual marriage immoral and completely unacceptable under their religious doctrines or beliefs.

However, testimony and written statements from various Christian churches and Buddhist groups made it clear that the minority position was by no means universal in the religious community.

The basic position of the minority then becomes that their religious-based position should determine the marriage law of the state of Hawaii, regardless of other religious beliefs or the civil rights of the individuals involved.

This is, of course, unacceptable to the majority, which seeks to protect the right of every church or religious group to believe and preach as they wish. But such groups have no right under our constitution to impose their beliefs on others through state law.

The "moral" position of the minority is based on the presumption that homosexuality is completely voluntary on the part of the individuals involved and therefore they are intentionally committing an "immoral" act and should be sanctioned. . . .

At the very least the jury is still out on the question of the causes of homosexual behavior. . . .

Whether the behavior is voluntary or not, the individual concerned is entitled to equal rights under the law. . . .

The protection of family values is another reason claimed by the minority and their witnesses for the banning of same-gender marriages. When you consider the high proportion of divorces, teenage pregnancies, single-parent families, and the not uncommon practice of couples living together without marriage, it would seem a bit ironic that the minority and their supporters would seek to prevent one group that wishes to promote marriage from doing so. Is it possible that there are many more troublesome areas where the minority and its supporters could productively promote family values than the one they have chosen here?

Other minority positions which seem questionable are the rejection of the relevance of the *Loving v. Virginia* case and the claim that homosexuals are not a suspect class and therefore—like criminals—can be subject to legal discrimination.

The United States Supreme Court some thirty years ago struck down a statute of the state of Virginia that prohibited interracial marriage (*Loving v. Virginia*, 388 US 1 [1967]). This case, which was cited by the Hawaii Supreme Court in its *Baehr* decision, raises the question of equal protection of the law. The opposition to interracial marriage (called miscegenation) was as emotional and passionate in the 1960s as the opposition to same-gender marriage now. Many of the same reasons, including destruction of existing society, were given then as they are now. The *Loving* case did not cause the collapse of society in Virginia or elsewhere, and the arguments now seem ridiculous, particularly in Hawaii. The minority apparently thinks our Supreme Court was misguided when it cited *Loving*. The majority agrees with the Supreme Court.

The minority attempt to reduce the status of homosexuals to that of a group that is somehow not entitled to certain constitutional rights deserves notice but not credence. . . .

CONCLUSIONS

The majority of the commission—while not all agree on every point—believe that they have prepared a reasonable report and suggested appropriate action to be taken by the legislature. The majority also is aware that its first recommendation— to allow same-gender couples to marry under state law—is vehemently opposed by many people of certain religious persuasions. The majority has also recommended the adoption of a comprehensive Domestic Partnership law. This would apply to all couples, regardless of gender, and apply most of the benefits and burdens of marriage to many in the community who not only live together, but also raise children without being married. We propose either of these solutions, or both.

LIST OF CONTRIBUTORS

Jennifer Black is a member of the Board of Contributors, Central Texans who write columns regularly for the *Waco Tribune-Herald*. She is an English instructor at McLennan Community College, Waco, Texas.

David Brooks is a columnist for the *New York Times*.

Patrick Buchanan is a conservative political commentator and writer.

George W. Bush is president of the United States.

Douglas Carl, known for his writings on counseling same-sex couples, is now deceased.

John B. Cobb Jr. is Emeritus Professor, Claremont School of Theology and Claremont Graduate School.

Robert J. Cordy is Associate Justice of the Supreme Judicial Court of Massachusetts.

Barbara J. Cox is a professor at California Western School of Law.

Ron Crews is president of the Massachusetts Family Institute.

John Derbyshire is a novelist and a contributing editor at the *National Review*.

Paula L. Ettelbrick is legal director of the Lambda Legal Defense and Education Fund and adjunct professor of law at New York School of Law.

Ed Fallon is a member of the Iowa House of Representatives.

David J. Garrow is the Presidential Distinguished Professor at Emory University Law School.

John M. Greaney is Associate Justice of the Supreme Judicial Court of Massachusetts.

Maurice Hamington is Assistant Professor of Philosophy at the University of Southern Indiana.

Jeffrey Hart is a contributing columnist for the *Conservative Chronicle.*

Larry A. Hickman is Professor of Philosophy at Southern Illinois University at Carbondale.

Derrick Z. Jackson is a columnist for the *Boston Globe.*

Jeff Jordan is Associate Professor of Philosophy at the University of Delaware.

Nicholas Kristof is a columnist for the *New York Times.*

Elizabeth Kristol is a writer, contributing to such publications as *Commentary* and the *Washington Post.*

Stanley Kurtz is Research Fellow, Hoover Institution, and contributing editor at *National Review Online.*

Daniel Maguire is Professor of Moral Theology at Marquette University.

Margaret H. Marshall is Chief Justice of the Supreme Judicial Court of Massachusetts.

Dennis O'Brien is President Emeritus at the University of Rochester, and author of *The Idea of a Catholic University.*

John O'Sullivan is Editor-at-Large of the *National Review.*

Dwight J. Penas, Attorney at Law, lives in Minneapolis, Minnesota.

Jonathan Rauch is a columnist for the *National Journal* and writer in residence at the Brookings Institution.

Dudley Rose is Assistant Dean for Ministerial Studies at Harvard Divinity School, and Senior Pastor, North Congregational Church, Cambridge.

Chivas Sandage is a poet and contributing writer for *Community News*, the newsletter of the Gay/Lesbian, Transgendered Community Center Project of Western Massachusetts.

Sam Schulman is a contributing writer for *Jewish World Review*. His essays have also appeared in the *Spectator* (London), *New York Press*, and *Commentary.*

Martha B. Sosman is Associate Justice of the Supreme Judicial Court of Massachusetts.

Francis X. Spina is Associate Justice of the Supreme Judicial Court of Massachusetts.

Glenn T. Stanton is Senior Research Analyst for Marriage and Sexuality at Focus on the Family.

Andrew Sullivan is an editor at the *New Republic.*

Lindsy Van Gelder is a contributing editor to *Ms.* magazine.